blackhawk   Kingfishers → green
                              ringed
mtern   orenpenia   Amazon
sun grebe   squirrel cuckoo

green   tat tiger
        W9-CBC-085   heron

The Birds of Costa Rica: A Field Guide

The Birds of Costa Rica

A FIELD GUIDE

RICHARD GARRIGUES

Illustrated by

ROBERT DEAN

A Zona Tropical Publication

FROM

COMSTOCK PUBLISHING ASSOCIATES

a division of

Cornell University Press

Ithaca, New York

Text and range maps copyright © 2007 by Richard Garrigues
Illustrations copyright © 2007 by Marc Roegiers and John K. McCuen

Cornell ISBN: 978-0-8014-4587-3 (cloth: alk. paper)
Cornell ISBN: 978-0-8014-7373-9 (pbk.: alk. paper)

Zona Tropical ISBN-10: 0-9705678-5-5
Zona Tropical ISBN-13: 978-0-9705678-5-7

Printed in China
10 9 8 7 6 5 4 3 2 1

Librarians: Cataloging-in-Publication Data for the Cornell edition are available from the Library of Congress.

Zona Tropical Editor in Chief: Mathias Black
Text Editor: David Featherstone
Book design: Zona Creativa S.A.
Designer: Gabriela Wattson

Table of Contents

Introduction

Graced with bounteous natural beauty, a stable democratic government, and friendly, peace-loving citizens, Costa Rica has become a popular destination for travelers from all over the world. Birds play a prominent role in attracting visitors, too. The shimmering quetzals, gaudy macaws, and comical toucans that populate tourism posters only begin to hint at the impressive avian diversity found throughout this small country.

The principal objective of this book is to help you correctly identify birds in Costa Rica. In part, this book evolved from seeing visitors and local birders—including naturalist guides—venturing into the field with the illustrated plates they had removed from the center of *A Guide to the Birds of Costa Rica* by F. Gary Stiles and Alexander F. Skutch (Cornell University Press, 1989). Although understandable from the perspective of minimizing gear weight, this practice has always seemed a shame since you end up leaving behind a valuable part of that wonderful guide, the text. In analyzing this practice, it became clear that people are tacitly deciding that they can look it up later if they want to know more about a particular species and are primarily interested in being able to make a proper identification in the field.

The aim of this publication is to provide the birder with an alternative. We hope that the illustrations, and the text that accompanies each one on the facing page, are of such quality that in most cases you will feel confident as to which species you have seen. In order to achieve this level of information, and to limit the size and weight of the book so that you will not think twice about taking it into the field, we have necessarily had to sacrifice material that, while interesting, is not directly pertinent to field identification. Fortunately, for most species found in Costa Rica, the bulk of this information (e.g., habits, nesting, range) already exists in the Stiles and Skutch volume, and we heartily recommend that any serious birder obtain a copy for further reference.

Likewise, we have chosen not to include pelagic species that you are extremely unlikely ever to see from the mainland shores, nor do we include the species known only from Cocos Island (some 350 miles off the Pacific coast of Costa Rica). A complete list of bird species reported from Costa Rica, including Cocos Island, can be found on page 341.

A Word on Taxonomy

Any field guide, as well as any bird checklist, is necessarily arranged in a linear sequence. Birds did not evolve on printed pages, however, and their true taxonomic relationships are really four dimensional— occurring in both time and space. Taxonomy (the science of naming species and determining their relationships to other species) is essentially an attempt by the human mind to impose a semblance of order on the complexity of the natural world.

Several taxonomic classifications are currently in use, and for the layout of this field guide we have decided to follow the order and nomenclature given in the American Ornithologist's Union's *Check-list of North American Birds, Seventh Edition*, including changes made in its 47th supplement. Nonetheless, throughout the presentation of species in this book, we have made slight changes to the checklist's sequence, both for design reasons and, whenever feasible, to place look-alike species on the same plates.

Also, as any birder who keeps lists of birds knows, taxonomic classifications periodically change as new information becomes available. In order to facilitate cross-referencing with information found in Stiles and Skutch, we have included a list of pertinent name changes (both English common names and scientific names) on page 335, in Taxonomic Notes.

About The Book

Each family of birds is introduced by a brief description that should help the novice birder determine to which group a bird belongs. This paragraph generally gives some behavioral information that applies to most or all of the family members found in Costa Rica. It also mentions some salient features to keep in mind when attempting to distinguish between similar-looking species within the same family.

Many species are illustrated by multiple images when, for example, there are significant plumage differences between sexes or between adult and juvenile stages. Generally, if juvenile birds resemble adults but are simply somewhat duller, they have not been illustrated. In a few cases, no illustration accompanies the species account, usually because that species is a very rare or accidental migrant and has only been seen a few times.

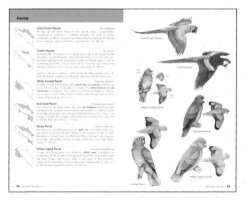

Sample spread of species accounts with illustrations.

On a given page, perched birds are nearly always represented at the same scale. Sometimes, however, there is a change of scale on a page; this is indicated with a horizontal line that spans the page. For design reasons, the scale can change from page to page, even within a family. Birds in flight are always shown at a smaller scale—the only exception is hummingbirds—but are to scale among themselves on a given page.

Corresponding to each species' illustration is a written account on the facing page. In addition to the species' English common name, you will find the scientific name (in italics); both terms are indexed separately at the end of the book. The account begins with the unique field marks to look for that will distinguish each species from similar ones. These features are highlighted in bold text. Please consult the Anatomical Features section (p. XIV) to clarify any body-part terms that may not be familiar to you. For definitions of non-anatomical terms, see the glossary on page 331.

Following the description of unique markings, we include information about how common a species is and where it occurs geographically. Please bear in mind that commonality can vary greatly throughout the mapped range, and is given as an approximate indication of a species' abundance. Also, the usage of terms varies somewhat from family to family; for example, a "common" raptor will never be as numerous as a "common" warbler.

To the left of most accounts is a thumbnail map of Costa Rica showing the species' range within the country. These maps are rather broad-stroke interpretations of where each species occurs, but, taken together with the above-mentioned written description of a species' geographic distribution, they indicate if you are at all likely to find the species in a given area. Please note that not every species account is accompanied by a map, either because a given species has only been seen a few times in Costa Rica or because the species is only known from widely scattered locations.

Example of a range map.

Location is everything in birding. Looking at the range maps in this book, you will realize that there are distinct patterns of bird distribution within the country. Thus, if you were birding on the Osa Peninsula and saw a wood-quail (p. 12), a quick look at the range maps would speed up the identification process by indicating that the only species to be expected in that part of the country is the Marbled Wood-Quail. Of course, the elimination process won't always be quite that simple, but you will often be able to significantly whittle down the number of candidates for an identification by first determining which species are possible in the region where you happen to be.

As a further aid to understanding where a given species is expected to occur, the map of Costa Rica on the inside front cover displays most of the geographic features and place names mentioned in the text.

The elevation ranges stated in the text are not rigid; some species—especially those that feed mostly on flower nectar or fruit—will readily wander up or down slope, beyond their normal elevations, in search of food. Likewise, juvenile birds seeking a territory to claim will sometimes show up in unexpected places, though they will rarely stay long.

One area worth special mention is the Guanacaste Cordillera, where the volcanoes are separated by low passes that do not act as strongly as barriers to the dispersal of Caribbean and Pacific lowland species as do the higher passes in mountain ranges farther to the south. Hence, it is not uncommon to find species that are otherwise confined to the Caribbean slope appearing on the Pacific-facing slopes of the Guanacaste volcanoes, and, to some extent, vice-versa. These distributional quirks may not always be indicated on the range maps or in the text, so be alert to this possibility when you are birding on the slopes of those volcanoes.

About a quarter of the species that occur in Costa Rica are seasonal migrants from North America, either passage migrants or winter residents. Passage migrants traverse Costa Rica in the fall on their way south, and again in the spring on their return trip north. Winter residents spend the fall and winter in Costa Rica before returning north in the spring. In this book, the description of most passage migrant species includes information about when it passes south and in what months it makes its return journey. For winter residents, the range of time cited is circumscribed by the earliest and latest periods of known occurrence, and note that most species will be represented by only a few individuals at either extreme of those dates.

Many species include some individuals that are passage migrants and others that are winter residents. Some passage migrants display behavior that is so similar to that of winter residents that it is difficult to tell them apart, and to thus know the precise time of occurrence in Costa Rica for either kind of migrant. When that is the case, the species is referred to as an *NA migrant*, and the text gives a single range of time that describes when you can expect either passage migrants or winter residents in Costa Rica; at either extreme of the time frame, you can expect a greater proportion of passage migrants, while only winter residents will occur during the middle of the time frame.

Note that a handful of species actually breed in Costa Rica and then migrate to South America during the second half of the year—these are called breeding residents.

Following the information on status and distribution is a comment on habitat and habits. This will give you an idea of where to expect to find a species within its mapped range, as well as offer an insight into how the bird might behave (e.g., foraging at a certain level of the forest, accompanying mixed species flocks, attending army-ant raids, etc.).

Unfortunately, most species that are found in mature forest (be it dry, humid, wet, or montane) are absent from much of the mapped range due to loss of habitat caused by deforestation. Note that many birds are closely associated with certain plants; when it is pertinent to identifying a bird, we cite the name of the plant or the genus to which it belongs.

Many species accounts include a description of vocalization. It is quite a challenge to transcribe what are often wonderfully complex sounds into a string of consonants and vowels that might approximate those sounds in some useful way for the reader. While these descriptions often include adjectives that help convey something of the quality of the sound, we have employed several other techniques to further describe how sounds are delivered. Accent marks show syllables that are emphasized, but are not noticeably louder (e.g., *huwít*). Capital letters indicate a stressed syllable that is distinctly louder (e.g., *klerEE*). An absence of punctuation marks or spaces indicates a very fast song (e.g., *bibidididi*). A slightly slower delivery is suggested by the use of dashes (e.g., *pee-a-weee*). The use of commas implies an even more pronounced pause between syllables (e.g., *doy, doy, doy, doy*). And, of course, these various styles can be used together to express more complex vocalizations (e.g., *tlee-dee, teedle-doo*). When a phrase is repeated at length, an ellipsis is used to save space (e.g., *kukláh-kukláh-kukláh...*).

Most birds produce a variety of sounds for different purposes; due to space limitations, however, only a description of the full song is usually given. Therefore, if you see a bird that you are sure fits the visual description and meets the range and habitat requirements for a given species, but is making a vocalization that doesn't fit the one described, chances are that it is simply producing an alternate call. Anyone with an interest in avian vocalizations should consult the commercially available recordings of Costa Rican bird sounds.

Sound does not always play an important role in identification. Cotingas, for example, rarely vocalize, while other birds are so readily seen and distinguishable that they can be identified without relying on sound. In some cases, therefore, the species description does not include vocalizations.

About 10 percent of the bird species that inhabit Costa Rica have very limited ranges and are considered regional endemics—in other words, they are species found only in the southern half of Central

America and nowhere else in the world. Assuming that these species will be of special interest to birders visiting from outside the region, they are noted in bold text as endemics and their geographic limits are given.

Judging the size of a bird can be extremely challenging. Many factors influence the impression of its size—lighting, distance, and whether it is viewed through optical equipment or the unaided eye. Also, remember that the measurements are from the tip of the bill to the tip of the tail, and do not include leg length (which can affect the impression of how big a bird is), nor is there any direct correlation between a bird's length and its mass (which can also affect the impression of size). As an example, both the Streak-chested Antpitta (p. 184) and the Long-billed Gnatwren (p. 236) are listed as measuring five inches (13 cm); upon seeing these birds in life, however, few people would say they are the same size. This is because the antpitta is a long-legged, chunky bird (attributes we tend to associate with being bigger, even though they are not part of the size calculation of the bird) that weighs ten times more than the slender, long-billed, long-tailed gnatwren, whose bill and tail length are included in the calculation. Nonetheless, by stating that these are both five-inch birds, you won't be expecting something the size of a turkey.

The measurements in the text have been rounded off to the nearest whole figure and should only be used as a general indication of size. One instance where the given measurements could be very useful, however, would be when two species are near each other, in more or less the same posture, and at the same distance from the observer. A perfect example would be if you had one of the yellowlegs (p. 70) standing on a mudflat within a meter of a Willet (p. 70). Both Greater and Lesser Yellowlegs are quite similar and, if seen alone, can't reliably be told apart by size. However, in this case, with the 15-inch Willet close by, one could determine if the yellowlegs was nearly the same size, and thus a Greater Yellowlegs (14"), or significantly smaller, and therefore a Lesser Yellowlegs (11").

This is a book by birders for birders, and we sincerely hope that you will find it useful in identifying birds in Costa Rica.

Anatomical Features

In the species descriptions, the author has used simple, nontechnical terms as much as possible. Nonetheless, in describing the various external features of birds, some technical terms become inevitable. If you are new to birding, you might want to take a few moments to familiarize yourself with the terms explained here. (See Glossary, page 331, for definitions of non-anatomical terms.) When trying to identify a bird, it is generally best to start by looking at various parts of the head. An inspection of the bill, for example, will often help you to identify the bird to the family level, if not to the species level.

THE BILL

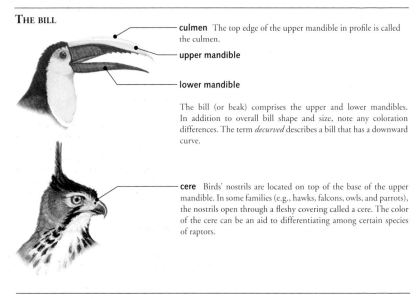

culmen The top edge of the upper mandible in profile is called the culmen.

upper mandible

lower mandible

The bill (or beak) comprises the upper and lower mandibles. In addition to overall bill shape and size, note any coloration differences. The term *decurved* describes a bill that has a downward curve.

cere Birds' nostrils are located on top of the base of the upper mandible. In some families (e.g., hawks, falcons, owls, and parrots), the nostrils open through a fleshy covering called a cere. The color of the cere can be an aid to differentiating among certain species of raptors.

LORE AND SUPRALORAL

supraloral The area above the lore.

lore The area between the base of the bill and the eye.

THE EYE AREA

superciliary The line of feathers extending from the base of the bill to above and behind the eye (thus including the supraloral feathers) is known as the superciliary. In many species, these feathers are of a different color than the contiguous head feathers, making them very useful in species identification.

eye line When the lore and the postocular stripe (see next page) are of the same color and set off from the surrounding feathers, they form an eye line.

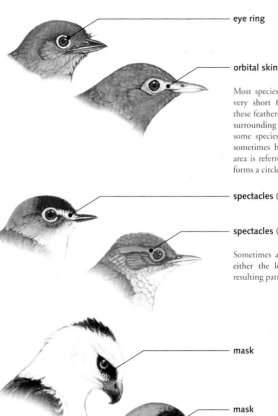

postocular stripe When a differently colored line of feathers extends behind the eye, it is referred to as a postocular stripe. Note that some birds show only a postocular spot.

eye ring

orbital skin

Most species of birds have a narrow ring of very short feathers around the eye. When these feathers are of a different color than the surrounding ones, they form an eye ring. In some species, the area around the eye (and sometimes beyond) is featherless. This bare area is referred to as orbital skin, or, when it forms a circle, as an orbital ring.

spectacles (formed with the lore)

spectacles (formed with a postocular stripe)

Sometimes an eye ring is the same color as either the lore or a postocular stripe; the resulting pattern is called *spectacles*.

mask

mask

The term *mask* is often used when the area around the eye is a darker color—usually black—than the rest of the head. More often than not, the mask includes the lore and ear coverts (see next page), but the term may be used in reference to little more than the lore.

Ear coverts, ear patch

ear patch The ear coverts, or cheek, are a distinct group of short feathers that cover the ear opening, which is located just below and behind the eye. When the feathers of the ear coverts, or sometimes just those along their outer border, are of a different color and contrast with the feathers surrounding them, the result is an ear patch.

Moustachial stripe, malar stripe, lateral throat stripe

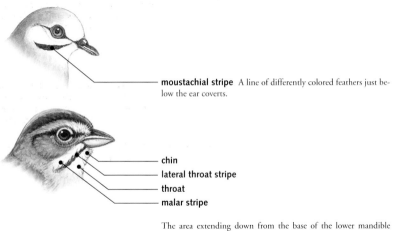

moustachial stripe A line of differently colored feathers just below the ear coverts.

chin
lateral throat stripe
throat
malar stripe

The area extending down from the base of the lower mandible between the cheek and throat is known as the malar, and when it is distinctly colored, it is called a malar stripe. A line between the malar and the throat is referred to as a lateral throat stripe. Though generally considered part of the throat, the area just below the base of the lower mandible is sometimes called the chin.

Gorget

gorget The highly iridescent throat feathers on certain species of hummingbirds are known as the gorget.

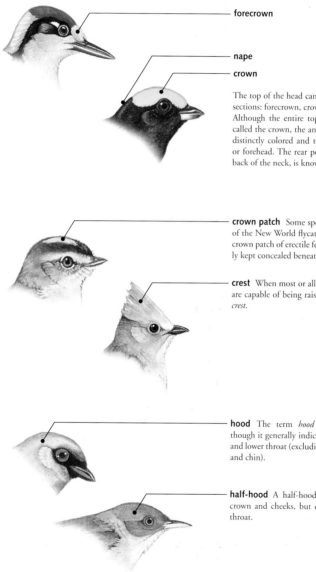

forecrown

nape

crown

The top of the head can be divided into three sections: forecrown, crown (or cap), and nape. Although the entire top of the head can be called the crown, the anterior portion is often distinctly colored and termed the forecrown, or forehead. The rear portion of the head, or back of the neck, is known as the nape.

crown patch Some species, including many of the New World flycatchers, have a colorful crown patch of erectile feathers that is generally kept concealed beneath the crown feathers.

crest When most or all of the crown feathers are capable of being raised, they are termed a *crest*.

hood The term *hood* has variable usage, though it generally indicates the crown, nape, and lower throat (excluding the forehead, eyes, and chin).

half-hood A half-hood is made up of the crown and cheeks, but does not include the throat.

NUCHAL COLLAR

nuchal collar A distinctly colored area across the nape.

UNDERPARTS, UPPERPARTS

Together, the throat, breast, flanks, belly, vent, and undertail coverts are known as the underparts. The vent is the feathered area around the anal opening; the undertail coverts are the feathers that cover the base of the underside of the tail. In technical parlance, the leg is referred to as the tarsus (plural: tarsi).

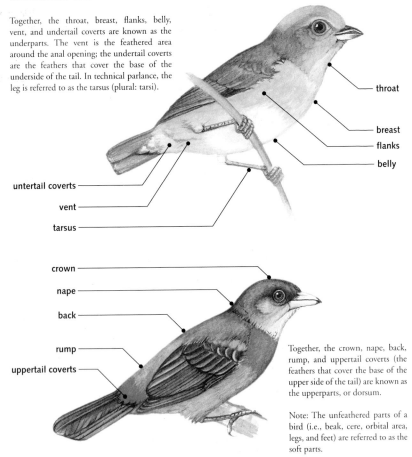

throat

breast

flanks

belly

untertail coverts

vent

tarsus

crown

nape

back

rump

uppertail coverts

Together, the crown, nape, back, rump, and uppertail coverts (the feathers that cover the base of the upper side of the tail) are known as the upperparts, or dorsum.

Note: The unfeathered parts of a bird (i.e., beak, cere, orbital area, legs, and feet) are referred to as the soft parts.

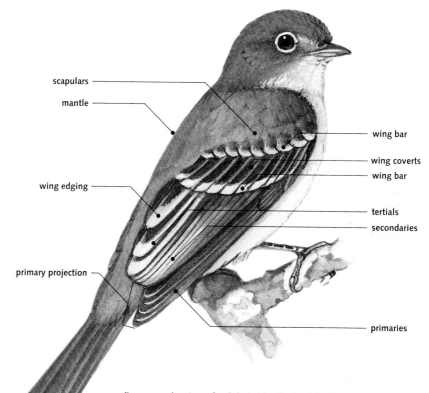

scapulars

mantle

wing bar

wing coverts

wing bar

wing edging

tertials

secondaries

primary projection

primaries

Features on the wings often help in identification. The feathers covering the juncture of the wing and body, corresponding to the shoulder, are known as the scapulars. Together, the scapulars and the upper back are termed the mantle. The several rows of feathers that cover the base of the flight feathers are the wing coverts. When the tips of these feathers are distinctly colored, they form wing bars.

The flight feathers are composed of three contiguous sets of feathers, which, from the inner to the outer portion of the extended wing, are known as tertials (three innermost feathers), secondaries, and primaries. When the wing is folded, these feathers stack up with the innermost of the three tertials on top and the outermost of the nine or ten primaries on the bottom.

A feature that is sometimes useful in identification is the distance that the tip of the outermost folded primary extends beyond the longest secondaries and tertials; this is known as the primary projection.

The term *wing edging* is used to describe a lighter color on the edge of each flight feather; this lighter color imparts a striped look to the wing.

SPECULUM

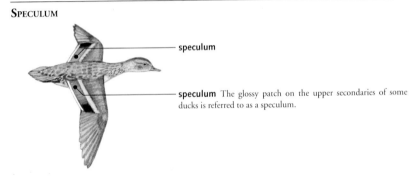

speculum

speculum The glossy patch on the upper secondaries of some ducks is referred to as a speculum.

UNDERWING

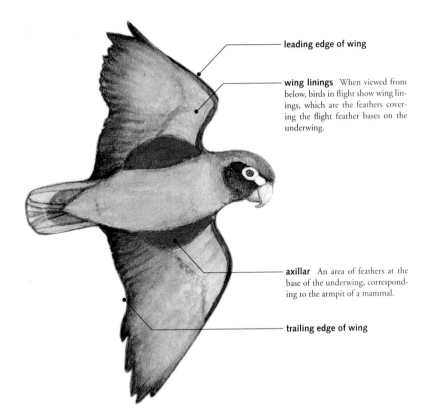

leading edge of wing

wing linings When viewed from below, birds in flight show wing linings, which are the feathers covering the flight feather bases on the underwing.

axillar An area of feathers at the base of the underwing, corresponding to the armpit of a mammal.

trailing edge of wing

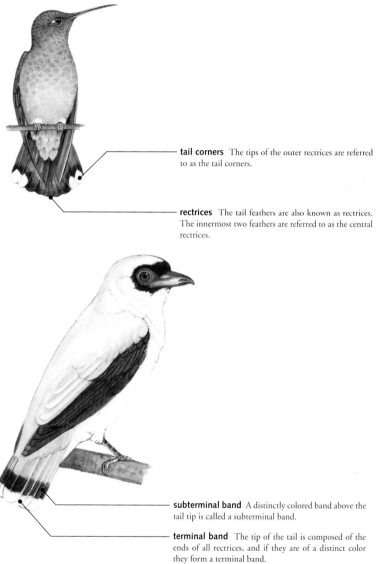

tail corners The tips of the outer rectrices are referred to as the tail corners.

rectrices The tail feathers are also known as rectrices. The innermost two feathers are referred to as the central rectrices.

subterminal band A distinctly colored band above the tail tip is called a subterminal band.

terminal band The tip of the tail is composed of the ends of all rectrices, and if they are of a distinct color they form a terminal band.

In addition to coloration or markings, note the shape of the tail, especially paying attention to whether the tip is square, rounded, notched, forked, tapering, or pointed. Also note the proportion of the tail length to the body.

Acknowledgements

First of all, I would like to thank Phillip Ostenso for having planted the seed that grew to become this book. My deepest thanks also go to my artist colleague, Robert Dean, for having been so ready, willing, and able to do the paintings that grace the pages of this guide; our publishers, John McCuen and Marc Roegiers, for having led us through the entire publication process, for having provided thoughtful criticism and suggestions, and for having taken us to some very good restaurants; their editor in chief, Mathias Black, who came on board near the end of the project, but just when there was the most to keep track of; editor, David Featherstone, for his impeccable attention to detail; and, finally, to Gabriela Wattson at Zona Creativa, for having designed a great-looking book.

Birders in Costa Rica all owe a debt to those ornithologists who have provided us with so much information about the region's bird life, and during the preparation of this book I drew invaluably from the work of Robert S. Ridgely, Alexander F. Skutch, Paul Slud, and F. Gary Stiles. Among my active birding colleagues here in Costa Rica, I must give special mention to Rafa Campos, Kevin Easley, Julio Sánchez, and, above all, Jim Zook, for having provided so much knowledge and a great deal of inspiration. Fortunately, many other people have also been willing to share information about Costa Rican birds. They include Willy Alfaro, Jaime Alvarado, Joel Alvarado, Rodolfo Alvarado, Eduardo Amengual, Hernán Araya, Rayner Araya, Gilbert Barrantes, Esteban Biamonte, Luis Campos, Neyer Campos, Ernesto Carman, Jhimmy Castiblanco, Erick Castro, Marino Chacón, Johel Chaves, Leonardo Chaves, Bill Clark, Paul Coopmans, Mariano Cruz, Rolando Delgado, Matt Denton, Gary Diller, Adolfo Downs, Steven Easley, Jesse Ellis, Melvin Fernández, Jeanne Fossani, Bob French, Abraham Gallo, Mark Garland, Charlie Gómez, Jean Jacques Gozard, Lou Hegedus, Rich Hoyer, Carlos Jiménez, Liz Jones, Henry Kantrowitz, Mathias Kümmerlen, Mark Lockwood, Daryl Loth, Eric Madrigal, Freddy Madrigal, Paco Madrigal, Daniel Martínez, Mike Mulligan, Paul Murgatroyd, Nancy Newfield, Gerardo Obando, Walter Odio, Winnie Orcutt, Gustavo Orozco,

Randall Ortega, Pablo Porras, Noble Proctor, Morris Quesada, Bob Quinn, Rafa Robles, Gary Rosenberg, César Sánchez, Luis Sánchez, Luis Sandoval, Alfredo Scott, Aaron Sekarak, Cagan Sekercioglu, Jorge Serrano, Alejandro Solano, Daniel Solano, Keith Taylor, Rachel Taylor, Bill Tice, Daniel Torres, Noel Ureña, Jay VanderGaast, Orlando Vargas, Alex Villegas, Max Vindas, Andy Walker, Lana Wedmore, Jan Westra, Pieter Westra, Drew Wheelan, Soo Whiting, John Woodcock, Bruce Young, and Rudy Zamora.

I should also thank all those fellow travelers who have accompanied me in the field during these years, for giving me a chance to practice bird identification skills. And I particularly wish to thank Carson Wade, for his periodic injections of wit and wisdom throughout the project.

And of course, my wife, Maricia, and my children, Leonardo, Daniel, David, Roberto, and Laura Carolina, who were kind enough to put up with my spending long hours at the computer these last five years. I truly appreciate their patience and understanding.

Richard Garrigues

I wish to thank the following people for having provided assistance in seeing birds I'd not seen before: Eduardo Amengual, Marino Chacón, Judy Davis, Kathy Erb, David Fisher, Michael and Patricia Fogden, Aisling French, Tony Godfrey, Larry Landstrom, Jamie Midgley, Pete Morris, Patrick O'Donnell, Alison and Michael Olivieri, Steve Pryor, Candy and Rich Stewart, Alex Villegas, Mark Wainwright, Roberto Wesson, and Jim Zook.

I must also thank Julio Sánchez and the Natural History Department at the Museo Nacional de Costa Rica for having graciously provided access to the bird collection.

And lastly, I am grateful to Zona Tropical Publications, and to Richard Garrigues, for giving me the opportunity to realize what, for several years, has been a major goal in my life.

Robert Dean

About the Author

Richard Garrigues has been birding since the age of sixteen, when a close encounter with a Black-and-white Warbler walking up a tree trunk just a few feet away from him in suburban New Jersey made a lasting impression. Since 1981, he has lived in Costa Rica, where for more than twenty years he has been leading birding and natural history tours. In April 2000, he published the first *Gone Birding Newsletter*, an online quarterly, and has been keeping readers up-to-date on rare bird sightings, new distribution data, and other pertinent local birding news ever since. This new field identification guide to the birds of Costa Rica is the fruition of a lifetime spent birding and writing about the natural world.

About the Illustrator

Robert Dean has been studying and painting neotropical birds for nine years, during which time he has been on birding trips throughout the Americas, both as a guide and as a tour participant. Born and raised in London, England, he was a professional musician for eighteen years before moving to Costa Rica, where he revitalized his childhood passion for wildlife and art. In addition to executing commissioned artwork for the Costa Rican Park Service, he has produced illustrations for Rainforest Publications on the wildlife of Costa Rica, Panama, and Peru.

Richard dedicates this book to the loving memory of Abbie Florence Rice, who gave him his first Peterson's.

Robert dedicates this book to the late Karen Mogensen, who started him on his Costa Rican adventure, and to his cat, Alice, who's been there through all of it.

Species Accounts and Illustrations

Tinamous

TINAMIDAE. These plump-bodied, small-headed, essentially tailless terrestrial birds are far more often heard than seen. Leg color, habitat, and voice are useful keys to identification, since CR's five native species are somewhat similar in appearance.

Great Tinamou
Tinamus major

Mostly grayish-brown, with **black barring posteriorly** and **gray legs**. Fairly common in lowlands and uncommon at middle elevations; to 1,700 m. Inhabits mature wet forests, where its far-carrying, clear, but quavering, whistled call is a characteristic sound. 17" (43 cm).

Highland Tinamou
Nothocercus bonapartei

Nearly as large as the Great Tinamou and also with **gray legs**, but note **rufous below**, becoming more buffy on belly; also has **buffy spots on back**. Fairly uncommon; occurs in middle-elevation forests (where there could be some overlap with Great Tinamou) and highland forests; from 1,200 to 2,500 m. The call is a monotonous series of harsh, nasal notes that completely lack the melodious quality of other CR tinamus. 15" (38 cm).

Little Tinamou
Crypturellus soui

A small **unpatterned** tinamou with **dull-yellow legs**. It is the most widespread member of the family in CR; found in wet and humid regions, from sea level to 1,500 m. This species' preference for tangled, dense, second-growth vegetation makes it exceedingly difficult to see. Its tremulous whistle brings to mind a horse's whinny. 9" (23 cm).

Thicket Tinamou
Crypturellus cinnamomeus

A **red-legged** and **heavily barred** tinamou of the dry forest. Fairly common in northwestern Pacific lowlands and foothills, to 1,000 m. Forages in both mature forest and second growth. A pure single-note whistle discloses its whereabouts. 11" (28 cm).

Slaty-breasted Tinamou
Crypturellus boucardi

The Caribbean counterpart of the Thicket Tinamou; both have **red legs**, but the Slaty-breasted Tinamou has an **unmarked gray breast**. Fairly uncommon in the northern half of the Caribbean lowlands, to 700 m. Roams the floor of mature forest. The characteristic call is an even, mellow tone with a distinct catch in the middle. 11" (28 cm).

Great Tinamou

Highland Tinamou

Little Tinamou

Thicket Tinamou

Slaty-breasted Tinamou

ANATIDAE. The peculiar broad bill readily identifies ducks and sets them apart from other species of similar behavior (e.g., grebes, cormorants, gallinules, and the sungrebe). However, in some species of the genera *Anas* and *Aythya*, females are quite similar and can be difficult to identify to the species level. Wing pattern in flight can be helpful, as well as paying close attention to the bill's size, shape, and color.

Black-bellied Whistling-Duck
Dendrocygna autumnalis

The **rose-pink bill and feet** of adult are unique among CR ducks. Juvenile has dusky bill and feet; told apart from Fulvous Whistling-Duck by grayish (not tawny) head and neck and plain back. In flight, all plumages show a **white wing stripe**. Abundant in Palo Verde and Caño Negro regions; fairly uncommon elsewhere, to 1,500 m. Found in freshwater marshes and ponds, as well as in flooded fields; frequently perches in trees; forages at night. Whistles a high-pitched *whit-whit-wee-wee-wee*. 21" (53 cm).

Fulvous Whistling-Duck
Dendrocygna bicolor

Perched or swimming birds could be mistaken for juvenile Black-bellied Whistling-Duck, but note **tawny head and neck** (not grayish). In flight, shows **all-dark wing** and **white U on rump**. Uncommon in Palo Verde and Caño Negro regions. Found in freshwater marshes and ponds, as well as in flooded fields. 19" (48 cm).

White-faced Whistling-Duck
Dendrocygna viduata

The white face is distinctive. This bird shows all-dark wings and tail in flight. Has not been seen in CR in nearly two decades, though possible in Palo Verde region. **Not illustrated**. 17" (43 cm).

Muscovy Duck
Cairina moschata

Female shows less white in wing than male. Biggest identification problem is determining if individuals are truly wild, since many domesticated birds exist in CR—these often show some white (in addition to the white in the wing) due to crossing with "barnyard ducks." Habitat, location, and their wariness of people are the best clues as to whether birds are truly wild. Fairly common in Palo Verde region; rare elsewhere in lowlands. Favors wooded wetlands and forested streams, but also feeds in open fields; perches and roosts in trees. Male 33" (84 cm); female 25" (64 cm).

Masked Duck
Nomonyx dominicus

Breeding male's **blue bill** and rich coloration are distinctive; **striped face** and **barred back** are diagnostic on female, juvenile, and nonbreeding male. In flight, all plumages show white in secondaries. Very uncommon in lowlands and middle elevations, to 1,500 m. Secretive, rarely venturing far from cover of aquatic vegetation; dives for food in shallow water. 13" (33 cm).

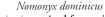

Cinnamon Teal
Anas cyanoptera

A **black bill** distinguishes the striking male of this species from the male Masked Duck; female is virtually identical to female Blue-winged Teal (p. 6) and very similar to both female Northern Shoveler and female Green-winged Teal (p. 6). Very rare winter resident in Palo Verde region, from Nov to March. Usually found in association with Blue-winged Teals. 16" (41 cm).

adult

adult

juv.

Black-bellied Whistling-Duck

Fulvous Whistling-Duck

male

male

Muscovy Duck

female/juv./
nonbreeding male

female/juv./
nonbreeding male

male

breeding
male

Masked Duck

Cinnamon Teal

American Wigeon
Anas americana

The male's **white crown** is distinctive; female has grayish head and neck. Both sexes have a **light-bluish bill with dark tip**. Uncommon winter resident from Oct to March; mostly in Palo Verde region, but also occurs in Caño Negro and Central Valley; to 1,500 m. Found on ponds and freshwater marshes. 20" (51 cm).

Mallard
Anas platyrhynchos

Female is much larger than other similarly plumaged CR species and has **orange bill with dark spot on upper mandible**. Breeding male's dark-green head similar to that of Northern Shoveler, but note bright-yellow bill and narrow white collar (male not illustrated). Very rare winter resident in Palo Verde region and Central Valley. 23" (58 cm).

Blue-winged Teal
Anas discors

The **white crescent** on male's face is diagnostic. Female virtually identical to female Cinnamon Teal (p. 4); also resembles female Northern Shoveler and female Green-winged Teal. In flight, both male and female show light-blue wing coverts (as do Cinnamon Teal and Northern Shoveler). Abundant NA migrant in Palo Verde, Caño Negro, and Central Valley; fairly uncommon elsewhere in lowlands and middle elevations; to 1,500 m; from Sept to April (a few present year-round). Prefers shallow ponds and freshwater marshes. 15" (38 cm).

Northern Shoveler
Anas clypeata

Contrasting dark and light pattern of male is unique. Female resembles female teals, but has a **spatulate bill** (grayish with orange edges) that is longer than the head. In flight, both sexes show bluish-gray wing coverts. Fairly common winter resident in Palo Verde region; uncommon in Caño Negro and Central Valley, to 1,500 m; from Oct to March. Found on ponds and freshwater marshes. 19" (48 cm).

Northern Pintail
Anas acuta

Male readily distinguished by **long neck with white stripe** extending up the side. Female best identified by her **slender build** and **pointed tail**; the latter is especially noticeable in flight, when **brown speculum** is also visible. Previously much more common, now a very uncommon winter resident in Palo Verde region; rare in Caño Negro and Central Valley, to 1,500 m; from late Sept to Feb. Favors ponds and open areas in shallow freshwater marshes. 21" (53 cm).

Green-winged Teal
Anas crecca

The male's **green and chestnut head** is definitive; female resembles other female teals and female Northern Shoveler. In flight, shows **buffy stripe** between **gray-brown wing coverts** and **green speculum**. Very casual winter resident; some reports from Palo Verde region and Central Valley. 14" (36 cm).

American Wigeon

female

male

female

male

Mallard

female

Blue-winged Teal

female

female

male

female

Northern Shoveler

female

female

male

female

male

Green-winged Teal

Northern Pintail

Ducks

Ring-necked Duck
Aythya collaris

Gray bill with white ring and black tip is diagnostic on both sexes. Male further distinguished from both male scaups by **black back** and **gray flanks**; female further set apart from female scaups by **dark eye** with **white eye ring**. In flight, both male and female show **gray secondaries and primaries**. Uncommon winter resident in Palo Verde region; very rare elsewhere, to 1,500 m; from late Oct to March. Forages by diving, hence found on deeper, open areas of ponds and marshes. 17" (43 cm).

Greater Scaup
Aythya marila

Nearly identical to Lesser Scaup and similar to Ring-necked Duck. Male and female best identified by a white wing stripe that extends from body to middle of primaries. One sighting of three birds in Gulf of Papagayo, Oct 1974. Most likely found on saltwater. 18" (46 cm).

Lesser Scaup
Aythya affinis

Nearly identical to Greater Scaup, but in flight shows white only in secondaries. Male similar to male Ring-necked Duck, though white back—barred with black—looks lighter; also note **white flanks**. Female set apart from female Ring-necked Duck by **yellow iris** and **no eye ring**; also note greater contrast between white feathers at base of bill and dark head. Uncommon winter resident in Palo Verde region and Central Valley, rare elsewhere; to 1,500 m; from mid-Nov to March. Found on freshwater ponds; forages by diving. 16" (41 cm).

Grebes

PODICIPEDIDAE. Superficially ducklike birds; found on ponds, lakes, and reservoirs. Skilled divers, grebes catch a variety of aquatic prey underwater, often resurfacing at some distance from where they submerged. The two resident species are best told apart by eye color and by bill shape and color.

Least Grebe
Tachybaptus dominicus

Smaller and somewhat darker than the Pied-billed Grebe; note **thin, black bill** and intense **yellow eye**. Common in the Central Valley and northwestern Pacific; fairly common elsewhere; to 1,500 m; extremely rare in Tortuguero region. 9" (23 cm).

Pied-billed Grebe
Podilymbus podiceps

Larger and somewhat lighter in body color than the Least Grebe; note **thick, pale bill** and **dark eye**. In breeding plumage, birds have a distinctive dark ring around the bill. Widespread but very uncommon, to 1,500 m. 13" (33 cm).

Eared Grebe
Podiceps nigricollis

Has thin, slightly upturned bill; also note red eye. A single CR record from April 1987 of two birds in breeding plumage on a glacial lake atop Mount Chirripó. **Not illustrated**. 13" (33 cm)

female

male

Ring-necked Duck

male

male

Greater Scaup

male

female

male

Lesser Scaup

adult

juv.

Least Grebe

breeding
adult

juv.

Pied-billed Grebe

Curassows, Chachalacas, & Guans

CRACIDAE. An essentially neotropical family of large, chickenlike birds. Despite their size, they are quite arboreal and can also fly well (although they frequently glide). Though attired in somber plumage, many species have brightly colored soft parts. In unprotected areas, they are sought after as game, and hence are increasingly rare. They feed on fruit and vegetation.

Great Curassow
Crax rubra

Large size and **curly crest feathers** render both sexes distinctive. Uncommon to rare in protected areas throughout the country, to 1,200 m. Individuals and pairs forage on the ground in mature forest, though they readily fly up into trees to escape danger as well as to roost. Males emit such a deep bass *uuuhm* that the sonic waves are almost felt. 36" (91 cm).

Gray-headed Chachalaca
Ortalis cinereiceps

Told apart from the Plain Chachalaca by **rufous primaries**, which are very obvious in flight and usually visible on perched birds. Fairly uncommon in wet lowlands and middle elevations, to 1,200 m. Favors forest edges and second growth; mostly arboreal and in small groups that typically fly in follow-the-leader fashion from one tree to the next. Produces a variety of sounds varying from soft, high notes to rather loud clucking, but does not say *chachalaca*. 20" (51 cm).

Plain Chachalaca
Ortalis vetula

Distinguished from Gray-headed Chachalaca by **lack of rufous in primaries**. Fairly common in hills of Nicoya Peninsula and very rare in northwestern lowlands. Somewhat arboreal; groups forage in dry forests, humid forests, and thickets. Gives the characteristic *chachaLAca* call at dawn and dusk. 21" (53 cm).

Black Guan
Chamaepetes unicolor

The **blue facial skin** should preclude confusion with vultures and all other large, black birds; also note red eye and reddish-pink legs. Fairly common in protected areas of highlands, uncommon to rare elsewhere; from 1,100 m to timberline. Mostly arboreal, usually seen singly or in pairs; favors mature forest, but also comes to fruiting trees in adjacent gardens. In flight, makes a startlingly loud rattle with its wings. **Endemic to CR and western Panama.** 24" (61 cm).

Crested Guan
Penelope purpurascens

The **red flap of bare skin on throat** and **white flecking on breast** differentiate this from species of similar size. Still fairly common in protected areas throughout the country, to 1,800 m in southern Pacific; elsewhere to 1,200 m. Surprisingly arboreal for its size; pairs or small groups forage at middle and upper levels of mature forest, advanced second growth, and forest edges. Utters a loud *klah-klah-klah*, repeated at length with varying pitch and speed; also produces a deep wing-rustling noise in flight. 35" (89 cm).

female

male

Great Curassow

Gray-headed
Chachalaca

Plain
Chachalaca

Black Guan

Crested Guan

Quails

ODONTOPHORIDAE. The New World quails are an essentially terrestrial family; their mottled brown dorsal patterns help provide camouflage. Most of the CR species are forest dwellers and very difficult to see, except perhaps briefly when a covey scurries across a trail. Their calls are the best clue to their presence in an area. The colors on the head and throat are key identification features.

Buffy-crowned Wood-Partridge
Dendrortyx leucophrys

Long legs and tail give it a chickenlike aspect; no other CR quail has **pale iris** and **streaked neck**. Uncommon in Central Valley, Dota region, and Cerro de la Muerte; from 1,000 to 2,800 m. Small coveys forage in thickets, second growth, forest openings, and shaded coffee plantations. This species' CR common name derives from its raucous call (*chir-ras-quá*). 13" (33 cm).

Marbled Wood-Quail
Odontophorus gujanensis

The **red orbital skin** and dark iris are distinctive. Fairly uncommon in southern Pacific lowlands and foothills, to 1,200 m. Small coveys roam the floor of mature wet forests and adjacent advanced second growth. At dawn and dusk, birds call with a repeated, rollicking *klá-ka-wáh-hah*. 10" (25 cm).

Black-eared Wood-Quail
Odontophorus melanotis

The **dark throat** and **rufous breast and belly** are diagnostic. Rare in Caribbean lowlands and foothills, to 1,000 m. Small coveys roam the floor of mature wet forests and adjacent advanced second growth. Its call is a repeated, gabbling *kukláh-kukláh-kukláh…* . **Endemic from Honduras to Panama.** 10" (25 cm).

Black-breasted Wood-Quail
Odontophorus leucolaemus

The only CR wood-quail with a **black breast**; the amount of **white on the throat** is variable, but helps in identification when visible. Fairly common at middle elevations of Caribbean slope and on Pacific slope of Guanacaste and Tilarán Cordilleras, from 700 to 1,800 m; uncommon in Dota region. Coveys forage on the floor of wet montane forests and adjacent advanced second growth. Covey members chorus a fast, rollicking *chu-chu-wi-chi-chú*. **Endemic to CR and western Panama.** 10" (25 cm).

Spotted Wood-Quail
Odontophorus guttatus

The combination of **streaked black-and-white throat** and **spotted underparts** is diagnostic. Raises crest when excited. Note existence of rufous morph. Uncommon on Central and Talamanca Cordilleras, from timberline down to 1,000 m on Pacific slope, and down to 1,500 m on Caribbean slope. Small coveys feed on the floor of mature highland forest, thickets, second growth, and forest openings. At dawn, birds repeat a loud *hu-wit, hu-wit, hu-wit-tsú*. 10" (25 cm).

Tawny-faced Quail
Rhynchortyx cinctus

The male's **tawny face** and **gray breast** are distinctive; female lacks tawny face, but note **white stripe on side of head** and **barring on underparts**. Rare in northern central Caribbean lowlands and foothills; also rare on Pacific slope of Guanacaste Cordillera; to 800 m. Pairs or small coveys move furtively on floor of mature wet forests. Makes a soft cooing sound. 7" (18 cm).

Buffy-crowned
Wood-Partridge

Marbled
Wood-Quail

Black-eared
Wood-Quail

Black-breasted
Wood-Quail

rufous
morph

Spotted
Wood-Quail

Tawny-faced Quail

female

male

Crested Bobwhite
Colinus cristatus

The **white-spotted underparts** set it apart from all but the Spotted Wood-Quail (p. 12), but note that the latter species occurs in different habitats. Northwestern Pacific race is common in northwestern Pacific and uncommon in Central Valley; to 1,500 m. Southern Pacific race is uncommon in lowlands on mainland side of Golfo Dulce; also reported from hills south of San Isidro de El General. Favors grasslands and brushy fields, foraging in coveys of up to a dozen or more birds. Whistles *whit, whit, WEit*. 8" (20 cm).

Boobies

SULIDAE. Found on the open ocean and rocky islets; a booby can be recognized in flight by its pointed beak, wings, and tail. In addition to plumage color and pattern, bill and leg color are important in sorting out the species. Normally, however, only one of the four possible species—the Brown Booby—is likely to be seen from shore. When feeding, boobies make spectacular headlong plunges into the water.

Brown Booby
Sula leucogaster

The **unmarked, dark-brown upperparts** and contrasting **white belly** facilitate identification; note that males on the Pacific side of CR have pale-gray heads. Juvenile closely resembles juvenile Red-footed Booby, but note darker head. This is the most commonly seen booby on both coasts, though more numerous on Pacific. Roosts and breeds on rocky islets; rarely comes very close to shore. 27" (69 cm).

Masked Booby
Sula dactylatra

Dark feet and **yellow bill** distinguish adult from rare Pacific white morph of Red-footed Booby. On juvenile, note white nuchal collar. Casual visitor to coastal waters; uncommon farther off shore. 34" (86 cm).

Blue-footed Booby
Sula nebouxii

The adult's **blue feet** are diagnostic; also note **white on rump and upper back**. Juvenile has dark feet and resembles male Pacific race of Brown Booby, but note white on rump and upper back. Occasionally appears along Pacific coast and in Gulf of Nicoya. 32" (81 cm).

Red-footed Booby
Sula sula

Red feet are distinctive in all adult morphs. Pacific dark morph has dark rump and tail, Caribbean dark morph has white rump and tail; rare Pacific white morph has black tail (compare with Masked Booby), Caribbean white morph has white tail. Juvenile has greenish feet and is very similar to juvenile Brown Booby, but is more uniformly dull brown. Generally not found close to shore; however, in recent years there have been a few dark morph birds regularly sighted on rocky islets off the northern end of Corcovado National Park. 28" (71 cm).

southern
Pacific race

northwestern
Pacific race

female

male

Crested Bobwhite

adult

juv.

adult

male Pacific
race

Brown Booby

Masked
Booby

adult

juv.

adult Caribbean
white morph

adult Pacific
dark morph

Red-footed
Booby

adult Pacific
dark morph

Blue-footed
Booby

adult

Pelicans

PELECANIDAE. Difficult to confuse with anything else; there is essentially only one species found in CR, the Brown Pelican, which is a common coastal inhabitant. Brown Pelicans soar effortlessly in large V-formations, skim low over the waves, plunge headfirst for fish, and roost on sandbars or in trees, especially mangroves.

Brown Pelican
Pelecanus occidentalis

The white head and neck of nonbreeding adults may suggest an American White Pelican, but note the **darker bill** and **grayish back feathers**. Though present on the Caribbean coast, it is far more common on the Pacific coast, where hundreds can be seen in a single day. 47" (116 cm).

American White Pelican
Pelecanus erythrorhynchos

Its **yellow-orange bill** and **white plumage** are obvious field marks. Very casual NA migrant; reported from Palo Verde (March, 1977), Caño Negro region (date uncited), and the Tortuguero canal system (late 1990s). **Not illustrated**. 61" (154 cm).

Cormorants

PHALACROCORACIDAE. Aquatic birds (of rivers, lakes, and coastal areas) that catch fish and other prey while diving underwater. When swimming on the surface, cormorants often look partially submerged, showing only their head, neck, and back. Birds are frequently seen perched with their wings outstretched as they dry their permeable plumage. Only one species occurs in Costa Rica.

Neotropic Cormorant
Phalacrocorax brasilianus

The **hooked tip of the bill** distinguishes this species from ducks, grebes, and the somewhat similar Anhinga. Very young birds have mostly white underparts. Common from lowlands to middle elevations, to 1,500 m. Favors slow-moving bodies of water. Generally silent except at roosts, where it utters deep grunts (hence the CR common name *pato chancho*, or pig duck). 26" (66 cm).

Anhingas

ANHINGIDAE. Anhingas are similar in appearance and habits to cormorants, and both families occur in similar habitats.

Anhinga
Anhinga anhinga

The Anhinga is differentiated from the Neotropic Cormorant by its longer, slimmer neck and **long, pointed bill**. Although fairly common, it is typically less numerous than the sympatric Neotropic Cormorant. Often swims so low in the water that only its head and neck are exposed; frequently soars. Usually silent. 35" (89 cm).

nonbreeding adult

breeding adult

juv.

Brown Pelican

juv.

adult

Neotropic Cormorant

male

female

Anhinga

Frigatebirds

FREGATIDAE. Graceful and elegant birds of coastal skies, frigatebirds have the greatest ratio of wing area to body weight of any bird in the world and can thus be seen soaring with ease on long, pointed wings or maneuvering skillfully as they harass gulls, pelicans, or boobies in hopes of making them drop their catch. They also pluck their own prey from the water's surface, but never actually dive into the water, in an attempt to keep their non-waterproof plumage dry.

Magnificent Frigatebird
Fregata magnificens

Birds undergo a series of plumage changes from juvenile to adult stage. Early juvenile has white head. As head darkens in later stages, several **short white wavy lines form on the axillars** (never present in Great Frigatebird); these are retained, except in adult males. The only frigatebird likely to be seen from the mainland. Very common along Pacific coast and fairly uncommon along Caribbean coast; on rare occasions, an individual can be seen inland, even soaring over the Central Valley. 40" (102 cm).

Great Frigatebird
Fregata minor

Very similar to Magnificent Frigatebird. Breeding resident on Cocos Island; accidental off Pacific coast. **Not illustrated**. 37" (94 cm).

Storks

CICONIIDAE. Large wading birds with long legs and long, impressive bills. The head and neck are featherless on both CR species. Often soar on thermal currents during the heat of the day.

Jabiru
Jabiru mycteria

Told apart from the much smaller Wood Stork by its **massive, slightly upturned bill**. In flight, shows **entirely white wings**. Juvenile is splotched gray-brown and white. Very uncommon in Palo Verde and Caño Negro regions. Forages in open freshwater marshes. 52" (132 cm).

Wood Stork
Mycteria americana

The **heavy, slightly decurved bill** differentiates it from the Jabiru and other white wading birds. In flight, the black flight feathers are diagnostic (King Vulture [p. 30] has similar black-and-white pattern, but short neck and legs). Very common in Caño Negro region and around Gulf of Nicoya; uncommon elsewhere in lowlands and in western Central Valley, to 900 m. Found in almost any open wetland habitat. 40" (102 cm).

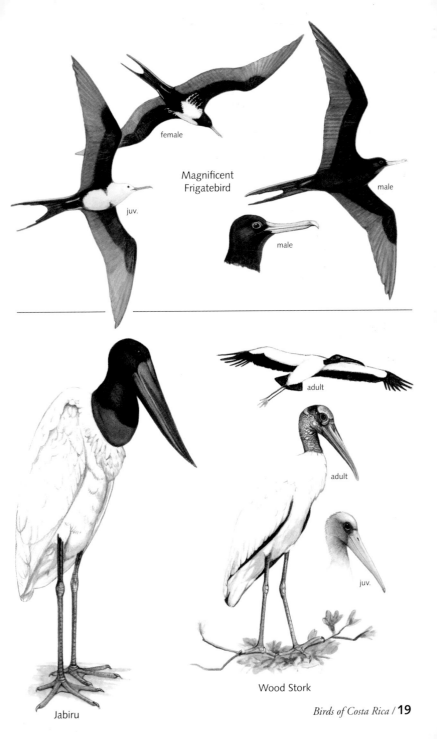

female

Magnificent
Frigatebird

male

juv.

male

adult

adult

juv.

Jabiru

Wood Stork

ARDEIDAE. These long-legged and long-necked birds are almost always found in wetland habitats. Apart from the odd-looking Boat-billed Heron (sometimes placed in its own monotypic family), all have long, pointed bills for spearing or snatching prey. Bill and leg color are important in differentiating among the similar-looking white herons and egrets.

Rufescent Tiger-Heron
Tigrisoma lineatum

Deep rufous head and neck of adult are diagnostic. Juvenile is virtually indistinguishable from juvenile Fasciated Tiger-Heron, but there is little range overlap. Uncommon in Caribbean lowlands, occasionally to 500 m. Moves slowly, often motionless; forages at edges of quiet streams or swamps within mature wet forest. 27" (69 cm).

Bare-throated Tiger-Heron
Tigrisoma mexicanum

Bare yellow skin on throat distinguishes both adult and juvenile from other tiger-herons (the similar Fasciated Tiger-Heron has no yellow on throat). Fairly common in lowlands, rarely above 500 m. More often in open habitats than other tiger-herons; found in a variety of wetland environments, including mangroves, marshes, and even roadside ditches. Utters a rolling, gravelly *wowrrh*. 30" (76 cm).

Fasciated Tiger-Heron
Tigrisoma fasciatum

Adult is similar to adult Bare-throated Tiger-Heron, but has **fine barring on cheeks and crown**; also note that the white throat feathers extend to base of bill. Juvenile is virtually identical to juvenile Rufescent Tiger-Heron, but there is little range overlap. Fairly uncommon in Caribbean foothills, between 100 and 900 m, north to Miravalles Volcano; has recently spread across Cerro de la Muerte highlands and down to Pacific foothills between Quepos and Uvita. Forages along rocky, fast-flowing streams in forested areas. 25" (64 cm).

Pinnated Bittern
Botaurus pinnatus

Similar to juvenile tiger-herons, but has **finely barred back of neck, streaking on throat and breast**, and overall **pale, sandy brown** coloration. In flight, shows dark-gray flight feathers. Very uncommon in lowlands, to 600 m. Camouflages well in tall grass of wet fields and in marsh vegetation. 26" (66 cm).

American Bittern
Botaurus lentiginosus

Distinguished from Pinnated Bittern by black malar stripe and unbarred back of neck; juvenile night-herons (p. 26) are stockier and have stouter bills. After going unreported in CR for nearly a century, there were two separate, unconfirmed sight reports in Central Pacific marshes, Nov 2003 and Jan 2004. At best, a very casual NA migrant. **Not illustrated**. 28" (71 cm).

Agami Heron
Agamia agami

Dark, rich coloration and **very long bill** are diagnostic. Juvenile is dull brown above, with slaty crown and white throat; resembles juvenile Tricolored Heron (p. 24), but neck is less reddish brown. Very uncommon in Caribbean lowlands and extremely rare in Golfo Dulce/Osa Peninsula. Quietly stalks in shallow streams or swamps within mature forest. 29" (74 cm).

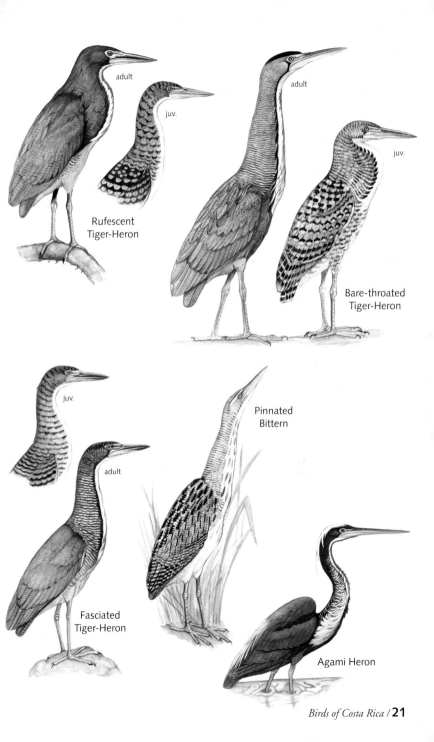

Rufescent
Tiger-Heron

adult

juv.

Bare-throated
Tiger-Heron

adult

juv.

juv.

adult

Fasciated
Tiger-Heron

Pinnated
Bittern

Agami Heron

Little Blue Heron
Egretta caerulea

Distinguished in all plumage phases by **two-toned bill** with **light blue-gray base** and **dark tip**; also note **dull-greenish legs**. Adult resembles dark morph Reddish Egret (p. 24) and somewhat resembles Tricolored Heron (p. 24). Juvenile is entirely white; summer residents (first-year birds) are white splotched with dark gray. Common and widespread NA migrant, from Sept to April; uncommon summer resident from April to Sept; to 1,500 m. Found in almost any open wetland habitat, and along wooded streams. 24" (61 cm).

Great Egret
Ardea alba

Largest of the white herons in CR, with **very long neck** (often held bent in an "S"), **yellow-orange bill**, and **black legs**. Common and widespread, to 1,500 m; resident population joined by NA migrants from Sept to April. Found in almost any open wetland habitat. 39" (99 cm).

Great Blue Heron
Ardea herodias

Large size and **gray coloration** should preclude confusion. A fairly common and widespread NA migrant, to 1,500 m; mostly from Sept to May, but some individuals present year-round. Found in almost any open wetland habitat. 46" (117 cm).

Cattle Egret
Bubulcus ibis

Distinguished from other white herons by **yellow-orange bill** (the Great Egret, which also has a yellow-orange bill, is twice the size and has a much longer neck). Breeding plumaged birds acquire orangish cast to crown, breast, and back. Since arriving in CR in 1954, has become very common and widespread to at least 2,200 m. Found in open wetland habitats, as well as in pastures, where it follows cattle and horses, grabbing the insects that those animals stir up. 20" (51 cm).

Snowy Egret
Egretta thula

Told apart from other white herons by **slender black bill**; also note black legs with **yellow feet** (juvenile has yellow-green on back of legs). Common and widespread, to 1,500 m; resident population joined by NA migrants from Sept to April. Found in almost any open wetland habitat, and along wooded streams. 24" (61 cm).

adult

first year

Great Egret

Little Blue Heron

adult

breeding

nonbreeding

Cattle Egret

juv.

Great Blue
Heron

Snowy Egret

Reddish Egret
Egretta rufescens

Adult dark morph similar to adult Little Blue Heron (p. 22) and adult pale morph similar to other white herons; however, both show **two-toned bill** with **pinkish base** and **black tip**. Juvenile dark morph is fairly uniformly dull gray, with dark bill and **pale iris**. Juvenile pale morph combines all-dark bill with all-dark legs and feet. Rare NA migrant in coastal lowlands, from Nov to April. Feeds actively in brackish water. 30" (76 cm).

Least Bittern
Ixobrychus exilis

Contrasting black and cinnamon pattern of male is diagnostic; female and juvenile are browner and duller, but still show distinctive **buffy wing patch** (especially noticeable in flight). Uncommon in lowlands, to 600 m. Difficult to see since it skulks in dense vegetation of freshwater marshes. 12" (30 cm).

Striated Heron
Butorides striata

Very similar to Green Heron, but sides of head and neck are gray or buffy. Known from a 1923 specimen taken near Cañas, Guanacaste and two recent sightings at Palo Verde, Oct 2003 and Feb 2004. 18" (48 cm).

Green Heron
Butorides virescens

Doesn't look very green, but small size, dark coloration, and **yellow-orange legs** (deep orange in breeding male) should aid in identification. Common and widespread, to 1,800 m; resident population joined by NA migrants from Sept to April. Found along almost any body of water; often hunts from low perch along the shoreline. 18" (48 cm).

Tricolored Heron
Egretta tricolor

Somewhat resembles adult Little Blue Heron (p. 22), but has **white belly**; also has longer, more slender bill. Juvenile somewhat resembles juvenile Agami Heron (p. 20), but neck is more reddish brown. Fairly uncommon but widespread NA migrant, to 1,000 m; mostly from Sept to May, but some individuals present year-round. Found in almost any open wetland habitat. 26" (66 cm).

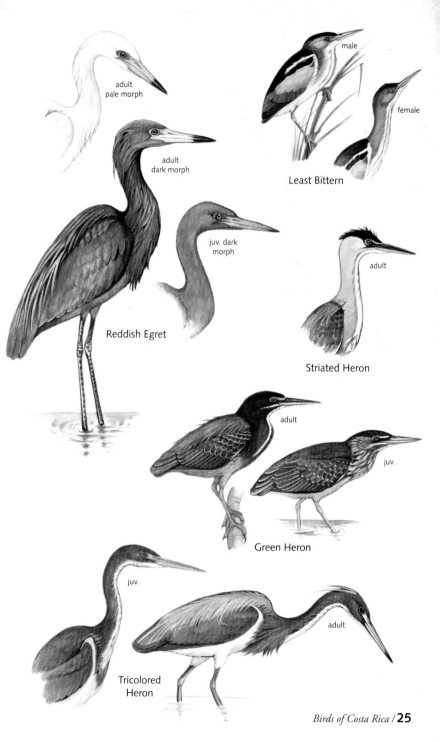

adult
pale morph

male

female

Least Bittern

adult
dark morph

juv. dark
morph

adult

Striated Heron

Reddish Egret

adult

juv.

Green Heron

juv.

adult

Tricolored
Heron

Herons

Black-crowned Night-Heron
Nycticorax nycticorax

Adult somewhat like Boat-billed Heron in coloration, but is **white below**; also note much narrower bill. Juvenile is very similar to juvenile Yellow-crowned Night-Heron, but note larger white spots on wing coverts and that **most of lower mandible is yellowish**. Fairly common in lowlands around Gulf of Nicoya, rare in Caribbean lowlands and Central Valley, to 1,000 m. Roosts by day in dense vegetation near water. 25" (64 cm).

Boat-billed Heron
Cochlearius cochlearius

The strange-looking **broad bill** is the definitive field mark. Somewhat like adult Black-crowned Night-Heron, but is darker below. Fairly common and widespread in lowlands, to 600 m. Colonies nest and roost by day in vegetation that overhangs ponds and streams. If bothered, makes a deep, throaty cackling *ka, ka, ka, cuaho, cuaho, cuah, cuah* and also loud beak-snapping noises. 20" (51 cm).

Yellow-crowned Night-Heron
Nyctanassa violacea

The head pattern on adult is distinctive. Juvenile can be told apart from juvenile Black-crowned Night-Heron by smaller spots on wing coverts and **all-dark bill**. Fairly common and widespread in lowlands; resident population joined by NA migrants from Oct to April. Roosts during the day in trees near water, especially mangroves, but often seen standing on mudflats and river banks in daylight. 24" (61 cm).

Spoonbills & Ibises

THRESKIORNITHIDAE. Large wading birds with long, distinctive bills—decurved in the ibises and flattened in the spoonbills. All fly with the neck and legs extended.

Roseate Spoonbill
Platalea ajaja

No other CR bird is **pink**; juvenile is much paler, but note unique bill shape. Fairly common in Caño Negro region and around Gulf of Nicoya; uncommon elsewhere in lowlands and in western Central Valley (to 900 m). Individuals and groups forage in shallow water of open wetland habitats. 32" (81 cm).

Black-crowned
Night-Heron

adult

juv.

Boat-billed Heron

adult

juv.

Yellow-crowned
Night-Heron

adult

juv.

Roseate Spoonbill

adult

juv.

Spoonbills & Ibises

White Ibis
Eudocimus albus

The **red bill and legs** set adult apart from white-colored herons and egrets. In flight, note **black wing tips**. Juvenile has mostly brownish upperparts, but the curved pinkish bill identifies it as an ibis (Whimbrel [p. 70] has striped head); also note white rump, belly, and underwing. Very common in Caño Negro region and around Gulf of Nicoya; uncommon elsewhere in lowlands and in western Central Valley (to 900 m). Probes in moist substrate of marshes and mudflats, also along streams; usually in small groups. 25" (64 cm).

Glossy Ibis
Plegadis falcinellus

In poor light, could be confused with Green Ibis, but always appears slimmer than that species. In good light, there should be no confusion. Fairly uncommon in wetlands of Palo Verde and Caño Negro regions. Small groups forage in freshwater marshes. 23" (58 cm).

White-faced Ibis
Plegadis chihi

Nearly identical to Glossy Ibis, but adult has red iris and reddish skin on face; juvenile is basically indistinguishable from Glossy Ibis. Known from one specimen taken in the Térraba Valley in the late 1800s. **Not illustrated**. 23" (58 cm).

Green Ibis
Mesembrinibis cayennensis

A **stocky**, dark ibis, which in good light shows bronzy green hues (compare with Glossy Ibis); feathers on back of head and nape often appear ruffled, giving it a slightly crested look. Uncommon in Caribbean lowlands, occasionally to 700 m. Prefers forested areas, where individuals or pairs forage in swamps or along streams; also found at edge of more open marsh habitat, as in Caño Negro. At dawn and dusk, gives a hollow, rolling *krwa-krwa-krwa-krwa*. 21" (53 cm).

Sunbittern

EURYPYGIDAE. The sole member of its family, the neotropical Sunbittern is restricted to gallery forests—both rushing, boulder-strewn mountain streams and slow-flowing lowland rivers and swamps. Its slow movements while foraging for invertebrates and small vertebrates and its cryptic coloration can make it difficult to spot.

Sunbittern
Eurypyga helias

The **long bill** and the shape of the body suggest a heron, but the **striped head pattern** eliminates any confusion. The spectacular sunburst pattern on the upper surface of the opened wings is also diagnostic. Uncommon in wet lowlands and foothills of Caribbean and southern Pacific (north to about Quepos), to 1,500 m. Emits a far-carrying, forlorn, rising whistled note lasting about one second. 18" (46 cm).

adult

White Ibis

juv.

Glossy Ibis

Green Ibis

New World Vultures

CATHARTIDAE. Often mistaken for hawks (and far more often seen) as they soar in search of carrion, their preferred food. The members of the genus *Cathartes* have a highly developed sense of smell, while the other genera rely on vision for locating food sources. These relatives of the storks and ibises have evolved strong, hooked beaks for ripping the flesh of dead animals. The color of their naked heads is important in determining species.

Black Vulture
Coragyps atratus

The **black head** differentiates it from the Lesser Yellow-headed Vulture and the Turkey Vulture. The juvenile King Vulture, also with a black head, is distinguished by its pale iris. The **white patch on primaries** (visible in flight) sets the Black Vulture apart from the three other CR vultures, as well as the Common and Mangrove Black-Hawks (p. 44). Generally the most commonly seen soaring bird countrywide below timberline, though less common in extensively forested areas. In addition to carrion, also feeds on human refuse and fruit (e.g., oil palm and bananas). 25" (64 cm).

Lesser Yellow-headed Vulture
Cathartes burrovianus

Not reliably told apart from Turkey Vultures unless **orange-yellow head** color is seen. Fairly common in Caño Negro region; casual in Pacific lowlands. An open country species that may feed primarily on dead fish. 25" (64 cm).

Turkey Vulture
Cathartes aura

Told apart from other vultures by its **red head**. Resident race distinguished from migrant Turkey Vultures by pale-bluish nape. In flight, all Turkey Vultures have distinctive **two-tone underwing pattern**, as does the Lesser Yellow-headed Vulture. The very similarly patterned Zone-tailed Hawk (p. 44) has feathered black head, yellow cere and legs, and faint tail bands; both species typically soar with wings held above the horizontal. Common resident countrywide, though uncommon above 2,000 m. Spectacular numbers of passage migrants (accompanied by Broad-winged and Swainson's Hawks) traverse CR from mid-Sept to late Oct and from late Jan to early May, mostly in Caribbean lowlands. 30" (76 cm).

King Vulture
Sarcoramphus papa

Adults are distinctive; even flying at a distance, the **black-and-white plumage pattern** should show (soaring Wood Stork [p. 18] is similarly patterned, but has long neck and legs). The blackish juvenile somewhat resembles other vultures in flight, but shows **uniformly dark underwing**; on perched juveniles, note **pale iris** and white flecking on underparts. Uncommon in lowlands and foothills, to 1,200 m. Prefers areas where mature forest still exists, though readily soars over open country. 32" (81 cm).

Black Vulture

juv.

adult

adult

Turkey Vulture

Lesser Yellow-headed
Vulture

adult

juv.

adult

King Vulture

ACCIPITRIDAE. A diverse, worldwide family of predatory birds characterized by keen vision (for finding prey), powerful feet with sharp talons (for catching and killing prey), and a sharp, hooked bill (for ripping prey apart). Except during spectacular migrations, most species are present at relatively low densities, which makes it less likely you will encounter them. Also, only a few species typically use exposed, obvious perches or soar regularly. Many juveniles can be very difficult to identify to species level.

Osprey
Pandion haliaetus

Dark eye line separates **white crown** from white underparts; soars on long, distinctively **crooked wings**. Common winter resident from early Sept to April, to 2,800 m; common passage migrant along coasts from early Sept to Oct and from March to April; uncommon summer resident from May to Aug. Found near water, from sea coasts to highland trout ponds; hunts for fish, typically by hovering, then plunging feet first into the water; perches on high, exposed branches. 23" (58 cm).

Gray-headed Kite
Leptodon cayanensis

Small gray head (often appears dovelike) contrasts with black back and white underparts; also note **bluish-gray soft parts**. In flight, recalls a hawk-eagle (p. 48), but combination of **black wing linings** and **white body** is unique. Juveniles are variable in plumage with pale, intermediate, and dark morphs—all have yellow-orange soft parts. Pale juvenile resembles Black-and-white Hawk-Eagle (p. 48), but is brown and white and has **unfeathered tarsi**. Fairly uncommon in lowlands and foothills, to 900 m. Perches in canopy and at forest edges; soars on broad wings. Call is a series of high, excited barking notes, lasting about 10 seconds. 20" (51 cm).

Harris's Hawk
Parabuteo unicinctus

Rufous shoulders and thighs of both adult and juvenile birds are diagnostic; in flight, note white rump and base of tail. Uncommon in lowlands of northwestern Pacific and Caño Negro region. Prefers open country with scattered trees for perching, but also uses utility poles; soars regularly. Utters a deep, harsh *raaaah*. 21" (53 cm).

Black-collared Hawk
Busarellus nigricollis

A very distinctive raptor. Uncommon in Caño Negro region and rare elsewhere in wet lowlands. Found near clear, calm water, where it feeds mainly on fish snatched from surface (seldom submerses itself in the manner of an Osprey). Perches at low to middle levels looking out over water; soars on broad, flat wings. 20" (51 cm).

Osprey

Gray-headed Kite

adult

adult

intermediate juv.

pale juv.

adult

adult

adult

juv.

Harris's Hawk

adult

adult

juv.

Black-collared Hawk

Hook-billed Kite
Chondrohierax uncinatus

In all plumages, can be recognized by decidedly **hooked bill**, **pale iris**, yellow-orange legs, and bare **greenish-yellow cere and lore**. The black morph is similar to the male Snail Kite, but the latter species has a yellow-orange to reddish cere. Rare in lowlands and foothills, to 1,000 m. Inhabits swamp forest and wooded areas near water, where it preys on snails and lizards. Occasionally soars on broad, oval wings that are pinched in at base of trailing edge. 17" (43 cm).

Snail Kite
Rostrhamus sociabilis

The **yellow-orange to reddish cere** distinguishes the male Snail Kite from the black morph Hook-billed Kite, which has a heavier, hooked bill; male further distinguished by **white basal half of tail** (especially obvious in flight). These features also differentiate female and juvenile birds from other streaked juvenile raptors and the adult female Northern Harrier (p. 40). Female resembles juvenile, but is darker. Fairly uncommon in Palo Verde and Caño Negro regions; casual at other lowland sites. Perches near the ground and flies low over freshwater marshes in search of snails. 17" (43 cm).

Double-toothed Kite
Harpagus bidentatus

Plumage pattern recalls a Broad-winged Hawk (p. 42), but the **dark stripe on center of white throat** is diagnostic. In flight, recalls an accipiter (p. 38), but the **puffy white undertail coverts** are conspicuous. Fairly common in wet lowlands and foothills, uncommon in northwestern Pacific lowlands and in Central Valley; to 1,700 m. Regularly soars on sunny mornings; perches at middle levels of forest, second growth, forest edges, and gardens; often follows foraging troops of White-throated Capuchins and Central American Squirrel Monkeys in order to catch the lizards and large insects that these mammals flush out. Calls with several high, thin *tsip* notes followed by two or three longer *tseeeah* notes. 14" (36 cm).

Hook-billed Kite

juv.

adult female

adult male

adult female

adult black morph

adult male

adult male

juv.

Snail Kite

adult

juv.

adult

Double-toothed Kite

Swallow-tailed Kite
Elanoides forficatus

Handsome and graceful in flight. The **long, forked tail** is diagnostic. Common breeding resident from late Dec to mid-Sept, mostly in foothills and mountains; generally absent from western Central Valley and northwestern Pacific; some year-round residents in southern Pacific and on Caribbean slope. Often in small groups (up to 50 or more in migration); usually consumes prey while in flight. 23" (58 cm).

Pearl Kite
Gampsonyx swainsonii

The **buffy yellow forecrown and cheeks** and **rufous flanks and thighs** readily identify this **tiny** raptor. First reported in CR in the mid-1990s, now fairly common along Pacific slope, to 1,000 m. Prefers open areas with scattered trees. 9" (23 cm).

White-tailed Kite
Elanus leucurus

The **white tail** and **black shoulders** are diagnostic. Since its arrival in CR in the mid-1950s, this species has now become fairly common countrywide to 1,500 m. Flies over open areas, including cities; often hovers while searching for prey. 16" (41 cm).

Plumbeous Kite
Ictinia plumbea

Adult and juvenile differentiated from adult and juvenile Mississippi Kite by **rufous on primaries**; also note that **wing tips extend beyond tip of tail** (noticeable when perched). Adult further differentiated from adult Mississippi Kite by two thin white bars on underside of tail. Breeding residents (from Feb to Sept) are fairly common in Caño Negro region and in mangroves and surrounding areas of northern half of Pacific coast; very uncommon elsewhere in lowlands. Passage migrants (from Feb to March and from July to Sept) are common along Caribbean coast. Perches on high, exposed branches and soars regularly, often catching insects on the wing. 14" (36 cm).

Mississippi Kite
Ictinia mississippiensis

Told apart from Plumbeous Kite by **white patch on upper surface of secondaries** and **all-black tail**. Juveniles of both species are very similar (see above). Common passage migrant in Caribbean lowlands and uncommon in Pacific lowlands and Central Valley, from mid-Sept to mid-Oct and from late March to early May. Mostly seen in obvious migratory groups, flying and soaring on long, pointed wings. 14" (36 cm).

Swallow-tailed Kite

Pearl Kite

adult

juv.

adult

White-tailed Kite

adult

adult

adult

adult

juv.

adult

juv.

Plumbeous Kite

Mississippi Kite

Bicolored Hawk
Accipiter bicolor

The **rufous thighs** on the two-toned gray adult are diagnostic. Juveniles are browner above, vary from white to buffy below, and do not always have rufous thighs; pale juvenile resembles pale morph Collared Forest-Falcon (p. 54), but has yellow (not greenish) cere and lacks dark crescent on ear coverts. In addition, pale juvenile resembles some juvenile Barred Forest-Falcons (p. 52), as well as adult Slaty-backed Forest-Falcon (p. 54), but lacks yellow orbital skin. Rare in humid and wet regions, to 1,800 m. Ambushes avian prey from perches at almost any level in mature wet forest, tall second growth, forest edges, and gardens. Gives a series of more than a dozen barking, trogonlike notes: *keh-keh-keh-keh...* . Male 14" (36 cm); female 17" (43 cm).

Tiny Hawk
Accipiter superciliosus

The shape and pattern of this **very small** hawk recall a Sharp-shinned Hawk, but Tiny Hawk never combines rufous barring below with dark gray above. **Noticeably darker crown** and lack of yellow orbital skin distinguish it from similarly patterned Barred Forest-Falcon (p. 52). Very uncommon in Golfo Dulce lowlands, in Caribbean lowlands and foothills, and also on Pacific side of northern cordilleras; to 1,500 m. Occasionally perches on exposed branches at edge of mature wet forest, but normally stays concealed in denser vegetation, from where it ambushes small birds, especially hummingbirds. Male 8" (20 cm); female 11" (28 cm).

Sharp-shinned Hawk
Accipiter striatus

In all plumages, nearly identical to the Cooper's Hawk; best told apart by **square tip of tail**. Also somewhat resembles Tiny Hawk (see above). Juvenile resembles Merlin (p. 50), but has **yellow iris**; on perched birds, also note that wings do not extend beyond base of tail. Uncommon NA migrant from mid-Oct to March, generally at middle elevations, from 500 to 2,500 m. Usually inconspicuous because it hunts for birds from cover of vegetation at edges of second growth, fields, and gardens; occasionally seen soaring. Male 11" (28 cm); female 14" (36 cm).

Cooper's Hawk
Accipiter cooperii

A large version of the Sharp-shinned Hawk, but with a **rounded tail tip**. Uncommon NA migrant from mid-Oct to March, from 700 to 3,000 m. Most often seen flying in the typical *Accipiter* manner of several flaps followed by a short sail. Male 15" (38 cm); female 18" (46 cm).

adult

juv.

juv.

Bicolored Hawk

adult

adult

juv.

adult
male

juv.

Sharp-shinned Hawk

Tiny Hawk

juv.

adult

adult

Cooper's
Hawk

Northern Harrier
Circus cyaneus

In all plumages, note **long wings and tail** and **white rump**. Somewhat similarly patterned female Snail Kite (p. 34) has short, unbarred tail and orangish cere. Very uncommon winter resident in Pacific lowlands, Caño Negro region, and Central Valley, from early Oct to early May, to 1,500 m; very uncommon passage migrant in Caribbean lowlands. Wintering birds hunt by flying low over open areas, gliding with wings held above horizontal; they readily perch on the ground. 20" (51 cm).

Crane Hawk
Geranospiza caerulescens

Differs from other essentially black raptors by combination of **red iris**, **dark-gray cere**, and long **orange-red legs**; in flight, note **white crescent across primaries** (juvenile has white on face and whitish barring on underparts). Uncommon but widespread in lowlands, to 500 m. Forages at middle and upper levels of mature forest and forest edges by reaching into bromeliads and knotholes with its long legs; soars infrequently. Utters a rather agitated, nasal scream: *keeur*. 19" (48 cm).

White Hawk
Leucopternis albicollis

No other CR raptor has an **all-white back**. Fairly uncommon in Caribbean lowlands and foothills, on Pacific slope of Guanacaste Cordillera, and from Carara south; rare above 1,200 m; also rare on southern Nicoya Peninsula. Perches placidly at middle levels of mature wet forest, advanced second growth, and forest edges; occasionally follows foraging troops of monkeys in order to catch the lizards and large insects that they flush out; soars regularly on broad wings. In flight, delivers a harsh, rasping *hee-EE-ah*. 23" (58 cm).

Barred Hawk
Leucopternis princeps

No other CR raptor combines a **blackish head and breast** with **finely barred underparts**; in flight, shows notably broad wings and short tail. Fairly common at middle elevations on Caribbean slope, from 400 to 1,600 m (up to 2,500 m in south); also fairly common on Pacific slope of Talamanca Cordillera, above 1,300 m; rare on Osa and Nicoya Peninsulas. Perches at middle levels of montane wet forest and forest edges, but most often seen soaring. In flight, it frequently vocalizes with loud, clear whistles (*whEE-er*) that are sometimes run together in a fast series. 24" (61 cm).

Semiplumbeous Hawk
Leucopternis semiplumbeus

The **orange cere and legs** and **white underparts** are diagnostic. Fairly uncommon in Caribbean lowlands, rarely above 500 m. Inhabits middle levels of mature wet forest, advanced second growth, and forest edges, perching quietly; does not soar. Calls with a short series of upslurred notes: *klerEE-klerEE-klerEE*. 15" (38 cm).

adult
male

juv.

Northern Harrier

adult
female

adult

juv.

adult

Crane
Hawk

White Hawk

Barred Hawk

Semiplumbeous
Hawk

Gray Hawk
Buteo nitidus

Adult possibly confused with Roadside Hawk, but has **gray barring below** (not rufous) and **all-gray wings** (no rufous in primaries); in flight, **black-and-white tail bands** recall a Broad-winged Hawk, but note overall gray coloration. Juvenile closely resembles juvenile Roadside and Broad-winged Hawks, but has **bold, teardrop spotting below**. Juvenile also similar to juvenile Common and Mangrove Black-Hawks (p. 44), but lacks barred undertail coverts. Common in northwest Pacific and lowlands of northern central Caribbean; fairly common in western Central Valley and in lowlands of southern Pacific; to 1,100 m. Prefers forest edges and open areas with scattered trees; uses exposed perches, including utility poles; soars regularly. Whistles a shrill, descending *PEE-yeeur*. 17" (43 cm).

Roadside Hawk
Buteo magnirostris

The **gray head and breast** together with **rufous barring** on rest of underparts readily identify perched adult (the somewhat similar adult Gray Hawk has gray barring below). In flight, the **rufous in primaries** is definitive. Juvenile recalls various other juvenile hawks with streaked underparts, but note **rufous barring on thighs**. Widespread and fairly common, to 1,500 m. Favors light woodlands and open areas with scattered trees, typically perching fairly low, even on fence posts; seldom soars. Delivers a squeaky, piercing *kwe-EEE-ee*. 15" (38 cm).

Broad-winged Hawk
Buteo platypterus

Plumage pattern of perched adult somewhat resembles that of Double-toothed Kite (p. 34), but note brown head and **dark stripe on side of throat**. In flight, looking from below, the **whitish flight feathers have black tips**; also note black-and-white tail bands (compare with Gray Hawk). Very rare dark morph (not illustrated) has dark-brown body and wing linings. Juvenile told apart from other juvenile hawks with streaked underparts by **dark malar stripe**. Abundant passage migrant from Oct to mid-Nov and from early March to May; traverses CR in spectacular flocks of soaring birds (usually with Turkey Vultures [p. 30] and Swainson's Hawks [p. 46]); to 3,500 m. Common and widespread winter resident, from Sept to May, mostly below 2,000 m. Perches at middle levels of forest edges; soars frequently. Whistles a high, even *pteeeeeee*. 16" (41 cm).

Short-tailed Hawk
Buteo brachyurus

In flight, both pale and dark morph birds show **dark tips on both the pale primaries and the darker secondaries**. The darkish tail is faintly banded and, despite the bird's name, not particularly short. Pale morph birds have head pattern like White-tailed Hawk, but head is brown not gray. Juveniles are quite similar to their respective adult morphs. Widespread, to 2,000 m. One of the most common soaring raptors in CR; rarely seen perched. Gives a high-pitched, harsh *keeeea*. 16" (41 cm).

White-tailed Hawk
Buteo albicaudatus

Adult resembles pale morph Short-tailed Hawk, but note **gray head** and **rufous shoulders** (visible on perched birds). In flight, note obvious **white tail** (which looks decidedly short) with single black subterminal band. On juveniles and rare dark morph adults, note **pale-gray tail that contrasts with dark body**. Very uncommon in northwestern Pacific; rare in Central Valley and intermontane valleys of southern Pacific; to 1,500 m. Prefers cleared areas; soars on broad wings and often hangs stationary in the wind. Repeats a shrill, whistled *kleewee*. 23" (58 cm).

Gray Hawk

adult

juv.

adult

Roadside Hawk

adult

adult

juv.

Broad-winged Hawk

adult

juv.

adult

adult dark morph

adult pale morph

juv. pale morph

adult pale morph

Short-tailed Hawk

White-tailed Hawk

Zone-tailed Hawk
Buteo albonotatus

In flight, most likely mistaken for a Turkey Vulture (p. 30), but note feathered black head, yellow cere and legs, and whitish tail bands. Rarely seen perched birds are similar to black-hawks, but have slimmer build, longer tail, and shorter legs. Uncommon in northwestern Pacific, south to Tarcoles, and in Central Valley, to 1,500 m; rare elsewhere in lowlands and foothills. Occurs in open, often marshy, areas. Flies with rocking motion and with wings held above the horizontal. 20" (51 cm).

Great Black-Hawk
Buteogallus urubitinga

The **slaty lores** and **barred thighs** differentiate perched adult from other black raptors; in flight, note **white rump and tail band**. Juvenile is very similar to juvenile Common and Mangrove Black-Hawks, but has more finely barred tail. Widespread but generally rare, becoming slightly more common in Palo Verde region and at middle elevations; to 1,600 m. Perches at middle levels of forest and forest edges, often near water; soars occasionally. Flight call is a drawn-out, screaming whistle that fluctuates slightly in pitch. 26" (66 cm).

Common Black-Hawk
Buteogallus anthracinus

Identical to Mangrove Black-Hawk in all aspects (and perhaps conspecific), but no range overlap. **Yellow lores** distinguish adult from other black raptors with yellow cere and legs; in flight, broad wings and short tail could suggest a Black Vulture (p. 30), but note **white tail band**. Juvenile is very similar to juvenile Great Black-Hawk, but has fewer and slightly wider tail bands; also resembles juvenile Gray Hawk (p. 42), but note barred undertail coverts. Common along Caribbean coast, rare elsewhere in Caribbean lowlands; almost always near water. Perches at lower and middle levels between sallies for crabs; soars regularly; often quite confiding. Whistles a series of ringing notes that rise in volume and pitch before fading. **Same illustrations as for Mangrove Black-Hawk**. 22" (56 cm).

Mangrove Black-Hawk
Buteogallus subtilis

Identical to Common Black-Hawk in all aspects (and perhaps conspecific), but no range overlap. Juvenile is very similar to juvenile Great Black-Hawk, but has fewer and slightly wider tail bands; also resembles juvenile Gray Hawk (p. 42), but note barred undertail coverts. Common along Pacific coast, especially in and around mangrove swamps, and also resident on Caño Island. **Same illustrations as for Common Black-Hawk**. 22" (56 cm).

Solitary Eagle
Harpyhaliaetus solitarius

Could be confused with Great Black-Hawk, but adult is **slate gray** (not black) with unbarred thighs; in flight, has enormous broad wings and **short tail barely extending past rear edge of wings**. Juvenile has heavy brown mottling that nearly forms a band across breast. Rare on Caribbean slope; also rare on Pacific slope of Talamanca Cordillera; from 500 to 2,200 m. Very rare in Golfo Dulce region and hills of Osa Peninsula. Perches at middle levels of mature wet forest and forest edges; soars regularly. Flight call is an even-pitched series of short, excited notes. 30" (76 cm).

adult

adult

juv.

Zone-tailed
Hawk

adult

adult

juv.

Great
Black-Hawk

adult

Common/Mangrove
Black-Hawk

juv.

adult

adult

Solitary Eagle

juv.

Swainson's Hawk
Buteo swainsoni

In all plumages (adults and juveniles of pale, intermediate, and dark morphs), note the distinctive flight silhouette with **long, narrow, pointed wings** and fairly long tail; intermediate in size between Broad-winged Hawks (p. 42) and Turkey Vultures (p. 30), both of which travel with Swainson's Hawks. Abundant and widespread passage migrant, from late Sept to Nov (when most numerous in Caribbean lowlands) and from late Feb to early May; to 3,500 m. Rare winter resident in Pacific lowlands and western Central Valley, from Oct to March, to 1,000 m. Migrates through CR in large, soaring flocks. 21" (53 cm).

Red-tailed Hawk
Buteo jamaicensis

In flight, adults of both resident and NA migrant races have diagnostic **orange-rufous tail**. Resident adult has **pale-rufous belly**; migrants are variable but typically show **dark streaking across belly**. Juvenile resident has heavily streaked underparts and buffy tail (grayish in most migrants) with narrow dark bands. Resident race (indicated on map) is fairly common in highlands above 1,500 m, uncommon from 1,500 m down to about 800 m; migrants (not indicated on map) are uncommon from Oct to April and can turn up almost anywhere, even in lowlands. Residents freely soar and often hang stationary in the wind; prefer partially cleared areas in montane regions and high, exposed perches. Screams a high, grating *keEEaah*. 22" (56 cm).

Harpy Eagle
Harpia harpyja

A massive bird of prey; adult recognized by **black band across upper breast**. In flight, wing linings have some black barring and spotting. Juvenile similar to smaller juvenile Crested Eagle, but has **double-pointed crest**. Now very rare and perhaps only on Osa Peninsula and in southern Talamanca Cordillera, to 2,000 m; formerly found on Caribbean slope. Hunts within the canopy of mature wet forest, mostly ambushing medium-sized mammals; does not soar. Call is a screaming *eeeeaa*. The national bird of Panama. Male 38" (97 cm); female 42" (107 cm).

Crested Eagle
Morphnus guianensis

Larger than any other raptor except the Harpy Eagle, which is twice the bulk. Adult pale morph similar to Harpy Eagle, but lacks black upper breast. Adult dark morph has bold barring on underparts. In flight, wing linings are white on pale morph and coarsely barred on dark morph. Juvenile closely resembles juvenile Harpy Eagle, but has **single-pointed crest**. Very rare in Caribbean lowlands and foothills and in southern Pacific, to 1,200 m. Perches at middle and upper levels of mature wet forest and forest edges; hunts medium-sized vertebrate prey; sometimes soars. Gives a shrill, rising, two-note whistle. 33" (84 cm).

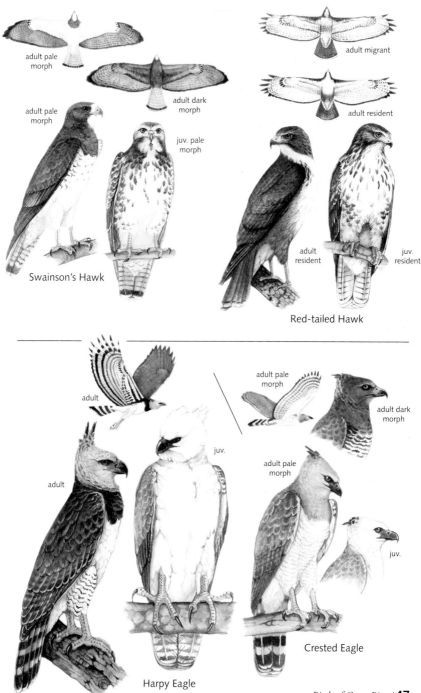

adult pale morph

adult dark morph

adult pale morph

juv. pale morph

Swainson's Hawk

adult migrant

adult resident

adult resident

juv. resident

Red-tailed Hawk

adult

adult

juv.

adult pale morph

adult dark morph

adult pale morph

juv.

Harpy Eagle

Crested Eagle

Hawks & Eagles

Black-and-white Hawk-Eagle
Spizastur melanoleucus

Closely resembles pale juvenile Gray-headed Kite (p. 32), but note **orange cere**, **yellow iris**, and **feathered tarsi**; also similar to juvenile Ornate Hawk-Eagle, but has **black mask** and **unbarred thighs**. Very rare in lowlands and foothills of Caribbean and southern Pacific slopes, to 1,200 m. Soars on flat wings; perches inconspicuously in canopy and at edges of mature wet forest. Whistles a series of clear notes: *klee, klee, klee… .* 23" (58 cm).

Ornate Hawk-Eagle
Spizaetus ornatus

The **tawny sides of head and chest** are diagnostic on adult. Juvenile distinguished by combination of pale head and breast and **barred thighs and flanks**. Uncommon in wet lowlands, foothills, and middle elevations of Caribbean and southern Pacific slopes, to 2,200 m. Perches at all levels inside mature wet forest; soars and vocalizes regularly. In flight, whistles a loud *wee-ew, weeh, weh, weh, weh*. 24" (61 cm).

Black Hawk-Eagle
Spizaetus tyrannus

Perched adult told apart from all other black raptors by **feathered tarsi with black-and-white barring**. In flight, no other dark raptor shows such **bold black-and-white barring on flight feathers**. Juvenile has unique combination of streaking on underparts and barred, feathered tarsi. Uncommon in wet lowlands, foothills, and middle elevations of Caribbean and southern Pacific slopes, to 2,000 m. Favors second growth, semi-open areas, and forest edges, often perching fairly low; soars freely and to great heights. Whistles a loud *weh, weh, WEEew*. 26" (66 cm).

Falcons

FALCONIDAE. Though the various species of this cosmopolitan family share no single obvious morphological characteristic to distinguish them from the closely related hawks and eagles, members of the genus *Falco* are typified by having long, pointed wings. Otherwise, the differences displayed by the various genera reflect their widely varying lifestyles, from carrion-eaters of open country to secretive bird-hunters of tropical forests. Females are larger than males in many species.

Red-throated Caracara
Ibycter americanus

Almost more suggestive of a guan than a raptor, but differentiated by **bare red facial skin**. Very uncommon in Golfo Dulce region and rare in Caribbean lowlands and foothills, to 1,200 m. Noisy pairs or small groups roam through upper levels of mature wet forest, second growth, forest edges, and gardens. Feeds largely on larvae extracted from wasp and bee nests. Makes raucous shouts similar to those of macaws (p. 98). 20" (51 cm).

Black-and-white
Hawk-Eagle

adult

Ornate
Hawk-Eagle

juv.

adult

adult

Black
Hawk-Eagle

juv.

adult

Red-throated
Caracara

American Kestrel
Falco sparverius

Somewhat similar to Merlin, but the **two bold bars on side of head** and the mostly **rufous tail** readily identify both sexes. Widespread but generally uncommon NA migrant from Sept to April, most likely in northern Pacific and Central Valley; to 1,800 m. Favors open fields, where it perches on posts, utility wires, and exposed branches of isolated trees; often hovers while hunting for insect prey. Gives a shrill, repeated *kli-kli-kli*, similar to that of Bat Falcon. 10" (25 cm).

Merlin
Falco columbarius

Told apart from American Kestrel by **dark tail** and **lack of bold facial pattern**; similar to juvenile Sharp-shinned Hawk (p. 38), but has dark iris and long wings that nearly reach the tip of the tail (noticeable when perched). In flight, has powerful steady wingbeats. Rare NA migrant from Sept to mid-March; mostly migrates along coasts, but can occur anywhere, even above timberline. Favors open areas, where it pursues small birds and insect prey. Male 10" (25 cm); female 13" (33 cm).

Aplomado Falcon
Falco femoralis

The bold head pattern, white throat and breast, dark belly band, and pale-rufous lower underparts are diagnostic. Known from only three reports in the last few decades, all in the Palo Verde region. Hunts from exposed perch in open country. **Not illustrated**. Male 15" (38 cm); female 17" (43 cm).

Bat Falcon
Falco rufigularis

Color of throat, upper breast, and sides of neck is always fairly uniform on a given bird, though it varies from individual to individual (white to pale rufous). The fine barring on the dark midsection also varies, from white to rufous. Very similar to Orange-breasted Falcon, but on that bird the upper breast and sides of neck are a different color than the throat. In flight, can look remarkably like a White-collared Swift (p. 116). Uncommon in wet lowlands and middle elevations; rare in northwest Pacific; to 1,500 m (rarely to 2,900 m). Found on high, exposed perches in partly to mostly cleared areas; captures fast-flying prey (swallows, swifts, hummingbirds, and bats) on the wing. Shrill *ki-ki-ki-ki...* is similar to call of American Kestrel. Male 10" (25 cm); female 12" (31 cm).

Orange-breasted Falcon
Falco deiroleucus

Bat Falcons with pale rufous throats are often incorrectly identified as Orange-breasted Falcons, but the latter species always shows **white throat above rufous breast**, and dark midsection has **coarse, white, scalloped barring**. No valid reports since the late 1950s; the few records are all from the foothills and middle elevations of the Caribbean slope. Hunts from exposed perch in forested terrain; captures birds in flight. **Not illustrated**. Male 13" (33 cm); female 15" (38 cm).

Peregrine Falcon
Falco peregrinus

Wide moustachial bar, giving a hooded appearance, distinguishes even streaked juvenile birds. Uncommon winter resident from mid-Sept to early May; regularly seen in Palo Verde and Caño Negro regions, near the mouth of the Tarcoles River, and in western Central Valley; very uncommon elsewhere in lowlands and foothills. Fairly common passage migrant along Caribbean coast from mid-Sept to Oct and from March to early May; occasionally in Central Valley and Pacific lowlands. Winter residents prefer open areas with concentrations of waterfowl; they attack prey in fast, powerful dives; regularly soar. Male 15" (38 cm); female 18" (46 cm).

American Kestrel

male

female

Merlin

male

juv. female

Bat Falcon

adult

adult

juv.

Peregrine Falcon

Falcons

Crested Caracara
Caracara cheriway

Distinctive adult has **black-and-white pattern** and **orange-red facial skin**. Similarly patterned brown-and-buff juvenile resembles both Yellow-headed Caracara and Laughing Falcon in flight, but note dark cap and belly. Common in northern Pacific lowlands and foothills; with deforestation, becoming increasingly common in southern Pacific lowlands and coastal foothills, northern central Caribbean lowlands, and western Central Valley; to 900 m. Prefers agricultural areas; perches high in trees as well as on ground; feeds primarily on carrion. 23" (58 cm).

Yellow-headed Caracara
Milvago chimachima

Adult similar to Laughing Falcon, but note **thin, dark line behind the eye**. Juvenile resembles adult, but has streaked head and underparts. In flight, both adult and juvenile resemble juvenile Crested Caracara, but lack dark cap and belly. Since first CR record in 1973, has become common in southern Pacific, to 1,200 m; rare north of Gulf of Nicoya, but apparently still spreading north—one adult seen in Caño Negro, Oct 2004. Found in agricultural areas; perches high in trees as well as on ground, and even on the backs of cattle; feeds mostly on carrion. Utters a dreadful, nasal scream: *reeeeaaah*. 16" (41 cm).

Laughing Falcon
Herpetotheres cachinnans

The **broad black mask** is diagnostic. In flight, shows **buffy patch in primaries** similar to that of Yellow-headed Caracara and juvenile Crested Caracara. Fairly common and widespread in lowlands and foothills, to 1,200 m; rarely to 1,800 m. Often perches conspicuously at forest edges and in open areas with scattered trees; feeds primarily on snakes. Calls mainly at dawn and dusk with a loud, far-carrying *gwa-co* (the first note higher and louder), thus its local common name: *guaco*. The full song is often given in duet, starting with single *gwa!* notes and accelerating into a crazed laughing cacophony. 20" (51 cm).

Barred Forest-Falcon
Micrastur ruficollis

Finely barred underparts distinguish adult from all but Tiny Hawk (p. 38), but note **yellow orbital skin** and lack of a dark crown. Underparts of juvenile vary from white to buff; the extent of barring also varies, from none to heavy; often with buffy nuchal collar; unbarred individuals resemble juvenile Bicolored Hawk (p. 38), but note yellow orbital skin. Fairly uncommon at middle elevations and in highlands, to 2,800 m; very uncommon in wet lowlands. Ambushes small vertebrate prey from low perches in mature forest, advanced second growth, and forest edges; also takes large insects, particularly at army-ant raids. Calls at dawn and dusk from high, concealed perch with a repetitious, barking *ehr!*. Male 13" (33 cm); female 15" (38 cm).

adult

juv.

adult

adult

adult

juv.

Crested Caracara

Yellow-headed Caracara

Laughing Falcon

gra
from
Biagua
times. 11

Falcons

Slaty-backed Forest-Falcon
Micrastur mirandollei

Adult told apart from juvenile Bicolored Hawk (p. 38) by **yellow orbital skin**. Juvenile has broad scalloping on underparts. Rare in Caribbean lowlands, west to San Carlos region. Ambushes vertebrate prey from low perches in mature wet forest and advanced second growth. From perch in lower canopy, calls at dawn and dusk with a series of about a dozen *haaah* notes that rise slightly in pitch and volume. Male 16" (41 cm); female 18" (46 cm).

Collared Forest-Falcon
Micrastur semitorquatus

Adult pale morph readily identified by **black crescent on ear coverts**; the similar pale juvenile Bicolored Hawk (p. 38) has yellow cere (not greenish). Variable juvenile morphs and rare adult dark morph best recognized by **long legs and tail** and **greenish cere and bare facial skin**. Fairly common in Pacific lowlands; very uncommon in Caribbean lowlands; also very uncommon at middle elevations on Pacific and Caribbean slopes, to 1,500 m. Hunts in lower levels of mature forest, gallery forest, and second growth. Calls at dawn and dusk from high perch with a loud, nasal *owh!*, somewhat like note of Laughing Falcon. Male 20" (51 cm); female 24" (61 cm).

Crakes & Rails

RALLIDAE. Many members of this widespread family are extremely difficult to see since they seldom leave the grassy cover of marsh habitat, and might go completely unnoticed if not for their frequent vocalizations. Their thin bodies facilitate moving through dense vegetation; they occasionally come into view along edges at dawn and dusk. Some species favor forested habitats, including mangroves, while gallinules, moorhens, and coots are relatively easy to see on or around ponds and open water in marshes. Colors of the head, bill, and legs are key field marks.

Gray-necked Wood-Rail
Aramides cajanea

The gray neck sets it apart from the smaller Rufous-necked Wood-Rail. Common and widespread in wet lowlands, foothills, and in Central Valley, to 1,400 m; uncommon in northwestern Pacific. Forages on the floor of mature forest, tall second growth, and even in forest remnants, usually near water; also in mangroves. The resounding call, most often heard at twilight and bringing to mind a group of drunken chickens, is given in chorus: *káh-klah, káh-klah, kah koh-ho-ho-ho-hah*. 15" (38 cm).

Rufous-necked Wood-Rail
Aramides axillaris

Similar to Gray-necked Wood-Rail, but **head and neck are rufous**; also note y mantle. Very uncommon in Gulf of Nicoya mangroves; also reported humid forest in Cerro Plano (near Monteverde) and swamp forest near de Upala. The call is a rollicking *ki-kyi-kip-kyip*, repeated numerous (28 cm).

Slaty-backed
Forest-Falcon

adult dark
morph

adult
pale morph

juv.

Collared
Forest-Falcon

Gray-necked Wood-Rail

Rufous-necked Wood-Rail

Uniform Crake
Amaurolimnas concolor

Looks and behaves like a small wood-rail (p. 54), but is **uniformly colored**; in silhouette, could be mistaken for the much more common Black-faced Antthrush (p. 186). Very uncommon in Caribbean lowlands and foothills, to 1,000 m; rare in Golfo Dulce region. Forages on the floor of swamp forest and near streams in mature wet forest and advanced second growth. Whistles a crescendoing series of six or more upslurred *suweee* notes. 8" (20 cm).

Ocellated Crake
Micropygia schomburgkii

White spots (with black borders) on upperparts and unbarred **brownish underparts** are diagnostic. Only CR record is a bird collected in grassland near Buenos Aires. Status unknown, but vocalizations recently reported from hills north of Buenos Aires may well be of this species. In alarm, gives a harsh, sizzling call; at dawn and dusk, sings a lengthy series of forceful notes: *pr-pr-pr-pr.* 6" (15 cm).

Ruddy Crake
Laterallus ruber

Distinguished by combination of **unbarred rufous underparts**, **dark-gray hood**, black bill, and olive green legs. Known in CR from two birds seen near a marsh between Miravalles Volcano and Tenorio Volcano in May 1955. Makes a whinnying *churr* similar to that of the White-throated Crake. 6" (15 cm).

White-throated Crake
Laterallus albigularis

Both Caribbean and Pacific races told apart from other crakes and rails in CR by **barred flanks** and **rufous breast**. Juvenile birds have gray breasts, but can be distinguished from Gray-breasted Crakes by lack of rufous nape. Common and widespread in wet lowlands and foothills; also common in Central Valley, to 1,500 m; rare north of Carara. Inhabits almost any damp grassy area; though very furtive, occasionally reveals itself at edges and openings. Frequently utters a loud, descending *churr*, lasting 5 seconds or more. 6" (15 cm).

Gray-breasted Crake
Laterallus exilis

Differentiated from similar crakes and rails by **ashy-gray breast** and **rufous nape**. Uncommon in Caribbean lowlands and the Golfo Dulce region. Prefers wet grassy areas with standing water; also occurs on riverbanks. Gives a series of up to ten high notes in rapid succession, with the first note slightly higher and longer: *teek, teetee-tee-teek.* Also makes a descending *churr* like the White-throated Crake, but softer and scratchier. 6" (15 cm).

Black Rail
Laterallus jamaicensis

No other CR rail (or crake) is as dark, especially on breast. Status unknown, but there are sight reports from Palo Verde, Caño Negro, and Golfo Dulce regions (dates uncited). Extremely furtive in marsh grass and wet pastures. On moonlit nights, gives a three-note call, with the last note lower (*ki-kee-doo*). 6" (15 cm).

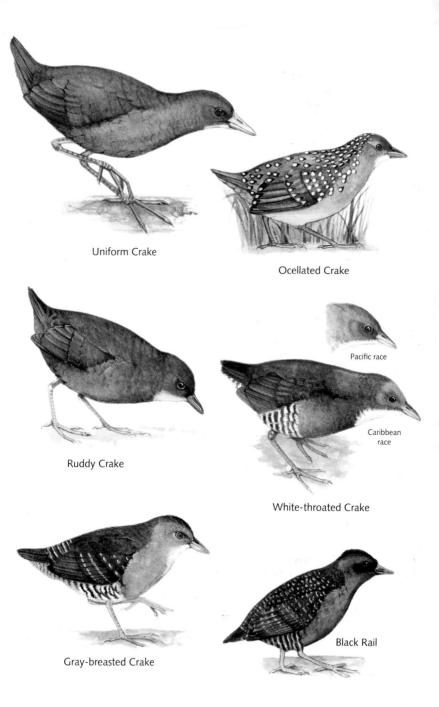

Uniform Crake

Ocellated Crake

Ruddy Crake

Pacific race

Caribbean race

White-throated Crake

Gray-breasted Crake

Black Rail

Sora
Porzana carolina

The **yellow bill** and **black face and throat** are diagnostic. Juvenile distinguished from adult by less black on face, darker bill, and dull buffy neck and breast; the similar but smaller Yellow-breasted Crake shows a distinct white superciliary. Fairly common NA migrant from Oct to early May, to 1,500 m. Favors the reedy edges of marshes and ponds. 8" (20 cm).

Yellow-breasted Crake
Porzana flaviventer

No other CR crake or rail has a **black eye line** and **white superciliary** (compare with juvenile Sora). Known from Palo Verde and Caño Negro regions; perhaps occurs in other suitable lowland sites. Inhabits the grassy margins of marshes and ponds. Utters a high, scratchy *kreerh*. 5" (13 cm).

Paint-billed Crake
Neocrex erythrops

Readily identified by combination of **red legs** and **two-tone bill** (which consists of a red base and a yellow-green tip). Status unknown; several sightings since 1985 in Caribbean and Golfo Dulce lowlands. Occurs in a variety of habitats, including wet pastures, rice fields, drainage ditches in banana plantations, and marshes. Sings a long series of accelerating and descending notes ending with several short, trilled *churr* notes. 8" (20 cm).

Spotted Rail
Pardirallus maculatus

The **speckled foreparts** make it distinctive. Status unknown; reported in the Central Valley from Cartago to Turrialba, and also in Palo Verde and Caño Negro regions. Favors tall reedy growth at edges of marshes. Produces a series of low, grunting, accelerating notes. 10" (25 cm).

Clapper Rail
Rallus longirostris

No other **large** CR rail has **barred flanks and belly**. Status unknown; reported in CR only from mangroves in Gulf of Nicoya, where first discovered in 1998. Mostly at dawn and dusk, produces a series of dry clacking notes that accelerates then slows. 14" (36 cm).

Purple Gallinule
Porphyrio martinica

Adult is instantly recognizable; juvenile has buffy brown neck, whereas juvenile moorhens and coots (p. 60) have grayish necks and juvenile jacanas (p. 60) show a white throat and breast. Fairly common and widespread, to 1,500 m. Walks through and clambers on vegetation around marshes, ponds, and riverbanks; rarely swims. Gives a high-pitched *kick*; also cackles like a hen. 13" (33 cm).

Sora

Yellow-breasted Crake

adult

juv.

Paint-billed Crake

Spotted Rail

Clapper Rail

adult

juv.

Purple Gallinule

Crakes & Rails

American Coot
Fulica americana

The distinctive **white bill and adjoining frontal shield** set it apart from the Common Moorhen. Juvenile very similar to juvenile Common Moorhen, but has lighter bill and lacks side stripe. Widespread, to 1,500 m; resident population joined by NA migrants from Oct to April. Swims on ponds and lagoons and occasionally dives. Makes a variety of clucking and cackling sounds. 15" (38 cm).

Common Moorhen
Gallinula chloropus

Similar to American Coot, but adult's **red frontal shield** (adjoined to mostly red bill) is diagnostic; also shows **white stripe on side**. Juvenile is very similar to juvenile American Coot, but has darker bill and white side stripe. Widespread, to 1,500 m, but absent from many suitable-looking sites. Favors marshes with floating vegetation; walks along reedy edges and is frequently seen swimming. Makes a variety of clucking and cackling sounds. 14" (36 cm).

Jaçanas

JACANIDAE. This small pantropical family is characterized by extremely long toes that effectively distribute the bird's weight, thus allowing it to walk over floating vegetation. Except for one monogamous African species, the females are polyandrous, courting two or more males whenever possible. Male mates of polyandrous females tend to nesting duties and rearing of the precocial chicks. These birds are relatively weak fliers that momentarily hold their wings vertically outstretched upon landing.

Wattled Jaçana
Jacana jacana

Resembles Northern Jaçana, but adult has a **black back** and a **red frontal shield** that extends into a short wattle on either side of the bill. Juvenile nearly identical to juvenile Northern Jaçana, but shows beginnings of red shield and wattle. Occasionally strays from Panama into the southern Pacific region of CR; has been seen at Laurel, Gamba, San Vito, and San Isidro de El General. 9" (23 cm).

Northern Jaçana
Jacana spinosa

Although this bird could recall a Common Moorhen or Purple Gallinule (p. 58), the **yellow-green flight feathers** are diagnostic. Juvenile is very differently plumaged and often mistaken for some type of shorebird, but the remarkably **long toes** and yellowish flight feathers set it apart; compare with juvenile Wattled Jaçana. Common and widespread, to 1,500 m. Conspicuous resident of marshes, ponds, wet pastures, and lowland riverbanks. Readily utters loud, high twittering notes, often with an agitated quality. 9" (23 cm).

American Coot

adult

Common Moorhen

adult

juv.

Wattled Jaçana

adult

adult

HELIORN
World. A
are eq

HIDAE. A small family, with one species in Africa, one in Asia, and one in the New ... three species have brightly colored, lobed feet. Though mostly seen swimming, sungrebes ...lly agile on land and on branches. Unlike true grebes (p. 8), the sungrebe rarely dives.

Sungrebe
Heliornis fulica

In size and behavior, suggests a duck or grebe, but none of these have **black and white striping on head and neck**. Fairly common in Caribbean lowlands; rare in Golfo Dulce region. Favors slow-moving rivers and streams with banks covered by overhanging vegetation, from which it gleans arthropods, frogs, and small lizards. Makes a nasal yapping *yeh-yeh-yeh!*. 11" (28 cm).

Limpkin

ARAMIDAE. Considered a relative of the cranes and the crakes and rails, the lone member of this family inhabits freshwater marshes and swamps in the New World tropics and subtropics, where it feeds primarily on apple snails. The common name alludes to the bird's awkward way of walking.

Limpkin
Aramus guarauna

Could bring to mind a juvenile ibis (p. 28), but its bill is less curved and its face is fully feathered. Fairly common only in Palo Verde and Caño Negro regions; very uncommon elsewhere in suitable habitat, including the Central Valley; to 1,500 m. Forages in freshwater marshes; perches on low limbs. Gives a loud, wailing *krrAAOOoow*. 26" (66 cm).

Thick-knees

BURHINIDAE. Thick-knees are terrestrial birds of arid, open habitats; they somewhat resemble long-legged plovers (p. 64). These birds remain mostly motionless throughout the day; their brown-and-gray streaked plumage affords them camouflage. Thick-knees have large eyes that correspond to their crepuscular and nocturnal foraging habits.

Double-striped Thick-Knee
Burhinus bistriatus

The combination of a **broad white superciliary** (bordered above by a blackish stripe) and a **short, stout bill** sets it apart from any of the shorebirds. In flight, shows a Willetlike wing pattern (p. 70). Fairly common in lowlands of northwestern Pacific, rare south to Jacó and in western Central Valley; to 800 m. Easily overlooked in daytime, when it stands or sits in pastures and cleared fields. Active and vocal at night, uttering a raucous, lengthy *pip-prri-pippridipip-pip-pip-pridipip…*. 19" (48 cm.)

male/nonbreeding
female

Sungrebe

breeding
female

Limpkin

Double-striped
Thick-Knee

CHARADRIIDAE. Most plovers resemble sandpipers (p. 68) in size, coloration, and habitat preference, but are characterized by large eyes and relatively short, stubby bills. Plovers pluck their prey from the ground surface, rather than probing in wet ground, as do sandpipers. They often remain motionless and attentive, then run down prey with a short burst of speed. The lapwing group, which contains larger, more boldly patterned species, is represented in CR by one recent arrival, the Southern Lapwing (p. 66).

Collared Plover
Charadrius collaris

Told apart from Wilson's Plover by **short, slender bill**, and from Semipalmated Plover by **all-black bill**, pinkish legs, and lack of nuchal collar. Uncommon on both coasts. Individuals or pairs forage among the flotsam above the high-tide line on beaches; they also forage on river tidal flats and gravel bars. 6" (15 cm).

Snowy Plover
Charadrius alexandrinus

Very pale; the only small plover in CR with **dark-gray legs** and **incomplete breast band**. Very rare passage migrant; possible on both coasts from Sept to Nov and from March to April. Individuals or pairs forage with other small plovers among the flotsam above the high-tide line on beaches; they also forage on river tidal flats and gravel bars. 6" (15 cm).

Wilson's Plover
Charadrius wilsonia

The **thick bill** sets it apart from the similarly patterned Collared Plover. Note all-black bill on Wilson's Plover as compared with orange base of bill on Semipalmated Plover. Common on Pacific coast and uncommon on Caribbean coast; resident population is joined by NA migrants from Sept to May. Forages with other small plovers on river tidal flats and gravel bars, and also among the flotsam above the high-tide line on beaches. 8" (20 cm).

Semipalmated Plover
Charadrius semipalmatus

The **orange legs** and **orange base of short, black-tipped bill** distinguish it from Collared Plover and Wilson's Plover, both with pinkish legs and black bills. Very common winter resident on Pacific coast and uncommon on Caribbean coast; from early Aug to early May. Passage migrants can occur inland (e.g., Caño Negro and Central Valley), from early Aug to Nov and from late March to early May. An uncommon summer resident, mostly along Gulf of Nicoya. Forages with other plovers and sandpipers on river tidal flats and gravel bars, and also on wave-lapped portions of beaches. 7" (18 cm).

Killdeer
Charadrius vociferus

Distinctively marked with **two breast bands**; in flight, shows **tawny rump**. Fairly common NA migrant from late Aug to May, to 1,500 m in Central Valley, where a resident population also exists. Favors grassy or plowed fields; also found around marshy ponds. Readily gives its characteristic *kill-deer* call. 10" (25 cm).

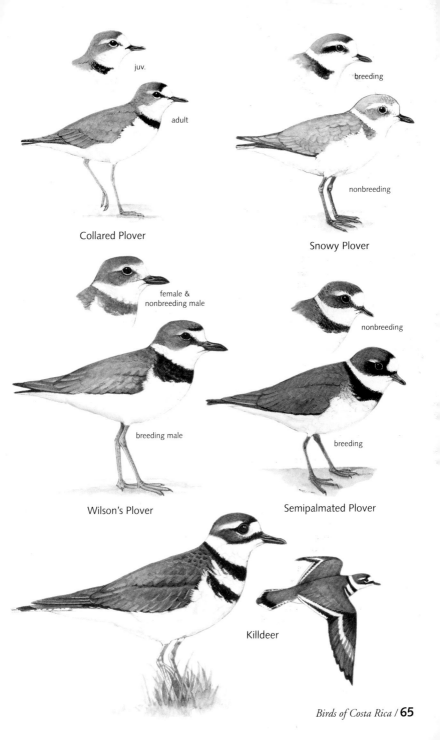

juv.

adult

Collared Plover

breeding

nonbreeding

Snowy Plover

female &
nonbreeding male

breeding male

Wilson's Plover

nonbreeding

breeding

Semipalmated Plover

Killdeer

Plovers

Black-bellied Plover
Pluvialis squatarola

The **black axillars**, visible in flight, are the definitive field mark in all plumages; on flying birds, also note **white wing stripe, rump, and tail base**. Standing birds in nonbreeding plumage can be recognized by their overall gray color, short bill, and large eye. (Compare with American Golden-Plover.) Common NA migrant on Pacific coast and fairly uncommon on Caribbean coast, from Aug to May; some juveniles are summer residents. Birds in breeding plumage occasionally seen in Aug and May. Mostly seen on tidal flats of rivers, but also on beaches and in mangroves; occasionally farther inland in migration. Whistles a melancholy *plee-uu-reee*, the middle note lower pitched. 11" (28 cm).

American Golden-Plover
Pluvialis dominica

Resembles Black-bellied Plover, but in flight shows **gray axillars and wing stripe**, and lacks white on rump and tail base. Standing birds in nonbreeding plumage show a slightly more well-defined supercilliary than do Black-bellied Plovers, but should be seen in flight to make positive identification. Breeding birds similar in pattern to breeding Black-bellied Plover, but have entirely black underparts. Very uncommon NA migrant, from mid-Aug to May, to 1,500 m in Central Valley; rare summer resident. Birds in breeding plumage occasionally seen in Aug and May. Prefers wet grassy fields, but also can occur on tidal flats. Gives a shrill *queet*. 10" (25 cm).

Southern Lapwing
Vanellus chilensis

Virtually unmistakable. First recorded in CR in 1997, this SA species has become established in lowlands of both Caribbean and Pacific slopes, to 800 m. Very uncommon; still spreading on both slopes. Pairs or family groups favor open grassy areas near water, including rivers, natural ponds, fish ponds, and sewage treatment plants. Aggressive in behavior and quite vocal; repeats a loud, agitated *KEEEAH, KEEAH, KEEAH…*; several individuals often join in. 14" (36 cm).

Oystercatchers

HAEMATOPODIDAE. The oystercatchers are a widespread and homogenous group of coastal waders, though a few species also occur farther inland. Their long, bladelike bills are specialized for feeding on various types of mollusks and are used both in dislodging the prey from rocky substrates and in extracting it from its shell.

American Oystercatcher
Haematopus palliatus

The **red-orange bill** and **entirely black head and neck** are diagnostic. The resident population (on Pacific coast only) is uncommon. NA migrants are uncommon on Pacific coast; and very uncommon on Caribbean coast; from Aug to May. Pairs forage on rocky points and along open beaches, both in intertidal zones and in shallow water. Emits a loud, piping whistle. 17" (43 cm).

nonbreeding

nonbreeding

breeding

Black-bellied Plover

nonbreeding

nonbreeding

breeding

American Golden-Plover

Southern
Lapwing

American
Oystercatcher

Stilts

RECURVIROSTRIDAE. The avocets and stilts form an attractive group of waders with boldly contrasting black-and-white plumage, long legs, and long bills (avocets have bills with notably upturned tips). They typically inhabit wetlands with shallow, open water, where they forage for aquatic invertebrates either by direct strikes or by sweeping with their long bills.

American Avocet
Recurvirostra americana

The **slender, upturned bill**, together with black-and-white pattern on wings and back, is diagnostic. A very casual NA migrant; four old records from Palo Verde region (from Dec to May), and one recent sighting at Lake Arenal. Forages in marshes and salt ponds. 18" (46 cm).

Black-necked Stilt
Himantopus mexicanus

The **extremely long red legs** and needlelike black bill are diagnostic. Resident population is common around Gulf of Nicoya; NA migrants present in lowlands and in Central Valley to 1,500 m, from Oct to May. Inhabits marshes, tidal flats, and ponds, including salt ponds; gregarious and often in groups of a dozen or more. These easily excited birds produce long series of sharp *kek* notes. 15" (38 cm).

Sandpipers

SCOLOPACIDAE. The members of this cosmopolitan family are known as waders or shorebirds, though not all species inhabit coastal areas. All of the species found in CR are nonbreeding migrants that nest at higher latitudes. During most of their stay in CR, they are clad in nonbreeding plumage, making identification even more of a challenge; but their relatively colorful and/or contrasting breeding plumage can sometimes be seen around the time of their fall arrival and spring departure. Bill shape and length, as well as length and color of legs, are often important identifying characteristics.

Marbled Godwit
Limosa fedoa

The **long, upturned bill** sets it apart from all other CR shorebirds, except for the very rare Hudsonian Godwit and American Avocet (none of the three share similar plumage). Fairly uncommon passage migrant from Aug to Sept and from March to April, uncommon winter resident from Aug to April, and rare summer resident on Pacific coast. One record from Caribbean coast: Tortuguero, Sept 2005. Favors mudflats and saltponds, often with Whimbrels and Willets (p. 70). In flight, gives a hoarse *kaWHEK*. 18" (46 cm).

Hudsonian Godwit
Limosa haemastica

The long, slightly upturned bill distinguishes it from all but the Marbled Godwit and American Avocet (none of the three share similar plumage). In flight, in all plumages, shows **black underwing and tail**, as well as **white tail base and wing stripe**. One CR record in late May, 1975, at a coastal lagoon near Puntarenas. **Not illustrated.** 15" (38 cm).

breeding

nonbreeding

American
Avocet

Black-necked
Stilt

Marbled
Godwit

Long-billed Curlew
Numenius americanus

Best told apart from Whimbrel by **lack of crown stripes**; body is buffy and, in flight, shows **cinnamon underwing**. Very rare NA migrant from mid-Nov to mid-April; reported only from Gulf of Nicoya. Usually in association with Whimbrels. 23" (58 cm).

Whimbrel
Numenius phaeopus

Long bill, decurved toward tip, sets it apart from all other CR shorebirds except Long-billed Curlew and juvenile White Ibis (p. 28), neither of which has **striped crown**. Very common NA migrant on Pacific coast and uncommon on Caribbean coast, from Aug to May; fairly uncommon summer resident on Pacific coast. Mostly found in brackish wetlands (e.g., mudflats and mangroves), less commonly along seashores; often with Willets. In flight, whistles a loud series of even-pitched *kyew* notes. 17" (43 cm).

Willet
Tringa semipalmata

Very drab in nonbreeding plumage, but note **gray legs** and straight, stout bill; easily identified in flight by **bold black-and-white wing pattern**. Very common NA migrant on Pacific coast and uncommon on Caribbean coast, from Aug to May; uncommon summer resident on Pacific coast. Mostly found in brackish wetlands (e.g., mudflats and mangroves), less commonly along seashores; often with Whimbrels. In flight, gives a loud *klee-klee-klee*. 15" (38 cm).

Solitary Sandpiper
Tringa solitaria

Resembles the Greater and Lesser Yellowlegs, but has **olive legs** and obvious **white eye ring**. In flight, note **dark wings, rump, and central rectrices**. Common NA migrant from Aug to May, to 2,000 m. Wades in shallow freshwater, constantly nodding its head. 8" (20 cm).

Greater Yellowlegs
Tringa melanoleuca

In all plumages, **bright-yellow legs** distinguish it from all but Lesser Yellowlegs. Differentiated from Lesser Yellowlegs by a **bill that is longer than the head**; also note **gray base** of bill. Uncommon NA migrant from Aug to May, to 1,500 m; rare summer resident. Wades in a variety of wetland habitat (e.g., puddles and river banks). Chimes three or four emphatic, slightly descending *tew* notes (similar to call of Lesser Yellowlegs). 14" (36 cm).

Lesser Yellowlegs
Tringa flavipes

Similar to Greater Yellowlegs, but **all-black bill is about equal in length to head**. Common NA migrant from Aug to May, to 1,500 m; uncommon summer resident. Wades in a variety of wetland habitats (e.g., puddles and river banks). Whistles one or two soft *tew* notes (similar to call of Greater Yellowlegs). 11" (28 cm).

Long-billed Curlew

Whimbrel

breeding

nonbreeding

Willet

nonbreeding

Solitary
Sandpiper

Lesser Yellowlegs

Greater Yellowlegs

Wandering Tattler
Tringa incana

In nonbreeding plumage, brings to mind a large, gray Spotted Sandpiper, but has **yellowish legs** and, in flight, shows **unmarked gray wings, rump, and tail**. Fairly uncommon NA migrant along Pacific coast, from late Sept to late April; rare summer resident. Individual birds forage along rocky coastline, constantly teetering tail up and down. 11" (28 cm).

Spotted Sandpiper
Actitis macularius

Spotted underparts readily identify birds in breeding plumage. In drab nonbreeding plumage, note **brown smudge on side of breast**. In flight, distinguished from Wandering Tattler by narrow but conspicuous **white wing stripe** and some white on sides of rump and tail. Very common and widespread NA migrant from late July to late May, to 2,200 m; rare summer resident. Found in any wetland habitat, from highland streams to seashore, usually individually. Teeters body and tail constantly; flies low with shallow, stiff wingbeats and short glides. 8" (20 cm).

Upland Sandpiper
Bartramia longicauda

Somewhat resembles a small Whimbrel (p. 70), but has **short, straight bill** and **yellow legs**; also note large eye. Uncommon passage migrant in Pacific lowlands and Central Valley, rare on Caribbean slope; from late Aug to Nov and from mid-March to late May. Favors areas with short grass; has upright posture and holds wings raised for a moment upon landing. 12" (31 cm).

Buff-breasted Sandpiper
Tryngites subruficollis

In shape, pattern, and habits, resembles the larger Upland Sandpiper, but has **unstreaked, buffy throat and breast**. Now very rare passage migrant in increasingly urbanized Central Valley, from late Aug to late Oct; could turn up in lowlands. Favors wet fields. Rather tame, but when flushed, flies rapidly and erratically. 8" (20 cm).

Ruddy Turnstone
Arenaria interpres

In all plumages, the **dark breast pattern** and **bright-orange legs** set it apart; also note pointed, wedge-shaped bill. Shows pied pattern in flight. Compare with similarly sized Surfbird. Common NA migrant on Pacific coast and fairly uncommon on Caribbean coast, from Aug to late May; uncommon summer resident. Individuals or groups forage on mud and sand exposed by the receding tide. In flight, gives a cackling rattle. 9" (23 cm).

Surfbird
Aphriza virgata

Size and shape similar to Ruddy Turnstone, but **legs and base of short, stout bill are yellowish**. In flight, shows white wing stripe, white rump, and **black subterminal tail band**. Fairly uncommon passage migrant on Pacific coast from mid-Sept to late Oct and from late April to May; rare winter resident, from Sept to May. Individuals or small groups favor rocky coastline. 10" (25 cm).

breeding

Wandering
Tattler

breeding

nonbreeding

Spotted Sandpiper

nonbreeding

Buff-breasted Sandpiper

Upland Sandpiper

breeding

breeding

nonbreeding

Surfbird

Ruddy Turnstone   nonbreeding

Sanderling
Calidris alba

In nonbreeding plumage, this is **the palest sandpiper**, with strongly contrasting black bill, eyes, and legs. Rufous head and breast are distinctive in breeding plumage. In both plumages, birds in flight show bold wing stripe. Common NA migrant from mid-Aug to early May along both coasts; very rare summer resident. The "classic" sandpiper that runs rapidly back and forth at the water's edge along sandy beaches; also found on mudflats and salt ponds. 8" (20 cm).

Semipalmated Sandpiper
Calidris pusilla

In all plumages, very similar to Western Sandpiper, but especially difficult to distinguish when in nonbreeding plumage. In breeding plumage, note lack of rufous on scapulars, crown, and ear coverts. Bill is shorter and straighter than on most Western Sandpipers. Distinguished from Least Sandpiper by black legs. Status difficult to judge given identification problems, but present as NA migrant from mid-Aug to early May, to 1,500 m; very rare summer resident. Forages more by picking prey from surface than by probing in substrate; found mostly on mudflats and sandbars near rivermouths, but also inland at edges of freshwater pools. In flight, gives a short, harsh *cherk*. 6" (15 cm).

Western Sandpiper
Calidris mauri

In breeding plumage, rufous on scapulars, crown, and ear coverts help distinguish it from the very similar breeding Semipalmated Sandpiper. In nonbreeding plumage, the two species are very difficult to distinguish. On average, bill is longer and more drooping than on Semipalmated Sandpiper. Distinguished from Least Sandpiper by black legs. Abundant NA migrant on Pacific coast and fairly common elsewhere, to 1,500 m, from early Aug to early May; uncommon summer resident. Typically forages by rapidly probing in substrate; mostly on mudflats and sandbars near rivermouths, but also inland at edges of freshwater pools. In flight, gives a high, thin *cheet*. 6" (15 cm).

Least Sandpiper
Calidris minutilla

Leg color and plumage pattern recall the significantly larger Pectoral Sandpiper; differentiated from similar-sized Semipalmated and Western Sandpipers by **yellowish legs**. Common NA migrant from early Aug to early May, to 1,500 m; rare summer resident. Small, loose groups forage near water's edge in both salt and freshwater habitats. In flight, trills a high, rising *trreeep*. 6" (15 cm).

Pectoral Sandpiper
Calidris melanotos

Distinguished in all plumages by **yellowish legs** and a **streaked breast that is clearly delineated from the white belly** (compare with smaller Least Sandpiper); also note pale base of bill. Fairly common NA passage migrant from early Aug to late Nov and from early April to late May; rare winter and summer resident. Mostly found in wet fields, much less commonly on mudflats and sandbars of lowland rivers; when flushed, flies low in rapid zigzag pattern. In flight, trills a harsh *trrrt*. 9" (23 cm).

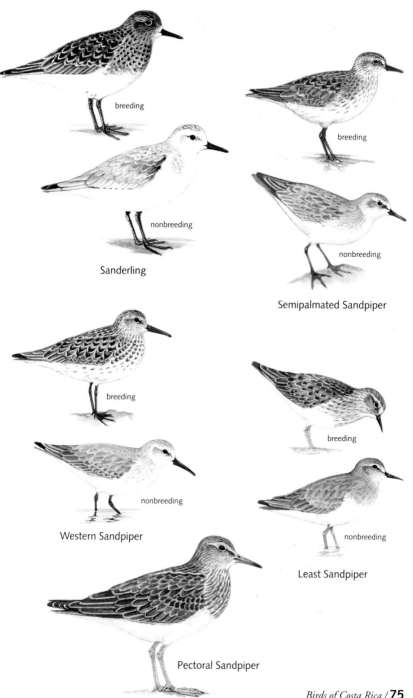

breeding

nonbreeding

Sanderling

breeding

nonbreeding

Semipalmated Sandpiper

breeding

nonbreeding

Western Sandpiper

breeding

nonbreeding

Least Sandpiper

Pectoral Sandpiper

White-rumped Sandpiper
Calidris fuscicollis

In flight, the **white uppertail coverts** are diagnostic (though otherwise distinct Curlew Sandpiper also has white uppertail coverts). On standing birds, note that wingtips extend beyond tip of tail; bill slightly decurved, with **reddish-brown base of lower mandible**. Rare passage migrant from early Sept to mid-Oct and from early April to late May, to 1,500 m. Forages near water's edge in both salt- and freshwater habitats. In flight, gives a high, mousy squeak: *tseek-tseek*. 7" (18 cm).

Baird's Sandpiper
Calidris bairdii

In flight, distinguished from very similar White-rumped Sandpiper by **dark center of rump and tail**; also note **slender, straight black bill** and buffy, faintly streaked breast. Very uncommon passage migrant from late Aug to early Nov and from early April to early June, on Pacific coast and in Central Valley, to 1,500 m. Favors wet grassy areas near water, but also found on mudflats with other sandpipers; rarely wades. In flight, trills a rough *krreeet*. 7" (18 cm).

Dunlin
Calidris alpina

In breeding plumage, has diagnostic black belly patch. Nonbreeding plumage is very drab gray, with brownish tinges on head and breast. In all plumages, note **sturdy bill that droops at tip** and, in flight, dark center of rump and tail. Very rare NA migrant known only from the Gulf of Nicoya, from late Dec to early May. Probes rapidly on mudflats and salt ponds. In flight, gives a harsh *krreet*. 8" (20 cm).

Curlew Sandpiper
Calidris ferruginea

In nonbreeding plumage, recalls a Dunlin, but has thinner, more decurved bill and, in flight, shows white uppertail coverts and wing stripe. The one CR record is from Colorado, on the Gulf of Nicoya, in early Nov (year uncited). **Not illustrated**. 8" (20 cm).

Stilt Sandpiper
Calidris himantopus

In breeding plumage, heavily barred underparts and rufous cheeks are distinctive. In drab gray nonbreeding plumage, note fairly long bill and **long, greenish legs** (the two dowitchers [p. 78] have longer bills and shorter legs). In flight, shows white rump and plain, dark wings. Fairly uncommon NA migrant around Gulf of Nicoya, from mid-Aug to late May; rare elsewhere on Pacific coast. Wades and probes like a dowitcher in both salt- and freshwater ponds. In flight, trills a soft, hoarse *trrrerp*. 9" (23 cm).

Red Knot
Calidris canutus

In all plumages, somewhat resembles the two dowitchers (p. 78), but note **short (about as long as the head), stout, straight bill** and **plump aspect**. In flight, shows **pale-gray rump and tail**. Uncommon NA migrant in Gulf of Nicoya, rare elsewhere along Pacific coast; from late Aug to late April. Forages on mudflats, moving slowly; rests in salt ponds. 10" (25 cm).

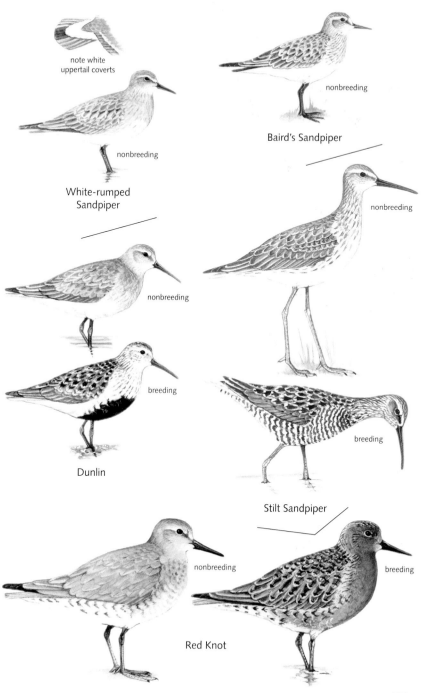

note white
uppertail coverts

nonbreeding

White-rumped
Sandpiper

Baird's Sandpiper

nonbreeding

nonbreeding

nonbreeding

breeding

Dunlin

breeding

Stilt Sandpiper

nonbreeding

breeding

Red Knot

Short-billed Dowitcher
Limnodromus griseus

Readily told apart from other shorebirds by **long, straight bill** and **pale superciliary**, but essentially identical to Long-billed Dowitcher, from which it is best differentiated by **evenly barred tail** (i.e., black and white bars of equal width). In flight, both species show white rump and lower back. Very common NA migrant on Pacific coast, uncommon elsewhere to 1,500 m, from early Aug to late May; uncommon summer resident. Probes deeply in shallow saltwater; in migration, can also occur in freshwater habitats. In flight, gives a clear, rapid *tu,tu,tu*. 11" (28 cm).

Long-billed Dowitcher
Limnodromus scolopaceus

Essentially identical to Short-billed Dowitcher. Indeed, bill is not noticeably longer than Short-billed Dowitcher's; best distinguished by **black tail with narrow white barring**. In flight, both species show white rump and lower back. Very uncommon NA migrant from late Oct to late April, to 1,500 m. Favors wet fields and freshwater ponds. In flight, gives a sharp *keek*, singly or in repetition. 11" (28 cm).

Ruff
Philomachus pugnax

Plumage, leg, and bill color vary with age and sex; somewhat resembles a plump yellowlegs (p. 70), though it has a short bill. Best identified in flight by **white V on uppertail coverts**; also has relatively deep, slow wingbeats for a shorebird. Two CR records from Chomes, in early Sept and late May (years uncited). **Not illustrated**. Male 11" (28 cm); female 9" (23 cm).

Wilson's Snipe
Gallinago delicata

Readily identified by **very long, straight bill** and **striped head and back**. Uncommon winter resident in lowlands and in Central Valley (to 1,500 m), from early Oct to late April; passage migrants can occur to 3,000 m. Individuals or pairs forage in wet fields; flight is swift and erratic. 10" (25 cm).

Wilson's Phalarope
Phalaropus tricolor

In nonbreeding plumage, could recall a Stilt Sandpiper (p. 76) or yellowlegs (p. 70), but note **very thin bill** and **white underparts**; also see Red-necked Phalarope. Fairly common passage migrant from late Aug to Oct and from mid-April to late May, mostly around Gulf of Nicoya; rare winter resident; also rare summer resident. Prefers salt ponds, but also found on mudflats and around freshwater pools; sometimes swims and spins on surface. 9" (23 cm).

Red-necked Phalarope
Phalaropus lobatus

In nonbreeding plumage, similar to Wilson's Phalarope, but has **black legs, white forehead**, and **streaking on back**. Fairly common passage migrant along Pacific coast from late Aug to early Nov, though much less common from April to May; very rare winter resident. Mostly found offshore, but also visits salt ponds and lagoons; plucks prey from water surface while floating and spinning. 8" (20 cm).

nonbreeding

breeding

nonbreeding

Short-billed Dowitcher

nonbreeding

Long-billed Dowitcher

Wilson's Snipe

nonbreeding

nonbreeding

Wilson's Phalarope

nonbreeding

nonbreeding

Red-necked Phalarope

breeding female

breeding male

breeding female

LARIDAE. Gulls and terns are uncommon along open beaches in CR; their greatest concentrations are found at river mouths, harbors, and the larger inlets. Gulls are stockier than terns and more often seen sitting on the water; largely scavengers, they do not dive for food. Terns are graceful birds that dive for fish and rarely sit on water. Identification to species can be challenging in adult birds and extremely difficult in juveniles. Here we treat only the species most likely to be seen from shore, exclude most of the rarities, and hope that "gullophiles" will forgive us.

Laughing Gull
Larus atricilla

Very similar to Franklin's Gull and best told apart in flight, when adult shows **gray upperwing with black tip** and first winter bird shows a **complete black tail band**. By far the most common gull in CR; juveniles are present year-round, accompanied by NA migrants from Sept to May. Opportunistically scavenges along tideline and around ports and fishing boats; rests on sandbars and on dikes that crisscross salt ponds and commercial shrimp ponds. 16" (41 cm).

Franklin's Gull
Larus pipixcan

Compared to Laughing Gull, flying adult shows **black band on primaries bordered by white on both sides**; first winter bird has black tail band interrupted by **white outer rectrices** (also note **white underparts**). Fairly common passage migrant on Pacific coast from Oct to Nov and from April to early June; rare winter resident. Casual on Caribbean coast. Scavenges less than Laughing Gull, often catches insects in flight over fields. 14" (36 cm).

Caspian Tern
Hydroprogne caspia

The **thick deep-red bill** (becoming **dusky toward tip**) distinguishes it from the very similar Royal Tern. In nonbreeding plumage, note dark streaks on crown. Very uncommon throughout the year on Pacific coast, mostly in Gulf of Nicoya. Prefers intertidal areas, where one or a few birds may be mixed among flocks of Royal Terns and Laughing Gulls. 21" (53 cm).

Royal Tern
Thalasseus maximus

Has a fairly straight, stout, **uniformly orange bill** (more yellowish in juvenile) that is intermediate in thickness between Caspian and Elegant Terns. Nonbreeding birds have white forehead and midcrown. The most common tern in CR; juveniles present year-round, accompanied by NA migrants from Sept to June. Feeds offshore, plunge-diving for fish; rests on sandbars, also on dikes that crisscross salt ponds and commercial shrimp ponds. 20" (51 cm).

Elegant Tern
Thalasseus elegans

Very similar to somewhat larger Royal Tern, but bill is proportionately longer and more slender, with slight drooping aspect. The color of the bill can vary from yellow in juvenile to orange or orange-red in adult (bill of adult often has a lighter colored tip). Uncommon NA migrant on Pacific coast, from Sept to early June; a few juveniles present from June to Aug; casual on Caribbean coast. Tends to accompany much more numerous Royal Tern. 17" (43 cm).

nonbreeding

breeding

bree

Laughing Gull

nonbreeding

breeding

breeding

first winter

Franklin's Gull

nonbreeding

breeding

Caspian Tern

nonbreeding

breeding

nonbreeding

breeding

Royal Tern

Elegant Tern

Gull-billed Tern
Gelochelidon nilotica

In nonbreeding plumage, more whitish than any other CR tern; also note **dark ear patch** and **thick all-black bill**. Uncommon NA migrant on Pacific coast, from Sept to May, with some juveniles present year-round; rare on Caribbean coast, though most likely April to May. Forages over intertidal areas and fields, rarely dives; instead swoops down and plucks prey from surface. 16" (41 cm).

Sandwich Tern
Thalasseus sandvicensis

The **yellow-tipped black bill** distinguishes this tern in all plumages. Fairly common NA migrant on both coasts, from Sept to May; juveniles, present June to Aug, are more common on Pacific coast. Generally the most numerous tern in CR after Royal Tern (p. 80), with which it associates. 16" (41 cm).

Common Tern
Sterna hirundo

The **tail's narrow, dark outer edge** is diagnostic, even on juvenile (with shorter, notched tail). Common passage migrant on both coasts, from Sept to mid-Nov and April to May; fairly uncommon winter resident on both coasts; uncommon summer resident from June to Aug in Gulf of Nicoya. An agile tern of sheltered waters; infrequently forages offshore. 14" (36 cm).

Forster's Tern
Sterna forsteri

In breeding plumage, similar to Common Tern, but with **darkest portion of tail on inside of fork**; nonbreeding birds have dark ear patch like that of Gull-billed Tern. Casual winter resident from Nov to March in Gulf of Nicoya. Often forages over freshwater, catching insects in flight. **Not illustrated**. 14" (36 cm).

Least Tern
Sternula antillarum

Notable for its small size and hurried wingbeats in flight. Uncommon, but can occur year-round in Gulf of Nicoya; rare elsewhere on Pacific coast and casual on Caribbean coast. Favors sheltered waters. 9" (23 cm).

Bridled Tern
Onychoprion anaethetus

Dark upperparts and pale underparts should preclude confusion. Similar Sooty Tern (*Onychoprion fuscatus*) is mostly pelagic and extremely unlikely to be seen from shore; note **narrow white superciliary** and **pale nuchal collar** on Bridled Tern. Breeds on rocky islets off Pacific coast from March to Sept (rare in other months); casual on Caribbean coast. Snatches prey from ocean surface by swooping, not diving. 14" (36 cm).

Large-billed Tern
Phaetusa simplex

Known from one bird that was photographed on Tortuguero River in March 2003. Stout, yellow bill and gray, white, and black upperparts are unique. **Not illustrated.** 14" (36 cm).

breeding

nonbreeding

Gull-billed Tern

breeding

nonbreeding

Sandwich Tern

breeding

nonbreeding

Common Tern

breeding

first winter

Least Tern

breeding

juv.

Bridled Tern

Gulls & Terns

Black Tern
Chlidonias niger

Distinctive in breeding plumage; in other plumages, the **dark smudge on side** below shoulder is diagnostic. Fairly common NA migrant on both coasts, from Sept to May; juveniles present June to Aug, though more common on Pacific coast. Found both offshore and over lowland wetlands; plucks small prey from water surface and also catches insects in flight. 10" (25 cm).

Brown Noddy
Anous stolidus

The **whitish cap** is distinctive. Uncommon along Pacific coast from April to Sept; rare on Caribbean coast. Most likely seen around rocky offshore islets; unlike most other terns, flies unswervingly and close to the ocean surface. 16" (41 cm).

Skimmers

RYNCHOPIDAE. The skimmers are closely related to gulls and terns, but their singular bill structure enables a unique foraging method: they keep their lower mandible open as they skim the water surface in search of small fish and shrimp. The use of tactile instead of visual cues allows skimmers to feed at night, when their prey are more often found near the surface.

Black Skimmer
Rynchops niger

The **red-and-black bill with elongated lower mandible** is diagnostic. Fairly common NA migrant in Gulf of Nicoya; rare elsewhere along the Pacific coast; from Sept to May. Rare summer resident on the Pacific coast, from June to Aug. From May to Oct occasional birds from SA are present and can be told apart by their entirely dark tail feathers. Usually seen resting on sandbars with gulls and terns. 18" (46 cm).

Pigeons & Doves

COLUMBIDAE. A cosmopolitan family of small-headed, full-breasted birds. Predominately feeding on seeds and fruits, the species of this family inhabit all regions and ecological niches in CR, from deep rain forest to city streets. Seen perched atop a distant tree or passing by in swift, strong flight, they could be mistaken for a raptor.

Rock Pigeon
Columba livia

The common "city pigeon" is one of the species most commensal with humans throughout the globe and should be recognizable, in all its numerous color patterns, to even nonbirders. In CR, it is often difficult to know if birds are truly wild or have a pigeon house nearby that they return to. However, if you really want to check off this species on your CR list, the birds around the National Theater in downtown San José are feral; they roost and nest on building ledges. 12" (30 cm).

nonbreeding

breeding

Black Tern

Brown Noddy

Black Skimmer

Rock Pigeon
(various color morphs)

Scaled Pigeon
Patagioenas speciosa

The **scaling on neck and underparts** is diagnostic; **bill mostly red** with white tip. Fairly common in intermontane valleys of southern Pacific, between 600 and 1,600 m, but to sea level in Dominical area; also common in Caño Negro region, but rare elsewhere in Caribbean lowlands. Stays in upper levels of trees in nonforest habitats. Coos with a low, loud *huu-hUU-huu*. 13" (33 cm).

Pale-vented Pigeon
Patagioenas cayennensis

Has **whitish belly and vent**. The multiple, soft colors on the head and neck distinguish it from any other similar arboreal pigeon; note the **all-black bill**. Common in wet lowlands, to 600 m. Stays in upper levels of trees in nonforest habitats. Coos with a three-part *hu-hu-huUUu*, sometimes introduced by a low *wuuu*. 12" (30 cm).

White-crowned Pigeon
Patagioenas leucocephala

A dark pigeon with a contrasting white crown. Accidental, but with several reports along Caribbean coast. **Not illustrated**. 13" (33 cm).

Red-billed Pigeon
Patagioenas flavirostris

Bill mostly whitish, with red base; the gray back feathers contrast subtly with the dull reddish-brown head, neck, and shoulders. Fairly common in northwestern Pacific, Central Valley, and middle elevations of Caribbean slope (to 2,000 m); uncommon elsewhere within mapped range. In middle and upper levels of trees in nonforest habitats. Coos with a forlorn *huUUu-hu-hu-huuu*. 12" (30 cm).

Band-tailed Pigeon
Patagioenas fasciata

The **bright yellow bill** and **white nape band** readily distinguish this large, gray pigeon. Common in highlands from timberline down to about 1,400 m; occasionally to 500 m, or lower. Typically perches in canopy at edges of oak forests and gardens, often in flocks. Makes a rather guttural *huhuUU, hu-huUU*; also produces loud wing-flapping sound. 14" (36 cm).

Short-billed Pigeon
Patagioenas nigrirostris

The lowland counterpart of the Ruddy Pigeon. Fairly uniformly colored, though slightly duller and darker on the back. Common in wet forest habitats, from sea level to 1,200 m; uncommon in Caño Negro region. Also very similar to Ruddy Pigeon in habits and voice, but call is accented differently: *hu, HU, hu-HU*. 10" (25 cm).

Ruddy Pigeon
Patagioenas subvinacea

A **uniformly ruddy-brown** pigeon, slightly more reddish on back than Short-billed Pigeon. Fairly common at higher elevations, from timberline down to 1,400 m, occasionally to 900 m. Hard to see since it perches in upper canopy of mature forest and adjacent tall second growth, though can be seen on gravel roads gathering pebbles. Frequently calls: *hu, hu-HU, hu*. 11" (28 cm).

Scaled Pigeon

Pale-vented
Pigeon

Red-billed
Pigeon

Band-tailed
Pigeon

Short-billed
Pigeon

Ruddy Pigeon

White-winged Dove
Zenaida asiatica

Perched bird somewhat resembles Mourning Dove, but the **white wing stripe** is obvious even on the folded wing. Common resident in northwestern Pacific (south to Jacó) and in western Central Valley (east to San José), to 1,200 m; resident birds are joined by NA migrants from Nov to May. Recent scattered reports from northern Caribbean slope. Found in fairly open, nonforested areas; often perches on wires and feeds along roadsides. Quite commensal with humans. Varied calls include a throaty "who-cooks-for-you." 11" (28 cm).

Mourning Dove
Zenaida macroura

This slim bird is somewhat similar to the White-winged Dove, but has a **long, tapering tail** that is edged with white. Also note **black spotting on folded wing**. An uncommon resident around southern flank of Irazú Volcano (to 2,300 m); also uncommon in region between Zarcero and San Ramón and in foothills northeast of Liberia. An uncommon winter resident in northwestern Pacific lowlands, from Oct to March. Forages on ground in agricultural areas. Call is a deep, melancholy *hu-WUU, hu, hu, hu.* 12" (30 cm).

Inca Dove
Columbina inca

Scaled pattern above and below is distinctive; has rufous primaries like smaller *Columbina* ground-doves, but long tail has white outer edges; also note **black bill**. Very common in northwestern Pacific and western Central Valley; still extending its range south along Pacific coast and east of Cartago; to 1,400 m. Forages on ground in fairly open areas. Gives an incessant *huuu-huup.* 8" (20 cm).

Common Ground-Dove
Columbina passerina

Unlike other small doves, has **pinkish-red basal half of bill**. Further distinguished from similar Plain-breasted Ground-Dove by scaling on upper breast. Very common in northwestern Pacific, south to Tarcoles; common in western Central Valley, and uncommon in eastern Central Valley and Caño Negro region, to 1,400 m. Forages on ground in open areas. Repeats an upwardly inflected *cuuup.* 6" (15 cm).

Plain-breasted Ground-Dove
Columbina minuta

Resembles Common Ground-Dove, but lacks scaling and spotting on breast; has **black bill**. Also similar to larger, browner female Ruddy Ground-Dove, but in flight shows rufous only in primaries and white on corners of tail (as does Common Ground-Dove). Fairly common in Caño Negro region and also in southern Pacific in Buenos Aires and Coto Brus Valley regions; uncommon in northwestern Pacific, western Central Valley, and Parrita/Quepos area. Individuals or pairs forage on ground in open areas. Repeats a rather rapid *huup.* 5" (13 cm).

Ruddy Ground-Dove
Columbina talpacoti

The male's bright reddish-brown body and contrasting light-gray head are diagnostic. Female resembles Plain-breasted Ground-Dove but is browner and has **no white in tail**; female also resembles female Blue Ground-Dove (p. 90), but has black markings on wing. Very common in wet lowlands and in eastern Central Valley, to 1,400 m; uncommon to rare in northwestern Pacific. Forages on ground in open areas. Repeats a low *hu-hUUp.* 7" (18 cm).

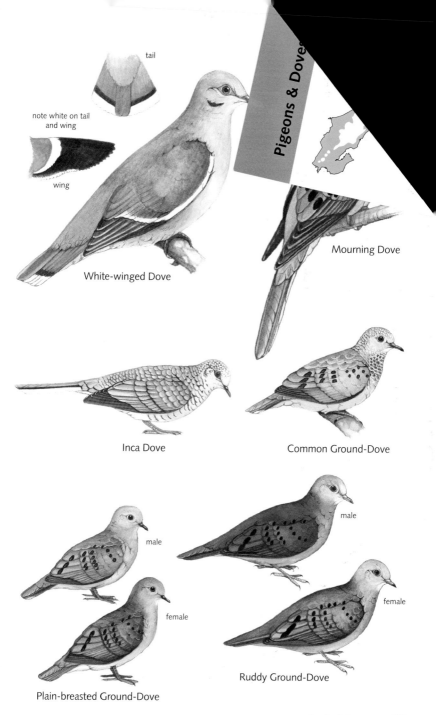

tail

note white on tail and wing

wing

White-winged Dove

Mourning Dove

Inca Dove

Common Ground-Dove

male

female

Plain-breasted Ground-Dove

male

female

Ruddy Ground-Dove

Blue Ground-Dove
Claravis pretiosa

The handsome male is not likely confused. Brown female has distinctive **chestnut wing markings** and a chestnut rump that contrasts with the dull-brown back; similar female Ruddy Ground-Dove (p. 88) has black wing markings. Fairly uncommon in wet lowlands and foothills; rare in northwestern Pacific; to 1,200 m. Prefers edges and openings in forested areas, often in pairs; more likely seen flying swiftly past or perched in a tree than on the ground. Call is an even, far-carrying *BUUP!*, repeated about once per second. 8" (20 cm).

Maroon-chested Ground-Dove
Claravis mondetoura

The only CR dove with **wing bars**; also has **white outer tail feathers**. Extremely rare in highlands, from 900 to 3,000 m. Forages on ground in dense undergrowth (especially seeding bamboo) at edges of highland forests. Gives a deep *wuup, wuup, wuup.* 9" (23 cm).

Gray-headed Dove
Leptotila plumbeiceps

Very much like White-tipped Dove, but with **red orbital skin**. Distinguished from Gray-chested Dove by **buffy cheeks** and **gray crown and nape**. Fairly common in Caño Negro region and on western side of Nicoya Peninsula, to 1,000 m; rare elsewhere in Pacific lowlands. Pairs or individuals forage on ground in humid forests and second growth. Call is deeper and hoarser than White-tipped Dove and given at about three-second intervals. 11" (28 cm).

White-tipped Dove
Leptotila verreauxi

Told apart from the other two *Leptotila* species by the **light-blue orbital skin**. Very common on Pacific side of CR and in Central Valley, to 2,200 m; uncommon in northern Caribbean plains, though likely increasing there and spreading east. Pairs or individuals forage on ground in light woodlands, gardens, and roadsides. Utters a low, mournful *whuuu*, lasting about one second (at intervals of six to seven seconds). 11" (28 cm).

Gray-chested Dove
Leptotila cassini

Differs from previous two species in having **golden-brown nape** (much more apparent on Pacific race) and darker gray breast; has red orbital skin. Common in wet lowlands and foothills, to 1,200 m. Pairs or individuals forage on ground in wet forests, at forest edges, and in shaded gardens. Its forlorn call, similar in quality to that of the White-tipped Dove, rises then falls slightly, lasting about 1.5 seconds. 11" (28 cm).

Blue Ground-Dove

male

female

Maroon-chested Ground-Dove

male

female

Gray-headed Dove

note white tips on tail

White-tipped Dove

Caribbean race

Pacific race

Gray-chested Dove

Birds of Costa Rica / **91**

Olive-backed Quail-Dove
Geotrygon veraguensis

The **white cheek stripe** readily identifies this otherwise dark quail-dove. Fairly uncommon in wet Caribbean lowlands, up to 500 m. Pairs or individuals forage on ground in wet forests; commonly walk on trails. Gives a hoarse, somewhat amphibian-like, *whu*. 9" (23 cm).

Chiriqui Quail-Dove
Geotrygon chiriquensis

Told apart from the male Ruddy Quail-Dove by its **gray crown** and **black moustachial stripe**. Uncommon to rare at middle elevations, between 600 and 2,400 m, from Rincón de la Vieja National Park south. Pairs or individuals forage on ground in humid montane forests; commonly walk on trails. Sings a sad, descending *whuuUUu*. **Endemic to CR and western Panama**. 12" (30 cm).

Purplish-backed Quail-Dove
Geotrygon lawrencii

Black moustachial stripe contrasts strongly with **pale face**. Uncommon in Caribbean foothills, from 400 to 1,000 m. Pairs or individuals forage on ground in wet forests; commonly walk on trails. Repeats a rising *hu-hua-hoooo*. 10" (25 cm).

Buff-fronted Quail-Dove
Geotrygon costaricensis

The **buff forehead** and **greenish nape** are diagnostic. Fairly uncommon at middle and upper elevations, between 1,200 and 3,000 m. Pairs or individuals forage on ground in wet montane forests; commonly walk on trails. Incessantly repeats a rising *wha, wha, wha, wha…* . **Endemic to CR and western Panama**. 11" (28 cm).

Violaceous Quail-Dove
Geotrygon violacea

A relatively plain quail-dove that might be confused with a *Leptotila* dove (p. 90), but has **chestnut-brown wings** and **violet back**. Uncommon on Pacific slopes of Guanacaste Cordillera, from 500 to 1,200 m; very rare and spottily distributed in Caribbean lowlands and foothills, to 600 m; also very rare on Nicoya Peninsula. Two recent sight records from Carara. Forages on ground in mature forests, but somewhat arboreal. Repeats a doubled *hu-hu*, the second note slightly lower pitched. 9" (23 cm).

Ruddy Quail-Dove
Geotrygon montana

The only CR quail-dove with a **brown moustachial stripe** (the Chiriqui Quail-Dove has a black moustachial stripe). Female is much duller brown than male, which is distinctly ruddy. Fairly uncommon in southern Pacific lowlands and foothills, to 1,200 m; rare in Caribbean lowlands and uncommon in foothills, to 1,000 m. Individuals forage on ground in wet forests; commonly walk on trails. Utters a deep, resonant *huuu*, similar to, but shorter than, call of Gray-chested Dove (p. 90). 9" (23 cm).

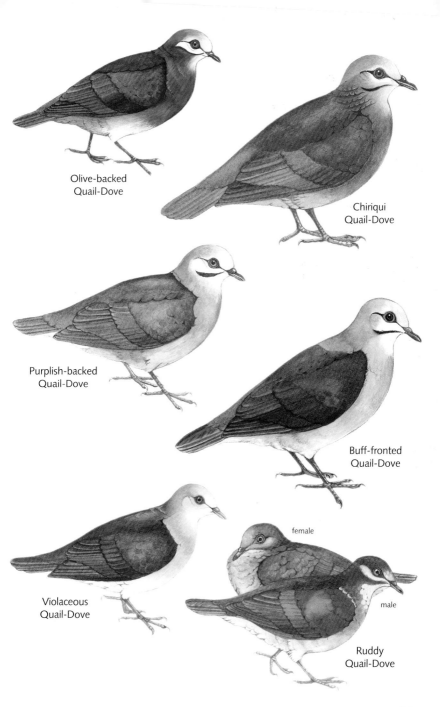

Olive-backed
Quail-Dove

Chiriqui
Quail-Dove

Purplish-backed
Quail-Dove

Buff-fronted
Quail-Dove

Violaceous
Quail-Dove

female

male

Ruddy
Quail-Dove

Parrots

PSITTACIDAE. From the large and gaudy Scarlet Macaw to the tiny Red-fronted Parrotlet, the unique bill shape should easily classify any member of this family. These brightly colored birds, however, can be uncannily difficult to see well because they fly silhouetted against the sky or blend in amid the vegetation. Listen for their vocalizations or the sound of falling pieces of fruit to help locate them. Plumage patterns on the head are important for distinguishing among congeners.

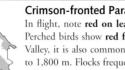

Sulphur-winged Parakeet
Pyrrhura hoffmanni

In flight, shows **bright yellow in wings**. On perched birds, note **red ear coverts**. Uncommon in Dota region and Talamanca Cordillera, between 1,600 and 3,000 m; descends in second half of year to as low as 700 m on both Caribbean and Pacific slopes. Small flocks forage in forest canopy, at forest edges, and in orchards. Flight call is quite high-pitched, with none of the screeching quality of other parakeets. **Endemic to CR and western Panama**. 9" (23 cm).

Crimson-fronted Parakeet
Aratinga finschi

In flight, note **red on leading portion of underwing** and long, pointed tail. Perched birds show **red forehead**. The most common parakeet in the Central Valley, it is also common on the Caribbean slope and in the southern Pacific; to 1,800 m. Flocks frequent gardens and forest edges; often found in *Erythrina* and palm trees. Produces a boisterous chattering *klee-klee-chee-chee...*, somewhat similar to call of other *Aratinga* parakeets. **Endemic from southeastern Nicaragua to western Panama**. 11" (28 cm).

[The following three species are mostly green and have blue flight feathers. They are distinguished by coloration on head and throat; also, no range overlap.]

Olive-throated Parakeet
Aratinga nana

Has **entirely green head** and dull **olive throat**. Fairly common throughout Caribbean lowlands, rarely to 700 m. Small flocks feed in fruiting trees in gardens and at forest edges. Calls are higher pitched and not as harsh as those of Crimson-fronted Parakeet. 9" (23 cm).

Brown-throated Parakeet
Aratinga pertinax

Has **pale-orange patch below eye** and **brownish throat, breast, and sides of face**. A recent arrival from Panama, now fairly common in lowland garden habitats, north to Gamba, and likely still spreading in southern Pacific. Makes a chatter similar to that of Crimson-fronted Parakeet. 10" (25 cm).

Orange-fronted Parakeet
Aratinga canicularis

Has **orange forehead** and **blue midcrown**. Fairly common in northwestern Pacific, south to Tarcoles; uncommon in western Central Valley, to 1,000 m. Flocks visit forests, agricultural areas, and mangroves. Screeching call similar to that of Crimson-fronted Parakeet. 9" (23 cm).

Sulphur-winged
Parakeet

Crimson-fronted
Parakeet

Olive-throated
Parakeet

Brown-throated
Parakeet

Orange-fronted
Parakeet

Birds of Costa Rica / **95**

Barred Parakeet
Bolborhynchus lineola

In flight, note **pointed tail** and uniform green color. Fine black barring difficult to observe unless birds are seen in good light. Fairly common in Talamanca Cordillera, quite uncommon in Central Cordillera; between 800 and 3,000 m. Flocks of twenty or more birds fly in close formation; seems partial to seeding bamboo. Flight call consists of soft, sweet chirping. 6" (15 cm).

Orange-chinned Parakeet
Brotogeris jugularis

Flight silhouette shows **short, pointed tail**. On perched birds, the small orange chin spot can be hard to see, but note the prominent **brown shoulders**. Common and widespread in lowlands and foothills, to 1,200 m. Noisy flocks prefer trees in clearings and at forest edges. Produces a near constant, shrill, harsh chatter. 7" (17 cm).

Red-fronted Parrotlet
Touit costaricensis

In flight, the only small CR parrot with a **square tail**. On perched birds, the **red forehead and wing patch** are diagnostic. A very uncommon species of Caribbean wet forests, mostly between 500 and 1,500 m, though can occur as high as 3,000 m and as low as sea level; rare north of Central Cordillera. Forages in forest canopy. Gives a shrill, querulous *chheee? chee, che-de-de-dee*. **Endemic to CR and western Panama**. 6" (15 cm).

Brown-hooded Parrot
Pionopsitta haematotis

Red axillars are an excellent field mark on flying birds. **Brownish head** with **white orbital ring** and **red ear patch** is distinctive. Fairly common in wet lowlands and at middle elevations, to 1,500 m. Forages in forest canopy and at forest edges; flies quickly with rocking motion and strong wingbeats. Call is a high-pitched *chreea, cheea*. 9" (23 cm).

Blue-headed Parrot
Pionus menstruus

Deep, floppy wingbeats recall White-crowned Parrot, but has distinctive **blue head**. Fairly common in Caribbean lowlands north to Parismina; also in southern Pacific lowlands, north to Sierpe, and in San Vito area. Likely still spreading north. Prefers gardens and forest edges. Typically gives doubled, metallic screech: *shreenk, shreenk*. 10" (25 cm).

White-crowned Parrot
Pionus senilis

Even in poor light, the **white forehead and midcrown** are often visible on both perched and flying birds; note **deep wingstroke**. (Compare with Blue-headed Parrot.) Common in wet lowlands and middle elevations, uncommon in Central Valley; to 1,800 m. Frequents gardens and forest edges. Very noisy, especially in flight, making a shrill chatter. 10" (25 cm).

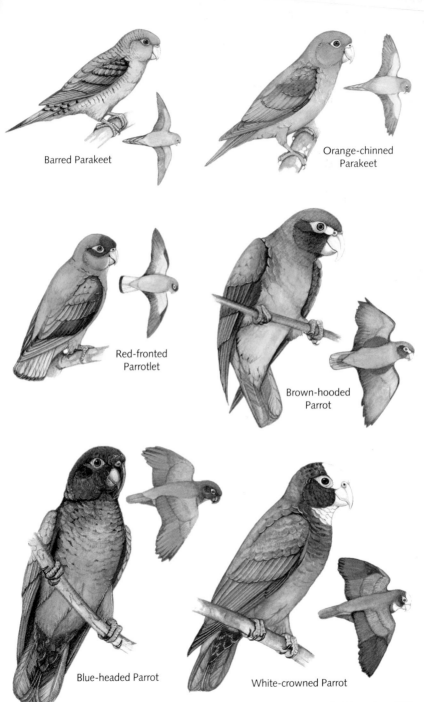

Barred Parakeet

Orange-chinned
Parakeet

Red-fronted
Parrotlet

Brown-hooded
Parrot

Blue-headed Parrot

White-crowned Parrot

Great Green Macaw
Ara ambiguus

Its large size and lovely blend of colors should render it unmistakable. Uncommon in northeastern Caribbean lowlands, rare south of Limón; occasionally to 800 m. Seasonal movements related to ripening of *Dipteryx* fruits. Loud *aak, raak* can be heard at a great distance. 33" (84 cm).

Scarlet Macaw
Ara macao

Unmistakable. This species is now readily found only in the Carara/Tarcoles area and on the Osa Peninsula. A few birds still remain in the Palo Verde area, and recent sightings in the northeastern Caribbean lowlands suggest it may be recolonizing areas where it has not been seen for at least fifty years. Flying birds announce themselves with a raucous, harsh *raaak, raaak*. 35" (90 cm).

[Species in the genus *Amazona*, which includes the following four species, fly with stiff, shallow wingbeats, not lifting the wings above the horizontal plane.]

White-fronted Parrot
Amazona albifrons

In flight, the only CR *Amazona* with **entirely blue secondaries**; male has red patch on leading edge of wing (absent in female). The **white forehead** and **red orbital skin** are distinctive. Very common in northwestern Pacific, to 1,200 m; rare in western Central Valley. Found in both wooded and open areas. Utters a raucous *ak-ak-ak-ak-ak*. 10" (25 cm).

Red-lored Parrot
Amazona autumnalis

Very similar to the Mealy Parrot, but note **red forehead** on both perched and flying birds. Common in wet lowlands and foothills, to 1,000 m. Prefers forest edges and gardens; more tolerant of deforestation than Mealy Parrot. On average, its varied calls are higher-pitched than those of Mealy Parrot; listen for its metallic *klink, klink, klink*. 13" (33 cm).

Mealy Parrot
Amazona farinosa

Best told apart from Red-lored Parrot by **dark cere**, wide white orbital ring, and absence of red on forehead. Common in wet lowlands, to 600 m. More dependent on forested tracts than Red-lored Parrot, although it also frequents forest edges and gardens. Among its many vocalizations, note deep *cheyup, cheyup*. 15" (38 cm).

Yellow-naped Parrot
Amazona auropalliata

A large, slow-flying parrot with distinctive **yellow nape**. Uncommon in northwestern Pacific, to 600 m; birds seen in Central Valley are possibly escaped cage birds. Forages high in trees. Makes a wide variety of deep utterances, without all the squawking of others in the genus. Unfortunately, its value as a pet bird has led to population decline. 14" (36 cm).

Great Green Macaw

CUCULIDAE.
culmen. Exce
tend to be
are usu

Scarlet Macaw

adult
male

juv.

adult
male

White-fronted Parrot

Red-lored Parrot

Mealy Parrot

Yellow-naped Parrot

Most cuckoos are slender birds with long tails; their narrow bills usually have an arched [cul]mt for the three species of ani, which are black, CR cuckoos are attired in brown tones and [s]urtive in their habits. Vocalizations are often the best clue to their presence, though migrants [are mostly] silent.

Black-billed Cuckoo
Coccyzus erythropthalmus

Narrow red orbital ring (yellowish-green on juvenile) distinguishes this species from the Yellow-billed Cuckoo and Mangrove Cuckoo. Also note **dark bill** and **small white tips on tail feathers**. A very uncommon passage migrant on Caribbean slope, rare on Pacific slope and in Central Valley; from late Sept to mid-Nov and from April to mid-May. Concealed amid shrubbery, it forages at forest edges, in second growth, and in gardens. 12" (30 cm).

Yellow-billed Cuckoo
Coccyzus americanus

Rufous primaries distinguish this species from the Black-billed Cuckoo and Mangrove Cuckoo. Also note **yellow bill** with dark culmen and tip, and **large white tips on tail feathers**. A fairly uncommon passage migrant, mostly on Caribbean slope, from Sept to mid-Nov and from mid-April to late May; a very rare winter resident, mostly in northwestern Pacific. Concealed amid shrubbery, it forages at forest edges, in second growth, and in gardens. 12" (30 cm).

Mangrove Cuckoo
Coccyzus minor

Black mask and **buffy underparts** (color varies in intensity from individual to individual) distinguish this from the previous two species. Upper mandible is black, lower mandible is yellow with black tip; also note large white tips on tail feathers. Fairly uncommon Central American migrant from Dec to June in northwestern Pacific lowlands; uncommon to rare in southern Pacific lowlands and in western Central Valley (to 1,100 m). Often sluggish; in CR, favors second growth and gardens over mangroves. Utters series of raspy, throaty notes. 12" (30 cm).

Pheasant Cuckoo
Dromococcyx phasianellus

Buffy breast with brown streaks and long, broad tail feathers distinguish this species from Striped Cuckoo. Very rare throughout Pacific slope, to 1,200 m in south. Skulks in undergrowth scrub at forest edges and in second growth. Whistles three- and four-note calls reminiscent of a Striped Cuckoo, but third note quivering. 15" (38 cm).

Striped Cuckoo
Tapera naevia

Overall color and pattern, plus habitat, could suggest a large sparrow, but note curved upper mandible. Distinguished from larger Pheasant Cuckoo by **plain breast** and unextravagant tail feathers. Fairly common in Caribbean lowlands, southern Pacific, and western Central Valley; to 1,100 m. Uncommon around Gulf of Nicoya and on Nicoya Peninsula. Inhabits brushy fields and second growth; forages in undergrowth; sings from exposed perches. Frequently whistles two clear notes, the second slightly higher, while raising and lowering crest feathers. Also sings a crescendoing five-note version: *tsee-tsee-tsee-TSEE-deep*. 12" (30 cm).

Black-billed
Cuckoo

Yellow-billed
Cuckoo

Mangrove
Cuckoo

Pheasant
Cuckoo

Striped
Cuckoo

Rufous-vented Ground-Cuckoo
Neomorphus geoffroyi

Not likely mistaken. Very rare in Caribbean foothills and lowlands, also on Pacific side of Guanacaste Cordillera; to 900 m. Dwells in understory of wet forest. Follows army-ant raids and, reportedly, peccaries to feed on the insects that they flush out. Produces a sharp cracking sound by snapping its bill shut; also utters a deep *hoof.* 19" (48 cm).

Squirrel Cuckoo
Piaya cayana

With **bright rufous upperparts** and **long tail**, not likely confused. Common and widespread, to 2,300 m. Found in gardens, second growth, and at forest edges; hops among branches in a squirrel-like manner in search of caterpillars. Among its various calls is an arresting *IK-weyeew.* In breeding season (from Jan to Aug), gives long series of dry *whip* notes. 18" (46 cm).

Lesser Ground-Cuckoo
Morococcyx erythropygus

The singular facial markings readily distinguish it; no other CR species has **bare yellow skin in front of the eye** and **blue skin behind the eye**. Fairly common in northwestern Pacific and in western Central Valley, to 1,200 m. Stealthily keeps to thickets and brushy fields, occasionally perches openly. At intervals, delivers a loud, long series of trilled whistles that accelerates then gradually slows. 10" (25 cm).

Greater Ani
Crotophaga major

Known from a handful of sightings of single birds at Tortuguero (in early 2003 and Dec 2004). Larger than the other two anis and further distinguished by pale iris and arched basal half of upper mandible. 18" (46 cm).

Smooth-billed Ani
Crotophaga ani

This and the Groove-billed Ani can be told apart from other essentially all-black birds of open country (cowbirds, grackles, and blackbirds) by their arched, laterally compressed bills. Smooth-billed Ani is very similar to adult Groove-billed Ani, but has **smooth, more highly arched bill**; virtually identical to juvenile Groove-billed Ani. Fortunately, little range overlap. Fairly common in southern Pacific, north to around Quepos; to 1,200 m. Groups of four to twelve forage on ground and perch low in fields and gardens. Typical call is a rising *weeeik.* 14" (36 cm).

Groove-billed Ani
Crotophaga sulcirostris

This and the Smooth-billed Ani can be told apart from other essentially all-black birds of open country (cowbirds, grackles, and blackbirds) by their arched, laterally compressed bills. Adult Groove-billed Ani is very similar to Smooth-billed Ani, but has **striations on the upper mandible**; juvenile virtually identical to Smooth-billed Ani. Fortunately, little range overlap. Common and widespread in lowlands and middle elevations, to 1,500 m; now extremely rare in southern Pacific. Small groups forage on ground and perch low in fields and gardens; often follow cattle to eat the insects they stir up. Common call is a tinkling *TEE-ho, TEE-ho.* 12" (30 cm).

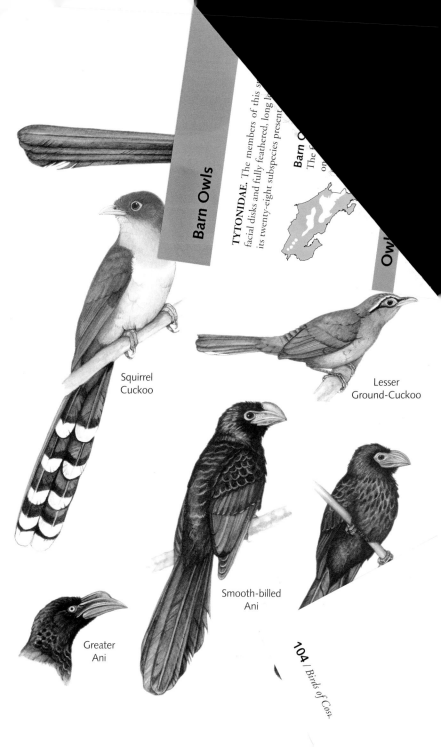

Barn Owls

TYTONIDAE. The members of this s
facial disks and fully feathered, long le
its twenty-eight subspecies presen

Barn C
The f
o

Ow

Squirrel
Cuckoo

Lesser
Ground-Cuckoo

Smooth-billed
Ani

Greater
Ani

...nall family of owls are distinguished by their heart-shaped
...gs. The familiar Barn Owl is cosmopolitan, with at least one of
...on every continent except Antarctica.

...wl *Tyto alba*

...acial disk is unique; CR's palest owl, but some individuals are quite buffy
...face and underparts. Fairly common and widespread, to 1,800 m. Forages
...or rodents by flying low over fields and marshes; prefers low perches (e.g.,
fence posts) at night, sometimes active at dusk and dawn. Gives a harsh shriek
khaaaaa. 16" (41 cm).

STRIGIDAE. Owls are characterized by stout bodies, rounded heads, round facial disks, and large,
forward-facing eyes. All CR species have relatively short tails and are somewhat cryptically colored in
shades of brown with a variety of mottling and streaking patterns. Chiefly nocturnal predators, owls
are renowned for their ability to hunt by sound and sight in the dark of night. At least two species
can be found in almost any given CR habitat below timberline. Vocalizations are extremely helpful
in detection and identification.

Spectacled Owl *Pulsatrix perspicillata*

A large owl without ear tufts; the **white X pattern on face** is distinctive. Birds
from northwestern Pacific often show barring on buffy underparts. Fairly
common and widespread, to 1,500 m. Roosts fairly low in trees, typically near
wooded streams. Call is a series of about six deep, muffled, chuckling notes that
sounds like a large sheet of tin being shaken. 19" (48 cm).

Crested Owl *Lophostrix cristata*

The conspicuous **white stripe** (buffy on some individuals) **from the tip of the
long ear tufts to the base of the bill** is diagnostic. Generally uncommon but
widespread, to 1,500 m. Roosts and hunts at low to middle levels of forest and
adjacent tall second growth; also at forest edges. Call is a deep, guttural *wk-wk-
wuUUuurr*. 16" (41 cm).

Striped Owl *Pseudoscops clamator*

Has **heavily streaked underparts** and **long ear tufts**; the white facial disk is
bordered by black. Fairly common in central Pacific lowlands, especially near oil
palms; uncommon elsewhere in mapped range, to 1,500 m. Favors open areas,
often seen perched on utility wires; nests and roosts on or near ground. Makes a
nasal, high-pitched *heeAHhh* that rises and falls. 15" (38 cm).

Barn Owl

Spectacled Owl

Crested Owl

pale morph

dark morph

Striped Owl

Birds of Costa Rica / **105**

Black-and-white Owl

Ciccaba nigrolineata

The only CR owl that has **black-and-white barring on underparts**. Fairly uncommon in wet lowlands; rare in dry forest and middle elevations, to 1,500 m. Forages at forest edges and in gardens, often near street lamps; roosts in lower and middle levels of large trees. Gives an ascending series of deep chuckling notes: *hwa, hwa, hwa, hwa, hwa, HWUU!* 15" (38 cm).

Mottled Owl

Ciccaba virgata

Has round head (no ear tufts), mottled dark-brown breast, and a streaked belly. Note **brown iris**. Fairly common and widespread, to 2,200 m. Forages at middle levels of forests, tall second growth, and forest edges; roosts fairly low in dense vegetation. Calls with deep, muffled notes followed by two loud notes and an additional muffled note: *whu, whu, WHUU, WHUU, whu.* 13" (33 cm).

Bare-shanked Screech-Owl

Megascops clarkii

Bright tawny facial disk lacks distinct rim. Fairly uncommon in highlands, from 900 m to timberline. Forages at forest edges and in forest canopy. Toots an evenly spaced *whu, whu, whu, whu*, with either second or third note emphasized. **Endemic from CR to northwestern Colombia**. 10" (25 cm).

Pacific Screech-Owl

Megascops cooperi

Very similar to Tropical Screech-Owl, but note that the dark border of the facial disk is less distinct. The two species are best distinguished by voice where their ranges overlap—in Central Valley and central Pacific lowlands. Fairly common in northwestern Pacific, to 1,000 m; uncommon in western Central Valley and rare east to Cartago. Hunts from low perches in trees, gardens, and open areas. Gives a short *hup* in a fast-paced series that rises then falls abruptly in pitch and tempo. 9" (23 cm).

Tropical Screech-Owl

Megascops choliba

Very similar to Pacific Screech-Owl, but note **distinct black facial disk border** (the rare rufous morph Tropical Screech-Owl [not illustrated] also has distinct black facial border). Fairly common in Central Valley and in intermontane valleys of southern Pacific, between 500 and 1,500 m; uncommon to rare in Tilarán Cordillera and in Pacific lowlands, from Orotina south. Hunts from low perches in trees, in both gardens and lightly wooded areas. Gives a bubbly, one-second trill followed by a slightly louder and questioning *POO!?* (this last note is sometimes doubled or tripled). 9" (23 cm).

Vermiculated Screech-Owl

Megascops guatemalae

In both rufous and gray morphs, has **unbordered facial disk** and shows more horizontal vermiculation than vertical streaking on underparts. Uncommon in wet lowlands and foothills of both the Caribbean slope and the southern Pacific (from Dominical south); to 1,000 m. Also in hills of Nicoya Peninsula, to 1,000 m. Inhabits lower levels of forest and advanced second growth. Makes a soft, crescendoing trill, lasting about ten seconds, that is easily mistaken for a Marine Toad's call. 8" (20 cm).

Black-and-white Owl

Mottled Owl

Bare-shanked Screech-Owl

Pacific Screech-Owl

Tropical Screech-Owl

Vermiculated Screech-Owl

rufous morph

gray morph

Unspotted Saw-whet Owl
Aegolius ridgwayi

The only **small** CR owl with **no barring or streaking below**. Rare in Central and Talamanca Cordilleras, from 2,500 m to timberline. Inhabits oak forests and parklike pastures. Pipes a series of even toots, reminiscent of Ferruginous Pygmy-Owl. 7" (18 cm).

[The three CR pygmy-owl species below are quite similar in appearance, but have slightly different vocalizations and little range overlap.]

Costa Rican Pygmy-Owl
Glaucidium costaricanum

Shows **white dots on brown crown** and **barring on sides of breast**; has both brown and rufous morphs. A fairly uncommon inhabitant of Central and Talamanca Cordilleras, from about 1,200 m to timberline. Active day and night in middle and upper levels of highland oak forests and at forest edges. Delivers a lengthy series of even notes, usually in couplets: *hao hao, hao hao, hao hao.* **Endemic from CR to western Panama**. 6" (15 cm).

Ferruginous Pygmy-Owl
Glaucidium brasilianum

Note **crown with short, light streaks**. Overall color varies from brown to rufous. Common in lowlands and foothills of northwestern Pacific and western Central Valley, rarer east of San José to Turrialba and south of Jacó to Dominical; to 2,200 m. Active day and night in lower and middle levels of forest edges and gardens. Gives a monotone series of rather staccato toots. 6" (15 cm).

Central American Pygmy-Owl
Glaucidium griseiceps

Note **grayish crown with white dots**, streaked belly, and absence of barring on flanks. Uncommon in wet Caribbean lowlands and foothills, to 800 m. Active day and night in lower and middle levels of mature forest, forest edges, and gardens. Whistles two to ten clear even notes that are faster and less labored than those of far more common Stripe-breasted Wren (p. 240). 6" (15 cm).

Burrowing Owl
Athene cunicularia

A pale-brown, round-headed, long-legged terrestrial owl. Accidental in CR. One specimen from north of Cartago, on the slopes of Irazú Volcano, in Dec 1900, and a possible sighting from northwestern Pacific lowlands, in the 1980s. **Not illustrated**. 9" (23 cm).

Short-eared Owl
Asio flammeus

In size, color, and pattern, somewhat similar to Striped Owl (p. 104), but has very short ear tufts and very fine streaking below. Known from two specimens taken near San José in Dec 1863 and Dec 1916. **Not illustrated**. 15" (38 cm).

Great Horned Owl
Bubo virginianus

The **dark ear tufts**, **tawny facial disk**, and **barred underparts** are a unique combination among CR owls. Very rare; known from Central Valley and northwestern Pacific. Apparently prefers to roost in (and hunt from) dense trees near open areas. Its call is an archetypal *hu-hoo, hooo, hooo.* **Not illustrated**. 20" (51 cm).

Unspotted
Saw-whet Owl

brown
morph

rufous
morph

Costa Rican
Pygmy-Owl

Ferruginous
Pygmy-Owl

Central American
Pygmy-Owl

Nightjars

CAPRIMULGIDAE. Cryptically plumaged and nocturnal, the nightjars can be tough to identify. Look for white or buff markings on the wings, tail, throat, and/or nape. Vocalizations are usually the most reliable way of determining species. The members of this widespread family are found in many different habitats; all nightjars hawk flying insects. Their eyes reflect bright orange-red when a beam of light is directed at them.

Common Pauraque
Nyctidromus albicollis

Roosting birds can be told apart from similar nightjars by conspicuous **buff spotting on wing coverts**, **chestnut cheeks**, and absence of nuchal collar; also note long, rounded tail. When flushed, male shows **bold white stripe across primaries and in outer tail feathers** (much less obvious in female). This is the common nightjar throughout lowlands and middle elevations, to 1,700 m. After dark, forages by flying up from ground in openings, especially roadsides and lawns; usually near woods, where it roosts (wonderfully camouflaged by day) in leaf litter. Whistles a slurred *kweeeuu!* often introduced by a stuttering series of *wik* notes. 11" (28 cm).

Chuck-will's-widow
Caprimulgus carolinensis

Male has white in tail (absent in female). Both sexes very similar to Rufous Nightjar, but have **grayish crown**; also resemble very rare Whip-poor-will. Very uncommon (or seldom detected) NA migrant from Oct to April, mostly in lowlands, rarely to 1,500 m. Known from a variety of habitats, including mature wet forest, second growth, forest edges, mangroves, and even rows of trees bordering fields; roosts primarily on low branches, but also on ground. Usually silent in CR. 12" (30 cm).

Rufous Nightjar
Caprimulgus rufus

Male has white in tail (absent in female). Both sexes very similar to the migrant Chuck-will's-widow, but have **rufous crown**; also resemble very rare Whip-poor-will. Rare in lowlands and foothills, to 1,000 m; found on Pacific slope from Parrita south and on Caribbean slope from Valle de la Estrella south. Favors second growth, thickets, and forest edges; roosts on ground or low perch. Male calls from low perch with loud chuck: *we-we-weeEo*. 11" (28 cm).

Whip-poor-will
Caprimulgus vociferus

Resembles Chuck-will's-widow and Rufous Nightjar, but is grayer with **heavy dark streaking on center of crown**; male shows white tips to outer rectrices (buff in female). Very rare (or undetected) NA migrant on Pacific slope and in Central Valley, from mid-Nov to late March, to 1,200 m. Perches low at forest edges when foraging; roosts on ground or low perches. Usually silent in CR. 10" (25 cm).

Dusky Nightjar
Caprimulgus saturatus

Little elevation overlap with other species; a dark nightjar with white tips to outer rectrices (tips are buff in female). Fairly common on Tilarán Cordillera, above 1,500 m; also fairly common on Central and Talamanca Cordilleras, from 1,800 m to just above timberline. Hunts from low perches at edge of montane forest and in clearings; also prefers low perches for roosting. Whistles a somewhat slurred *whEE-per-whEE*, the last note slightly higher pitched. **Endemic to CR and western Panama**. 9" (23 cm).

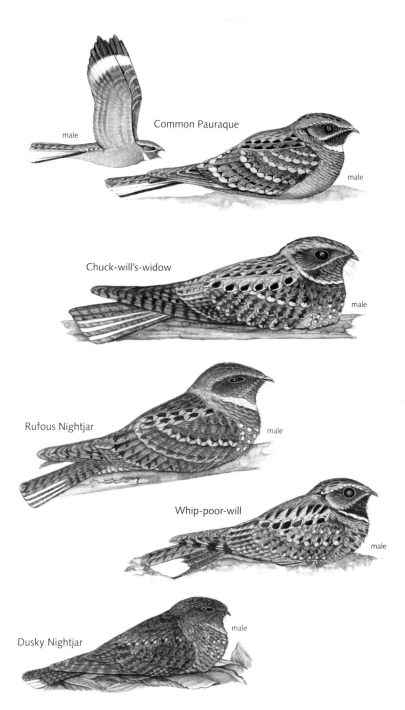

Common Pauraque

male

male

Chuck-will's-widow

male

Rufous Nightjar

male

Whip-poor-will

male

Dusky Nightjar

male

White-tailed Nightjar
Caprimulgus cayennensis

The **buff nuchal collar** (tawny on female) is definitive; in male, underside of tail is mostly white and upperside has narrow white stripes; no white in tail of female. Uncommon on Pacific slope and rare on southern Caribbean slope, to 800 m. Favors open, grassy areas, where it perches on ground, both for hunting and roosting. Sings a high, thin *pik-speeeeea*, the last note rising, then falling. 8" (20 cm).

Lesser Nighthawk
Chordeiles acutipennis

Very similar to Common Nighthawk; in flight, the white band in the wing (buff on female) is nearer the tip and the wing tip is not as sharply pointed as in Common Nighthawk. All of these field marks are very subtle! When roosting, wing tips reach tip of tail. Resident on Pacific slope, where most common near coast. Abundant passage migrant, mostly along Caribbean coast, from mid-Sept to early Nov. Can be seen at dusk and dawn foraging over open areas, often near water. Roosts lengthwise on low branches, especially in mangroves. 9" (23 cm).

Common Nighthawk
Chordeiles minor

Very similar to Lesser Nighthawk, but in flight the white band (buff on female) is nearly halfway between the wing tip and the bend in the wing; and the wing tip is pointed. All of these field marks are very subtle! When roosting, the wingtips extend beyond the tail tip. Abundant passage migrant, from early Sept to early Nov and from mid-March to April; mostly along Caribbean coast, though occurs farther inland, too; also on the Pacific slope and in the Central Valley. Uncommon breeding resident at lower elevations on Pacific slopes of Guanacaste Cordillera, and in Térraba region; from April to Aug. Comes out at dusk to feed on flying insects. Roosts on ground or lengthwise on low branches. In flight, gives a nasal *beeeznt*. 10" (25 cm).

Short-tailed Nighthawk
Lurocalis semitorquatus

In flight, no obvious field marks, but can be recognized by batlike flight (few CR bats are as large) and decidedly **short tail**. When roosting, wing tips project beyond tip of tail. Uncommon in wet lowlands and foothills of Caribbean and southern Pacific, to 1,200 m. Flies at treetop level over forested areas and adjacent clearings and streams, emerging at last light of day and going to roost at first light. Roosts lengthwise on branches of canopy tree. Flight call is a hard *kit-kit-kit*. 9" (23 cm).

Ocellated Poorwill
Nyctiphrynus ocellatus

Less variegated than other CR nightjars; males are very dark brown, females are more ruddy; white spots on belly may be hard to see on roosting birds. In flight, shows narrow white tips to outer rectrices; no white in wing. Known only from southeast of Brasilia de Upala, where status of population is uncertain. Inhabits young second growth adjacent to more mature forest. From the ground or low perch, males sing a trilled *kwreeeo*. **Not illustrated**. 8" (20 cm).

White-tailed
Nightjar

male

Lesser
Nighthawk

male

male

Common
Nighthawk

male

male

Short-tailed
Nighthawk

Birds of Costa Rica / **113**

Potoos

NYCTIBIIDAE. A Neotropical family of nocturnal birds that resemble the nightjars (p. 110), but one noticeable difference is their habit of perching upright, both while roosting and hunting. Distinguishing between species present in CR can be very difficult without hearing vocalizations.

Great Potoo
Nyctibius grandis

More than twice the bulk of the other two CR species; also note large head uniformly mottled with brown and buff and **lacking any obvious markings**. Has bright orange-yellow eye-shine, as does the Common Potoo. Uncommon in wet lowlands of Caribbean and of Osa Peninsula and Golfo Dulce, to 600 m. On day roosts, typically perches crosswise on a high limb inside mature forest or at forest edges; at night, sallies for flying insects from high, exposed perch. Gives a loud, throaty *WAAAAuur* that falls off slightly at the end and also a quick, hollow *WAU!*; most often heard on moonlit nights. 20" (51 cm).

Common Potoo
Nyctibius griseus

Virtually identical to Northern Potoo in appearance and habits—separable only by voice. Similar to Great Potoo, but with a **pale cheek stripe bordered below by a dark malar stripe**. Has bright orange-yellow eye-shine, as does the Great Potoo. Fairly uncommon in lowlands and foothills of southern Pacific and very uncommon in wet Caribbean lowlands and foothills, to 1,200 m. Often perches quite low, at the tip of a more or less vertical snag (or even fence post), appearing amazingly like an extension of the perch itself (especially in cryptic pose); seems to prefer more open areas than Great Potoo. The call is a sweet and mournful, resonant, descending *KWUU-UU, KUU, KUU, kwuu, kwuu*. **Same illustrations as for Northern Potoo**. 15" (38 cm).

Northern Potoo
Nyctibius jamaicensis

Virtually identical to Common Potoo in appearance and habits—**separable only by voice**. Combines the gruff, throaty sound of a Great Potoo with the cadence of the song of a Common Potoo. If no vocalization is heard, identification can be based on geographic location, but caution is urged in areas of proximity (Caño Negro region and Jacó area), where the status of these two species is unclear. Uncommon in northern Pacific and western Central Valley. **Same illustrations as for Common Potoo**. 15" (38 cm).

Oilbird

STEATORNITHIDAE. The sole member of this family is unique in being the world's only nocturnal avian frugivore. Roosts and nests colonially in caves and dark ravines; navigates using echo-location.

Oilbird
Steatornis caripensis

Resembles a very large nightjar (p. 110), but coloration is a **rich rufous-brown with white spots**; has red eye-shine. No CR population has yet been discovered, but specimens have been collected from Cerro de la Muerte and Monteverde; an individual was photographed dayroosting in Corcovado National Park; and there is an additional sight report from above Horquetas de Sarapiquí. Feeds at night on palm and wild avocado fruits taken in hovering flight. Emits a slow series of clicks in flight. 18" (46 cm).

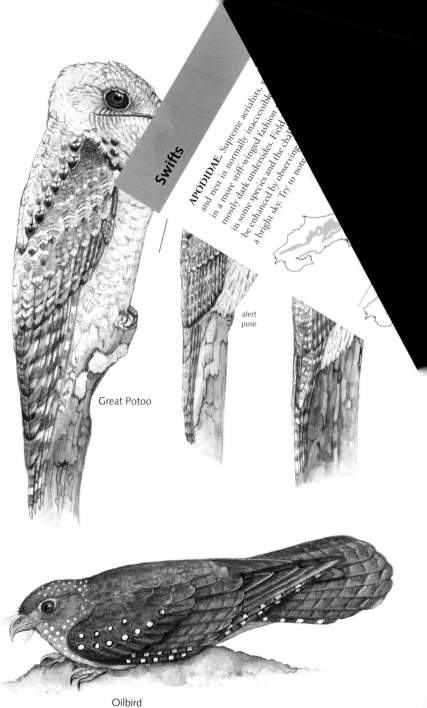

Swifts

APODIDAE: Supreme aerialists, s... and nest in normally inaccessible... in a more stiff-winged fashion... mostly dark undersides. Field... in some species and the cha... be enhanced by observing... a bright sky. Try to note...

Great Potoo

alert
pose

Oilbird

wifts reportedly even copulate on the wing, landing only to roost
places such as cliffs, hollow trees, and behind waterfalls. They fly
than the superficially similar swallows and martins (p. 232) and have
dentification can be quite difficult given the lack of obvious field marks
enging viewing conditions under which they are often seen. Viewing can
them against a dark background (e.g., trees or hillsides) rather than against
coloration of throat and rump.

White-chinned Swift   *Cypseloides cryptus*

A relatively large, dark swift with a **squat head** and a **short, square tail**; the
subtle whitish facial markings, which are diagnostic, are not likely to be seen
in the field. Similarly plumaged Black Swift has a notched tail and a more
elongated head. Difficult to distinguish from the similarly shaped Spot-fronted
Swift, though each species has distinctive (but subtle) facial markings. Rare in
highlands; occasionally descends to adjacent foothills and lowlands to forage.
6" (15 cm).

Black Swift   *Cypseloides niger*

Males have a noticeably notched tail, females less so. Larger than any other CR
swift—except White-collared Swift, which also shows a somewhat notched tail.
Similarly sized, all-dark White-chinned Swift has a shorter, square tail and a
squat head. Very uncommon in Tilarán, Central, and Talamanca Cordilleras,
descending to lower elevations to forage. 7" (18 cm).

Spot-fronted Swift   *Cypseloides cherriei*

Under ideal viewing conditions, shows a **white spot both in front of and
behind the eye**; otherwise, virtually impossible to distinguish from the similarly
shaped White-chinned Swift. Very uncommon, mostly on Pacific slope from
Central Valley south, but also recently recorded in Puerto Viejo de Sarapiquí
area. 5" (13 cm).

Chestnut-collared Swift   *Streptoprocne rutila*

The **chestnut collar** is definitive, though birds can look entirely dark under poor
viewing conditions and most females and juveniles show little or no chestnut
around the neck. Fairly common in intermontane valleys of southern Pacific,
less common elsewhere in highlands and southern Pacific lowlands, and rare in
Caribbean lowlands. 5" (13 cm).

White-collared Swift   *Streptoprocne zonaris*

The **large size** and obvious **white collar** facilitate identification, though in poor
light it could be mistaken for a Black Swift; also, lone individuals could possibly
be mistaken for a Bat Falcon (p. 50). Widespread and generally very common,
though uncommon in northwestern Pacific. Usually seen traveling and foraging
in groups of a dozen or more (up to 100+), commonly with other, smaller swift
species. 9" (23 cm).

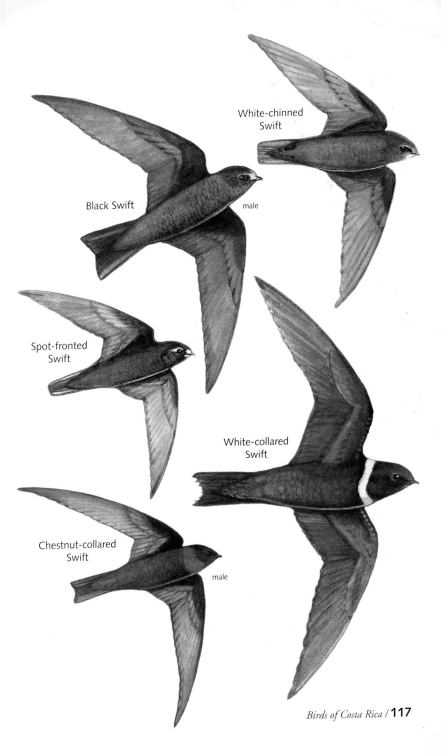

White-chinned
Swift

Black Swift

male

Spot-fronted
Swift

White-collared
Swift

Chestnut-collared
Swift

male

Costa Rican Swift
Chaetura fumosa

The obvious **pale rump patch** is the defining field mark (no range overlap with Gray-rumped Swift); also note decidedly pale throat. Vaux's Swift has pale rump, but it is less distinct than on Costa Rican and Gray-rumped Swifts. Common in southern Pacific lowlands and foothills, to 1,200 m. **Endemic from CR to northern Colombia.** 4" (10 cm).

Gray-rumped Swift
Chaetura cinereiventris

Nearly identical to Costa Rican Swift (no range overlap), but with slightly larger **pale rump patch**. Vaux's Swift has pale rump, but it is less distinct than on Gray-rumped and Costa Rican Swifts. Common in Caribbean lowlands, to 600 m. Often forages in groups of a dozen or more. 4" (10 cm).

Vaux's Swift
Chaetura vauxi

The **throat is clearly paler than the lower underparts**; the rump is also paler than rest of upperparts, but with less contrast than in Costa Rican and Gray-rumped Swifts. Fairly common in highlands and middle elevations, from 600 to 2,200 m; occasionally reaches adjacent lowlands. Usually seen in pairs or small groups. 5" (13 cm).

Chimney Swift
Chaetura pelagica

Compared to the previous three species, the Chimney Swift is more **monochromatic**; throat and rump show little contrast with rest of body. Common passage migrant on Caribbean slope from late Aug to early Nov and from mid-March to late April; mostly along coast, but occasionally to 1,000 m. In migration, displays a unidirectional flight pattern that sets it apart from other CR swifts, none of which are migratory. 5" (13 cm).

Lesser Swallow-tailed Swift
Panyptila cayennensis

Slender build; **long, pointed tail** and **striking, contrasting pattern** all help in identification. Note that the forked tail is normally held closed in flight. Fairly uncommon in wet lowlands and foothills of both Pacific and Caribbean slopes, and rare in Central Valley; to 1,000 m. Usually seen singly or in pairs, seldom found in groups of more than six; typically accompanies other swift species. 5" (13 cm).

Great Swallow-tailed Swift
Panyptila sanctihieronymi

Virtually identical to Lesser Swallow-tailed Swift in shape and color pattern, but nearly twice the length and more than double the bulk. In other words, size alone is all you have to go by, so caution is urged. An accidental bird from northern Central America; only a handful of sight reports from Puerto Viejo de Sarapiquí, Tortuguero, and San Isidro de El General. 8" (20 cm).

Costa Rican
Swift

Gray-rumped
Swift

Vaux's Swift

Chimney
Swift

Lesser
Swallow-tailed Swift

Great
Swallow-tailed Swift

Hummingbirds

TROCHILIDAE. As many of their common names imply (e.g., emerald, goldentail, mountain-gem), hummingbirds are veritable avian jewels. These birds have a number of evolutionary adaptations for feeding on flower nectar, the most notable of which is their unique ability to hover and fly backward, indeed in any direction. Bill shape and size influence their feeding behavior and are also important features for identifying them. The brilliant colors displayed by many species, particularly among males, are the result of feather structure (vs. pigmentation) and are only visible from certain angles. Males of many species are quite vocal, though most produce little more than a monotonous series of thin, high-pitched notes. In a number of species, especially the hermits, groups of males (up to twenty or more at some sites) gather to sing for the purpose of attracting females. In these assemblages, known as leks, individual males are usually spaced apart by a meter or more (and can be frustratingly difficult to see amid the vegetation). Although hummingbirds are found in virtually every habitat in CR, the greatest species diversity occurs at middle elevations.

Green Hermit
Phaethornis guy

Combination of **dark blue-green upperparts** and **white-tipped central rectrices** is diagnostic. Common in foothills and middle elevations, from 500 to 2,000 m. Forages in lower levels of mature wet forest and forest edges. Males lek in low, dense vegetation inside forest. 6" (15 cm).

Stripe-throated Hermit
Phaethornis striigularis

Coloration similar to larger Long-billed Hermit, but note **tapering tail with buff tips**. (Despite its name, CR race shows no obvious streaking on throat.) Common in wet lowlands and foothills, to 1,000 m; uncommon between 1,000 and 1,600 m and in northwestern Pacific lowlands. Forages low in mature forest, advanced second growth, forest edges, and gardens. Males lek inside forest, using perches less than a meter above the ground. 4" (10 cm).

Long-billed Hermit
Phaethornis longirostris

Brownish coloration should distinguish this hermit from all but the Stripe-throated Hermit, but note **elongated white-tipped central rectrices**. Common in wet lowlands, and very uncommon from 500 to 1,200 m. Forages in lower levels of mature wet forest, advanced second growth, and forest edges. Males lek in low, dense vegetation inside forest. 6" (15 cm).

Bronzy Hermit
Glaucis aeneus

Similar to Band-tailed Barbthroat, but note **rufous base of outer rectrices** and **pale-cinnamon throat**. Fairly uncommon in wet lowlands, and rare from 400 to 1,200 m. Forages low at forest edges and in wet thickets, visiting *Heliconia* and banana flowers. 4" (10 cm).

Band-tailed Barbthroat
Threnetes ruckeri

The **white base of the outer rectrices** and the **dark throat** differentiate this species from the Bronzy Hermit. Fairly common in wet lowlands, to 800 m; rarely to 1,200 m. Visits *Heliconia*, *Calathea*, and banana flowers at lower levels of mature wet forest, advanced second growth, and forest edges. Males form small leks in low, dense vegetation inside forest. 4" (10 cm).

female

male

Green
Hermit

Stripe-throated
Hermit

Long-billed
Hermit

Bronzy
Hermit

Band-tailed
Barbthroat

Birds of Costa Rica / **121**

White-tipped Sicklebill
Eutoxeres aquila

Has an **extremely decurved bill** and is the only CR hummer with **streaked underparts**. Very uncommon in Caribbean foothills and adjacent lowlands and in southern Pacific; to 1,200 m. Feeds primarily on *Heliconia* flowers in lower levels of mature wet forest, advanced second growth, and forest edges; perches on inflorescence while feeding. 5" (13 cm).

Violet Sabrewing
Campylopterus hemileucurus

Male is unmistakable with its **glittering-violet** hues and large **white tips on outer rectrices**. Female is less distinctive, but readily recognized by **decurved bill, violet throat**, and **white in tail**. Common at middle elevations, from 1,000 to 2,400 m; some descend to lower elevations from Nov to April, occasionally even to sea level. Found at lower levels of mature wet forest, often at openings and forest edges. Males lek in low, dense vegetation inside forest. 6" (15 cm).

Fiery-throated Hummingbird
Panterpe insignis

The spectacular forecrown, throat, and breast colors can be difficult to see, so note the **thin, straight bill** with pinkish basal half of lower mandible and the small white spot behind the eye. The **bluish rump** and **blue-black tail** set it apart from the Magnificent Hummingbird. Very common in Central and Talamanca Cordilleras, mostly above 2,000 m; uncommon from Miravalles Volcano south through Tilarán Cordillera, above 1,500 m. From March to July—throughout its range—occasionally descends to as low as 700 m. Active at all levels of forests, forest edges, and clearings. Often very pugnacious; utters a screechy sputter. **Endemic to CR and western Panama**. 4" (10 cm).

Magnificent Hummingbird
Eugenes fulgens

The male's **violet forecrown** and **turquoise throat** are distinctive; the all-green back and rump further distinguish it from the Fiery-throated Hummingbird. The female can be recognized by her large size, fairly **straight black bill**, **postocular stripe**, and **gray underparts**. Common in highlands of Central and Talamanca Cordilleras, from 1,800 m to timberline; fairly uncommon down to 1,300 m on Caribbean slope. Frequents edges and openings in highland oak forest, also in gardens. 5" (13 cm).

Green-crowned Brilliant
Heliodoxa jacula

The small **violet-blue throat patch** is the definitive field mark on the otherwise sparkling-green male. The **short white malar stripe** distinguishes the female from other species with **greenish-spotted underparts** (Scaly-breasted Hummingbird, Blue-chested Hummingbird, Charming Hummingbird, and White-necked Jacobin [p. 124]). Note that juvenile male has **pale-rufous malars and chin** (and may be responsible for many reports of Fiery-throated Hummingbird at lower than normal elevations). Common at middle elevations, from 700 to 2,200 m; from Feb to June, occurs as low as 100 m. Visits all levels of wet montane forest, second growth, and forest edges; prefers to perch (vs. hover) when feeding. 5" (13 cm).

White-tipped
Sicklebill

male

Violet
Sabrewing

female

throat colors
displayed

Fiery-throated
Hummingbird

male

juv.

female

male

female

Magnificent
Hummingbird

Green-crowned
Brilliant

Scaly-breasted Hummingbird

Phaeochroa cuvierii

A **drab** hummer, but note **white tips to the outer rectrices**; also note pink basal half of lower mandible. The breast does not appear conspicuously scaly. Female Green-crowned Brilliant (p. 122) has short white malar stripe; female Blue-chested Hummingbird, Charming Hummingbird, and White-necked Jacobin show some blue on chest. Common in dry and humid Pacific lowlands and intermontane valleys of southern Pacific, and in Caño Negro region; uncommon in wet lowlands of southern Pacific and in Sarapiquí region. Found at lower and middle levels along forest edge, in second growth and gardens, as well as in mangroves. Male sings rather well for a hummingbird; often sings from fairly high perch in second growth and gardens. 5" (13 cm).

Purple-crowned Fairy

Heliothryx barroti

No other CR hummer has **entirely white underparts**; also note short bill and long, tapering tail. Fairly uncommon in lowlands and middle elevations, to 1,600 m. Mostly at middle and upper levels of mature wet forest and tall second growth, but at all levels of forest edges and gardens. 5" (13 cm).

Blue-chested Hummingbird

Amazilia amabilis

Virtually identical to Charming Hummingbird, but no range overlap (sometimes considered conspecific). Males of both species can be recognized by their **green crown**, **violet-blue chest**, and **bronzy-black tail**. Females of both species have **dappled breast with bluish center**; can be told apart from more heavily spotted female White-necked Jacobin by relatively long, straight bill with **pink basal half of lower mandible**. Also compare female with Scaly-breasted Hummingbird and female Green-crowned Brilliant (p. 122). Fairly uncommon in wet Caribbean lowlands, to 500 m. Found at lower and middle levels of forest edges and gardens. Males form small leks at middle levels of forest edges. 4" (10 cm).

Charming Hummingbird

Amazilia decora

Virtually identical to Blue-chested Hummingbird, but no range overlap (see previous species account). Fairly uncommon in southern Pacific lowlands and foothills, to 1,200 m. Found at lower and middle levels of forest edges and gardens. Males form small leks at middle levels of forest edges. **Endemic to CR and western Panama**. 4" (10 cm).

White-necked Jacobin

Florisuga mellivora

Male's **royal blue head** and extensive **pure white on underparts and tail** are distinctive; the white nape sometimes does not show. Female's all-dark bill distinguishes her from Scaly-breasted Hummingbird and female Blue-chested and Charming Hummingbirds. Female Green-crowned Brilliant (p. 122) has short white malar stripe. Fairly common in wet lowlands and foothills, to 1,000 m. Forages at all levels of forest edges and gardens; often seen zipping back and forth in mid-air catching insects. 5" (13 cm).

Scaly-breasted
Hummingbird

Purple-crowned
Fairy

female

male

female

male

Blue-chested
Hummingbird

female

Charming
Hummingbird

male

female

male

White-necked
Jacobin

Canivet's Emerald
Chlorostilbon canivetii

Both sexes virtually identical to Garden Emerald (often considered conspecific); the only notable difference is bill color—**reddish lower mandible with black tip**. Male color pattern very similar to Steely-vented Hummingbird, but note **forked tail and entirely green back and rump**. Female's facial pattern is identical to that of female Garden Emerald; this feature sets both apart from other similarly plumaged female hummers. Common on Pacific slopes of Guanacaste and Tilarán Cordilleras; fairly uncommon elsewhere in northwestern Pacific and western Central Valley; to 1,500 m. Feeds on small flowers in brushy pastures, forest edges, and gardens. 3" (8 cm).

Garden Emerald
Chlorostilbon assimilis

Both sexes virtually identical to Canivet's Emerald (often considered conspecific); but have **entirely black bill**. Male color pattern very similar to Steely-vented Hummingbird, but note **forked tail and entirely green back and rump**. Female's facial pattern is identical to that of female Canivet's Emerald; this feature sets both apart from other similarly plumaged female hummers. Fairly common in intermontane valleys and uncommon elsewhere in southern Pacific; to 1,500 m. Also occurs on Caribbean slope in Reventazón River watershed. **Endemic to CR and Panama**. 3" (8 cm).

Steely-vented Hummingbird
Amazilia saucerrottei

Color pattern very similar to male Canivet's and Garden Emeralds, but note **coppery rump** separating green back and steely blue tail. Common in northwestern Pacific, to 1,200 m. Fairly uncommon in Caño Negro region, in Central Valley (east to Turrialba), and in Dota region south to Fila Costera (above Dominical); to 1,600 m. Feeds at lower and middle levels of forest openings and edges, second growth, and gardens. 4" (10 cm).

Blue-tailed Hummingbird
Amazilia cyanura

Similar to Steely-vented Hummingbird, but with **rufous patch in wings**. Distinguished from Stripe-tailed Hummingbird (p. 132), which also has rufous patch on wings, by **blue tail** with no white in outer rectrices. Very rare; reported from Central Valley, Sarapiquí, Monteverde, Carara, and Nicoya Peninsula. Feeds at lower and middle levels of forest edges and gardens. 4" (10 cm).

Alfaro's Hummingbird
Amazilia alfaroana

Resembles Steely-vented Hummingbird, but has turquoise forecrown. Known only from one female collected on the upper Pacific slope of Miravalles Volcano, Sept 1895. Previously classified as Indigo-capped Hummingbird (*Amazilia cyanifrons*). **Not illustrated**. 4" (10 cm).

Violet-crowned Woodnymph
Thalurania colombica

Male can appear all-dark, but in good light shows dazzling **green throat and breast** with **purple crown, shoulders, and belly**. Female more likely to cause confusion, but **U-shaped pale-gray throat and breast** contrast with darker belly. Common in wet lowlands and foothills, to 900 m on Caribbean slope and 1,200 m in southern Pacific; rare north of Quepos. Inhabits lower and middle levels of mature wet forest, second growth, and forest edges. 4" (10 cm).

Canivet's
Emerald

female

male

male

female

Garden
Emerald

Steely-vented
Hummingbird

male

female

Blue-tailed
Hummingbird

Violet-crowned
Woodnymph

Blue-throated Goldentail
Hylocharis eliciae

Could possibly recall a Rufous-tailed Hummingbird, but has **golden-green tail** and **thick, coral-red bill** with black tip. Fairly common in lowlands and foothills of Pacific slope, to 1,200 m; uncommon on Caribbean slope, to 900 m. Prefers lower and middle levels of forest openings and edges, second growth, and gardens. Males lek from thin twigs and vines at middle levels of second growth and forest openings. 4" (10 cm).

Bronze-tailed Plumeleteer
Chalybura urochrysia

In poor light, appears mostly dark, but note diagnostic **pinkish-red feet**. Uncommon in wet Caribbean lowlands and foothills, to 900 m. Feeds in lower levels of mature wet forest, second growth, and forest edges; frequently visits *Heliconia* clumps. 4" (10 cm).

Cinnamon Hummingbird
Amazilia rutila

Dorsal coloration similar to Rufous-tailed Hummingbird, but has **entirely pale-rufous underparts**; female Purple-throated Mountain-gem (p. 134) has white postocular stripe and lacks rufous in tail. Fairly common in northwestern Pacific south to Tarcoles and in western Central Valley; to 1,000 m. Accidental on Caribbean slope, where reported from Sarapiquí and Turrialba. Frequents forest edges, second growth, and gardens. 4" (10 cm).

Rufous-tailed Hummingbird
Amazilia tzacatl

The only CR hummer that combines **rufous rump and tail** with **green breast**. Widespread; very common in wet habitats, to 1,600 m, but uncommon from 1,600 to 2,200 m. Uncommon in northwestern Pacific lowlands. The common hummer found in most human-altered habitats; very aggressive and often engages in chases. 4" (10 cm).

Green-breasted Mango
Anthracothorax prevostii

Male potentially confused with Rufous-tailed Hummingbird, but has **black stripe down throat and center of breast** (**bordered by blue**); also note maroon (not rufous) tail. Female is unique in having **dark median stripe on whitish underparts**. Fairly common in Palo Verde and Caño Negro regions, uncommon elsewhere in northwestern Pacific; also uncommon in Central Valley and northern central Caribbean lowlands; rarely above 1,000 m. There are recent reports from the southern Pacific lowlands of individuals that are either this species or the Veraguan Mango; one of these two species appears to be expanding its range. Feeds at all levels of forest edges, gardens, and mangroves. 5" (13 cm). *

Veraguan Mango
Anthracothorax veraguensis

Both sexes nearly identical to Green-breasted Mango, but note **blue-green** (not black) **median stripe**. Status uncertain in CR, though may be expanding its range north from Panama into southern Pacific lowlands. 5" (13 cm).

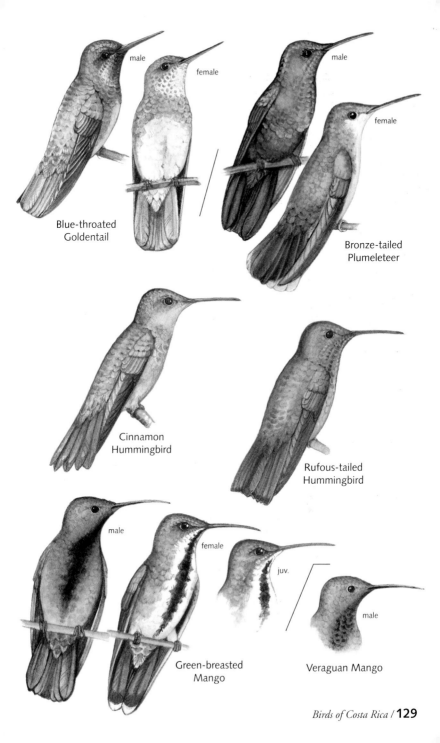

Blue-throated
Goldentail

male

female

Bronze-tailed
Plumeleteer

male

female

Cinnamon
Hummingbird

Rufous-tailed
Hummingbird

male

female

juv.

Green-breasted
Mango

male

Veraguan Mango

White-bellied Emerald
Amazilia candida

Male and female virtually identical, though female has white tips to tail corners. On both sexes, note **bronze-green tail with dark subterminal band** and **pinkish lower mandible with black tip**. Easily confused with female Mangrove Hummingbird, but latter has mostly dark tail. Possibly confused with female Ruby-throated Hummingbird, but latter has all-black bill and white postocular spot. Very rare or perhaps casual migrant from northern Central America. Four old records (San José, Coronado de Térraba, Puerto Jimenez, and near Turrialba) and two recent reports from Pacific side of Nicoya Peninsula (Dec 1999 and Dec 2000). Most likely at forest edges and gardens. 4" (10 cm).

Mangrove Hummingbird
Amazilia boucardi

Male's **bluish-green throat and chest**, **white belly**, and **dark forked tail** are diagnostic. Female resembles very rare White-bellied Emerald, but has mostly dark tail with bronze-green central rectrices. Uncommon in mangroves, from Gulf of Nicoya south to Golfo Dulce, and also around Tamarindo. Forages at lower and middle levels of mangrove swamps and adjacent vegetation; prefers nectar of flowers from the buttressed Tea Mangrove (*Pelliciera rhizophorae*). **Endemic to CR**. 4" (10 cm).

Ruby-throated Hummingbird
Archilochus colubris

Male unique—no other CR hummer combines a **red gorget** with a **black, forked tail**; female told apart from similarly plumaged female hummers by the combination of **white postocular spot**, **white tail corners**, and dull-green crown. Juvenile male resembles female, but shows a few red throat feathers. Fairly common winter resident in northwestern Pacific and western Central Valley, uncommon in Caño Negro region and southern Pacific, casual elsewhere; from mid-Oct to mid-April; mostly below 1,000 m, but can occur as high as 2,300 m. Favors brushy fields, second growth, and gardens. 3" (8 cm).

Brown Violet-ear
Colibri delphinae

Distinguished by **brown color** and **violet ear patch**; also note fairly short, straight bill. Uncommon in wet foothills and middle elevations, including hills of Osa Peninsula, from 400 to 1,600 m. Feeds on a variety of plants with small flowers. Occurs in forest canopy; also found at all levels of forest edges and gardens. 4" (10 cm).

Green Violet-ear
Colibri thalassinus

Told apart from other mostly green hummers by **violet ear patch**. Very common in highlands, from Tilarán Cordillera south; between 1,400 m and timberline, though some descend to 900 m from March to Oct. Visits an assortment of flowers at all levels of forest edges and gardens. From high, exposed perches, males incessantly sing a typically two-note song. 4" (10 cm).

White-bellied
Emerald

male

male

female

Mangrove
Hummingbird

male

female

Ruby-throated
Hummingbird

Brown
Violet-ear

Green
Violet-ear

Snowy-bellied Hummingbird
Amazilia edward

Note sharp distinction between **glittering-green breast** and **white belly**; the upper edge of the belly forms an arch. Also note **coppery rump and lower back**. Uncommon in hills and intermontane valleys of southern Pacific, from 300 to 1,600 m. Forages at forest edges, gardens, and brushy fields. **Endemic to CR and Panama**. 4" (10 cm).

[Females of *Eupherusa* could be mistaken for females of *Elvira*, but the former have rufous in the wing.]

Stripe-tailed Hummingbird
Eupherusa eximia

The **rufous wing patch** is shared by the Black-bellied Hummingbird and the rare Blue-tailed Hummingbird (p. 126). Male set apart from male Black-bellied Hummingbird by green underparts; set apart from Blue-tailed Hummingbird by white in tail. Female distinguished from nearly identical female Black-bellied Hummingbird by more obvious wing patch and less white in tail. Uncommon at middle elevations, from 800 to 2,000 m; note some seasonal altitudinal movements (up to 500 m higher or lower than its normal range). Inhabits mature wet montane forest, often at forest openings and edges. 4" (10 cm).

Black-bellied Hummingbird
Eupherusa nigriventris

Male has distinctive **black face and underparts**; female resembles female Stripe-tailed Hummingbird, but has reduced rufous wing patch and **entirely white outer three rectrices**. Fairly uncommon at middle elevations on Caribbean slope from Central Cordillera south, between 900 and 2,000 m, moving lower from April to Sept (down to 600 m). Prefers mature wet montane forest and forest openings and edges. **Endemic to CR and western Panama**. 3" (8 cm).

White-tailed Emerald
Elvira chionura

Male and female similar to respective sexes of Coppery-headed Emerald (no range overlap), but with **straight bill**; also note that male has green crown and that female has more distinct black subterminal tail band. Fairly common at middle elevations on southern Pacific slope, from 800 to 2,200 m. Found in mature montane forest, as well as at forest edges and in gardens. **Endemic to CR and western Panama**. 3" (8 cm).

Coppery-headed Emerald
Elvira cupreiceps

The noticeably **decurved bill** sets it apart from the White-tailed Emerald (no range overlap); also note coppery crown and rump of male and narrow black subterminal band on white outer rectrices of female. Fairly common at middle elevations on Caribbean slope, south to Reventazón River; from 600 to 1,500 m; also fairly common on Pacific slope of Guanacaste and Tilarán Cordilleras, from 1,200 to 1,500 m. Feeds at all levels in mature wet montane forest and forest edges. Males form small leks at middle levels of forest edges. **Endemic to CR**. 3" (8 cm).

Snowy-bellied
Hummingbird

male

female

Stripe-tailed
Hummingbird

male

female

Black-bellied
Hummingbird

male

female

White-tailed
Emerald

male

female

Coppery-headed
Emerald

Long-billed Starthroat
Heliomaster longirostris

The facial pattern and **long, straight bill** are distinctive. Distinguished from Plain-capped Starthroat by **postocular spot** and **blue-green forecrown**. Fairly uncommon in intermontane valleys and surrounding slopes of southern Pacific, to 1,200 m; very uncommon in southern Pacific lowlands; rare in Caribbean lowlands and foothills and in eastern Central Valley (to 1,400 m). Visits flowering trees in gardens and at forest edges. 4" (10 cm).

Plain-capped Starthroat
Heliomaster constantii

Resembles Long-billed Starthroat, but has a **white postocular stripe** and lacks colorful crown. Fairly uncommon in northwestern Pacific and western Central Valley, to 1,000 m; very rare in intermontane valleys of southern Pacific. Forages at middle and upper levels of second growth and forest edges; also visits flowering trees in fields. 5" (13 cm).

Green-fronted Lancebill
Doryfera ludovicae

The **long, thin, slightly upturned bill** is the best field mark on this rather dark hummer; also note **bronzy crown** and small white spot behind eye. Uncommon at middle elevations and in highlands, from Tilarán Cordillera south, between 800 and 2,300 m. Visits clusters of hanging, pink/red epiphytic flowers (Ericaceae) at upper and middle levels of mature forest and forest edges; regularly hawks insects along mountain streams, sometimes perching on rocks in midstream between sallies. 5" (13 cm).

White-bellied Mountain-gem
Lampornis hemileucus

The only CR hummer that combines **white postocular stripe**, **white belly**, and **green back**. Fairly uncommon at middle elevations on Caribbean slope, from Tilarán Cordillera south, between 700 and 1,500 m. Forages at middle and lower levels of wet montane forest, mostly at openings and edges. **Endemic to CR and western Panama**. 4" (10 cm).

Purple-throated Mountain-gem
Lampornis calolaemus

The **white postocular stripe**, **purple throat**, and **turquoise forecrown** identify the male; the female is nearly identical to the female White-throated Mountain-gem, but has brighter green tail. Female could be mistaken for a Cinnamon Hummingbird (p. 128), but has postocular stripe and lacks rufous tail. Common at middle elevations and in highlands, from Guanacaste Cordillera to northern end of Talamanca Cordillera, between 1,000 and 2,500 m. From May to Sept, some descend to as low as 300 m. Feeds at all levels of wet montane forest, second growth, forest edges, and gardens. **Endemic to Nicaragua and CR**. 4" (10 cm).

White-throated Mountain-gem
Lampornis castaneoventris

Male similar to male Purple-throated Mountain-gem, but has **white throat** and **pale-gray tail**. Female virtually identical to female Purple-throated Mountain-gem, but has dull bronzy-green tail. Fairly common in Talamanca highlands, from 1,800 m to timberline (from May to Sept, some descend to 1,500 m). Forages at middle and lower levels of oak forests, forest edges, and gardens. **Endemic to CR and western Panama**. 4" (10 cm).

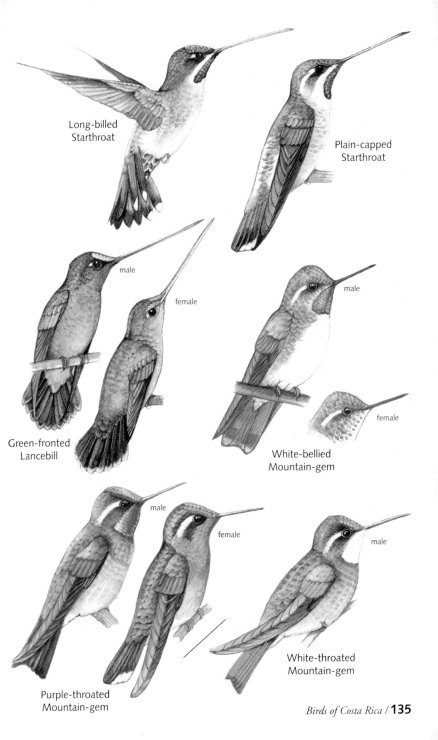

Long-billed
Starthroat

Plain-capped
Starthroat

male

female

Green-fronted
Lancebill

male

female

White-bellied
Mountain-gem

male

female

Purple-throated
Mountain-gem

male

White-throated
Mountain-gem

Birds of Costa Rica /

Hummingbirds

Black-crested Coquette
Lophornis helenae

Male told apart from male White-crested Coquette by green crown; **long, wiry, black crest feathers**; and spotted belly. Female very similar to female White-crested Coquette, but note **spotted belly**. Uncommon in Caribbean foothills and adjacent lowlands, south to watershed of Reventazón River; rare in Central Valley; to 1,200 m. Visits trees with small flowers in forest canopy, forages down to lower levels at forest edges and in gardens, often coming to *Stachytarpheta*. Very beelike in flight. 3" (8 cm).

White-crested Coquette
Lophornis adorabilis

Male similar to male Black-crested Coquette, but has **white crest**, green gorget with long tufts extending back, and pale-rufous belly. Female very similar to female Black-crested Coquette, but note **pale-rufous belly**. Uncommon in southern Pacific and rare in Central Valley, east to Turrialba; to 1,400 m. Visits trees with small flowers in forest canopy; forages down to lower levels of forest edges and gardens. Very beelike in flight. **Endemic to CR and western Panama.** 3" (8 cm).

Rufous-crested Coquette
Lophornis delattrei

Male has long rufous crest feathers, female has rufous forehead; both sexes have dull-greenish bellies. Known in CR from four male specimens taken in San Pedro (east of San José) between 1892 and 1906, all in October. No recent records. **Not illustrated**. 3" (8 cm).

Green Thorntail
Discosura conversii

Small size and white rump band could suggest a coquette, but male's **long tail** and lack of crest plumes should dispel any confusion; female shows distinctive **white malar stripe**. Fairly uncommon in Caribbean foothills and middle elevations, from Tilarán Cordillera south, between 400 and 1,600 m; rare visitor to adjacent lowlands. Visits trees with small flowers in forest canopy; forages down to lower levels at forest edges and in gardens. Very beelike in flight. Male 4" (10 cm); female 3" (8 cm).

Snowcap
Microchera albocoronata

Male is instantly recognizable; female told apart from other similar female hummers by **short, straight bill** and absence of green spotting on grayish-white underparts. Uncommon on Caribbean slope, from 300 to 900 m; some descend to adjacent lowlands during latter half of year. Forages on small flowers in canopy and edges of both mature wet forest and second growth. **Endemic from southern Honduras to western Panama.** 3" (8 cm).

Violet-headed Hummingbird
Klais guimeti

The conspicuous **white spot behind the eye** and the **violet crown** (more bluish in female) are diagnostic. Fairly common in Caribbean foothills and adjacent lowlands, to 1,000 m; fairly uncommon in southern Pacific, from 300 to 1,200 m; recent scattered sightings (2005 and 2006) in northern and central Pacific lowlands. Feeds on a variety of plants with small flowers, in forest canopy and at lower levels of forest edges and gardens. When foraging, flies slowly, with body held horizontal and tail cocked up. 3" (8 cm).

female

White-crested
Coquette

male

female

male

Black-crested
Coquette

female

male

Green
Thorntail

female

Snowcap

male

female

male

Violet-headed
Hummingbird

Birds of Costa Rica / **137**

Magenta-throated Woodstar
Calliphlox bryantae

On male, the combination of relatively **long tail**, **whitish patch on each side of rump**, and **magenta gorget** is distinctive. Female somewhat resembles female Scintillant and Volcano Hummingbirds, but the combination of a **white postocular spot** and a **whitish patch on each side of rump** should clinch the identification. Uncommon at middle elevations, from 700 to 1,800 m. Often feeds on low-growing flowers at forest edges, but tends to perch on high, exposed twigs; foraging flight is slow and insectlike, with body held horizontal and tail cocked up. **Endemic to CR and western Panama**. Male 4" (10 cm); female 3" (8 cm).

Scintillant Hummingbird
Selasphorus scintilla

Male's **brilliant orange gorget** distinguishes it from the male Volcano Hummingbird; female has **rufous tail feathers** with black subterminal band. Fairly common at middle elevations on Pacific slopes of Central and Talamanca Cordilleras, and uncommon on Caribbean slopes, from 900 to 2,200 m; rare at upper elevations of Tilarán Cordillera. Typically feeds low at forest edges, brushy pastures, and gardens. **Endemic to CR and western Panama**. 3" (8 cm).

Volcano Hummingbird
Selasphorus flammula

Three races occur in CR; males distinguished by color of gorget; females identical (labels on illustrations indicate geographic distribution of each race). Both sexes very similar to respective sexes of Scintillant Hummingbird; male's gorget color is diagnostic (though varying from rose-red to purplish with either green or gray overtones); female has **bronzy-green central rectrices**. Common in Central and Talamanca Cordilleras, above 1,800 m; very uncommon below 1,800 m (down to 1,200 m), mostly from March to July. Forages at forest edges, gardens, and overgrown open areas; also in paramo. **Endemic to CR and western Panama**. 3" (8 cm).

male

female

Magenta-throated
Woodstar

female

male

Scintillant
Hummingbird

male
Irazú &Turrialba
Volcanoes

male
Talamanca
Cordillera

male
Poás & Barva
Volcanoes

female

Volcano
Hummingbird

TROGONIDAE. Trogons are colorful and fairly sedentary birds of forests and forest edges. Females have somewhat duller plumage than males. To distinguish between similarly plumaged species, note bill, eye, and eye ring color, as well as undertail pattern.

Black-headed Trogon   *Trogon melanocephalus*
The only yellow-bellied trogon in CR with a **pale-blue orbital ring** and **blue-gray bill**; female distinguished from female Violaceous Trogon by **extensive white tips** on underside of tail feathers. Common in northwestern Pacific lowlands and foothills, south to Carara, and in Caño Negro region. Frequents lower and middle levels of dry and gallery forests, forest edges, and gardens. The call is an accelerating series of chucks, rising in pitch and then terminating with several quickly descending notes. 11" (28 cm).

Violaceous Trogon   *Trogon violaceus*
Male is only CR trogon with a **yellow orbital ring**. Female's orbital ring is whitish and elliptical; distinguished from female Black-headed Trogon by **narrow barring on tail**. Widespread and common in wet lowlands and foothills, uncommon in drier areas; to 1,400 m. Occurs in gallery forest, at forest edges, and gardens, usually at middle or upper levels. The call—often given from a high perch—is a series of even-pitched notes (*kyew, kyew, kyew...*) that are higher pitched than those of the Slaty-tailed Trogon (p. 144). 9" (23 cm).

Black-throated Trogon   *Trogon rufus*
Male's combination of **green head**, **blue orbital ring**, and **yellow bill** is diagnostic; female is only CR trogon with **yellow belly** and **brown upperparts**. Common in wet lowlands and foothills, to 1,200 m. Favors lower and middle levels of mature wet forest and adjacent advanced second growth. The call—more whistled than that of other trogons—is a slow, deliberate series of two to five notes, reminiscent of a Chestnut-backed Antbird (p. 178), but all notes even-pitched. 9" (23 cm).

Black-headed
Trogon

male

female

Violaceous
Trogon

male

female

Black-throated
Trogon

male

female

Baird's Trogon
Trogon bairdii

The only orangish-red bellied trogon in CR with a **pale-blue orbital ring** and **blue-gray bill** (female's bill is dark gray). Common in lowlands and foothills of southern Pacific, to 1,200 m. Favors lower and middle levels of mature wet forest. The chuckling call begins at a moderate pace, then rises in both pitch and tempo before slowing and dropping. **Endemic to CR and western Panama.** 11" (28 cm).

Elegant Trogon
Trogon elegans

Some range overlap with Orange-bellied Trogon, but male Elegant Trogon is the only red-bellied trogon in CR with both **orange orbital ring** and **yellow bill**; and female is the only CR trogon with a **white ear patch**. Uncommon in northwestern Pacific lowlands and foothills, to 800 m. Stays in middle and upper levels of mature dry and humid forests. The call consists of several harsh, guttural, almost froglike croaks. 11" (28 cm).

Collared Trogon
Trogon collaris

Respective sexes virtually identical to Orange-bellied Trogon in every aspect, including voice, habitat, and habits. **The only difference is the color of the belly, which is red**. No range overlap with similar Elegant Trogon. Fairly common in central and southern highlands, from 800 to 2,800 m; descends to foothills on both Pacific and Caribbean slopes, from June to Dec. Found in middle levels of mature wet montane forest, forest edges, and gardens. The call is a series of sweet, down-slurred *caow, caow* notes, with several seconds of silence between each couplet. 10" (25 cm).

Orange-bellied Trogon
Trogon aurantiiventris

Respective sexes virtually identical to the Collared Trogon in every aspect, including voice, habitat, and habits. **The only difference is the color of the belly, which is orange**. Common in wet northwestern highlands, where the Collared Trogon is absent; uncommon farther south, where the two species' ranges overlap; from 700 to 2,300 m. **Endemic to CR and western Panama.** 10" (25 cm).

Baird's Trogon

male

female

Elegant Trogon

male

female

Collared Trogon

male

female

Orange-bellied Trogon

male

female

Resplendent Quetzal
Pharomachrus mocinno

A large, chunky trogon. The unique males have **four extended uppertail coverts** (not true tail feathers) that dangle up to 30" (76 cm) beyond the squared-off tail tip. Female quetzals are the only trogons combining **green head**, **gray belly**, and **red vent**. Fairly common in highlands of Tilarán, Central, and Talamanca Cordilleras (on both Pacific and Caribbean slopes); from 1,400 to 3,000 m. In the northern part of their CR range (Tilarán Cordillera), they are altitudinal migrants (most of the year they occur from 1,600 m down to 1,400 m; from about Sept to Nov, however, they descend the Caribbean slope, where most then occur between 800 and 500 m). Inhabits middle levels of mature wet montane forest, forest edges, advanced second growth, and even enters gardens when ripe fruit is available; feeds mostly on members of the avocado family. The call is a throaty *kyow, kyow*; in flight, gives a brisk *wicka-wicka*. 14" (36 cm).

Slaty-tailed Trogon
Trogon massena

The only CR trogon with an **unpatterned dark-gray tail**; also note **orange-red bill** (though female's upper mandible is black). Common in wet lowlands and foothills, to 1,200 m. Forages in middle and upper levels of mature wet forest, though often lower at forest edges and in gardens. Typically calls with a series of monotonous barking notes (*aah, aah, aah, aah...*), lower pitched than that of Violaceous Trogon (p. 140). 12" (30 cm).

Lattice-tailed Trogon
Trogon clathratus

The only CR trogon with a **pale iris**. Underside of tail is dark-gray with faint white barring. Fairly uncommon in Caribbean foothills, south from Rincón de la Vieja, from 100 to 1,000 m. Call is a fast-paced series of notes rising in pitch, then falling abruptly at the end. **Endemic to CR and western Panama**. 12" (30 cm).

Resplendent
Quetzal

male

female

Slaty-tailed
Trogon

male

female

Lattice-tailed
Trogon

female

male

Motmots

MOMOTIDAE. Handsome birds of the forest interior and forest edges. Typically perching from one to four meters above the ground, motmots often remain inactive for long intervals as they scan their surroundings for suitable prey—large invertebrates and small reptiles and amphibians. All CR species, except the Tody Motmot, have racquet-tipped tails, which they habitually swing, pendulum-like. Vocalizations are helpful for locating perched individuals.

Blue-crowned Motmot

Momotus momota

The **intense blue ring that separates the black crown and sides of head** readily distinguishes this species from other CR motmots. The common motmot of the Central Valley and middle elevations, to 2,000 m, and the only motmot in the southern Pacific region; confined to evergreen patches in northern Pacific lowlands. Prefers forest edges and shady gardens. Typically calls with a slow series of low, doubled notes: *hoop-hoop, hoop-hoop…* . 16" (41 cm).

Keel-billed Motmot

Electron carinatum

A mostly **greenish motmot with a rufous forehead** and a blue superciliary that extends back to nearly the end of the black mask. A rare resident of Caribbean foothill forests along the Guanacaste and Tilarán Cordilleras, from 300 to 900 m. Inhabits lower levels of mature wet forest. Said to make a sound like a cackling hen. 13" (33 cm).

Rufous Motmot

Baryphthengus martii

The **largest motmot**, with a very long tail; similar to the Broad-billed Motmot, but note that the **rufous on the underside extends all the way to the belly** (not just the breast). Fairly common in Caribbean lowlands and foothills, to 1,000 m. Inhabits lower levels of mature wet forest. Song is a deep, bubbling, rolling hooting that is most often heard at dawn. 18" (46 cm).

Broad-billed Motmot

Electron platyrhynchum

Like a small version of the Rufous Motmot, but note that it has a **blue-green chin** and that the rufous only extends to the lower breast. Common in Caribbean lowlands and foothills, to 1,000 m. Inhabits lower and middle levels of mature wet forest. The call is a throaty *awnk*. 12" (30 cm).

Tody Motmot

Hylomanes momotula

The **smallest motmot** and the only one **without a dark spot on the breast**. Note also the white moustachial stripe and lack of tail racquets. Very uncommon and easily overlooked resident of a narrow elevation belt on the Guanacaste volcanoes, from 500 to 1,000 m. Perches at lower levels of humid forest. Reportedly makes a call somewhat like that of the Ferruginous Pygmy-Owl (p. 108). 7" (18 cm).

Turquoise-browed Motmot

Eumomota superciliosa

An exquisite motmot with **large area of featherless shaft** on central rectrices. The common motmot of northern Pacific lowlands and foothills; rare in western Central Valley; to 900 m. Inhabits dry and humid forests, forest edges, and even tree-lined roadsides. The call is a hoarse *qwahk*. The national bird of Nicaragua. 13" (33 cm).

Blue-crowned
Motmot

Keel-billed
Motmot

Rufous Motmot

Broad-billed
Motmot

Tody Motmot

Turquoise-browed
Motmot

Kingfishers

ALCEDINIDAE. The six New World members of this cosmopolitan family all live up to their name and dive for fish. Disproportionately large, stout, pointed bills are a trademark of the kingfishers. Similar-looking species can be told apart by observing details of plumage, as well as by size differences—though this can sometimes be deceptive. In the five resident breeding species, the male has more rufous on the breast than does the female; the reverse is true of the migrant Belted Kingfisher.

Ringed Kingfisher
Ceryle torquatus

The largest kingfisher in this hemisphere and, of the two with **blue-gray upperparts**, the only one with **mostly rufous underparts** (see Belted Kingfisher). Widespread and fairly common in lowlands and Central Valley, to 1,500 m. Found along rivers and streams, as well as lakes, lagoons, and large ponds. The flight call is a loud, rasping *krek*. Also makes a loud, even rattle. 16" (41 cm).

Green Kingfisher
Chloroceryle americana

The most common kingfisher in CR. Distinguished from Amazon Kingfisher by **white spotting on the wings** and **white on outer tail feathers** (especially obvious in flight); female further told apart from female Amazon Kingfisher by **two green breast bands**. Potentially encountered at any suitable wetland site (e.g., rainwater pools, small streams, and wide rivers), to 1,200 m. Typically uses low perches, even rocks in waterways. The ticking call resembles the sound made by striking two pebbles against each other. 7" (18 cm).

Belted Kingfisher
Ceryle alcyon

Similar to the Ringed Kingfisher, but note the **extensively white underparts**. Male has no rufous on underparts. Fairly common NA migrant from mid-Sept to early May. Found along rivers and streams, as well as lakes, lagoons, and large ponds; also occurs along seashores of both coasts. Makes an uneven rattle, not as loud as the Ringed Kingfisher. 13" (33 cm).

American Pygmy Kingfisher
Chloroceryle aenea

This miniscule kingfisher is distinguished from the larger Green-and-rufous Kingfisher by **white belly and vent**. Uncommon in lowlands, to 600 m. Favors swamp forests, mangroves, and shaded streams; occasionally found in more exposed situations. The call is like a soft rendition of the Green Kingfisher's. 5" (13 cm).

Green-and-rufous Kingfisher
Chloroceryle inda

The only **green-backed kingfisher with entirely rufous underparts** (female has dark-green band across breast); the smaller American Pygmy Kingfisher has white belly and vent. An uncommon to rare inhabitant of lowland Caribbean swamp forests and shaded streams. Rarely perches or flies above eye level. The call is a harsh *drit-drit-drit*. 9" (23 cm).

Amazon Kingfisher
Chloroceryle amazona

Like a large version of the much more common Green Kingfisher, but the **wings and tail lack white**; female further told apart from female Green Kingfisher by **white on center of breast**. Fairly common along lowland rivers, streams, ponds, lakes, and lagoons; to 1,200 m in Reventazón River watershed and in southern Pacific. Calls with a single harsh *chirt*, which is sometimes repeated in rapid succession to make a rattle. 11" (28 cm).

male

female

Ringed Kingfisher

male

female

Green Kingfisher

female

male

Belted Kingfisher

male

female

American Pygmy Kingfisher

male

female

Green-and-rufous Kingfisher

male

female

Amazon Kingfisher

Puffbirds

BUCCONIDAE. The black-and-white or brown-toned puffbirds are a somber-looking group of sit-and-wait predators. Most of these stout birds have rather short tails; their bills end in hooks or slight curves (vs. the sharp point of kingfishers [p. 148]).

White-necked Puffbird
Notharchus macrorhynchos

A large, thick-bodied puffbird with a **white forehead** and nuchal collar (compare with Pied Puffbird). Widespread and fairly uncommon in lowlands, to 600 m. Typically perches high on exposed branches at forest edges and in clearings with scattered trees. The rarely given vocalization is a weak, high-pitched twitter. 10" (25 cm).

White-fronted Nunbird
Monasa morphoeus

The **long coral-red bill** and **white forehead and chin** on an otherwise dark-gray bird should preclude confusion. Formerly common resident of Caribbean slope, to 800 m; populations in many areas seem to be declining. Favors mature forests and adjacent semi-cleared areas. Much more vocal than other local puffbirds, nunbirds have a wide repertoire of sounds, and even join in communal choral groups that utter agitated, squabbling, whistled notes. 11" (28 cm).

Pied Puffbird
Notharchus tectus

Like a small version of the White-necked Puffbird, but with a **black forehead**; also note the **narrow white superciliary**, **white scapular patch**, and white tips to underside of tail feathers. Uncommon in wet Caribbean lowlands, to 300 m. Prefers forest edges and partially cleared areas. The high-pitched call consists of a series of emphatic, crescendoing, buzzy, whistled notes. 6" (15 cm).

Lanceolated Monklet
Micromonacha lanceolata

Distinctively patterned, though its small size and sedentary habits can make it hard to see. A rare resident of Caribbean foothills and middle elevations, from 400 to 1,300 m. Perches fairly low in forests and at forest edges, usually not far from streams. The thin, whistled call rises in pitch. 5" (13 cm).

White-whiskered Puffbird
Malacoptila panamensis

Not readily confused; the **chunky proportions**, **streaked underparts**, and **white whiskers** are diagnostic. Fairly common in humid and wet lowlands and foothills, to 1,000 m. Perches inconspicuously in understory of mature forest. Calls are high-pitched, soft, and reedy. 8" (20 cm).

White-necked
Puffbird

White-fronted
Nunbird

Pied
Puffbird

Lanceolated
Monklet

female

male

White-whiskered
Puffbird

Jacamars

GALBULIDAE. Classic sit-and-wait predators; with their bills held upwards, jacamars actively survey their environment for insect prey, which they catch in swift flight. Their stoic manner and green-and-rust colors allow them to easily go undetected. In CR species, males have white throats, females pale rufous.

Great Jacamar
Jacamerops aureus

Larger and **chunkier** than the Rufous-tailed Jacamar, with a bill more the size and shape of a motmot's (unlike a motmot [p. 146], the Great Jacamar does not have racquet tail-tips). Female has pale-rufous throat. Extremely rare in Caribbean lowlands and foothills, to 600 m. Typically perches fairly high in mature wet forest canopy. Makes a long, high-pitched, three-note whistle, as well as an assortment of odd noises, including a catlike meowing. 12" (30 cm).

Rufous-tailed Jacamar
Galbula ruficauda

When perched, gives the impression of an oversized hummingbird. Fairly common in wet forest habitats, to 1,200 m. Prefers forest edges and openings, often perching near eye level. The call note is a sharp *peep!* with a squeaky quality. The song is a long series of squeaks that increases in pitch and rhythm. 9" (23 cm).

Barbets & Toucans

RAMPHASTIDAE. Toucans, the quintessential neotropical birds, are readily recognized by their oversized beaks. Bill color patterns are important for distinguishing among the similar-looking species. Also included in the same family are the New World barbets, with two species in CR.

Prong-billed Barbet
Semnornis frantzii

No other species combines a **stout blue-gray bill** with an **ochraceous head and breast**. Common at middle elevations and in highlands, from 800 to 2,400 m. Inhabits epiphyte-laden montane wet forests and adjacent gardens, where the fast-paced, hollow-sounding, even-pitched duets of this species are a characteristic sound. **Endemic to CR and western Panama**. 7" (17 cm).

Red-headed Barbet
Eubucco bourcierii

Red head and **yellow bill** of male are distinctive. Likewise, the female's facial pattern is unique among CR species. Fairly uncommon at middle elevations from Tilarán Cordillera south; between 400 and 1,800 m. Forages at middle and upper levels of wet forests, often accompanying mixed flocks. Rarely vocalizes. 6" (15 cm).

Emerald Toucanet
Aulacorhynchus prasinus

The only CR toucan with **green breast and belly**. The race that occurs in CR and western Panama has a distinctive **dark-blue throat**. Fairly common at middle elevations, from 800 to 2,400 m. Forages at middle levels in montane wet forests and adjacent gardens and second growth. Quite vocal; most calls have a harsh, barking quality. 12" (30 cm).

male

Great Jacamar

male

female

Rufous-tailed
Jacamar

Prong-billed
Barbet

male

female

Emerald Toucanet

Red-headed Barbet

Chestnut-mandibled Toucan
Ramphastos swainsonii

The bicolored, **yellow and dark-brown bill** distinguishes it from the Keel-billed Toucan. Common in Caribbean and southern Pacific lowlands (north to Carara), rising to foothills and, less commonly, middle elevations; to 1,200 m. Inhabits forested and semi-open areas. Its song, which is completely different from the Keel-billed Toucan's, is a sonorous *tee de, te de, te de*. 22" (56 cm).

Keel-billed Toucan
Ramphastos sulfuratus

Note the **bright, multicolored bill** on this slightly smaller counterpart of the Chestnut-mandibled Toucan. Common in Caribbean lowlands; fairly common at middle elevations on Caribbean slope; also fairly common at middle elevations of Pacific slope, from northwestern corner of the country to western end of Central Valley, to 1,400 m; rare in northwestern Pacific lowlands. Inhabits forested and semi-open areas. Common call is a dry, rather froglike croak, repeated at length (similar to that of Yellow-eared Toucanet). 18" (46 cm).

Collared Araçari
Pteroglossus torquatus

A **slimly proportioned** toucan. Distinguished from the Fiery-billed Araçari by mostly **chalky-white upper mandible** and black belly band (no range overlap). Common in Caribbean lowlands, becoming less common in foothills, to 1,000 m; uncommon in northern Pacific, where usually found in gallery forest. Small groups travel through mature wet forests, forest edges, and adjacent gardens. Most often heard vocalization is a high-pitched, two-note "hiccup." 16" (41 cm).

Fiery-billed Araçari
Pteroglossus frantzii

The central and southern Pacific slope counterpart of the Collared Araçari, this species has a **red-orange upper mandible**. Additionally, the belly band is red, not black. Small groups travel through mature wet forests, forest edges, and adjacent gardens. The call is a high-pitched, two-note "hiccup." **Endemic to CR and western Panama**. 17" (43 cm).

Yellow-eared Toucanet
Selenidera spectabilis

The only CR toucan with an **entirely black throat, breast, and belly**. Also, the only CR toucan in which the sexes can be told apart in the field: male has yellow on side of head. Very uncommon in Caribbean foothills and adjacent lowlands, from 100 to 1,200 m; also occurs on Pacific slopes of Guanacaste volcanoes. Forages at middle and upper levels of mature forest. Its grating, croaking call resembles that of the Keel-billed Toucan. **Endemic from southeastern Honduras to northwestern Colombia**. 14" (35 cm).

Chestnut-mandibled
Toucan

Keel-billed
Toucan

Woodpeckers

PICIDAE. Th...
like bills tha...
while per...
Food c...
flight...

Collared
Araçari

female

Yellow-eared
Toucanet

Fiery-billed
Araçari

male

woodpeckers are a widespread and familiar family distinguished by their strong, chisel-
enable them to peck into wood; they also have stiff tail feathers that help support them
hed on vertical trunks. Their presence is often detected by the sound of tapping on wood.
nsists largely of wood-boring insects, but many species also eat fruit and even hawk insects in
. Among CR species, males show more red markings on the head and/or face than do females.

Acorn Woodpecker
Melanerpes formicivorus

The **striking facial pattern** facilitates identification; in flight, large white
patches on wings and rump are visible. Common in highlands, mostly above
1,800 m, but occasionally down to 1,000 m. Forages at all levels (including on
ground) of oak forests and adjacent gardens; often hawks insects. Very vocal;
commonly chortles a scratchy *wic-ka, wic-ka, wic-ka.* 9" (23 cm).

Golden-naped Woodpecker
Melanerpes chrysauchen

Recalls a Black-cheeked Woodpecker (no range overlap), but has **yellow nape**.
Fairly uncommon in wet forests of southern Pacific, from Carara south, to
1,500 m. Forages at middle levels of forests and forest edges. Gives several short
rattles: *wret, wret, wret.* **Endemic to CR and western Panama**. 7" (18 cm).

Black-cheeked Woodpecker
Melanerpes pucherani

Similar to Golden-naped Woodpecker (no range overlap), but has a **red nape**.
Common in Caribbean lowlands and foothills, to 900 m. Prefers gardens and
forest edges, but also found at openings in mature wet forest, foraging at middle
and upper levels; commonly feeds on fruit. Makes a fairly high-pitched, rattling
chirrr, chirrr, chirrr. 7" (18 cm).

Hoffmann's Woodpecker
Melanerpes hoffmannii

Told apart from Red-crowned Woodpecker by **yellow-orange nape and belly**
(though see note below). Common in northwestern Pacific and in Central Valley,
east to Turrialba; to 2,000 m; uncommon in Caño Negro and Arenal regions.
Prefers gardens, second growth, and open areas with a few trees; forages at all
levels. Makes a harsh, sputtering rattle. **Endemic from southern Honduras to
CR**. 7" (18 cm).

Red-crowned Woodpecker
Melanerpes rubricapillus

Very similar to Hoffmann's Woodpecker, but has **red nape and belly**. (Most birds
from Carara to Quepos are apparently hybrids with Hoffmann's Woodpecker;
they have orange napes and bellies.) Common in southern Pacific, to 1,500 m.
Prefers gardens, second growth, and open areas with a few trees; forages at all
levels. Utters a long, rattling chatter. 7" (18 cm).

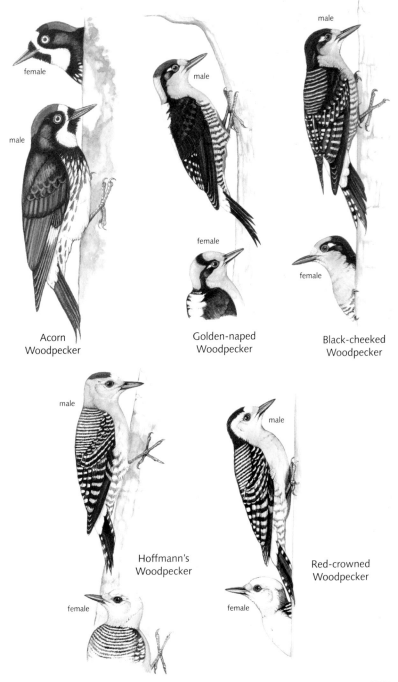

female

male

Acorn
Woodpecker

male

female

Golden-naped
Woodpecker

male

female

Black-cheeked
Woodpecker

male

female

Hoffmann's
Woodpecker

male

female

Red-crowned
Woodpecker

Golden-olive Woodpecker
Piculus rubiginosus

Distinguished from Rufous-winged Woodpecker by **gray crown** and **whitish cheeks**. Fairly common at middle elevations, between 800 and 2,000 m. Forages at middle and upper levels of forest; often at lower levels in adjacent second growth and gardens. Utters a rising, sputtering rattle. 8" (20 cm).

Hairy Woodpecker
Picoides villosus

CR race is smaller and darker than NA races; not likely confused with other CR woodpeckers. Fairly common in highlands, from 1,500 m to timberline. Found in montane forests and adjacent gardens; forages at all levels, actively pecking at small stems. Gives a sharp *speek* that is louder than the similar note of the Smoky-brown Woodpecker. 7" (18 cm).

Smoky-brown Woodpecker
Veniliornis fumigatus

No other CR woodpecker is so **uniformly brown**; the congeneric Red-rumped Woodpecker has barred underparts. Fairly uncommon in northern half of Caribbean slope and onto Pacific face of Tilarán Cordillera, to 1,800 m; also fairly uncommon in intermontane valleys of southern Pacific, between 400 and 1,800 m. Forages at lower and middle levels of forest edges. Gives a sharp *zick* that is softer than the similar note of the Hairy Woodpecker. 6" (15 cm).

Rufous-winged Woodpecker
Piculus simplex

Resembles Golden-olive Woodpecker, but its **cheeks are olive-brown** (also note pale iris); male further distinguished by **red crown**, female distinguished by **olive-brown crown**. (Despite its name, rufous color is rarely visible in folded wing.) Uncommon in Caribbean lowlands and foothills, and rare in southern Pacific; to 900 m. Forages at middle and upper levels of wet forest, and at lower and middle levels in adjacent gardens. Call is a vigorous, jaylike *cheea, cheea, cheea, cheea*. **Endemic from eastern Honduras to western Panama.** 7" (18 cm).

Red-rumped Woodpecker
Veniliornis kirkii

Similar to Smoky-brown Woodpecker, but with **barred underparts** (red rump not very visible). Rare in southeastern Caribbean lowlands; also rare in southern Pacific lowlands, north to Carara. Forages in forest canopy and at lower levels of adjacent second growth; also in mangroves. Gives a falling, nasal *keeer*, similar to note of Great Kiskadee (p. 210). 6" (15 cm).

Olivaceous Piculet
Picumnus olivaceus

This miniature woodpecker is not likely confused with other CR woodpeckers, though its small size and behavior could suggest a Plain Xenops (p. 168). Fairly common in intermontane valleys of southern Pacific, to 1,400 m, and in lowlands (except for mainland side of Golfo Dulce) north to Tarcoles; uncommon in Caño Negro region. Favors forest openings, forest edges, and second growth; actively pecks vines and twigs at lower and middle levels, not using tail to support itself. Makes a thin twittering sound. 4" (10 cm).

female

male

Golden-olive
Woodpecker

male

female

Hairy
Woodpecker

male

female

Smoky-brown
Woodpecker

male

female

Rufous-winged
Woodpecker

female

male

Red-rumped
Woodpecker

female

male

Olivaceous
Piculet

Chestnut-colored Woodpecker
Celeus castaneus

Similar to Cinnamon Woodpecker, but on the Chestnut-colored Woodpecker the **head is paler than the back**, and the back and underparts are the same chestnut color. Fairly common in wet Caribbean lowlands, uncommon in foothills, to 700 m. Forages at middle and upper levels of forest, forest edges, and nearby gardens. Whistles a falling *skeew* succeeded by a nasal *keh, keh, keh*. 9" (23 cm).

Pale-billed Woodpecker
Campephilus guatemalensis

Both sexes have noticeably more **red on head** than the red-crested Lineated Woodpecker. Further distinguished by white stripe that begins on neck and by whitish bill. Common in lowlands; less common at middle elevations, to 1,400 m. More commonly found in forest habitat than the Lineated Woodpecker; forages at all levels of forests, occasionally visits forest edges and adjacent gardens. Its characteristic sound is a loud, sharp, double rap; its call is a sputtering, laughing rattle. 13" (33 cm).

Cinnamon Woodpecker
Celeus loricatus

Similar to Chestnut-colored Woodpecker, but **head and back are the same color**, and the underparts are lighter than the back. Fairly uncommon in wet Caribbean lowlands; somewhat more common in foothills, to 900 m. Found in forest canopy; drops to lower levels at forest edges and in adjacent second growth. Call is a forceful, descending *dwee, dwee, dwe, dwit*. 8" (20 cm).

Lineated Woodpecker
Dryocopus lineatus

Combination of **red crest** and **white stripe that begins at base of dark bill** distinguishes both sexes from similar Pale-billed Woodpecker. (Be aware that lighting can make it difficult to accurately determine bill color on these two species.) Fairly common in lowlands and middle elevations, to 1,400 m. Generally prefers more open habitat than Pale-billed Woodpecker; forages at all levels. Gives an emphatic *wick-wick-wick-wick-...* .13" (33 cm).

Yellow-bellied Sapsucker
Sphyrapicus varius

The **white wing patch** is diagnostic in all plumages. In CR, adult females are seen more often than males or juveniles. A very uncommon NA migrant from Oct to March, most likely in highlands, rare in lowlands. Favors gardens and forest edges. Generally does not vocalize in CR. 8" (20 cm).

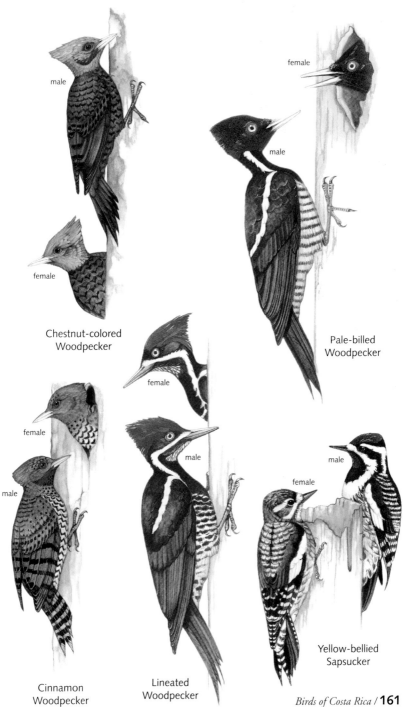

male

female

Chestnut-colored
Woodpecker

female

male

Pale-billed
Woodpecker

female

male

Cinnamon
Woodpecker

female

male

Lineated
Woodpecker

female

male

Yellow-bellied
Sapsucker

FURNARIIDAE. A large and varied family of neotropical birds that are essentially insectivorous. Most are attired predominantly in shades of brown. Their habits and habitats are diverse, though many favor the company of mixed species flocks. The majority of ovenbird species dwell in middle and upper elevation forests; most woodcreepers, in turn, occur in lowland forests. (Until recently, woodcreepers [p. 168] were placed in a separate family, Dendrocolaptidae.)

Pale-breasted Spinetail
Synallaxis albescens

The **proportionately long tail** and **rufous crown and wing coverts** distinguish it from all but the much darker Slaty Spinetail. Fairly common in brushy fields of southern Pacific, to 1,200 m. Usually stays low and hidden in vegetation, but sings from exposed perches. Tirelessly utters a sharp, scratchy *zwee-bit, zweebit*. 6" (15 cm).

Slaty Spinetail
Synallaxis brachyura

Similar to Pale-breasted Spinetail, but nonrufous parts are **dark, sooty gray**. Common in wet lowlands and foothills, to 1,200 m. Dwells in low overgrown tangles in open areas and, unlike Pale-breasted Spinetail, sings from concealment. Repeatedly gives a somewhat wrenlike, descending, stuttering *ch-ch-ch-chirrr*. 6" (15 cm).

Red-faced Spinetail
Cranioleuca erythrops

Rufous wings, tail, and half-hood contrast with mostly olive-brown body. Fairly common at middle elevations, from 700 to 2,000 m. Forages acrobatically on mossy limbs of mature wet forest and at forest edges, mostly at middle levels; often rummages in dead leaf clusters; accompanies mixed flocks. Delivers a high, rapid, slightly descending series of staccato notes. 6" (15 cm).

Spotted Barbtail
Premnoplex brunnescens

No other CR furnariid combines such **dark brown** plumage with **buffy spots on underparts**; note **pale tawny throat**. Common at middle elevations, from 500 to 2,300 m. Climbs trunks and hangs upside-down below limbs in lower and middle levels of mature wet forest, advanced second growth, and at forest edges; accompanies mixed flocks. Produces a sharp *speep!*, followed by a very rapid string of slightly duller, drier notes. 6" (15 cm).

Ruddy Treerunner
Margarornis rubiginosus

No other CR furnariid is so **uniformly reddish-brown** with **whitish throat and superciliary**. Common in highlands, from 1,500 m to timberline. Forages in moss and epiphytes at all levels of wet montane forest, forest edges, and adjacent gardens. Climbs trunks and hangs upside-down below limbs; accompanies mixed flocks. Rapidly twitters high, thin notes. **Endemic to CR and western Panama**. 6" (15 cm).

Pale-breasted
Spinetail

adult

juv.

Slaty
Spinetail

adult

juv.

Red-faced
Spinetail

Spotted
Barbtail

Ruddy
Treerunner

Buffy Tuftedcheek
Pseudocolaptes lawrencii

The **buffy throat and flared-out cheek feathers** readily distinguish it; no other CR furnariid has **wing bars**. Uncommon in highlands, from 1,600 m to timberline. Forages actively and noisily in epiphytes (especially bromeliads), in wet montane forest, forest edges, and adjacent gardens. Call note is a sharp *sfik!* 8" (20 cm).

Striped Woodhaunter
Hyloctistes subulatus

Similar to Lineated Foliage-gleaner, but has **blurred streaking on breast**; also similar in pattern to several woodcreepers, but does not climb up trunks. Uncommon in wet foothills of Caribbean and southern Pacific slopes, from 400 to 1,200 m, and rare in wet lowlands of both slopes. Inhabits middle and lower levels of mature forest. Pokes into dead leaf clusters and epiphytes; accompanies mixed flocks. Utters a loud *kyip-kyip-kyip-kyip-kyip*. 7" (18 cm).

Buff-throated Foliage-gleaner
Automolus ochrolaemus

Similar to Scaly-throated Foliage-gleaner, but **eye ring and superciliary are buffy**. Fairly common in lowlands and foothills, to 1,200 m. Actively forages in dense undergrowth of mature wet forest and adjacent advanced second growth; accompanies mixed flocks. Gives a sputtering, nasal trill that slows and drops slightly at the end. 7" (18 cm).

Buff-fronted Foliage-gleaner
Philydor rufum

The **ochraceous forehead, superciliary, and underparts** distinguish it from other furnariids. Rare at middle elevations, from 800 to 2,300 m. Forages actively in middle levels of wet forest; accompanies mixed flocks. Calls with a hard *skik*. 7" (18 cm).

Lineated Foliage-gleaner
Syndactyla subalaris

Resembles Striped Woodhaunter, but has **crisp**, **pale-buffy streaking on breast**. Juvenile, with its tawny throat, resembles larger Streak-breasted Treehunter (p. 166), but has **tawny postocular stripe**. Fairly uncommon at middle elevations, from 1,400 to 2,200 m; rare down to 800 m. Favors lower and middle levels of openings in mature wet forest. Pokes into dead leaf clusters and epiphytes; accompanies mixed flocks. Gives a crescendoing series of about ten rapid, dry notes. 7" (18 cm).

Scaly-throated Foliage-gleaner
Anabacerthia variegaticeps

Similar to Buff-throated Foliage-gleaner, but **eye ring and superciliary are ochraceous**; scaling on throat is faint. Rare at middle elevations, from 800 to 1,800 m. Forages in leaf clusters, epiphytes, and vines at middle levels of mature wet forest and advanced second growth; accompanies mixed flocks. Call is a loud, sharp squeak. 6" (15 cm).

note flared-out
cheek feathers

Buffy
Tuftedcheek

Striped
Woodhaunter

Buff-throated
Foliage-gleaner

Buff-fronted
Foliage-gleaner

adult

juv.

Scaly-throated
Foliage-gleaner

Lineated
Foliage-gleaner

Birds of Costa Rica / **165**

Ruddy Foliage-gleaner
Automolus rubiginosus

A dark reddish-brown foliage-gleaner with underparts lighter than rest of body. Fairly common in the hills surrounding the Coto Brus Valley; unconfirmed reports from Monteverde area; from 1,100 to 1,400 m. Actively forages in dense undergrowth and lower levels of mature humid forest and adjacent advanced second growth; often in pairs. Whistles a nasal *ka-kwik*. 8" (20 cm).

Streak-breasted Treehunter
Thripadectes rufobrunneus

The **tawny throat** and **streaked breast** distinguish this large, dark furnariid. Somewhat similar juvenile Lineated Foliage-gleaner (p. 164) has tawny postocular stripe. Fairly common in middle elevations and highlands, from 1,200 to 2,500 m. Actively forages in dense undergrowth and lower levels of mature wet forest and adjacent advanced second growth; accompanies mixed flocks. Utters a scratchy *cheh-brah, cheh-brah, cheh-brah…*, with a scolding quality. **Endemic to CR and western Panama**. 8" (20 cm).

[The three CR leaftossers are all quite similar. Best distinguished by throat color, though that can be difficult to see when the bird hops about the dimly lit forest floor. Could be mistaken for a thrush (p. 246), but a leaftosser is plumper and has shorter legs and a longer bill.]

Scaly-throated Leaftosser
Sclerurus guatemalensis

Has **scalloped pattern on white throat** and on brown breast and sides of head; **lacks rufous rump** of the Gray-throated Leaftosser and Tawny-throated Leaftosser. Uncommon in wet lowlands and foothills of both Pacific and Caribbean slopes, to 1,000 m. Forages on the ground in mature forest by flicking leaves with bill. Sings a fairly high-pitched song lasting 3 seconds and increasing in pitch and volume, then dropping, with the last three or four notes lower and weaker. 6" (15 cm).

Gray-throated Leaftosser
Sclerurus albigularis

Similar to both Scaly-throated and Tawny-throated Leaftossers, but note **gray throat** and **reddish-brown breast**. Uncommon in middle elevations of northern half of CR, from 600 to 1,500 m. Forages on the ground in mature wet forest by flicking leaves with bill. Repeats a quick phrase of five to seven notes, the first three or four high descending notes are followed by one or two sharp, higher notes. 6" (15 cm).

Tawny-throated Leaftosser
Sclerurus mexicanus

Similar to Scaly-throated and Gray-throated Leaftossers, but the **tawny throat** is diagnostic. Uncommon in middle elevations, from 700 to 1,800 m. Forages on the ground in mature wet forest by flicking leaves with bill. Whistles four or more thin, wheezy, descending notes, each slightly shorter than the previous. 6" (15 cm).

Ruddy
Foliage-gleaner

Streak-breasted
Treehunter

Scaly-throated
Leaftosser

Gray-throated
Leaftosser

Tawny-throated
Leaftosser

Birds of Costa Rica / **167**

Plain Xenops
Xenops minutus

The prominent **white malar stripe** and **short, upturned bill** are distinctive; plain underparts separate it from Streaked Xenops. Fairly common in lowlands and foothills of southern Pacific and in Caribbean foothills, uncommon in Caribbean lowlands, and rare in northwestern Pacific; to 1,500 m. Forages at all levels in mature wet forest, forest edges, second growth, and gardens; behaves like an Olivaceous Piculet (p. 158), pecking into vines and dead twigs. Accompanies mixed flocks. Gives a fast, high-pitched trill. 5" (13 cm).

Streaked Xenops
Xenops rutilans

Resembles Plain Xenops, but has **streaked underparts**. Rare in middle elevations and highlands, from Central Cordillera south, between 1,200 and 2,500 m. Forages at all levels in mature wet forest and at forest edges; behaves much like a Plain Xenops. The call consists of two to six thin, hissing notes. 5" (13 cm).

[Adapted for climbing up tree trunks, woodcreepers superficially resemble the woodpeckers, although they glean and probe for their prey, rather than peck into wood. All CR woodcreepers have rufous wings and tail, so it is necessary to concentrate on other field marks for species identification. Bill shape, size, and color are very important; also try to note any markings on the head and underparts (e.g., streaking, spotting, barring, eye ring, eye line, malar stripe, etc.).]

Black-banded Woodcreeper
Dendrocolaptes picumnus

The only CR woodcreeper with **streaked breast** and **barred belly**; also note stout, dusky bill. Rare at middle elevations of Caribbean slope, from 500 to 2,000 m; also on Pacific side of Tilarán Cordillera and in Dota region. Forages at all levels in mature wet forest. Sings a fast series of twelve or more notes, which diminish in pitch and intensity. 11" (28 cm).

Northern Barred-Woodcreeper
Dendrocolaptes sanctithomae

Fine black barring on brown head, back, and underparts is diagnostic, but can be difficult to detect in dim light; has straight, stout, dark bill. Common in wet lowlands of both Pacific and Caribbean slopes; less common in foothills, to 1,300 m; and rare in dry lowlands. Forages at middle and lower levels of mature forest, advanced second growth, and adjacent gardens; often accompanies army-ant swarms. Calls at dawn and dusk with a penetrating *doh-wee, doh-wee, doh-wee, doh-wee*, each part upslurred; call is similar to that of Tawny-crowned Greenlet (p. 228). 11" (28 cm).

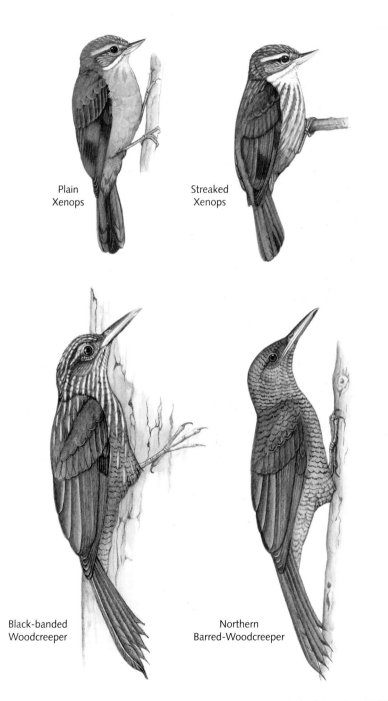

Plain
Xenops

Streaked
Xenops

Black-banded
Woodcreeper

Northern
Barred-Woodcreeper

Plain-brown Woodcreeper
Dendrocincla fuliginosa

Has **straight, black bill**; an essentially unmarked bird, though note **dark malar stripe** separating **pale cheeks and throat**. Fairly uncommon in wet Caribbean lowlands and foothills, to 900 m. Forages at middle and lower levels of mature forest and advanced second growth; often accompanies army-ant swarms. Call is a sharp, metallic *speeyk*. 8" (20 cm).

Ruddy Woodcreeper
Dendrocincla homochroa

No other woodcreeper is so **uniformly rufous**; also note straight, brownish bill and **gray lores**. Fairly uncommon in northern Pacific slope foothills and in intermontane valleys of southern Pacific, between 500 and 1,200 m; uncommon to rare elsewhere in Pacific lowlands, Caribbean foothills, and Caño Negro region. Forages in lower levels of humid and dry forests; often accompanies army-ant swarms. 8" (20 cm).

Tawny-winged Woodcreeper
Dendrocincla anabatina

Has **straight, black bill**; rufous wings and tail contrast with olive-brown upperparts; note pale-buffy throat. Fairly common in Pacific lowlands and foothills, from Carara south, to 1,500 m. Forages at middle and lower levels of mature wet forest and advanced second growth, also in mangroves; often accompanies army-ant swarms. Song is a lengthy, agitated *whe-whe-whe-whe…*, lasting up to a minute. 7" (18 cm).

Long-tailed Woodcreeper
Deconychura longicauda

Brown breast with buffy spots and a bicolored bill with pale lower mandible could suggest a Spotted Woodcreeper (p. 172), but note **plain-brown back** and thinner bill. Uncommon in Pacific lowlands from Carara south; rare in foothills of Caribbean and southern Pacific, to 1,200 m. Forages mostly at lower levels in mature wet forest. 7" (18 cm).

Wedge-billed Woodcreeper
Glyphorhynchus spirurus

Told apart from other woodcreepers by **short bill with slightly upturned lower mandible**. Common in lowlands and foothills of Caribbean slope and of Pacific slope (from Carara south), to 1,500 m. Forages at middle and lower levels of mature wet forest and advanced second growth. Sings a quick *wididididi* that falls then rises. 6" (15 cm).

Olivaceous Woodcreeper
Sittasomus griseicapillus

Unpatterned gray head and underparts are diagnostic; has short, straight, dark bill. Fairly common at middle elevations of Pacific slope, from 700 to 1,500 m; uncommon in lowlands of northern Pacific (including mangroves) and at middle elevations on Caribbean slope. Forages actively at middle levels in relatively open areas within forest and at forest edges. Gives a high, rapid, rattling trill. 6" (15 cm).

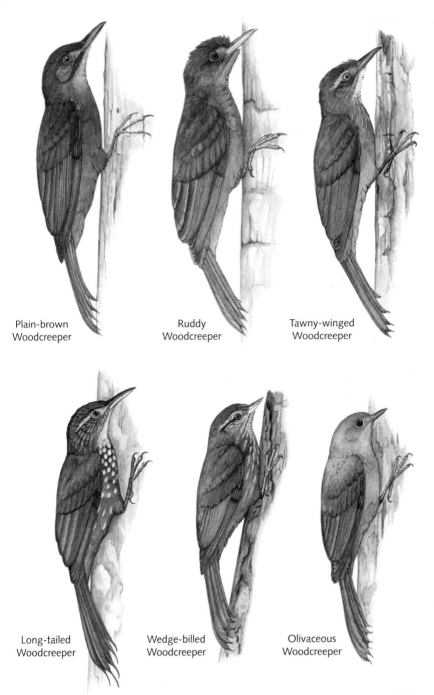

Plain-brown
Woodcreeper

Ruddy
Woodcreeper

Tawny-winged
Woodcreeper

Long-tailed
Woodcreeper

Wedge-billed
Woodcreeper

Olivaceous
Woodcreeper

Streak-headed Woodcreeper
Lepidocolaptes souleyetii

Very similar to the Spot-crowned Woodcreeper, but note **pinkish-brown bill** and **streaked crown** (not spotted); also note that there is very little range overlap. The shape of the bill (thin, decurved) distinguishes this species from the Cocoa and Ivory-billed Woodcreepers. Common and widespread in lowlands; uncommon at middle elevations, to 1,500 m. Forages at all levels in garden habitats. Gives a two- or three-second, descending trill. 8" (20 cm).

Spot-crowned Woodcreeper
Lepidocolaptes affinis

Has **slender, decurved, pale bill** and **spotted crown**. One of three CR woodcreepers found above 1,700 m (Strong-billed Woodcreeper [p. 174] and Black-banded Woodcreeper [p. 168] are both very rare). Also compare with Streak-headed Woodcreeper. Fairly common in Talamanca Cordillera and uncommon on Central Cordillera, from timberline down to 1,500 m, rarely to 1,000 m. Forages at all levels, both in garden habitats and mature oak forests; often accompanies mixed flocks. Gives one or two high, nasal squeaks followed by a fairly even, two- or three-second trill that drops off and slows slightly at the very end. 8" (20 cm).

Cocoa Woodcreeper
Xiphorhynchus susurrans

Resembles Streak-headed and Ivory-billed Woodcreepers, but has **straight, stout bill with dark upper mandible** and **lighter lower mandible**. Common in wet lowlands and foothills, to 900 m; rare in dry lowlands. Forages at all levels of forest edges, second growth, and gardens; occasionally found in mature forest. Very vocal, but typically calls hidden from view; gives a series of seven or more emphatic notes (*wheet, wheet, wheet…*), rising slightly then falling off at the end. 9" (23 cm).

Black-striped Woodcreeper
Xiphorhynchus lachrymosus

The **bold scaling on head, back, and underparts** is diagnostic. Uncommon in wet lowlands; rare in adjacent foothills, to 1,200 m. Forages in middle and upper levels of mature wet forest and at forest edges. Sings a jerky, descending, laughing whinny. 9" (23 cm).

Spotted Woodcreeper
Xiphorhynchus erythropygius

Though not overly conspicuous, this species has a more obvious **eye ring** than any other CR woodcreeper; note **olive-brown underparts with buffy spots**; bicolored bill is stout and straight. Similar to Long-tailed Woodcreeper (p. 170), but note thicker bill and streaking on back. Common at middle elevations, from 800 to 1,700 m; uncommon at lower elevations in foothills, and rare in wet lowlands. Forages at all levels in mature wet forest and advanced second growth; often with mixed flocks. Gives two or three slurred, descending whistles, each slightly lower pitched. 9" (23 cm).

Ivory-billed Woodcreeper
Xiphorhynchus flavigaster

Similar to Streak-headed and Cocoa Woodcreepers, but has **straight, stout, pale bill**; also note dusky malar stripe. Fairly uncommon in northwestern Pacific and Caño Negro region, to 900 m. Frequently forages on major limbs of trees in evergreen forest and at forest edges. Gives a loud, laughing, descending whinny. 9" (23 cm).

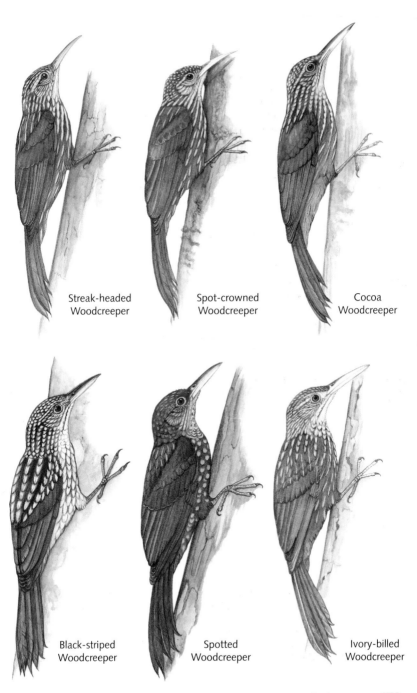

Streak-headed
Woodcreeper

Spot-crowned
Woodcreeper

Cocoa
Woodcreeper

Black-striped
Woodcreeper

Spotted
Woodcreeper

Ivory-billed
Woodcreeper

Ovenbirds & Woodcreepers

Strong-billed Woodcreeper   *Xiphocolaptes promeropirhynchus*
This bird has a **stout bill** that is slightly decurved and laterally compressed. Rare in foothills and middle elevations of Caribbean slope, from Tilarán Cordillera south, between 500 and 1,700 m; very rare on southern Pacific slope of Talamanca Cordillera. Inhabits mature wet forest; often begins foraging near base of tree and works its way far up trunk. At dawn and dusk, repeats a loud *KEW-WEE* about ten times. 12" (30 cm).

Brown-billed Scythebill   *Campylorhamphus pusillus*
The **long, slim, extremely decurved bill** is diagnostic. Fairly uncommon in Caribbean foothills and middle elevations, from Tilarán Cordillera south, between 300 and 1,500 m; uncommon in Pacific foothills and middle elevations, from Dota region south, between 300 and 2,500 m; rare in lowlands of Osa region. Forages at all levels in mature wet forest; often accompanies mixed flocks. Whistles a stuttering series of loud, cascading notes (lasting five seconds). 9" (23 cm).

Typical Antbirds

THAMNOPHILIDAE. Most members of this large neotropical family live in forests, where their overall dark coloration blends well with the shadows. Many are quite vocal, which aids greatly in locating them. None routinely eat ants—the common name antbird derives from the fact that a few species habitually follow foraging army ants, which flush out hidden arthropods that the birds eagerly consume. Encountering an ant swarm attended by a variety of antbirds and other species is one of the great neotropical birding experiences.

Fasciated Antshrike   *Cymbilaimus lineatus*
Male resembles male Barred Antshrike, but is more finely barred and has **red iris**; female unmistakable. Fairly common in wet Caribbean lowlands, and rare in Caño Negro region and foothills, to 1,200 m. Pairs hop methodically through tangled vegetation of forest edges and second growth, at low to middle levels. Delivers four to eight clear notes (*kwew, kwew, kwew, kwew*) at the same pitch, but each note rises at the end. 7" (18 cm).

Barred Antshrike   *Thamnophilus doliatus*
Male similar to male Fasciated Antshrike, but with broader white barring and **pale-yellow iris**; female is only cinnamon-rufous bird in CR with **streaked sides of head**. Common in northwestern Pacific and Caño Negro region; uncommon in wet lowlands and foothills, to 1,400 m. Pairs typically stay low in thickets, forest edges, and second growth. Call is a fast-paced series of chuckling notes that accelerates before ending in a higher-pitched, nasal *wek!*. 6" (15 cm).

Strong-billed
Woodcreeper

Brown-billed
Scythebill

female

male

Fasciated Antshrike

female

male

Barred Antshrike

Great Antshrike
Taraba major

On male, the combination of mostly black upperparts and mostly white underparts is distinctive; on female, the combination of reddish-brown upperparts and mostly white underparts is distinctive. In both sexes, any doubts as to identification are dispelled by the heavy, hooked bill and **bright-red iris**. Fairly common in wet lowlands and foothills, to 1,100 m. Prefers dense tangles and thickets of forest edges and new second growth, now and then rising to lower branches of small trees. Proclaims presence with an accelerating, descending, bouncy chuckle that ends in a soft, nasal *wrray*. 8" (20 cm).

Black-hooded Antshrike
Thamnophilus bridgesi

The **white speckling on shoulder** distinguishes male from other basically black birds. In female, pale streaking on head and breast is diagnostic. Common in southern Pacific, to 1,200 m; rare north of Carara, to Tenorio Volcano. Pairs inhabit lower levels of mature forest, second growth, and forest edges; often with mixed flocks. Gives an accelerating series of staccato notes that ends in a longer, lower note. **Endemic to CR and western Panama**. 6" (15 cm).

Russet Antshrike
Thamnistes anabatinus

The **thick bill with hooked tip** differentiates it from other cinnamon/rufous birds. Fairly common in Caribbean foothills and in southern Pacific lowlands and foothills, to 1,500 m; rare in Caribbean lowlands. Behaves more like a foliage gleaner (p. 164) than an antshrike—individuals or pairs travel with mixed flocks in middle levels of mature wet forest, advanced second growth, and forest edges, often poking into dead leaf clusters. Gives a thin *tsweetsip*. 6" (15 cm).

Western Slaty-Antshrike
Thamnophilus atrinucha

Male has prominent **white spotting on tips of wing coverts** and **white tips on tail feathers**; female is larger and less active than similarly plumaged female antvireos (p. 180) and antwrens (p. 182). Common in Caribbean lowlands and rare in Caribbean foothills, to 1,000 m; also a small population in evergreen forests of Santa Rosa National Park. Pairs forage in lower levels of mature wet forest, tall second growth, and cacao plantations. Call is a fast-paced series of fairly even-pitched chuckling notes that ends with a single, higher-pitched *wek!*. 6" (15 cm).

Dusky Antbird
Cercomacra tyrannina

Compared with smaller Slaty Antwren (p. 182), note proportionately longer tail. Common in wet lowlands and foothills of Caribbean and southern Pacific, to 1,200 m; very uncommon north of Carara. Rather wrenlike; pairs favor low dense vegetation in forest openings, forest edges, and second growth. Frequently gives a series of emphatic staccato notes, the first three rising slightly in pitch, then leveling and accelerating slightly. 6" (15 cm).

male

female

Great
Antshrike

male

female

Black-hooded
Antshrike

Russet Antshrike

male

female

Western
Slaty-Antshrike

male

female

Dusky Antbird

Birds of Costa Rica / **177**

Immaculate Antbird
Myrmeciza immaculata

No other antbird with **blue orbital skin** is so **uniformly patterned**. Fairly uncommon at middle elevations of Caribbean slope, from Miravalles Volcano south, between 500 and 1,700 m; rare at middle elevations of southern Pacific slope, between 900 and 1,700 m. Pairs or small groups forage on or near the ground in mature wet forest and adjacent advanced second growth, habitually lowering and raising their tails; often with army-ant swarms. Quite noisy; intones six to ten forceful, even-pitched notes. 7" (18 cm).

Chestnut-backed Antbird
Myrmeciza exsul

The **dark slaty head** and **chestnut-brown back** distinguish it from other antbirds with blue orbital skin. Female of Caribbean race has chestnut-brown underparts; female of Pacific race has rufous underparts. Very common in wet lowlands and foothills of southern Pacific, but rare north of Carara; fairly common in Caribbean lowlands and foothills; to 1,200 m. Pairs forage near the ground (or even on the ground) in mature wet forest. Whistles two or three clear, labored notes, the last one lower (reminiscent of Black-faced Antthrush [p. 186] and Black-throated Trogon [p. 140]); also gives a nasal, raspy *hyaah*. 6" (15 cm).

Bare-crowned Antbird
Gymnocichla nudiceps

Bare blue forecrown on male is diagnostic; **rufous wing bars and underparts** set female apart from other antbirds with blue orbital skin. Common in Caño Negro region; uncommon in wet lowlands of Caribbean and southern Pacific; rare in foothills, to 1,200 m. Pairs stay low in dense growth of forest openings, forest edges, and second growth. Particularly fond of *Heliconia* thickets; joins army-ant swarms. Delivers a series of even-pitched, whistled notes that accelerates and weakens toward end. 6" (15 cm).

Bicolored Antbird
Gymnopithys leucaspis

The mostly **white underparts** differentiate it from other antbirds with blue orbital skin. Fairly uncommon in wet lowlands and foothills of Caribbean and southern Pacific slopes, to 1,600 m; rare on Pacific slopes of Guanacaste Cordillera. Pairs or small groups forage near the ground in mature wet forest and adjacent advanced second growth, almost exclusively at army-ant swarms. Frequently utters a harsh *nhyarr*; sings a series of high notes which increase in pitch and pace, then slow down and descend (similar to song of Ocellated Antbird). 6" (15 cm).

Ocellated Antbird
Phaenostictus mcleannani

This striking antbird has an **extended blue orbital area** and **bold scalloping** on back and underparts. Uncommon in Caribbean lowlands and foothills, to 1,200 m. Pairs or small groups forage near the ground in mature wet forest and adjacent advanced second growth, almost exclusively at army-ant swarms. Song quite similar to that of Bicolored Antbird, but more dulcet; also gives a descending, buzzy *dzjeer*. 8" (20 cm).

female

Immaculate
Antbird

male

female
caribbean race

Chestnut-backed
Antbird

male

female

male

Bare-crowned
Antbird

Bicolored
Antbird

Ocellated
Antbird

Typical Antbirds

Dull-mantled Antbird
Myrmeciza laemosticta

Told apart from other dark-brown birds by its **red iris** and **white spotting on shoulders**. Fairly common in Caribbean foothills, from 300 to 900 m. Forages on or near the ground in dense vegetation, mostly along streams and ravines in mature wet forest. Sings a series of about eight high, emphatic whistled notes, the first two or three upwardly inflected, and the remaining notes downwardly inflected; also utters a shrill, blurred downwardly inflected *bzhew.* 6" (15 cm).

Spotted Antbird
Hylophylax naevioides

Multi-patterned male is distinctive; female, though somewhat less striking, is also distinctive. Common on both Caribbean and Pacific slopes of Guanacaste Cordillera, between 600 and 800 m; fairly uncommon in Caribbean lowlands and foothills, to 1,000 m. Individuals and pairs forage in the understory of mature wet and humid forests and adjacent advanced second growth, very often with army ants. Sings a soft, sweet, buzzy, descending series of eight to ten doubled notes: *zpeeda, zpeeda, zpeeda... .* 4" (10 cm).

Plain Antvireo
Dysithamnus mentalis

Female resembles Tawny-crowned Greenlet (p. 228), but has **dark iris**. Male told apart from male Spot-crowned Antvireo by **plain crown and breast**. Fairly common in Caribbean foothills and middle elevations, from 400 to 1,500 m; rare in adjacent lowlands. Fairly common in southern Pacific foothills and middle elevations, rarely to 2,500 m; uncommon in lowlands, north to Parrita. Pairs inhabit understory of mature wet forest and advanced second growth. Song is a series of accelerating and descending chuckling notes. 4" (10 cm).

Spot-crowned Antvireo
Dysithamnus puncticeps

Both sexes resemble Streak-crowned Antvireo (little range overlap), but have **indistinct streaking on throat and breast**. Male resembles male Plain Antvireo, but note spots on crown. Fairly common in Caribbean lowlands and foothills, from Cahuita south, to 800 m. Pairs and small groups forage at lower levels of mature wet forest and adjacent gardens. Delivers a fast, rolling series of notes that rise, level off, then descend as they increase in tempo. 4" (10 cm).

Streak-crowned Antvireo
Dysithamnus striaticeps

Both sexes resemble Spot-crowned Antvireo (little range overlap), but have **distinct streaking on throat and breast**. Fairly common in Caribbean foothills, to 800 m; very uncommon in Caribbean lowlands, south to about Limón. Pairs join mixed flocks in lower and middle levels of mature wet forest and adjacent advanced second growth. Song similar to Plain Antvireo, but rises initially in pitch and intensity before accelerating and descending. **Endemic from southeastern Honduras to CR.** 4" (10 cm).

Dull-mantled
Antbird

female

male

Spotted Antbird

male

female

Plain Antvireo

male

female

Spot-crowned
Antvireo

male

female

Streak-crowned
Antvireo

male

female

Slaty Antwren
Myrmotherula schisticolor

Male and female resemble respective sexes of Dusky Antbird (p. 176), but are smaller and have shorter tail. Fairly common in Caribbean foothills and middle elevations, from 700 to 1,500 m. Fairly common on Pacific slope of Guanacaste and Tilarán Cordilleras, from 1,000 to 1,500 m; also fairly common on Pacific slope of Talamanca Cordillera, from 700 to 2,000 m; uncommon in Pacific lowlands, from Carara south. Pairs forage actively with mixed flocks at lower levels of mature wet forest and adjacent advanced second growth. Whistles a high, soft *tswee-tswee-tswee-tswee*, each note upwardly inflected. 4" (10 cm).

Rufous-rumped Antwren
Terenura callinota

In size and color pattern, resembles a small flycatcher or warbler; **rufous rump** is diagnostic; also note **dark cap**. Rare at middle elevations of Caribbean slope, from Tilarán Cordillera south, between 700 and 1,200 m. Forages actively (warblerlike) at middle levels of mature wet forest and forest edges, usually with mixed flocks. 4" (10 cm).

Dot-winged Antwren
Microrhopias quixensis

The combination of a **single broad white wing bar**, **white dots on shoulder**, and **broad white tail tips** is diagnostic. Common in southern Pacific lowlands and foothills, and uncommon in Caribbean lowlands and foothills; to 1,000 m. Pairs and small groups forage actively with mixed flocks in lower levels of mature wet forest and adjacent advanced second growth. Sings a series of high, fast notes, which rise initially in pitch and intensity before descending; also gives a sharp s*peEa*. 4" (10 cm).

Checker-throated Antwren
Myrmotherula fulviventris

Black-and-white throat pattern on male is diagnostic; female has **pale iris** and **blackish wing coverts** (compare with female White-flanked Antwren). Fairly uncommon in Caribbean lowlands and foothills, to 900 m. Pairs and small groups forage actively with mixed flocks in lower levels of mature wet forest and adjacent advanced second growth, mostly investigating dried leaves. Utters a monosylabic series of high, thin *tsit* notes, the first few notes somewhat more emphatic. 4" (10 cm).

White-flanked Antwren
Myrmotherula axillaris

The male's **white flanks** are diagnostic; female has **dark iris**, **gray cap**, and **white flanks** (compare with female Checker-throated Antwren). Fairly uncommon in Caribbean lowlands and foothills, to 900 m. Pairs are typically found in mixed flocks, foraging actively at lower and middle levels of mature wet forest and adjacent advanced second growth. Whistles a series of high *tswee* notes that drop in pitch and intensity. 4" (10 cm).

male

male

female

female

Slaty
Antwren

Rufous-rumped
Antwren

male

male

female

female

Dot-winged
Antwren

Checker-throated
Antwren

male

female

White-flanked
Antwren

Ground Antbirds

FORMICARIIDAE. The ground antbirds (antpittas and antthrushes) have dark plumage and are big-eyed, two adaptations for life in the dim rain forest understory. The plump antpittas have upright postures—accentuated by their long legs and very short tails—and move by hopping. Antthrushes typically walk with their short tails cocked up, suggesting a miniature chicken or a forest rail. Species of this family are heard more often than seen.

Ochre-breasted Antpitta
Grallaricula flavirostris

Rather like a **tiny** version of the Thicket Antpitta, but with **yellowish bill** and **white vent**. Also note prominent buffy eye ring. Rare at middle elevations on Caribbean slope, between 700 and 1,500 m, from Tilarán Cordillera south; also rare at middle elevations on Pacific slope, between 900 and 1,800 m, from Dota region south. Slightly less terrestrial than the larger antpittas, but still stays in understory of mature wet forests. Habitually twists from side to side. Sings a high trill with a rattling quality. 4" (10 cm).

Thicket Antpitta
Hylopezus dives

Larger than the somewhat similar Ochre-breasted Antpitta; further distinguished by **dark bill** and **reddish-orange vent**. Also note ochraceous breast, which is finely streaked with black. Fairly uncommon in wet Caribbean lowlands and foothills, to 900 m. Very difficult to see since it favors the cover of dense thickety vegetation at forest edges, in young second growth, and along streams. Presence revealed by a series of about twelve whistled notes that rise slightly in pitch and volume, then end abruptly, lasting about two seconds (compare with Black-headed Antthrush [p. 186]). **Endemic from Honduras to western Colombia.** 5" (13 cm).

Streak-chested Antpitta
Hylopezus perspicillatus

Has prominent buffy eye ring, **buffy spotted wing bars**, **dark malar stripe**, and heavy black streaking on breast. Fairly common in southern Pacific, uncommon on Caribbean slope; to 1,200 m. Prefers relatively open areas in understory of mature wet forest; habitually inflates and deflates abdomen. Its song (of up to ten notes) lasts four seconds. The first three notes rise slightly; the following notes are even pitched and slower; the last few notes are coupled. 5" (13 cm).

Black-crowned Antpitta
Pittasoma michleri

The rotund shape and **boldly scalloped underparts** set this species apart. Rare in Caribbean foothills, from Tilarán Cordillera south, between 300 and 800 m. Stays on or near the ground in mature wet forest; accompanies army-ant swarms. Gives a long-winded series of sharp *pip* notes, rapid at first, then gradually slowing, the whole phrase lasting for thirty seconds or more. **Endemic from CR to northwestern Colombia**. 7" (18 cm).

Scaled Antpitta
Grallaria guatimalensis

This bird's plump shape, **scaled upperparts**, and **rufous underparts** are diagnostic. Rare at middle elevations, from 800 to 1,600 m. Stays on or near the ground in mature wet montane forest, sometimes hopping along trails. Produces a low, hollow, crescendoing series of trills lasting about three seconds. 7" (18 cm).

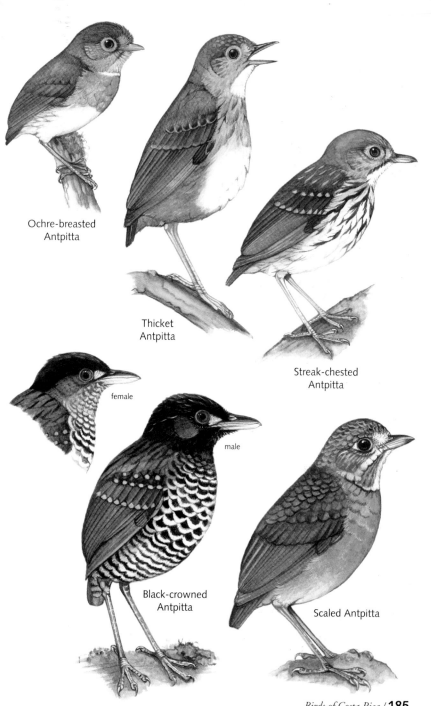

Ochre-breasted
Antpitta

Thicket
Antpitta

Streak-chested
Antpitta

female

male

Black-crowned
Antpitta

Scaled Antpitta

Ground Antbirds

[The three CR antthrushes can be told apart by the color and pattern of the head and by the color of the breast; their respective vocalizations are quite distinct. Note that there is little range overlap.]

Black-headed Antthrush
Formicarius nigricapillus

The **entirely black head and breast** are diagnostic. Uncommon in Caribbean foothills and middle elevations, from 400 to 1,200 m. Struts through leaf litter of mature forest and advanced second growth; accompanies army-ant swarms. Whistles a series of fast, hollow notes that rise in pitch, then level off, lasting about five seconds (longer than similar call of Thicket Antpitta [p. 184]). 7" (18 cm).

Black-faced Antthrush
Formicarius analis

Note the **dark-gray breast**. Common in wet lowlands and foothills, to 500 m on Caribbean slope (higher in south) and 1,500 m in southern Pacific. Struts through leaf litter of mature forest and advanced second growth. Whistles a labored *pyee, pyew, pyew*; the first note (accented and higher) is usually followed by two or three notes, but sometimes by as many as ten or more (compare with call of Chestnut-backed Antbird [p. 178]). 7" (18 cm).

Rufous-breasted Antthrush
Formicarius rufipectus

The **rufous breast** is diagnostic. Fairly uncommon at middle elevations of Caribbean slope, from Tilarán Cordillera south, between 800 and 1,800 m. Inhabits the floor of mature forest and advanced second growth, often beneath dense undergrowth. Whistles a clear, two-note *pyew, pyew*, the second note slightly higher. 7" (18 cm).

Tapaculos

RHINOCRYPTIDAE. CR's tapaculo is the northernmost member of this essentially South American family of mostly small dark birds, many with very limited distribution. Basically terrestrial and extremely furtive, they are heard far more often than seen.

Silvery-fronted Tapaculo
Scytalopus argentifrons

The **frosty stripe across the male's brow** is a good field mark; females are browner, without brow line; both have **barred flanks**. Common from timberline down to 1,500 m on Pacific slope, and down to 1,200 m on Caribbean slope, from Miravalles Volcano south. Inhabits dense undergrowth in wet montane forests, especially along streams and ravines. At intervals, utters a characteristic series of rapid, emphatic, staccato notes that increase in volume, then decrease in pace, lasting five seconds or more. **Endemic to CR and western Panama.** 4" (10 cm).

Black-headed
Antthrush

Black-faced
Antthrush

Rufous-breasted
Antthrush

female

Silvery-fronted
Tapaculo

male

Tyrant Flycatchers

TYRANNIDAE. Both the largest New World bird family and the most diverse CR family (78 species). Most species have a definite flycatcher jizz (upright posture, rather drab plumage). Bill size, shape, and color are important characteristics for sorting out species. Habits, habitat, and voice are also helpful in species identification. Some species have colorful crown patches that they display when excited. Illustrations show these, even though they are normally concealed.

Yellow-bellied Tyrannulet
Ornithion semiflavum

Small size, **obvious white superciliary**, yellow underparts, and absence of wing bars are diagnostic. Very similar to Brown-capped Tyrannulet, but note **gray crown** (ranges only overlap in the Caño Negro region). Very uncommon in lowlands from Caño Negro west to Guanacaste Cordillera, and from Carara south to Golfo Dulce; to 600 m. Forages at forest edges and in gardens. Whistles five or six high, fairly even-pitched, slightly accelerating notes. 3" (8 cm).

Brown-capped Tyrannulet
Ornithion brunneicapillus

Very similar to Yellow-bellied Tyrannulet, but has **brown crown**. Fairly common throughout Caribbean lowlands and into lower middle elevations, to 900 m. Forages actively with mixed flocks in mid- to upper canopy of forests and forest edges; more often heard than seen. Gives a high-pitched, emphatic series of whistled notes that, after an initial one or two notes, rapidly descend the scale. 3" (8 cm).

Yellow Tyrannulet
Capsiempis flaveola

Yellow underparts, wing bars, and superciliary recall a Yellow-winged Vireo (p. 228) in pattern (but no range overlap). Common in wet lowlands of both Caribbean and Pacific slopes; fairly uncommon in foothills, to 600 m on Caribbean slope and 1,200 m in southern Pacific. Pairs forage low in overgrown brushy areas. Quite vocal, utters sputtering series of *wheep* or *wee-deep* notes. 4" (10 cm).

[The stubby body, unique facial markings, and broad bill distinguish the three CR spadebills from other flycatchers.]

Stub-tailed Spadebill
Platyrinchus cancrominus

Virtually identical to White-throated Spadebill, though slightly paler; best told apart by habitat and voice in narrow zone of overlap. Uncommon in evergreen forests of northwestern Pacific lowlands, south to Parrita; also uncommon in humid forests on Pacific slope of northern cordilleras, to 1,300 m. Keeps within three meters of forest floor. Call is a dry, rapid *kitidid* or *ti-di*. 4" (10 cm).

Golden-crowned Spadebill
Platyrinchus coronatus

Greenish back and obvious **golden-rust crown** set it apart from the other two spadebills. Fairly common in understory of lowland wet forests and advanced second growth, to 700 m in Caribbean foothills and 1,200 m in southern Pacific. Produces a very high-pitched, rapid, hissing trill that undulates slightly and lasts about two seconds; could easily be mistaken for an insect noise. 3" (8 cm).

White-throated Spadebill
Platyrinchus mystaceus

Virtually identical to Stub-tailed Spadebill, but darker (and little range overlap). Common in understory of middle-elevation wet forests, from 700 to 2,100 m. Call is a sharp, squeaky *squik!*. 4" (10 cm).

Yellow-bellied
Tyrannulet

Brown-capped
Tyrannulet

Yellow
Tyrannulet

Stub-tailed
Spadebill

Golden-crowned
Spadebill

White-throated
Spadebill

Mouse-colored Tyrannulet
Phaeomyias murina

The **buffy wing bars** and **pinkish base of lower mandible**, together with **brownish upperparts**, should differentiate it from other tyrannulets. Rare and only recently discovered in CR (1996); possible in intermontane valleys of southern Pacific; stays low in second growth and scrub. 5" (13 cm).

Rough-legged Tyrannulet
Phyllomyias burmeisteri

The **yellow wing bars** and **bicolored bill** set it apart from the somewhat similar Paltry Tyrannulet. The **white superciliaries meet on the forehead**— superciliaries do not meet on the forehead of the similar Yellow-crowned Tyrannulet (little or no range overlap). A rare resident of middle and upper elevations, from 800 to 2,800 m, in forest canopy and at forest edges. Call is a high, piercing *tseEe*; six of these notes in rapid succession constitute the song. 4" (10 cm).

Paltry Tyrannulet
Zimmerius vilissimus

Bright yellow wing edging and **no wing bars** differentiate it from the Rough-legged and Yellow-crowned Tyrannulets—indeed from all other small, short-billed flycatchers, and even warblers. Common and widespread, from lowlands to timberline, though rare in Central Valley and northwestern Pacific. Frequents gardens, forest edges, and second growth, dining on mistletoe and other berries, as well as insects. Call is a whistled *peee-yer* that falls slightly at the end. 4" (10 cm).

Yellow-crowned Tyrannulet
Tyrannulus elatus

Unlike other CR flycatchers that have concealed crown patches, this species frequently displays its crown patch, which is bright yellow. Otherwise distinguished from Paltry Tyrannulet by **yellowish wing bars** and **yellow belly**. Set apart from Southern Beardless-Tyrannulet by a more obvious superciliary and a dark-gray crown. Little or no range overlap with Rough-legged Tyrannulet (see above). Uncommon in gardens and forest edges in southern Pacific, to 1,200 m. Spreading north from Panama; has reached Carara, where first reported in 2002. Whistles a clear *pray TEER*. 4" (10 cm).

Northern Beardless-Tyrannulet
Camptostoma imberbe

Small and drab, with a **slight crest**, **dingy wing bars**, and **short bill**. Duller and with less distinct wing bars than Southern-Beardless Tyrannulet. Fairly common in dry forest habitat and scrub, up to 800 m, including western Central Valley. Calls with a shrill *peeeuh*. 4" (10 cm).

Southern Beardless-Tyrannulet
Camptostoma obsoletum

Very similar to Northern-Beardless Tyrannulet (note rather small area of range overlap), but brighter and with more **conspicuous wing bars**. Set apart from Yellow-crowned Tyrannulet by a less obvious superciliary and by brownish-gray crown. Fairly common in southern Pacific lowlands; uncommon in southern Pacific foothills, to 1,200 m; rare north of Carara, where mostly confined to gallery forest. Prefers second growth and gardens; often holds tail cocked up. Sings four to six slightly descending *psee* notes; call is a high *wheer*. 4" (10 cm).

Mouse-colored
Tyrannulet

Rough-legged
Tyrannulet

Paltry
Tyrannulet

Yellow-crowned
Tyrannulet

Northern
Beardless-Tyrannulet

Southern
Beardless-Tyrannulet

Yellow-bellied Elaenia
Elaenia flavogaster

The **parted crest**, revealing a white crown patch, is distinctive. When crest is not raised, this species looks nearly identical to a Lesser Elaenia that *has its crest raised*; so, in zones of overlap, note absence of pale wing patch. Widespread and fairly common in most of CR, though rare in northwestern Pacific; to 2,200 m. Found in semi-open habitats and gardens, where it forages at middle levels, frequently eating berries. Often appears agitated due to the raised crest and somewhat irritated quality of the freely given call, which is a loud, wheezy *wheeeur*. 6" (15 cm).

Lesser Elaenia
Elaenia chiriquensis

Very similar to Yellow-bellied Elaenia, but note **pale wing patch** formed by edges of folded secondaries. At most, only raises a slight crest (never parted down the middle); white crown patch best seen from behind. Fairly common in intermontane valleys of southern Pacific, uncommon in Cartago/Paraiso area; status uncertain on lower western slopes of Miravalles Volcano. Prefers gardens and scrubby open areas with small trees. Calls with scratchy notes. 5" (13 cm).

Mountain Elaenia
Elaenia frantzii

Olive-green above with **obvious wing bars** (appear spotted) and wing edging; has a **round head**. Common in highlands, from timberline down to about 1,200 m. Found at forest edges and in gardens; eats mostly berries. Gives a loud whistled *pseer*. 6" (15 cm).

Northern Scrub-Flycatcher
Sublegatus arenarum

Distinguished from the three CR members of the genus *Elaenia* (see above) by **more distinct contrast on underparts**. Distinguished from the Panama Flycatcher (p. 208) by **small bill** and **faint supraloral stripe**. Fairly uncommon in mangroves and adjacent scrub around the Gulf of Nicoya; rare in similar habitat around the Golfo Dulce. Whistles a clear *weep*. 6" (15 cm).

Rufous-browed Tyrannulet
Phylloscartes superciliaris

The rufous brow and other distinct facial markings facilitate identification of this otherwise rather nondescript bird. Note, however, that the rufous brow is not always obvious. Quite uncommon in wet forests on the northern half of the Caribbean slope, from 500 to 1,300 m. Accompanies mixed flocks, foraging like a warbler in midcanopy vegetation and at forest edges. Call is a sharp, emphatic *screesh*. 4" (10 cm).

Piratic Flycatcher
Legatus leucophaius

Recalls the much larger Sulphur-bellied Flycatcher (p. 212), but has a **short black bill**, **unstreaked olive-brown back**, and **dusky tail** (not rufous). Common breeding resident from lowlands to about 1,500 m; migrates to SA after breeding (most gone by late Sept), begins returning in late Jan. Favors gardens and forest edges, typically perches in treetops. Named for its habit of expropriating other birds' nests by pestering the builders until they abandon the structure. Often-heard call is a high, ringing *bee-ee* that rises and falls, followed after a pause by a series of three to six fast notes: *bidididi*. 6" (15 cm).

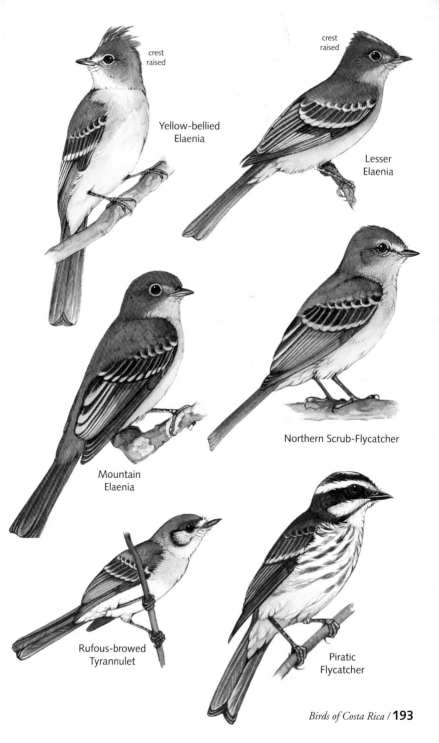

crest raised

Yellow-bellied Elaenia

crest raised

Lesser Elaenia

Northern Scrub-Flycatcher

Mountain Elaenia

Rufous-browed Tyrannulet

Piratic Flycatcher

Yellow-olive Flycatcher

Tolmomyias sulphurescens

The **pale iris** distinguishes this species from the nearly identical Yellow-margined Flycatcher. Set apart from similarly plumaged Greenish Elaenia by **wide bill** and pale iris. Common and widespread, to 1,400 m. Forages at lower and middle levels of second growth, forest edges, and gardens. The conspicuous nest, in the form of an upside-down U, is made of fine black fibers. Call is a shrill, sibilant *tssssp*. 5" (13 cm).

Yellow-margined Flycatcher

Tolmomyias assimilis

Nearly identical to the Yellow-olive Flycatcher, but has **dark iris** and **darker gray head**. Fairly uncommon in Caribbean lowlands and foothills, to 600 m in northern half of CR, and 1,000 m in south. Forages from middle to upper levels of wet forests and forest edges. Call is an emphatic *tssk, tssp, tssp, tssp*. 5" (13 cm).

Greenish Elaenia

Myiopagis viridicata

Nondescript, with indistinct facial markings; the **black bill is narrow and rounded** (note **pale base of lower mandible**). Could suggest Yellow-olive Flycatcher, but that species has gray head, pale iris, and broad, flat bill. Relatively uncommon on Pacific side of country and in Caño Negro area; rare in Reventazón River watershed; to 1,500 m. Found singly at forest edges and in second growth. Call is a somewhat buzzy *cheez*. 5" (13 cm).

Olive-striped Flycatcher

Mionectes olivaceus

The **whitish triangular spot behind the eye** combined with narrow streaking on the breast identifies this slender-billed flycatcher. Common at middle elevations, from about 800 to 2,200 m; some descend to base of mountains on Caribbean slope from July to Jan. Forages for insects and fruits at lower to middle levels of wet forest and at forest edges. Males produce a soft, shrill, undulating sound. 5" (13 cm).

Sepia-capped Flycatcher

Leptopogon amaurocephalus

The **dark-brown crown** and **ochre wing bars** distinguish it from the Slaty-capped Flycatcher. Rare on Caribbean slope of Guanacaste, Tilarán, and Central Cordilleras, to 1,300 m; very rare in intermontane valleys of southern Pacific. Keeps to lower levels of mature wet forest and advanced second growth. Call is a single, loud, harsh note. 5" (13 cm).

Slaty-capped Flycatcher

Leptopogon superciliaris

Similar to Sepia-capped Flycatcher, but has **gray crown** and **conspicuous dark ear patch**. Fairly common on Caribbean slope, from Tilarán Cordillera south; also common on Pacific slope of Talamanca Cordillera; from 500 to 1,600 m. Forages at middle levels of wet forest; typically accompanies mixed flocks. Call is a high, sharp *tswit*. 5" (13 cm).

Yellow-olive
Flycatcher

Yellow-margined
Flycatcher

Greenish Elaenia

Olive-striped
Flycatcher

Sepia-capped
Flycatcher

Slaty-capped
Flycatcher

Common Tody-Flycatcher
Todirostrum cinereum

This pert little bird is distinguished from the Black-headed Tody-Flycatcher by its **entirely yellow underparts** and **yellow iris**; also note two-tone coloration. Common and widespread, to 1,600 m, though less common in northwestern Pacific. Forages actively in lower levels of vegetation in gardens, second growth, and along streams. Calls with high, staccato *chip* notes, which often run together very rapidly. 4" (10 cm).

Black-headed Tody-Flycatcher
Todirostrum nigriceps

Similar to the Common Tody-Flycatcher, but has **white throat** and **dark iris**; also note that the **yellow-green back contrasts with the black cap**. Uncommon in Caribbean lowlands and foothills, to about 1,000 m. Difficult to see since it stays high in trees of advanced second growth, forest edges, and gardens. Gives a series of high *chip* notes, which trail off toward the end. 3" (8 cm).

Black-capped Pygmy-Tyrant
Myiornis atricapillus

The **white spectacles** distinguish it from other diminutive but large-billed flycatchers. Fairly common in Caribbean lowlands and foothills, to 600 m. Inhabits wet forests, advanced second growth, and forest edges, though small size makes it difficult to spot. The buzzy call is easily mistaken for an insect or amphibian. 3" (8 cm).

Slate-headed Tody-Flycatcher
Poecilotriccus sylvia

Told apart from other small flycatchers with gray heads and olive backs by the **long, straight, thick, black bill**. Found from sea level to about 1,000 m, though relatively common only in wet southern Pacific. Stays low in dense vegetation in second growth and more open areas of forests. Call, which is very similar to that of the Northern Bentbill, is a short *trrr*. 4" (10 cm).

Scale-crested Pygmy-Tyrant
Lophotriccus pileatus

The very rarely raised **rufous-tipped black crest feathers** are a noticeable and unique feature, even when not raised. Common on Caribbean slope, from 300 to 1,700 m, and on Pacific slope, from 750 to 1,700 m. Also found in higher hills of Osa Peninsula. Prefers middle levels of wet forests and tall second growth. Produces an assertive series of dry, wooden *chik* notes. 3" (8 cm).

Northern Bentbill
Oncostoma cinereigulare

The **curved bill tip** is diagnostic. Common in wet lowlands and uncommon in northwestern Pacific; occasionally found as high as 1,100 m. Although typically forages from one to six meters above the ground in second growth and more open areas of forests, its small size, drab color, and staid manner, combined with darting flight, make it difficult to see. The often-heard, soft, rolling *perrrrrr* alerts one to its presence; call is slightly longer than the very similar call of the Slate-headed Tody-Flycatcher. 4" (10 cm).

Common
Tody-Flycatcher

Black-headed
Tody-Flycatcher

Black-capped
Pygmy-Tyrant

Slate-headed
Tody-Flycatcher

crest not
raised

Scale-crested
Pygmy-Tyrant

Northern
Bentbill

Ruddy-tailed Flycatcher

Terenotriccus erythrurus

The combination of small size, **gray head**, and **rufous wings, tail, and underparts** is distinctive. Fairly common in wet lowland and foothill forests, to 1,200 m. Perches in lower and middle levels of forest; has habit of periodically raising wings above back, then lowering them, in one quick motion. Call is a high *speeee spit*. 3" (8 cm).

Ochre-bellied Flycatcher

Mionectes oleagineus

A slim, plain olive bird with a noticeably **ochre-colored belly**. Quite common in wet forests of lowlands and foothills, to 1,200 m; uncommon in gallery forests of northwestern Pacific lowlands. Stays low inside mature forest and second growth; also comes to forest edges and gardens. Often flicks one wing up over the back, then the other. Males sing incessantly from low perches, producing a series of sharp *chip* notes that is followed by a number of louder, more emphatic notes. 5" (13 cm).

Tawny-chested Flycatcher

Aphanotriccus capitalis

The **tawny chest** resembles that of Sulphur-rumped Flycatcher, but note **wing bars** and entirely olive-green back and rump. Very uncommon on northern half of Caribbean slope, to 1,000 m. Inhabits lower and middle levels of tall second growth, overgrown forest edges, and streamside thickets. Whistles a quick, upslurred *speeya*. **Endemic to Nicaragua and Costa Rica.** 5" (13 cm).

Bran-colored Flycatcher

Myiophobus fasciatus

The brownish upperparts and streaked breast might suggest a female Blue-black Grassquit (p. 296) or a female Indigo Bunting (p. 312), both of which share the same habitat; but note **flat bill**, **whitish wing bars**, and **white patch on secondaries**. Fairly common in intermontane valleys of southern Pacific, between 700 and 1,200 m. Stays low in second growth and scrub. Repeats a whistled *whee, whee, whee…* . 5" (13 cm).

Sulphur-rumped Flycatcher

Myiobius sulphureipygius

Nearly identical to the Black-tailed Flycatcher, but has darker, **tawny chest and flanks**; also note hint of a dusky bar below eye; the two species are usually found in different habitats. Light-yellow rump could suggest a Buff-rumped Warbler (p. 270), but note lack of superciliary. Fairly common in lowland and foothill wet forests, to 1,200 m. Forages at lower and middle levels, often with mixed flocks. Call is an explosive *swit!*. 5" (13 cm).

Black-tailed Flycatcher

Myiobius atricaudus

Distinguished from nearly identical Sulphur-rumped Flycatcher by paler breast; usually found in different habitat. Light-yellow rump could suggest a Buff-rumped Warbler (p. 270), but note lack of superciliary. Uncommon in southern Pacific lowlands and foothills, to 1,200 m; rare north of Carara. Prefers forest edges, second growth, and edges of mangrove swamps. Call is a colorless *whit*. 5" (13 cm).

Ruddy-tailed
Flycatcher

Ochre-bellied
Flycatcher

Tawny-chested
Flycatcher

Bran-colored
Flycatcher

Sulphur-rumped
Flycatcher

Black-tailed
Flycatcher

Bright-rumped Attila
Attila spadiceus

The combination of **long, hooked bill**, **red iris**, and **bright yellow rump** is diagnostic. A common and widespread bird, to 1,800 m. Found in mature forests, second growth, forest edges, and gardens. Very vocal (though difficult to see when calling); gives an increasingly emphatic *wit, wi-deet, wi-deet, wi-deet, wheeew*, the last note dropping down; also makes a fast *we-hir,we-hir,we-hir,we-hir,we-hir,we-hir* that rises and falls. 8" (20 cm).

Rufous Mourner
Rhytipterna holerythra

Virtually identical to the slightly larger Rufous Piha (p. 214)—best told apart by voice. Fairly common in wet lowlands and foothills, to 1,200 m. Mostly inside mature forest and tall second growth, at middle to upper levels; often accompanies mixed flocks. Whistles a loud, slow, somewhat sad *wheea-tseer* that rises and falls. 8" (20 cm).

Torrent Tyrannulet
Serpophaga cinerea

The only CR bird found along mountain streams that has **blackish cap, wings, and tail**. (The American Dipper [p. 250], which shares the same habitat, is plumper and more uniformly grayish.) A common inhabitant of swift, rocky, highland streams, between about 2,200 and 500 m (occasionally lower on Caribbean slope), from Tilarán Cordillera south. Forages from river rocks and along banks, often pumps tail. Call is a shrill *tseep*. 4" (10 cm).

Long-tailed Tyrant
Colonia colonus

The **two elongated central tail feathers** continue (up to 4" [10 cm]) beyond rest of tail in males; slightly less in females. If the tail feathers cannot be seen, the broad **whitish superciliary and back stripe** are diagnostic. Fairly common in Caribbean lowlands, to about 600 m. Forages from exposed perches in forest clearings and gardens, and along rivers; often in pairs. Call is a sweet, rising *sweeE*. Including elongated central tail feathers, its total length is: 10" (25 cm).

Royal Flycatcher
Onychorhynchus coronatus

Rarely opens spectacular crest, but the closed crown feathers still facilitate the identification by giving the bird a **peculiar hammerheaded appearance**. Also note the **cinnamon rump** and **tawny tail** that contrast with the brown upperparts. Fairly uncommon in Pacific lowlands; also fairly uncommon in Caño Negro region and rare in rest of Caribbean lowlands; to 900 m. Found at lower levels of humid forest, forest edges, and particularly along wooded streams, where it constructs a pendant nest nearly two meters long. Call is a resonant, whistled *keyerink*. 7" (18 cm).

Eye-ringed Flatbill
Rhynchocyclus brevirostris

As its name suggests, this species has a **prominent eye ring** and a **wide, flat bill**. Fairly uncommon in wet forests, from sea level to about 2,000 m; most likely found at middle elevations. Seems lethargic; perches upright in midcanopy, often with mixed flocks. Call is a sharp, harsh *sweezp*. 6" (15 cm).

Bright-rumped
Attila

Rufous
Mourner

Torrent
Tyrannulet

Long-tailed
Tyrant

female

male
(crest raised)

Royal
Flycatcher

Eye-ringed
Flatbill

Ochraceous Pewee
Contopus ochraceus

Larger than the very similar Tufted Flycatcher (p. 206). Rare in Talamanca Cordillera and on Irazú and Turrialba Volcanoes, from 2,200 to 3,000 m. Sallies from exposed perches in treefall gaps and other openings in oak forests; shakes tail upon landing. Call is a shrill *pit, pit, pit*. **Endemic to CR and western Panama**. 7" (18 cm).

Dark Pewee
Contopus lugubris

The **obvious crest** and absence of wing bars distinguish this species from the wood-pewees and the Tropical Pewee. Fairly common at middle and upper elevations, from 1,200 to 2,200 m. Sallies from high exposed perch at forest edges or in gardens, often near streams. Repeats a staccato *pik*. **Endemic to CR and western Panama**. 7" (18 cm).

Olive-sided Flycatcher
Contopus cooperi

White median underparts separate **dusky sides and flanks**, forming unique vest. Looks shorter tailed than other *Contopus*. Fairly common passage migrant from late Aug to late Oct and from mid-March to late May, virtually anywhere below timberline; rare winter resident. Makes long sallies after flying insects, typically returning to the same high exposed perch. Sometimes utters a sharp *pip, pip, pip*. 7" (18 cm).

[The following three species are very difficult to distinguish. Bill color and vocalizations are useful aids in identification. These species can be told apart from the *Empidonax* (p. 204) by their less distinct eye rings and wing bars. Also compare them with the Dark Pewee.]

Western Wood-Pewee
Contopus sordidulus

On the lower mandible, the anterior half (sometimes more) is black; base is orange. A common and widespread passage migrant from late July to mid-Nov and from late March to early June; rare winter resident and possibly a breeding resident in highlands. Found in virtually any habitat where there is an exposed perch. Birds habitually return to the same perch after a sally. Call is a downslurred *peeur*. 6" (15 cm).

Eastern Wood-Pewee
Contopus virens

Lower mandible is orange with dark tip. Very common passage migrant, from mid-Aug to late Nov and from mid-March to mid-May, sea level to 1,500 m, rarely to 2,500 m; rare winter resident, to 1,200 m. Occurs in virtually any habitat where there is an exposed perch. Birds habitually return to the same perch after a sally. Call is a rising *pee-wee*; sometimes whistles its full *pee-a-weee*. 6" (15 cm).

Tropical Pewee
Contopus cinereus

Lower mandible is orange with dark tip. Combination of **bill color**, **pale lores**, and **yellowish belly** is diagnostic. Also note that **crown is darker than rest of head**. Fairly common in Caribbean lowlands and foothills, to 1,000 m; uncommon in Central Valley and in southern Pacific, to 1,300 m; also uncommon in mangroves around Gulf of Nicoya. Frequents gardens, pastures with brush, and forest edges; tends to perch quite low and does not regularly return to the same perch after a sally. Call is a rapid, bubbly, trill. 5" (13 cm).

Ochraceous
Pewee

Dark Pewee

Olive-sided
Flycatcher

Western Wood-Pewee

Eastern
Wood-Pewee

Tropical Pewee

[The *Empidonax* flycatchers on this page are very similar and are among the most difficult birds in Costa Rica to identify to species level. Variable plumage, due to wear and molt, and infrequently given single-note vocalizations only exacerbate the situation. They are also very similar to the wood-pewees and Tropical Pewee (p. 202), but note more distinct eye ring and wing bars.]

Alder Flycatcher
Empidonax alnorum
Willow Flycatcher
Empidonax traillii
Formerly considered conspecific, the two are so alike in aspect and behavior that it is best to regard them as *Empidonax* sp. (or Traill's Flycatcher—the former common name) when seen in the field. Both have an indistinct eye ring, brownish-olive upperparts, white throat, light brownish wash on breast, and pale-yellow lower underparts. Abundant passage migrants from early Sept to early Nov and from mid-Mar to late May, from lowlands to 1,500 m. The Willow Flycatcher is a very uncommon winter resident from Dec to Feb, during which time the Alder Flycatcher is absent. Prefer low perches in fairly open situations (e.g., brushy fields, gardens, hedges, forest edges). Calls are very hard to distinguish; songs are occasionally heard during spring migration (mid-March to late May). The Alder Flycatcher sings a burry *weebyew* and the Willow Flycatcher sings a scratchy *fitz-bew*. 6" (15 cm).

Acadian Flycatcher
Empidonax virescens
Note **longer primary projection** than any other *Empidonax* in CR. Has narrow eye ring, olive upperparts, whitish throat, olive wash on breast, whitish middle of breast, and pale yellow on rest of underparts. Fairly common passage migrant, from mid-Sept to early Nov and from early March to mid-May; uncommon winter resident, from mid-Sept to mid-May; mostly in Caribbean lowlands, but possible elsewhere, to 1,200 m. Most likely in understory of forests and at forest edges, in dense vegetation. Its note is a loud, squeaky *pseeip*. 6" (15 cm).

Yellow-bellied Flycatcher
Empidonax flaviventris
The most readily identifiable of the NA migrant empids, it is the only one with a **dull-yellowish throat**. Told apart from the resident Yellowish Flycatcher (p. 206) by its evenly circular eye ring and overall olive coloration. Common in lowlands and foothills, to 1,500 m, from late Aug to late May. Inhabits lower levels of forest and second growth. Frequently whistles a clear, rising *tsu-wee*, reminiscent of a wood-pewee. 5" (13 cm).

White-throated Flycatcher
Empidonax albigularis
This resident empid is browner than the migrant empids; note **obvious white throat contrasting with brownish chest**. Fairly common around the western and southern base of Irazú Volcano; uncommon along northeastern flank of Guanacaste, Tilarán, and Central Cordilleras; very rare in intermontane valleys of southern Pacific; mostly from 500 to 1,500 m. Forages from low, exposed perches in brushy pastures and marshy areas. Makes a buzzy, rising *pisseep*. 5" (13 cm).

Least Flycatcher
Empidonax minimus
Smaller and grayer than other migrant empids. It has an **obvious eye ring** and a fairly **short bill**; also has the shortest primary projection of any of the migrant empids. A rare NA migrant, from Oct to April; to 1,200 m. Stays at lower levels of second growth and forest edges. Call is a sharp *pit*. 5" (13 cm).

Alder/Willow
Flycatcher

Acadian Flycatcher

Yellow-bellied
Flycatcher

White-throated
Flycatcher

Least Flycatcher

Yellowish Flycatcher

Empidonax flavescens

Somewhat resembles Yellow-bellied Flycatcher (p. 204), but brighter yellow below; also note that **uneven eye ring extends behind the eye**. Common at middle and upper elevations, from 800 to 2,500 m. Inhabits lower and middle levels of mature wet forest and adjacent second growth and gardens. Call is a single, high *tseew*. 5" (13 cm).

Black-capped Flycatcher

Empidonax atriceps

The **black crown** and **strongly elliptical eye ring** distinguish this small native empid. Common in highlands, from about 2,200 m to above timberline. Forages at all levels of forest edges, brushy pastures, and gardens; often quite low and confiding. Call is a single *pwip*. **Endemic to CR and western Panama**. 4" (10 cm).

Tufted Flycatcher

Mitrephanes phaeocercus

The smart **crest** and **bright ochre breast** are key characteristics. Smaller than the Ochraceous Pewee (p. 202), which is similar in behavior and habitat. Common at middle and upper elevations, from 500 to 3,000 m. Perches on exposed twigs in treefall gaps and other openings in mature forest, also at forest edges and gardens; often in pairs. Typically shivers its wings and tail upon alighting after a sally, and often gives a quick, spirited series of *pip*'s. 5" (13 cm).

Fork-tailed Flycatcher

Tyrannus savana

Two-tone coloration and **extremely long tail** are diagnostic. A fairly common resident of intermontane valleys of southern Pacific, from 100 to 1,200 m; very uncommon in Cartago area and casual elsewhere (e.g., northwestern Pacific and Caribbean lowlands). Found in open areas, where it often perches very low in trees or on bushes, if not on the ground. Produces a dry, scratchy, creaking sound. Including elongated outer tail feathers, its total length is: 14" (36 cm).

Scissor-tailed Flycatcher

Tyrannus forficatus

The **pearl-gray upperparts**, **salmon flanks and wing linings**, and **extremely long tail** are diagnostic. A common winter resident in northwestern Pacific lowlands and foothills, less common in Central Valley (where occasionally found above 2,000 m), rare in southern Pacific lowlands, and casual in north central Caribbean lowlands; from Oct to April. Prefers open areas with scattered trees, but also perches on fences and wires. Gives a flat *pik*. Including elongated outer tail feathers, its total length is: 13" (33 cm).

Black Phoebe

Sayornis nigricans

Unlike any other CR flycatcher in coloration; dark bill, eye, and legs differentiate it from similarly patterned thrushes (p. 246). Common in Central Valley and at middle elevations, from 500 to 2,200 m; uncommon on Pacific slope of Guanacaste and Tilarán Cordilleras. Almost always near water, often perching on river rocks, but also on wires, buildings, and the ground. Gives a quick, shrill *chirp*. 7" (18 cm).

Yellowish
Flycatcher

Black-capped
Flycatcher

Tufted
Flycatcher

Fork-tailed
Flycatcher

Scissor-tailed
Flycatcher

Black Phoebe

Great Crested Flycatcher
Myiarchus crinitus

The gray and yellow underparts are brighter, and their junction more sharply defined, than in other *Myiarchus* flycatchers; also note **pale base of lower mandible**. Common winter resident on Pacific slope and fairly common on Caribbean slope, to 1,400 m; from late Sept to early May. Also common passage migrant on both Pacific and Caribbean slopes, to 1,800 m. Possible in almost any wooded habitat, even in mangroves and gardens. Call is a rising *wheep*. 8" (20 cm).

Brown-crested Flycatcher
Myiarchus tyrannulus

Browner above and paler below than Great Crested Flycatcher, with **all-black bill**. Difficult to tell apart from Nutting's Flycatcher; if possible, note gray-brown rump. Common in northwestern Pacific and uncommon in western end of Central Valley; to 900 m. Favors open habitats—such as brushy pastures—and forest and mangrove edges. Call is a repetitious, sharp *whip*. 8" (20 cm).

Ash-throated Flycatcher
Myiarchus cinerascens

A **very pale** *Myiarchus*, with a proportionately shorter and slimmer bill than the Great Crested Flycatcher. Accidental in CR, with an old record (March 1934) from near Ciudad Quesada and a recent report (Oct 2001) from Punta Uva, Limón. 7" (18 cm).

Dusky-capped Flycatcher
Myiarchus tuberculifer

The decidedly **darker crown** distinguishes it from other members of the genus. A common and widespread bird, to 1,800 m. Forages at low and medium heights in gardens and at forest edges. Whistles a somewhat mournful *wheeew* that rises and falls slightly; fairly similar to call of both Nutting's and Panama Flycatchers. 6" (15 cm).

Nutting's Flycatcher
Myiarchus nuttingi

Very similar to Brown-crested Flycatcher and not easily distinguished in the field, though it is slightly smaller and slimmer; if possible, note cinnamon rump. Uncommon in northwestern Pacific and western end of Central Valley; to 1,200 m. Favors lower and middle levels of deciduous and humid forest; also found at forest edges. Whistles a *peer* reminiscent of Dusky-capped Flycatcher, but higher pitched and less melancholy. 7" (18 cm).

Panama Flycatcher
Myiarchus panamensis

Told apart from other *Myiarchus* flycatchers by having **no rufous in wings and tail**. Distinguished from Northern Scrub-Flycatcher (p. 192) by large bill and absence of facial markings. Fairly common in Pacific mangroves, from Gulf of Nicoya south. Whistles a clear *wheer* similar to that of Dusky-capped Flycatcher, sometimes followed by a long, fast, rolling trill. 8" (20 cm).

Great Crested
Flycatcher

Brown-crested
Flycatcher

Ash-throated
Flycatcher

Dusky-capped
Flycatcher

Nutting's
Flycatcher

Panama
Flycatcher

Boat-billed Flycatcher
Megarhynchus pitangua

Very similar to the Great Kiskadee, but the bill is much wider and thicker and the **broad white superciliaries do not quite meet on the nape**. Back, wings, and tail are olive in adult; juvenile has some rufous on the wings and could thus be confused with the Great Kiskadee, so check the bill. Widespread and fairly common in gardens and at forest edges, up to 2,200 m. Produces a rattling call reminiscent of most CR *Melanerpes* woodpeckers (p. 156). 9" (23 cm).

Great Kiskadee
Pitangus sulphuratus

Distinguished from adult Boat-billed Flycatcher by **brown back**, **mostly rufous wings and tail**, and **white superciliaries that meet on the nape**; also note narrower and thinner bill (juvenile Boat-billed Flycatcher has some rufous in the wings, so check the bill). The similar White-ringed Flycatcher, which also has white superciliaries that meet on the nape, is smaller and has no rufous in wings and tail. The Great Kiskadee frequently exposes a yellow crown patch. Common and widespread in gardens and clearings, to 1,800 m. A very vocal bird, its English common name is an onomatopoeic version of the loud three-note call: *kis-ka-dee* (somewhat similar to call of Gray-capped Flycatcher). 9" (23 cm).

Golden-bellied Flycatcher
Myiodynastes hemichrysus

Of all the large flycatchers with bright yellow underparts, the only one with a **dark lateral throat stripe**. Fairly common at middle elevations of Caribbean slope, from Miravalles Volcano south, between about 800 and 1,800 m; also on Pacific slope of Tilarán and northern Talamanca Cordilleras, to 2,300 m. Found at middle levels of gaps in wet forest. Call is a high, squeaky *spee-ah*. **Endemic to CR and western Panama.** 8" (20 cm).

White-ringed Flycatcher
Conopias albovittatus

Like a Social Flycatcher, but with proportionately larger bill, **broad white superciliaries joining on the nape**, and **black ear coverts**. Told apart from larger Great Kiskadee by lack of rufous in wings and tail. Fairly common in wet Caribbean lowlands and foothills, to 500 m; uncommon in Caño Negro region. Favors forest edges, where it perches at middle to upper levels. Calls with a rapid, sputtering series of *beep*'s. 6" (15 cm).

Social Flycatcher
Myiozetetes similis

The broad white superciliaries do not quite meet on the nape and the ear coverts are dark gray (compare with White-ringed Flycatcher and Rusty-margined Flycatcher [p. 328]); also note the short bill. A very common and widespread species, to 2,200 m. Found at lower and middle levels in gardens and along streams. Calls with an agitated *chip, cheer-de-cheer-de, chip* that alternates up and down (song of birds in southern Pacific has a squeakier and less colorful quality). 6" (15 cm).

Gray-capped Flycatcher
Myiozetetes granadensis

Like a Social Flycatcher, but with **gray crown and nape**, and **narrow white superciliaries ending just behind the eye**. The Tropical Kingbird (p. 212) lacks superciliaries. Common in wet lowlands; less common in foothills and middle elevations, to 1,500 m. Forages at lower and middle levels in gardens and along streams. Call is a single, short *wick*; also makes an agitated, squeaky *bee-be-dee*, recalling a Great Kiskadee. 6" (15 cm).

Boat-billed
Flycatcher

Great
Kiskadee

Golden-bellied
Flycatcher

White-ringed
Flycatcher

Social
Flycatcher

Gray-capped
Flycatcher

Streaked Flycatcher
Myiodynastes maculatus

Very similar in appearance to Sulphur-bellied Flycatcher, but differs in having **pink basal half of lower mandible**, **cream-colored superciliary**, **thin malar stripe**, and whitish belly. Fairly common in Pacific lowlands and Caño Negro region; less common at middle elevations of Pacific slope, to 1,200 m; casual on Caribbean slope. Prefers middle and upper levels of gardens and forest edges. Call is a harsh, squeaky *pick-pyew*. 8" (20 cm).

Sulphur-bellied Flycatcher
Myiodynastes luteiventris

Similar to Streaked Flycatcher, but differs in having **mostly black bill** (pale at very base of lower mandible), **white superciliary**, **thick malar stripe**, and yellowish belly. Also compare with Piratic Flycatcher (p. 192). Common passage migrant, from early March to mid-May and from early Aug to mid-Oct; common breeding resident from April to Sept. Migrants can show up almost anywhere, to 2,200 m. Breeding resident nests in northern half of CR, including the Central Valley, to 2,000 m; it does not nest in Caribbean lowlands. A noisy inhabitant of gardens and forest edges, typically at upper levels. Call is a high, squeaky *swee-eeah*. 8" (20 cm).

Tropical Kingbird
Tyrannus melancholicus

Very similar to Western Kingbird, but the **tail appears notched** when the bird is perched; in flight, note little contrast between olive back and dark olive-brown tail. Gray-capped Flycatcher (p. 210) has obvious white brow and bright yellow on upper breast. The very rare Gray Kingbird is white below. One of the most common birds in CR, to 2,200 m. Pairs or individuals inhabit gardens and open areas, often perching on utility wires. Call is a spritely *bee, bibididi*. 8" (20 cm).

Western Kingbird
Tyrannus verticalis

Very similar to Tropical Kingbird, but the **tail appears square tipped** when the bird is perched; in flight, note contrast between olive back and black tail, which shows narrow white outer edges. Uncommon winter resident, from Nov to April, in northwestern Pacific and western Central Valley; rare in southern Pacific; to 1,000 m. Favors gardens and open areas; a number of individuals are often found in the same area. Sometimes gives a shrill series of *pik*'s. 8" (20 cm).

Eastern Kingbird
Tyrannus tyrannus

The two-toned coloration and noticeable **white-tipped tail** are distinctive. In flight, note **dark underwing**. A very common passage migrant in Caribbean lowlands, uncommon elsewhere; from early Sept to late Oct and from mid-March to early May; to 1,700 m. Migrates through Caribbean lowlands in huge numbers, flying in flocks of dozens of individuals. Usually silent in migration. 8" (20 cm).

Gray Kingbird
Tyrannus dominicensis

Brings to mind a Tropical Kingbird, but is paler and lacks yellow on underparts. In flight, note **pale underwing**. A very rare passage migrant along the Caribbean coast, from Sept to early Oct and in March. Most reports are of single birds accompanying flocks of Eastern Kingbirds. 9" (23 cm).

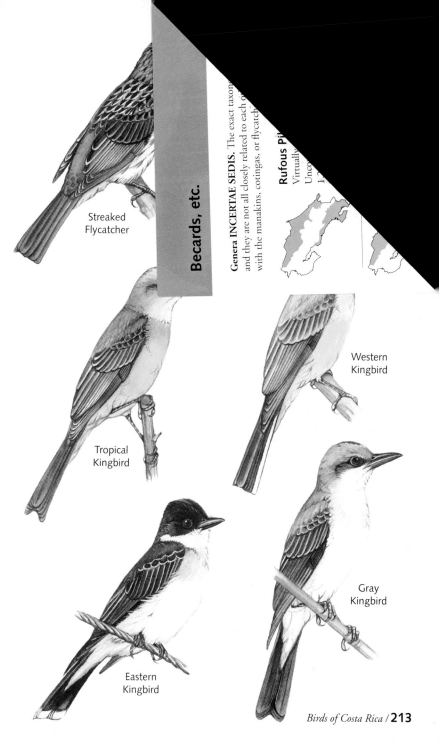

Streaked
Flycatcher

Becards, etc.

Genera INCERTAE SEDIS. The exact taxon[...] and they are not all closely related to each o[...] with the manakins, cotingas, or flycatch[...]

Rufous Pi[...]
Virtuall[...]
Unco[...]
1[...]

Tropical
Kingbird

Western
Kingbird

Eastern
Kingbird

Gray
Kingbird

mic placement of these species is currently uncertain,
...her. In the past, some of these species have been included
...rs, or even placed in their own family (e.g., Tityridae).

...na   *Lipaugus unirufus*
...identical to the Rufous Mourner (p. 200)—best told apart by voice.
...mmon on Caribbean slope, fairly common on southern Pacific slope; to
...00 m. Favors middle levels of mature wet forest, where often not easy to see
because it perches placidly and its periodic vocalizations are quite ventriloquial.
Delivers a loud, vibrant *PEEAAH!* and also a whistled *whee-ur-weet*. 9" (23 cm).

Thrushlike Schiffornis   *Schiffornis turdina*
A nondescript olive-brown bird. Similar to female Tawny-crested Tanager
(p. 280), but note smaller bill and "big-eyed" look. Little or no range overlap with
the much larger Mountain Robin (p. 250). Fairly common in southern Pacific, to
1,700 m; fairly uncommon in Caribbean foothills, to 1,000 m; very uncommon
in Caribbean lowlands. Usually found singly in understory of mature wet forest;
somewhat sluggish and confiding; perches sideways on vertical stems. Whistles a
clear protracted note, a shorter slurred note, and a quick final note: *pweeeee-huwi-
pit.* 6" (15 cm).

Speckled Mourner   *Laniocera rufescens*
No other rufous bird shows **dark wing coverts with pale rufous tips**; also
note indistinct scalloping on breast. (Compare with Rufous Piha [this page]
and Rufous Mourner [p. 200].) Rare in Caribbean lowlands and foothills, and
in southern Pacific from Quepos south; to 800 m. Perches quite motionlessly
at lower and middle levels of mature wet forest, often near a stream or swamp;
accompanies mixed flocks. Seldom heard; displaying males sing a clear *tlee, dee*,
with a distinct pause between notes. 8" (20 cm).

Gray-headed Piprites   *Piprites griseiceps*
The combination of **white eye ring**, **yellow throat**, and **lack of wing bars** is
distinctive. Rare in Caribbean lowlands and foothills, to 1,000 m. Accompanies
mixed flocks in lower and middle levels of mature wet forest and adjacent tall
second growth. Call is a liquid *whit!*; sings an undulating two-second phrase of
quick, sputtering notes. **Endemic from eastern Guatemala to CR.** 5" (13 cm).

Cinnamon Becard   *Pachyramphus cinnamomeus*
Told apart from female Rose-throated Becard (p. 216) and all other cinnamon/
rufous species by faint **buffy supraloral stripe** and **dusky lores**. Unlike other
CR becards, male and female are virtually identical. Common in Caribbean
lowlands and foothills, to 900 m; very uncommon in Pacific coastal lowlands,
from Gulf of Nicoya south. Caribbean-slope birds are found at lower and middle
levels of gardens and forest edges; Pacific birds favor vicinity of mangroves.
Whistles a high, melancholy, descending *twee, twee-tee-tee-tee.* 6" (15 cm).

Rufous Piha

Thrushlike
Schiffornis

Speckled
Mourner

Gray-headed
Piprites

Cinnamon
Becard

Rose-throated Becard
Pachyramphus aglaiae

Male of resident race has **black crown** and **gray body**, male of migrant race is mostly dark with gray belly; females of both races are identical to each other. Neither race shows rose in throat. Female's contrasting **dark crown** distinguishes her from Cinnamon Becard (p. 214). Resident race is fairly common in lowlands of northwestern Pacific; uncommon in central and southern Pacific; to 1,200 m. Migrant race is very rare in Caribbean lowlands, from Nov to March. Pairs forage at middle and upper levels of mature dry forest, at edges of humid forest, and in gardens. Gives a sharp, upwardly inflected *swee-ah*. 7" (18 cm).

Barred Becard
Pachyramphus versicolor

Both sexes are uniquely patterned. Fairly uncommon in highlands, from Tilarán Cordillera south, between 1,500 and 3,000 m. Individuals or pairs forage in middle levels of montane forest, forest edges, and adjacent gardens; often with mixed flocks. Sings an energetic series of about ten notes: the first three notes rise in pitch, the following notes then maintain the same pitch but increase in pace until the last note, which drops in pitch. 5" (13 cm).

Black-and-white Becard
Pachyramphus albogriseus

Similar to White-winged Becard, but male has **gray back** and **white supraloral stripe**; female has distinctive **chestnut cap**. Rare at middle elevations, from Tilarán Cordillera south, mostly on Caribbean slope, from 500 to 1,800 m; descends to adjacent lowlands during latter half of year. Individuals or pairs accompany mixed flocks at middle levels of mature wet forest. Calls with a very high, thin *sweea, sweea, sweea, sweea*. 6" (15 cm).

White-winged Becard
Pachyramphus polychopterus

Male distinguished from male Black-and-white Becard by **black upper back** and **black lores** (female somewhat similar to female Black-and-white Becard, but note absence of chestnut on crown). Female resembles a flycatcher in coloration and behavior, but note **buffy wing bars and wing edging**, and **buff-tipped tail feathers**. Fairly uncommon in wet lowlands and foothills, rare in northwestern Pacific; to 1,200 m. Individuals or pairs inhabit middle levels of second growth, forest edges, and gardens; found mostly in gallery forest in the northwest. Sings a fast series of sweet *chew* notes, the first followed by a slight pause. 6" (15 cm).

Masked Tityra
Tityra semifasciata

The **red orbital area** and **red basal half of bill** differentiate both sexes from the Black-crowned Tityra. Common and widespread, to 1,800 m. Pairs or small groups visit fruiting trees in gardens and at forest edges. Frequently makes dry, buzzy squeaks that could suggest an insect noise or a bathtub toy. 8" (20 cm).

Black-crowned Tityra
Tityra inquisitor

Similar to Masked Tityra, but note **all-dark bill**. Male has **black crown**. Female has **chestnut sides of face**; chestnut color can appear reddish in certain light, thus increasing the resemblance to a female Masked Tityra. Widespread but fairly uncommon, to 1,200 m. Pairs or small groups visit fruiting trees in gardens and at forest edges. Infrequent vocalizations are softer than those of Masked Tityra. 7" (18 cm).

male
resident race

female

Rose-throated
Becard

female

male

Barred
Becard

female

male

Black-and-white
Becard

female

male

White-winged
Becard

male

female

Masked
Tityra

male

Black-crowned
Tityra

female

Cotingas

COTINGIDAE. This incredibly varied group of neotropical birds shows no single shared morphological trait that aids the observer in assigning them to this family. Likewise, internal anatomy, vocalizations, and behavior differ widely among the sixty or so species currently placed here. Fortunately, the seven species found in CR should not present any great identification challenges.

Yellow-billed Cotinga
Carpodectes antoniae

Male and female very similar to respective sexes of Snowy Cotinga (but no range overlap); note **yellow bill**. Very uncommon in southern Pacific lowlands, to 800 m. Actively forages for fruit in canopy of mature wet forest and in tall trees of adjacent open areas; also found in mangroves. Generally silent. **Endemic to CR and western Panama**. 8" (20 cm).

Snowy Cotinga
Carpodectes nitidus

Male and female very similar to respective sexes of Yellow-billed Cotinga (but no range overlap); note **grayish bill**. Also, tends to be more sluggish in its movements and not known to visit mangroves. Uncommon in Caribbean lowlands, rarely to 700 m. **Endemic from northern Honduras to western Panama**. 8" (20 cm).

Lovely Cotinga
Cotinga amabilis

Very similar to Turquoise Cotinga, but no range overlap. Colorful male not likely confused (compare, however, with male Blue Dacnis [p. 290]); overall size, shape, and coloration of female could bring to mind a dove or thrush, but none of these appear **scaled above** and **spotted below**. Rare in Caribbean foothills, from Miravalles Volcano to near Panama; to 1,700 m. Feeds on fruit in canopy of mature wet forest and in tall trees of adjacent open areas. 8" (20 cm).

Turquoise Cotinga
Cotinga ridgwayi

Both sexes very similar to Lovely Cotinga, but no range overlap (compare male with male Blue Dacnis [p. 290]). Male has **black eye ring** and shows black feather bases on shoulders and back; overall size, shape, and coloration of female could bring to mind a dove or thrush, but none of these appear **scaled above** and **spotted below**. Uncommon in southern Pacific, to 1,800 m. Perches and feeds in canopy of mature wet forest, as well as partially cleared areas. **Endemic to CR and western Panama**. 7" (18 cm).

Purple-throated Fruitcrow
Querula purpurata

The male's magenta throat can be difficult to see in backlight conditions—and the female and juvenile are entirely black—but the **broad, light-gray bill** and chunky proportions (with broad wings and short tail) should distinguish this species from other medium-sized black birds. Fairly common in wet Caribbean lowlands, to 500 m. Noisy groups of four or more birds move through middle and upper levels of mature wet forest, forest edges, and adjacent gardens, sometimes with mixed flocks. Gives a querulous, throaty *quaah, quaah*. 11" (28 cm).

male

male

female

Yellow-billed
Cotinga

Snowy
Cotinga

male

male

female

female

Lovely
Cotinga

Turquoise
Cotinga

male

female

Purple-throated
Fruitcrow

Cotingas

Three-wattled Bellbird
Procnias tricarunculatus

The adult male is unique; the female somewhat resembles a flycatcher in coloration, but note her large size and lack of any facial markings. Juvenile males look like females, but have short wattles. Fairly common breeding resident, from March to June, in Tilarán Cordillera (to 1,500 m) and Talamanca Cordillera (to 2,400 m), though also breeds in Guanacaste and Central Cordilleras and on hills of Nicoya Peninsula; disperses to lower elevations after breeding, probably following regular annual routes. Forages at middle and upper levels of mature wet forest, humid forest, and advanced second growth. Males call from high, bare perches with sounds that include a very loud *EENK!* and an extremely high-pitched utterance. **Endemic from eastern Honduras to western Panama**. Male 12" (30 cm); female 10" (25 cm).

Bare-necked Umbrellabird
Cephalopterus glabricollis

Though the adult male's spectacular scarlet throat sac is only inflated during breeding displays, its size and **distinctive crest** should preclude identification problems; even females, which are smaller and have shorter crests, are fairly distinctive. Uncommon on Caribbean slope from Miravalles Volcano south. Breeds from March to June at middle elevations, from 800 to 2,000 m; then migrates to foothills and contiguous lowlands, from 500 down to 50 m. Inhabits lower and middle levels of mature wet forest. Generally silent, though wings produce a deep rustling in flight; displaying males emit a deep, hollow *huuU!* **Endemic to CR and western Panama**. Male 17" (43 cm); female 14" (36 cm).

Manakins

PIPRIDAE. A neotropical family of small woodland birds. Predominantly frugivorous; their bills are short with a wide base. Males sport bright and/or contrasting plumage, while females are generally greenish; juvenile males resemble females and take a year or more to acquire adult plumage. The males perform courtship displays that vary from subtle to sublime. Females tend to the nesting chores.

White-collared Manakin
Manacus candei

The dapper male is unmistakable. Female and juvenile of this species are virtually identical to those of the Orange-collared Manakin (no range overlap); they can be distinguished from other small olive-green birds (e.g., flycatchers and euphonias) by their **bright-orange legs**. Common in Caribbean lowlands and foothills, to 900 m. Stays in lower levels of second growth and forest edges. Gives a rippling *brrrreee* and a high *peee-peuw*; displaying males produce loud snapping and popping noises with their wings. **Illustration of female and juvenile same as for Orange-collared Manakin**. 4" (10 cm).

Orange-collared Manakin
Manacus aurantiacus

Male's **orange collar** is distinctive; female and juvenile of this species are virtually identical to those of White-collared Manakin (no range overlap). Female lacks protruding central rectrices of female Long-tailed Manakin (p. 222). Fairly common in southern Pacific lowlands and foothills, to 1,100 m. Inhabits lower levels of mature wet forest, second growth, and forest edges. Calls with a slightly rising *chewwe*; in addition to wing snapping, displaying males also make a buzzing noise. **Endemic to CR and western Panama. Illustration of female and juvenile same as for White-collared Manakin**. 4" (10 cm).

male

female

Three-wattled
Bellbird

breeding
male

female

Bare-necked
Umbrellabird

male

male

female/juv.

White-collared
Manakin

White-collared/
Orange-collared Manakin

Orange-collared
Manakin

Long-tailed Manakin
Chiroxiphia linearis

Male very similar to male Lance-tailed Manakin, but note very long central rectrices; juvenile male also has red crown. Female virtually identical to female Lance-tailed Manakin (no range overlap). Female similar to female Orange-collared Manakin (p. 220). Common in northwestern Pacific and western Central Valley; uncommon elsewhere in its range; to 1,500 m. Forages at lower and middle levels of forest and advanced second growth. Calls include a liquid *who-wee-do* and a nasal *waahh*. Males display on low perches, while emitting an undulating *chur-wu, chur-wu*, with an underlying buzzy chatter. **Illustration for female Long-tailed Manakin same as for female Lance-tailed Manakin.** Male 10" (25 cm); female 6" (15 cm).

Lance-tailed Manakin
Chiroxiphia lanceolata

Male very similar in appearance and behavior to male Long-tailed Manakin, but note short central rectrices; juvenile male also has red crown. Female virtually identical to female Long-tailed Manakin (no range overlap). Fairly common near Panama border in southern Pacific, from 1,000 to 1,500 m. Feeds at middle levels of humid forest and second growth. **Illustration for female Lance-tailed Manakin same as for female Long-tailed Manakin.** 6" (15 cm).

White-ruffed Manakin
Corapipo altera

All-dark male has distinctive **white throat**. Female shows greater contrast between **grayish throat** and rest of body than do other female manakins. Common in middle elevations; from 400 to 1,000 m on Caribbean slope, from 1,000 to 1,500 m in southern Pacific, and above 600 m on Osa Peninsula. From July to Jan, often moves to lower elevations. Feeds at lower and middle levels of mature forest, second growth, and forest edges. Makes a high, squeaky, rolling *spweeea*. 4" (10 cm).

Blue-crowned Manakin
Pipra coronata

The **glittering-blue crown** on the otherwise black male is distinctive; female has **brighter green upperparts** than other CR manakins. Common in southern Pacific lowlands and foothills, to 1,400 m; uncommon near Panama border on Caribbean slope, to 1,200 m. Found in lower levels of mature wet forest and advanced second growth. Displaying males give a fast, bubbly series of notes followed by a harsh *per-rreck!*. 4" (10 cm).

White-crowned Manakin
Pipra pipra

Male not likely confused; female has decidedly **grayish head** and **dark-red iris**. Uncommon on Caribbean slope of Central and Talamanca Cordilleras, from 500 to 1,500 m. Favors lower and middle levels of mature wet forest and adjacent advanced second growth. Periodically utters a harsh, upwardly inflected *screeaah!*. 4" (10 cm).

Red-capped Manakin
Pipra mentalis

Male is readily identified; female is **dull olive-green** with **pale pinkish bill**. Common in wet lowlands and uncommon in foothills, to 1,100 m. Favors mature wet forest, but also occurs in second growth and sometimes gardens; feeds at lower and middle levels. Produces a looping, drawn-out *sp, sp, spweeeeee*, followed by a sharp *spip!*. 4" (10 cm).

juv. male

male

male

Long-tailed
Manakin

female

Long-tailed/
Lance-tailed Manakin

Lance-tailed
Manakin

male

male

female

White-ruffed
Manakin

female

Blue-crowned
Manakin

male

male

female

female

Red-capped
Manakin

White-crowned
Manakin

Sharpbill

OXYRUNCIDAE. Currently placed in this monotypic family, the Sharpbill has often been considered one of the Cotingidae, or even a member of the Tyrannidae. It has a very spotty distribution throughout the neotropics, from CR to southeastern Brazil.

Sharpbill
Oxyruncus cristatus

Seen from below, it could be confused with the Speckled Tanager (p. 288), but note the **plain olive upperparts** and **sharply pointed bill**. Very uncommon in middle-elevation forests of Caribbean slope from Miravalles Volcano south, between 500 and 1,400 m. Stays at upper levels of mature wet forest and forest edges; joins mixed flocks, though quite unobtrusive. Makes a high, buzzy, arcing trill: *tseeeeeuuuuuh.* 7" (18 cm).

Vireos

VIREONIDAE. A New World family that includes vireos, greenlets, shrike-vireos, and peppershrikes. Generally attired in drab olive along with green, yellow, and/or white; most species (except the greenlets) have fairly strong, hooked bills. The vireos resemble wood-warblers (p. 254), but have heavier bills and tend to be less active. Most species sing frequently if not very melodically.

Yellow-throated Vireo
Vireo flavifrons

The **bright yellow spectacles, throat, and breast**, together with **white wing bars**, are a unique combination. A common and widespread NA migrant, from late Sept to late April, to 1,800 m. Found in a variety of habitats, but typically in gardens and second growth, and at forest edges; often accompanies mixed flocks. Makes a descending series of harsh, fast notes: *cheh-cheh-cheh-cheh-cheh-cheh.* 5" (13 cm).

White-eyed Vireo
Vireo griseus

The only vireo in CR that combines **yellow spectacles**, **white wing bars**, and **white throat**. Juvenile has a dark iris. A very rare NA migrant known from a handful of records along the Caribbean coast; one record from the Puerto Viejo de Sarapiquí area (Jan 2004); and one report of a bird seen and heard in Monteverde (March 1997). Song, which may be heard in March or April, is harsh and fast with a burry quality. 5" (13 cm).

Mangrove Vireo
Vireo pallens

A **drab** vireo with **yellow lores** and **narrow white wing bars**. Fairly common in Pacific mangroves, south to Tarcoles. Will often respond if one makes pishing and squeaking noises. Sings a scratchy, monotone *chi-chi-chi-chi-chi-chi-chi.* 4" (10 cm).

Blue-headed Vireo
Vireo solitarius

The **white throat and spectacles contrast with the gray-blue head**. A rare NA migrant, from late Sept to late March. The few records suggest it could show up just about anywhere, though more likely on Pacific slope or in highlands. 5" (13 cm).

Sharpbill

Yellow-throated
Vireo

White-eyed
Vireo

Mangrove
Vireo

Blue-headed
Vireo

Philadelphia Vireo
Vireo philadelphicus

Could be mistaken for a nonbreeding Tennessee Warbler (p. 254), but has thicker bill and is more sluggish. Similar to Brown-capped Vireo, but distinguished by **gray cap** and **yellow throat**. Has more **obvious eye line** than rare Warbling Vireo and, although the amount of yellow on the undersides is variable, always shows some **yellow on the breast and throat**. Fairly common and widespread NA migrant, though somewhat less common on Caribbean side of CR, from late Oct to late April, to 2,200 m. Forages at lower and middle levels of second growth, forest edges, and gardens; often with mixed flocks. Generally silent. 5" (13 cm).

Brown-capped Vireo
Vireo leucophrys

Similar to Philadelphia Vireo, but with noticeably **brown cap**; also has **white throat**. Fairly common in middle and upper elevations, between 1,500 and 2,500 m, from Tilarán Cordillera south. Forages at middle and upper levels of second growth, forest edges, and gardens; often with mixed flocks. Sings a short, lively warble of alternating higher and lower notes. 5" (13 cm).

Warbling Vireo
Vireo gilvus

Like a pale Philadelphia Vireo, but note **subtle line through eye** and **absence of yellow on throat**. Also compare with a nonbreeding Tennessee Warbler (p. 254). A very rare NA migrant, from late Sept to late April; mostly in northern half of CR, to 800 m. Makes a nasal mewing. 5" (13 cm).

Yellow-green Vireo
Vireo flavoviridis

Similar to Red-eyed Vireo, but with much more yellow below and less distinct facial striping. Common breeding resident on Pacific side of CR from lowlands to about 1,500 m, rather uncommon on Caribbean slope; migrates to SA after breeding (most gone by late Oct), begins returning in late Jan. Forages at middle and upper levels of second growth and gardens. Sings short simple phrases repetitiously, often while hidden in vegetation. 6" (15 cm).

Red-eyed Vireo
Vireo olivaceus

The **white superciliary** (**bordered above and below by black**) is fairly distinctive. Usually quite pale below, but some birds show yellow on flanks and vent, thus causing confusion with Yellow-green Vireo. A very common and widespread passage migrant, from mid-Aug to late Nov and from late March to late May; to 2,000 m. Can turn up almost anywhere. Generally silent. 6" (15 cm).

Black-whiskered Vireo
Vireo altiloquus

Resembles both Yellow-green and Red-eyed Vireos; the definitive **dark malar stripe** is not always easy to see and wet or molting birds of the previous two species could appear to have such a mark. A casual NA migrant on Caribbean side of CR. Seems to favor dense undergrowth in relatively open areas. Generally silent. **Not illustrated**. 6" (15 cm).

Philadelphia
Vireo

Brown-capped
Vireo

Warbling
Vireo

Yellow-green
Vireo

Red-eyed
Vireo

Yellow-winged Vireo
Vireo carmioli

No other vireo or warbler in CR combines **yellow wing bars** with **yellow underparts** (resembles Yellow Tyrannulet [p. 188], but no range overlap). Common in highlands of Central and Talamanca Cordilleras, from 1,500 m to timberline. Forages at all levels in mature forests, forest edges, and gardens; often accompanies mixed flocks. Sings a leisurely series of two- and three-note phrases with distinct pauses between each phrase. **Endemic to CR and western Panama**. 4" (10 cm).

Scrub Greenlet
Hylophilus flavipes

No similar bird has both a **pale iris** and a **pink bill**. Uncommon on southern Pacific slope, to 900 m. Stays low in dense scrub in open areas; also in bamboo plantations. Sings a sweet and simple w*e-cher, we-cher, we-cher, we-cher, we-cher, we cher, wee*. 5" (13 cm).

Tawny-crowned Greenlet
Hylophilus ochraceiceps

Brings to mind a female Plain Antvireo (p. 180), but note **pale iris**. Fairly common on Caribbean slope (more common in foothills) and in southern Pacific (more common in lowlands); to 1,200 m. Forages actively at lower and middle levels of mature wet forest. Small, noisy groups often accompany mixed flocks. Utters an agitated *doy, doy, doy, doy* (like a Northern Barred-Woodcreeper [p. 168]) and a high, shrill whistle (like a Scaly-breasted Wren [p. 244]). 4" (10 cm).

Lesser Greenlet
Hylophilus decurtatus

Like a wood-warbler in size, pattern, and behavior; somewhat resembles the very rare Nashville Warbler (p. 254), but only shows some yellow on the flanks (not on throat, breast, and vent). Coloration like that of the breeding male Tennessee Warbler (p. 254), but note **white eye ring**. Very common and widespread, to 1,500 m. Forages actively in middle and upper levels of forests, forest edges, and advanced second growth; usually in small groups and with mixed flocks. Repetitiously and leisurely sings a short, warbled phrase: *chi-uree*. 4" (10 cm).

Rufous-browed Peppershrike
Cyclarhis gujanensis

The **rufous superciliary**, **gray head**, and **yellow underparts** are a unique combination. Fairly common in middle elevations and highlands from Tilarán Cordillera south, between 700 and 2,400 m. Also fairly common in northwestern Pacific and in Caño Negro region, and in mangroves of Gulf of Nicoya and central Pacific coast. Highland birds frequent forest edges and gardens, lowland birds are more likely in gallery forest and mangroves; forages at all levels. From a high, hidden perch, incessantly sings rather grosbeaklike musical phrases, periodically switching to another song from its ample repertoire. 6" (15 cm).

Green Shrike-Vireo
Vireolanius pulchellus

The only **bright-green** bird with a **yellow throat**. Caribbean slope birds have blue foreheads. Fairly common in wet forests of Caribbean slope and southern Pacific, to 1,200 m. More often heard than seen (sings tirelessly from high in the forest canopy); occasionally forages at lower levels along forest edges. Caribbean birds whistle a clear *peeta-peeta-peeta*; Pacific birds utter a single-syllabled series (*peer-peer-peer*). 6" (15 cm).

Yellow-winged
Vireo

Scrub
Greenlet

Tawny-crowned
Greenlet

Lesser
Greenlet

Rufous-browed
Peppershrike

Green
Shrike-Vireo

CORVIDAE. A widespread family that is familiar to many birders. CR's five representatives are all omnivorous, noisy, active foragers, though one species, the Black-chested Jay, is a bit more furtive.

White-throated Magpie-Jay — *Calocitta formosa*

Unmistakable. Common throughout the northwestern Pacific, to 1,200 m. Seems to be extending its range south along the Pacific coast, with recent sightings south of Dominical; also spreading in northern central region, with recent reports from the region between Arenal and Guápiles; has entered western Central Valley (to Santa Ana and Belén). Noisy groups travel through both forested and more open areas, including gardens. Varied vocalizations range from raspy scolding notes to sweet oriole-like chirping. 19" (48 cm).

Black-chested Jay — *Cyanocorax affinis*

Plumage pattern similar to Brown Jay, but has **blue-violet upperparts** and **yellow iris**. Uncommon in southern Caribbean lowlands, north to Valle de la Estrella; recently found near San Vito in southern Pacific. Small groups move through all levels of vegetation in forests, forest edges, and gardens. Not as bold or obvious as other jays in CR. Among its many calls is a liquid *chew-chew-chew-chewp*. 13" (33 cm).

Brown Jay — *Cyanocorax morio*

No other CR jay is **dark brown above**. Juvenile has yellow bill and eye ring. Common at middle elevations, to 2,300 m; fairly uncommon in Caribbean and Pacific lowlands. Boisterous parties roam through trees, avoiding mature-forest habitats. Gives a rather shrill and agitated *piyah, piyah*; makes an audible popping noise with its special throat sac. 15" (38 cm).

Azure-hooded Jay — *Cyanolyca cucullata*

A distinctive bird, with a **powder-blue crown** that contrasts with a **deep-blue body**. Fairly common at middle elevations of Caribbean slope, from 800 to 2,000 m; also on Pacific side of Tilarán Cordillera and in Dota region. Groups forage at all levels in mature wet forest. Has a number of calls, including a screeching *eet-eet*, a hoarse *aaak*, and a shrill *eenk, eenk*. 11" (28 cm).

Silvery-throated Jay — *Cyanolyca argentigula*

The **silvery-white throat** is diagnostic on this small, dark jay. Very uncommon in highlands of Irazú and Turrialba Volcanoes and Talamanca Cordillera, from 2,000 to 3,200 m. Pairs or groups forage at middle and upper levels of mature oak forests. Utters a harsh *nyah-nyah-nyah-nyah*. **Endemic to CR and western Panama**. 10" (25 cm).

White-throated
Magpie-Jay

Black-chested Jay

adult

juv.

Brown Jay

Azure-hooded Jay

Silvery-throated Jay

HIRUNDINIDAE. The swallows and martins are often compared to the similarly sized swifts (p. 116), another group of streamlined aerialists that ply the skies in pursuit of flying insects. Swallows and martins have deeper wingstrokes, however, and all but the male Purple Martin (p. 234) have paler undersides. And, unlike swifts, they are frequently seen perched on wires, branches, or even buildings. Unendowed vocalists, most produce little more than high-pitched twittering.

Blue-and-white Swallow — *Pygochelidon cyanoleuca*

Distinguished from following three species by **black undertail coverts**. Common at middle and upper elevations, from 500 to 3,100 m; occasionally to sea level, as at Dominical. Small groups forage over open areas, in both urban and rural settings; often fairly high. 4" (10 cm).

Mangrove Swallow — *Tachycineta albilinea*

The **white rump** sets it apart from the Blue-and-white Swallow and the following two species; also note **white line above lore**. Common in lowlands; uncommon at higher elevations, to 1,000 m. Forages by skimming low over water surfaces and fields, often far from mangroves. 5" (13 cm).

Tree Swallow — *Tachycineta bicolor*

Very similar to Blue-and-white Swallow, but note **white undertail coverts**. Distinguished from Mangrove and Violet-green Swallows by **absence of white on rump**. A rare NA migrant (though in some years irruptive), from Sept to April; to 1,500 m. Individuals forage over open areas (often near water), accompanying other swallows, except in irruptive years, when large monospecific flocks can occur. 6" (15 cm).

Violet-green Swallow — *Tachycineta thalassina*

Resembles previous three species, but note **white extending onto sides of rump**; also note white on sides of face. A casual winter resident, from Nov to March, with scattered reports countrywide. Forages fairly high in the air, usually in the company of other swallows. 5" (13 cm).

Cliff Swallow — *Petrochelidon pyrrhonota*

Members of the race most commonly seen in CR (*pyrrhonota*) can be identified from below by **dark throat** and **squarish tail**, and from above by **pale forehead** and **pale-buff rump**. However, one race (*melanogaster*) has rufous forehead and more richly colored rump, and is thus readily confused with the very rare Cave Swallow. An abundant passage migrant, from mid-Aug to early Nov and from March to mid-May, to 1,500 m; rare winter resident in northwestern lowlands. Migrants move steadily through in company of Bank Swallows (p. 234) and Barn Swallows (p. 236); occasionally feed over open areas. 5" (13 cm).

Cave Swallow — *Petrochelidon fulva*

A very casual NA migrant. Only three recent reports from CR, each of individuals in association with Barn Swallows (p. 236): Abangaritos (Jan 2002), Chomes (Feb 2002), and Filadefia (Nov 2005). With so few sight reports in CR, difficult to say which race visits the country, though it is most likely *pallida*, which has a pale, tawny forehead and an even paler throat. 5" (13 cm).

Blue-and-white
Swallow

Mangrove
Swallow

Swallows

Tree
Swallow

Violet-green
Swallow

pyrrhonota
race

Cliff
Swallow

pallida
race

Cave
Swallow

Purple Martin
Progne subis

Male—the only CR swallow or martin with dark underparts—could be mistaken for a swift (p.116), but in good light shows **shiny blue-black plumage**. Female resembles Gray-breasted Martin, but has **grayish forehead and nape**. Fairly common passage migrant in Caribbean lowlands, though mostly along coast, from mid-Aug to mid-Oct and from Feb to April; rare in Central Valley and on Pacific slope. Migrating flocks often fly higher than other species of migrating swallows. 8" (20 cm).

Gray-breasted Martin
Progne chalybea

Resembles female Purple Martin, but lacks gray on forehead and nape. The **dark, steely-blue upperparts** distinguish it from the Northern Rough-winged Swallow; both species have dingy underparts. Fairly common and widespread in both town and country, to 1,700 m. Forages over open areas, often near water; roosts and nests in tree cavities, as well as under bridges and in open-ended iron beams of buildings (e.g., gas and bus stations). 7" (18 cm).

Brown-chested Martin
Progne tapera

In color and pattern like a Bank Swallow, though larger. A very casual SA migrant: one report of nine individuals from Golfito area in early Oct 2004; another report of one individual (with Gray-breasted Martins) near Cortés in late March 2006. Also several reports from San José area, but none in last twenty years. Forages over open areas, accompanying other swallows and martins. 7" (18 cm).

Bank Swallow
Riparia riparia

The gray-brown upperparts and white underparts with a **gray-brown breast band** separate it from all but the larger, casual Brown-chested Martin. An abundant passage migrant; from mid-Aug to early Nov, generally along coasts, but also elsewhere, to 1,500 m; from March to mid-May, mostly along coasts. A casual winter resident. Passage migrants move steadily through in company of Barn and Cliff Swallows; occasionally feed over open areas. 5" (13 cm).

Northern Rough-winged Swallow
Stelgidopteryx serripennis

Differentiated from Southern Rough-winged Swallow by **uniformly gray-brown back and rump** and dingy throat and breast (throat sometimes with buffy wash). Similar but larger Gray-breasted Martin has dark, steely-blue upperparts. A fairly common resident of foothills and mountains in northern half of country, to 1,800 m. Joined from late Aug to early May by NA migrants, which are common in Pacific lowlands and uncommon in Caribbean lowlands. Pairs or small groups of resident birds forage over open areas, usually quite low; migrants often congregate in groups of twenty or more. 5" (13 cm).

Southern Rough-winged Swallow
Stelgidopteryx ruficollis

A **pale rump that contrasts with the brown back and the cinnamon throat** distinguishes this bird from Northern Rough-winged Swallow. Fairly common resident on Caribbean slope (to 1,000 m) and on southern Pacific slope (to 1,800 m); after breeding, from Aug to Feb, can occur in Central Valley and northwestern lowlands. Pairs or small groups forage over open areas, frequently near water. 5" (13 cm).

male

female

Purple Martin

Gray-breasted
Martin

Brown-chested
Martin

Bank
Swallow

Northern
Rough-winged
Swallow

Southern
Rough-winged
Swallow

Swallows

Barn Swallow
Hirundo rustica

Long, forked tail is distinctive; also note **uniformly dark-blue upperparts**, white subterminal markings on tail, and rufous forehead (paler on juvenile). Juvenile and molting birds don't have the characteristic long tail, but still show a distinct notch. Very abundant and widespread NA migrant, from early Aug to early June; rarely to 3,000 m. In migration, occurs virtually everywhere, but with largest numbers flying low along coasts (often with Cliff Swallows [p. 232] and Bank Swallows [p. 234]); winter residents prefer open fields. 5" (13 cm).

Gnatwrens & Gnatcatchers

SYLVIIDAE. The relatively few New World members of this large family of Old World warblers are all small, active birds.

Tawny-faced Gnatwren
Microbates cinereiventris

Its general shape and habits could suggest a wren (p. 238), but note the **tawny face** and **white throat**. Fairly common in Caribbean lowlands and foothills, to 1,000 m. Inhabits understory of mature wet forests. Sometimes accompanies mixed flocks; often follows raiding army ants. Makes a wrenlike chatter and a shrill *peeea*. 4" (10 cm).

Long-billed Gnatwren
Ramphocaenus melanurus

The **long thin bill** and **long narrow tail** (with white feather tips) should preclude any confusion. Common in humid areas from sea level to 1,200 m; restricted to evergreen patches in northwestern Pacific. Pokes about in thickets and tangled vines at forest edges and openings, and in adjacent second growth. Frequently sings a staccato trill, which can vary in quality from wooden to dulcet, lasting about two seconds and often rising slightly at the end. 5" (13 cm).

White-lored Gnatcatcher
Polioptila albiloris

Very similar to Tropical Gnatcatcher, but much more common within its range. Breeding male has entirely black cap (despite its name, lores are black). Nonbreeding male (from about Sept to Jan) and female are distinguished from respective sexes of Tropical Gnatcatcher by **narrow white superciliary**. Also compare with Chestnut-sided Warbler (p. 258). Fairly common in northwestern Pacific, to 700 m; uncommon (and usually near mangroves) from Puntarenas to Tarcoles. Pairs forage in shrubs and small trees in second growth, forest edges, and open areas; often holds tail cocked up. Makes a complaining *iyaah* and a high, emphatic *tsee-tsee-tsee-tsee-tsee-tsee*. 4" (10 cm).

Tropical Gnatcatcher
Polioptila plumbea

Where range overlaps with White-lored Gnatcatcher, be sure to check for the **broad white superciliary** in both sexes. Also compare with Chestnut-sided Warbler (p. 258). Common in wet lowlands and middle elevations, to 1,200 m; uncommon in northwestern Pacific and western Central Valley. Pairs forage actively at all levels in second growth, forest edges, and gardens; often holds tail cocked up. Gives a nasal *myew*; song is a descending series of fast, high chirps. 4" (10 cm).

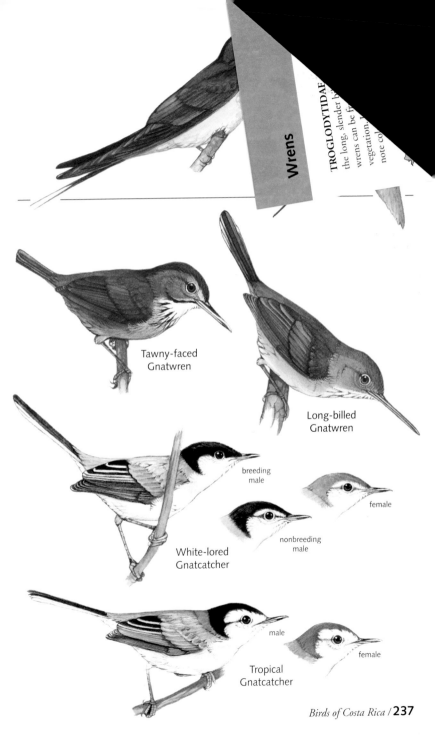

Wrens

TROGLODYTIDAE
the long, slender b
wrens can be fr
vegetation.
note co

Tawny-faced
Gnatwren

Long-billed
Gnatwren

White-lored
Gnatcatcher

breeding
male

nonbreeding
male

female

Tropical
Gnatcatcher

male

female

Barring on the wings and/or tail is a key characteristic of this family. Also note
ll, which is slightly curved in many species. Though active and very vocal, many
ustratingly difficult to see since they forage for arthropods in dense tangles and thick
Learning their calls is the best way of detecting their presence. Once a bird is actually seen,
or and markings on head, throat, and breast.

Rufous-naped Wren
Campylorhynchus rufinucha

A large, bold species that might be mistaken for a Great Kiskadee or its look-
alikes (p. 210) because of the **black-and-white striped head**; none of those birds,
however, have barring on the wings and tail. Very common in northwestern
Pacific and into the western half of the Central Valley; to 1,000 m. Forages
at middle and lower levels of dry forest, second growth, and gardens, often
around human habitations. Pairs and family members call back and forth with a
potpourri of both musical and grating notes. 7" (18 cm).

Band-backed Wren
Campylorhynchus zonatus

The **boldly spotted breast** and **banded back** distinguish this large wren
(Spot-breasted Wren has a plain-brown back). Fairly common in Caribbean
lowlands and foothills, to 1,200 m. Forages on branches and trunks of trees
at middle and lower levels of forest edges and gardens; often conspicuous.
Utters a squeaky, scratchy series of notes that have a certain lilting rhythm.
7" (18 cm).

Rock Wren
Salpinctes obsoletus

A rather drab wren, but note **fairly long tail with black subterminal band and
buff tip**. A true habitat specialist; found only in open situations (e.g., grassy
hillsides, rocky slopes, and ravines) along the Pacific face of the Guanacaste
Cordillera, between about 500 and 1,500 m. The feeble song is a sequence of
short phrases, each consisting of four to ten repeated notes—some shrill, some
sweet. 6" (15 cm).

Rufous-breasted Wren
Thryothorus rutilus

White speckling on black cheeks and throat and **bright rufous breast** are
unique traits among CR wrens. Common in foothills and middle elevations of
southern Pacific, between 300 and 1,600 m, reaching sea level in the Carara area;
uncommon in Pacific foothills from Tenorio Volcano south to western Central
Valley, between 300 and 900 m. Tends to forage fairly high in trees at forest
edges and in gardens. The song consists of several brisk musical phrases, not as
mellow or full-bodied as those of other members of the genus. 5" (13 cm).

Spot-breasted Wren
Thryothorus maculipectus

A **brown-backed** wren with a **heavily spotted breast** (Band-backed Wren has a
banded back). Fairly uncommon in lowlands of Caño Negro region. Forages in
lower and middle levels of trees in gardens, as well as in low, dense vegetation.
The sweet, whistled song is slightly less complex than that of many others in the
genus. 5" (13 cm).

Rufous-naped
Wren

Band-backed
Wren

Rock Wren

Rufous-breasted
Wren

Spot-breasted
Wren

Stripe-breasted Wren
Thryothorus thoracicus

The only wren in CR with **streaked throat and breast**. Common in Caribbean lowlands and foothills, to 1,000 m. Pairs forage in lower levels of mature wet forest and forest edges. Delivers a series of clear, even-pitched whistles that recall the vocalization of the Central American Pygmy-Owl (p. 108). Also quickly repeats a short phrase of dulcet tones, then switches to another phrase. **Endemic to Nicaragua, CR, and Panama**. 5" (13 cm).

Riverside Wren
Thryothorus semibadius

This bird has **rich rufous upperparts** and **finely barred black-and-white underparts** (the Rufous-and-white Wren has mostly white underparts). Common in southern Pacific lowlands and foothills, to 1,200 m. Pairs or small groups forage low in dense vegetation inside mature wet forests and at forest edges (despite its name, not confined to riversides); regularly comes into view. Has loud, sweet, fast-paced songs that are not quite as explosive as those of the Bay Wren. **Endemic to CR and western Panama**. 5" (13 cm).

Bay Wren
Thryothorus nigricapillus

The **chestnut body** and **white throat and facial markings** readily differentiate the Bay Wren (like most birds in this genus, however, it can be difficult to see). Common in Caribbean lowlands and foothills, to 1,000 m. Almost always found near watercourses, working its way through thick shrubbery. The powerful voice veritably explodes from vegetation with rapidly repeated phrases. 6" (15 cm).

Rufous-and-white Wren
Thryothorus rufalbus

Bright rufous upperparts and heavier **black streaking on cheeks** distinguish this from the Plain Wren; **mostly white underparts** set it apart from the Riverside and Banded Wrens. Common in foothills of northwestern Pacific and western Central Valley, from 300 to 1,100 m; also common in evergreen forest and mangroves of northwestern lowlands, south to Carara; uncommon in Térraba River basin. Call is a deep, rich sequence of toots and trills abruptly ending on a higher pitched note. 6" (15 cm).

Plain Wren
Thryothorus modestus

A fairly drab, brown-backed wren; the combination of **white superciliary**, **white throat**, and **buffy flanks** is diagnostic. (Compare with Rufous-and-white Wren.) The duller and grayer birds of the Caribbean lowlands were once considered a separate species: Canebrake Wren (*T. zeledoni*). Common on Pacific slope and in the Central Valley, to 2,000 m; fairly common in Caribbean lowlands; uncommon in northwestern Pacific lowlands. Forages at lower levels of overgrown vegetation in nonforest habitats. The CR common name derives from its typical song: *chinchirigüt*. 5" (13 cm).

Banded Wren
Thryothorus pleurostictus

Though this species resembles several other CR wrens, the **black barring on the sides and flanks** is unique. Very common in northwestern Pacific lowlands and western Central Valley, to 800 m. Forages in understory of dry forests, thickets, and also mangroves. A fine singer; the clear musical phrases often contain a rattling *kreeEEee* (like the sound produced by one of those cork-lined bird call devices). 5" (13 cm).

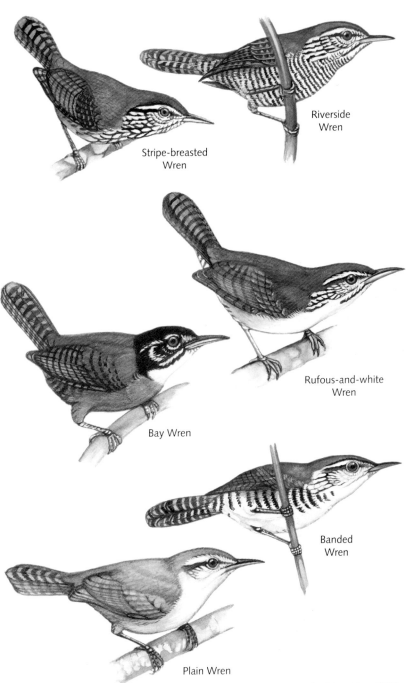

Stripe-breasted
Wren

Riverside
Wren

Bay Wren

Rufous-and-white
Wren

Banded
Wren

Plain Wren

Black-bellied Wren
Thryothorus fasciatoventris

The **immaculate white throat and breast** contrast sharply with the black belly, which is finely barred posteriorly. Common in southern Pacific lowlands, to 500 m. Prefers to conceal itself within dense *Heliconia* thickets and vine tangles along streamsides and forest edges. Its rich, liquid phrases and slurred musical *chooup* reveal its presence. **Endemic from CR to western Colombia.** 6" (15 cm).

Black-throated Wren
Thryothorus atrogularis

A **dark-brown** wren with **black throat and chest**. Fairly common in Caribbean lowlands and foothills, to 1,100 m. Skulks in dense, overgrown vegetation; far more often heard than seen. Sings a loud series of about five whistles and chirps, terminating in either a trill or three even short whistles. **Endemic to Nicaragua, CR, and western Panama.** 6" (15 cm).

Ochraceous Wren
Troglodytes ochraceus

Similar to the House Wren, but note **rich cinnamon-brown coloration** and **prominent buffy superciliary**. Common at middle and upper elevations, from Tilarán Cordillera south, between 900 and 3,000 m. Forages on epiphyte-laden trunks and branches at middle levels of mature wet montane forests and adjacent gardens; often with mixed flocks. The thin song is rapid and high-pitched. **Endemic to CR and western Panama.** 4" (10 cm).

House Wren
Troglodytes aedon

A small, brown, fairly unpatterned bird; it does show **narrow barring on the wings and tail** and an **indistinct superciliary**. Common and widespread, to 2,800 m; uncommon in northwestern Pacific. Usually around buildings and in weedy pastures. Vocalizes from an exposed perch; utters a spirited, bubbly song that mixes musical trills and chattering (similar to song of Tropical Parula [p. 256]). 4" (10 cm).

Sedge Wren
Cistothorus platensis

The only **streak-backed** wren in CR, where it is fairly common in wet fields in the vicinity of Cartago. Its limited habitat is rapidly disappearing, however. Generally skulking, it occasionally makes a short, low flight over the grass before dropping down into cover. From atop a clump of vegetation, sings variable phrases, often with a scratchy and/or shrill quality. 4" (10 cm).

Timberline Wren
Thryorchilus browni

The **white edging on the primaries** is diagnostic. Fairly common in highlands above 2,700 m. Forages in bamboo and dense shrubbery. The wrenlike song, neither full-bodied nor exceedingly musical, is a rapid delivery of high warbles and trills. **Endemic to CR and western Panama.** 4" (10 cm).

Black-bellied
Wren

Black-throated
Wren

Ochraceous
Wren

House Wren

Sedge
Wren

Timberline
Wren

Song Wren
Cyphorhinus phaeocephalus

The **thickish bill** and large area of **blue-gray orbital skin** could suggest some antbirds (see species on p. 178), but note the **barring on the wings and tail**, which no antbird has. Fairly uncommon in Caribbean lowlands, reaching foothills along Guanacaste Cordillera, to 1,000 m. Small groups forage on or near the ground in mature wet forest and adjacent advanced second growth, sometimes accompanying other species. The amazing song incorporates clear, melodious whistles superimposed on harsh, henlike clucking; several birds often join together in song. 5" (13 cm).

White-breasted Wood-Wren
Henicorhina leucosticta

A **small, short-tailed** wren with white superciliary, black-and-white streaked cheeks, and **white throat and breast** (the lowland counterpart of the Gray-breasted Wood-Wren). Very common in Caribbean lowlands and foothills, to 1,200 m; common at middle elevations in southern Pacific, to 1,800 m; rare in southern Pacific lowlands. Active and noisy, it mostly forages on or near the ground in mature wet forest and adjacent advanced second growth. Produces an often-heard chattering, a piercing *cheet* call note, and quite a variety of clear, whistled phrases (similar to song of Gray-breasted Wood-Wren). 4" (10 cm).

Gray-breasted Wood-Wren
Henicorhina leucophrys

The highland counterpart of the White-breasted Wood-Wren, but note **gray breast**. Abundant from 800 m to timberline. Dwells in understory of wet montane forest and forest edges. Its loud, lengthy, rollicking melody is one of the most commonly heard and attention-grabbing sounds in its habitat. Utters a chatter similar to that of the White-breasted Wood-Wren. 4" (10 cm).

Scaly-breasted Wren
Microcerculus marginatus

A close relative of the Nightingale Wren (no range overlap), though it is lighter colored and has a **pale throat and breast**. (Despite its name, the CR race does not have scaling on the breast.) Common in wet lowlands and foothills on both sides of the southern half of CR, to 1,700 m. Walks along the floor of mature wet forest, often near streams and ravines. After a quick introductory phrase of several short notes, the "song"—consisting of widely-spaced, successively lower-pitched, shrill, whistled notes—sometimes lasts several minutes; the whistled notes could recall those of a Tawny-crowned Greenlet (p. 228). 4" (10 cm).

Nightingale Wren
Microcerculus philomela

A **small, dark**, essentially terrestrial wren with an **extremely short tail** (no range overlap with similar Scaly-breasted Wren). Fairly common in foothills and adjacent lowlands on the northern half of the Caribbean slope, to 1,200 m. Prefers mature wet forest. Since very difficult to see, one should learn to enjoy (and settle for) the extraordinary vocalization that unhurriedly wanders up and down the scale, not quite staying in key. 4" (10 cm).

Song Wren

White-breasted
Wood-Wren

Gray-breasted
Wood-Wren

Scaly-breasted
Wren

Nightingale
Wren

Thrushes

TURDIDAE. The CR members of this widespread family sport rather drab plumage, though some species have bright orange or yellow bill, legs, and/or eye ring. Juveniles of most species have spotted plumage. Many are more pleasing to the ear than to the eye (the Clay-colored Robin [p. 250], for example, was named the national bird of Costa Rica for its melodious song).

Slaty-backed Nightingale-Thrush
Catharus fuscater

The **pale iris** distinguishes it from other nightingale-thrushes. Similar to the larger Sooty Robin (p. 248), but has **whitish belly** (no range overlap). Common at middle elevations of Caribbean slope, between 800 and 1,800 m; also common at upper elevations of Pacific slope of Tilarán Cordillera and in the Dota region. Forages in forest understory; at dawn and dusk, often hops along trails. Song recalls that of Black-faced Solitaire (p. 248), but is lower pitched and less complex—lacks final shrill note; typical version slides up, then down the scale: *tlee-dee, teedle-doo.* 7" (18 cm).

Black-headed Nightingale-Thrush
Catharus mexicanus

Most closely resembles Slaty-backed Nightingale-Thrush, but note **dark iris** and contrast between **dark-olive back** and **black crown**. Common in Caribbean foothills, between 300 and 1,000 m; uncommon on Pacific slope of Guanacaste and Tilarán Cordilleras, between 700 and 1,300 m. Stays low in mature forests. Song has a flutelike quality typical of nightingale-thrushes, but with some slightly harsh and fuzzy parts. 6" (15 cm).

Black-billed Nightingale-Thrush
Catharus gracilirostris

A relatively slender nightingale-thrush with a **black bill**; also note **brown wash across breast** that separates gray throat from gray belly. Very common in highlands, from 2,200 m to timberline; less common above timberline. Inhabits understory of oak forests and adjacent gardens and clearings, also in paramo; often very confiding. Its song, though somewhat muddled, retains the flutelike essence of the genus. **Endemic to CR and western Panama**. 6" (15cm).

Orange-billed Nightingale-Thrush
Catharus aurantiirostris

This species and both the Slaty-backed and Black-headed Nightingale-Thrushes all have orange bills, but note **brown back**. (Southern CR race has distinctly gray crown.) Similar to Ruddy-capped Nightingale-Thrush, but has eye ring. Fairly common at middle elevations on the Pacific slopes of the Tilarán, Central, and Talamanca Cordilleras, from 500 to 2,200 m; also on higher hills of Nicoya Peninsula. Forages at low levels in tangled second growth, shady gardens, and coffee plantations. Song is varied, faster, and less musical than that of other nightingale-thrushes. 6" (15 cm).

Ruddy-capped Nightingale-Thrush
Catharus frantzii

Told apart from other nightingale-thrushes by its **bicolored bill** and distinctly **reddish-brown crown**. Absence of eye ring further sets it apart from Orange-billed Nightingale-Thrush. Common in highlands, from 1,500 to 2,500 m. Forages close to the ground in montane forests; at dawn and dusk, comes out into the open in adjacent gardens and clearings. Sings varied phrases with distinctive quality of nightingale-thrushes. 6" (15 cm).

Slaty-backed
Nightingale-Thrush

Black-headed
Nightingale-Thrush

Black-billed
Nightingale-Thrush

northern
CR race

Orange-billed
Nightingale-Thrush

Ruddy-capped
Nightingale-Thrush

Veery
Catharus fuscescens

Distinguished from Swainson's and Gray-cheeked Thrushes by redder upperparts and less distinct breast spotting. An uncommon passage migrant, from Sept to Oct and from March to April; mostly near Caribbean coast, occasionally into foothills, and even Central Valley. Stays on or near ground in mature forest and second growth, typically near water and with other migrant thrushes. 7" (18 cm).

Swainson's Thrush
Catharus ustulatus

The **prominent buffy spectacles** differentiate it from the very similar Gray-cheeked Thrush. Also compare with Veery. A widespread and very common passage migrant, from late Sept to mid-Nov and from late March to mid-May; an uncommon winter resident; from sea level to 2,800 m. More arboreal than other migrant thrushes; occurs in a wide range of habitats. Spring migrants often sing rising, flutelike phrases. 7" (18 cm).

Gray-cheeked Thrush
Catharus minimus

Closely resembles Swainson's Thrush, but has only **pale, indistinct eye ring**. Also compare with Veery. An uncommon passage migrant, from late Sept to mid-Nov, on Caribbean side of CR and in Central Valley; a very rare winter resident on both sides of CR. Stays on or near ground in second growth and gardens, usually near water and with other migrant thrushes. 7" (18 cm).

Wood Thrush
Hylocichla mustelina

The **heavily spotted underparts** and **rufous crown** are diagnostic. A fairly uncommon NA migrant, from Oct to April, from sea level to 1,700 m. Usually seen on or near the ground in mature wet forest or advanced second growth. In alarm, utters a quick *pik-pik-pik*. 8" (20 cm).

Black-faced Solitaire
Myadestes melanops

No other CR thrush with **orange bill and legs** is so **uniformly slate gray** or has a **contrasting black face**. Common at middle and upper elevations, from 1,000 to 2,800 m; descends to 400 m on Caribbean slope in second half of year. Dwells in lower and middle levels of montane wet forests. Most often seen while feeding on berries; extremely difficult to locate when singing. Its unhurried, ethereal song is a characteristic feature of montane wet forests; it combines pure flutelike tones with a shrill note that sounds like a rusty gate hinge. (If flutelike tones are heard without shrill note, could suggest song of Slaty-backed Nightingale-Thrush [p. 246].) **Endemic to CR and western Panama**. 7" (18 cm).

Sooty Robin
Turdus nigrescens

No other **entirely black plumaged** bird in CR has **orange bill, eye ring, and legs**; also note **pale iris**. Distinguished from similar Slaty-backed Nightingale-Thrush (p. 246) by black belly (no range overlap). Common above 2,400 m. Forages on ground in open areas and at forest edges. Call is a harsh, jaylike *ret-ret-ret*. **Endemic to CR and western Panama**. 10" (25 cm).

Veery

Swainson's
Thrush

Gray-cheeked
Thrush

Wood Thrush

juv.

adult

Black-faced
Solitaire

s
they
Dipper

a
on l
aquatic
streams.

Soo

Thrushes

White-throated Robin
Turdus assimilis

The **streaked throat bordered below by a bold white crescent** is distinctive; also note yellow eye ring, bill, and feet. Fairly common on Pacific slope; very uncommon on Caribbean slope; from 800 to 1,800 m. During second half of year, some birds move to lower elevations. Prefers middle levels of mature forests and adjacent second growth. A talented vocalist that sings surprisingly varied phrases ranging from tuneful whistles to thin trills, all typically given in couplets. 9" (23 cm).

Clay-colored Robin
Turdus grayi

CR's nondescript national bird, *el yigüirro*, can be distinguished from the Mountain Robin and the Pale-vented Thrush by its **yellow-green bill**. Widespread and common, to 2,400 m, though uncommon in northwestern Pacific. A true garden-variety bird that hops on the ground in typical robin fashion; routinely flicks its tail upon landing. From March through June, tirelessly whistles melodic phrases that are responsible for its status as the national bird of Costa Rica. 9" (23 cm).

Mountain Robin
Turdus plebejus

A dull, dark robin with a **black bill**. Compare with Clay-colored Robin and Pale-vented Thrush. Fairly common at middle and upper elevations, from 1,200 m to timberline. Mostly arboreal, in highland, forest edges, and adjacent gardens. Sings a monotonous series of notes that vary in pitch and duration from phrase to phrase. 10" (25 cm).

Pale-vented Thrush
Turdus obsoletus

The distinctive **white belly and vent**, together with the **dark bill**, distinguish this species from the Clay-colored and Mountain Robins. Fairly common in Caribbean foothills, from 600 to 1,200 m; migrates to lowlands at base of mountains in second half of year. Mostly arboreal; occurs in wet forests and advanced second growth. Sings with the sweet unmistakable caroling of a robin; the varied phrases are delivered slightly faster than those of the Clay-colored Robin and with fewer pauses between the phrases. 9" (23 cm).

Dippers

CINCLIDAE. The five members of this family are unique among the passerines for their ability to swim (and even walk) underwater. When standing on boulders in the middle of rushing streams, typically bob up and down, raising and lowering their short tails. The CR race of the American is paler than its northern relatives.

American Dipper
Cinclus mexicanus

No other small bird found along mountain streams is so **plump** and so **grayish overall** (compare with Torrent Tyrannulet [p. 200]). Fairly common at middle and upper elevations of Caribbean slope, from 700 to 2,500 m; less common Pacific slope of Central and Talamanca Cordilleras. Forages on river rocks for insects, sometimes disappearing below the water's surface; flies low along Call is a sharp, buzzy *dzeet*. 7" (18 cm).

White-throated
Robin

Clay-colored
Robin

Mountain
Robin

Pale-vented
Thrush

American
Dipper

Birds of Costa Rica / **251**

Mockingbirds

MIMIDAE. A New World family of birds characterized by long tails and thin, narrow bills; most species have brown or gray plumage. Members of this family display a variety of habits; some species are extremely furtive, others are downright brazen.

Gray Catbird
Dumetella carolinensis

The only gray bird in CR that has a **black cap** and a **rufous vent**. A fairly common winter resident (from early Sept to early May) and passage migrant, throughout Caribbean lowlands; note, however, that passage migrants can show up almost anywhere in the country. Usually difficult to see since it forages in tangled second growth and forest edges; most commonly shows itself in early morning. Gives a *mew* reminiscent of a cat. 8" (20 cm).

Tropical Mockingbird
Mimus gilvus

Fairly nondescript, but note **white-tipped tail feathers** and **narrow wing bars**. There have been breeding pairs in the center of Siquirres and Limón for a number of years now. Additional reports from Tortuguero, Arenal, San Isidro de El General, the area north of Dominical, and a site near Bagaces suggest that this species is establishing itself in CR. Prefers open areas (including fields, soccer fields, and urban gardens). An accomplished singer; despite its name, it rarely imitates other species. 10" (25 cm).

Silky-Flycatchers

PTILOGONATIDAE. A family of four species with limited distribution ranges; the two CR representatives are highland endemics. Despite the common name, the members of this family are more closely related to the thrushes and waxwings than to the tyrant flycatchers, and they eat fruit more often than they eat insects.

Long-tailed Silky-Flycatcher
Ptilogonys caudatus

The **prominent crest**, long tail, and unique coloration are diagnostic. Fairly common in Central and Talamanca Cordilleras, from 1,600 m to timberline. Found in forests, forest edges, and gardens; typically perches upright at tips of branches located near the top of tall trees, but can be seen as low as eye level when it feeds on fruits in shrubs. Makes a wooden and staccato (but sweet) chittering. **Endemic to CR and western Panama**. 9" (23cm).

Black-and-yellow Silky-Flycatcher
Phainoptila melanoxantha

Size and rotund shape could suggest a robin (p. 250), but **yellow flanks** (male also has yellow rump) are diagnostic. Fairly common in highlands, above 1,200 m in Guanacaste and Tilarán Cordilleras, and from 1,800 m to timberline in Central and Talamanca Cordilleras. Rather sedentary; feeds on berries at middle levels of montane forests and forest edges. Gives a high, thin *tsip*. **Endemic to CR and western Panama**. 8" (20 cm).

Gray Catbird

Tropical
Mockingbird

Long-tailed
Silky-Flycatcher

female

male

Black-and-yellow
Silky-Flycatcher

Waxwings

BOMBYCILLIDAE. A boreal family of sleek, crested birds. Typically travel in gregarious flocks, feeding on berries and occasionally flycatching in the manner of a kingbird. In silhouette, the upright stance of perched birds could suggest the Eastern Kingbird (p. 212).

Cedar Waxwing *Bombycilla cedrorum*
Crest, **black mask**, and relatively **short, squared-off tail** are distinctive. Occurs as an infrequent, though irruptive, NA migrant between Dec and mid-May; most likely in highlands. Small flocks (sometimes lone individuals) visit trees in clearings and gardens. In flight, gives a high, thin, hissing trill. 7" (18 cm).

Wood-Warblers

PARULIDAE. A New World family of small, active birds characterized by thin, pointed bills. Wood-warblers are easily confused with vireos (p. 224), but vireos have heavier bills and are typically more methodic in their movements. Furthermore, vireos—both resident and migrant species—freely vocalize, whereas the migrant warblers seldom utter more than a *chip* note when away from their breeding grounds. More than three quarters of the fifty-three warbler species reported in Costa Rica are NA migrants, many of which present identification challenges. A number of species are very similar, and, to add to the confusion, a given species often shows a range of plumage variations. From about mid-March, many NA migrants begin to molt into their distinctive breeding plumage. Check for wing bars, streaking on the breast and back, as well as any distinctive facial pattern or coloration.

Orange-crowned Warbler *Vermivora celata*
Similar to Tennessee Warbler in behavior and coloration, but note **yellow undertail coverts** and **blurry streaking on underparts**. Juvenile generally paler. A very casual NA migrant, with only a handful of scattered records. Reported up to 1,500 m. 5" (13 cm).

Tennessee Warbler *Vermivora peregrina*
In all plumages, shows **thin eye line**, **pale superciliary**, and **whitish undertail coverts**. (Note that adult female and nonbreeding male are virtually identical.) Breeding male resembles Lesser Greenlet (p. 228), but note eye ring on latter species. Adult female and nonbreeding male could be confused with Philadelphia and Warbling Vireos (p. 226), but note thin bill and white undertail coverts. Abundant NA migrant, from early Sept to early May, to 2,300 m. Forages at all levels of forest edges and gardens; often in small flocks that feed on flower nectar and insects. Face sometimes tinted orange from pollen. 5" (13 cm).

Nashville Warbler *Vermivora ruficapilla*
Pattern is very similar to that of Lesser Greenlet (p. 228), but has **bright-yellow underparts**; drab juvenile female virtually identical to Lesser Greenlet. (Nashville Warbler also closely resembles female and juvenile *Oporonis* warblers [p. 270], but is essentially arboreal.) A very casual NA migrant, to 1,500 m. 5" (13 cm).

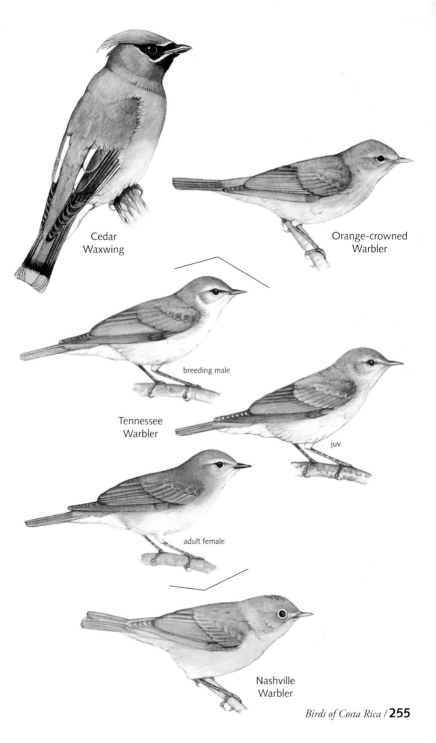

Cedar
Waxwing

Orange-crowned
Warbler

breeding male

Tennessee
Warbler

juv.

adult female

Nashville
Warbler

[The Blue-winged Warbler and Golden-winged Warbler frequently hybridize; the resulting hybrids are classified as either Brewster's Warbler or Lawrence's Warbler. There are only a few records for either hybrid in CR.]

Blue-winged Warbler
Vermivora pinus

The only **mostly yellow** warbler with a **narrow, dark eye line** and **two white wing bars**. Rare NA migrant, from mid-Sept to late April; most likely in Caribbean lowlands and middle elevations, to 1,500 m. Forages at middle levels of second growth and in gardens. 5" (13 cm).

Golden-winged Warbler
Vermivora chrysoptera

The large **yellow shoulder patch** and **striped facial pattern** (less distinct in female and juvenile but still obvious) readily identify this species. Fairly common NA migrant at middle elevations and in highlands, to 2,500 m; fairly uncommon in Caribbean lowlands; rare in Pacific lowlands; from early Sept to late April. Prefers middle levels of forests and forest edges; often accompanies mixed flocks. 5" (13 cm).

Northern Parula
Parula americana

Breeding male has prominent breast band; nonbreeding (and juvenile) male and adult female show less distinct breast band; juvenile female lacks breast band entirely. In all plumages, told apart from similar Tropical Parula by **two wing bars**, yellow throat, and **broken eye ring**. Rare NA migrant, from late Oct to early April; to 1,200 m. Forages at middle and upper levels of forest edges, second growth, and gardens. 4" (10 cm).

Tropical Parula
Parula pitiayumi

Somewhat similar to Northern Parula, but note **single wing bar**, orangish tint to upper breast and throat, and **dark mask**. Similar to Flame-throated Warbler, but little range overlap. A resident warbler. Fairly common on Caribbean slope; fairly uncommon on Pacific slope; from 600 to 1,800 m. Forages at middle and upper levels of forest edges, second growth, and gardens. Sings a series of high, fast notes and trills that recall song of House Wren (p. 242). 4" (10 cm).

Flame-throated Warbler
Parula gutturalis

Orange-red throat is distinctive, even on drab juvenile. Similar to Tropical Parula, but little range overlap. Fairly common in highlands of Central and Talamanca Cordilleras, from 1,600 m to timberline. Pairs or small groups forage at middle and upper levels of forests, forest edges, and adjacent gardens; often accompanies mixed flocks. Gives a high, drawn-out, buzzy, arcing note. **Endemic to CR and western Panama**. 5" (13 cm).

Magnolia Warbler
Dendroica magnolia

The **white tail band** sets it apart in all plumages; also note **yellow rump**. (Adult female is very similar to breeding male, but drabber.) Very uncommon NA migrant, from mid-Sept to late April, to 1,500 m. Forages at lower and middle levels in gallery forest, thickets, and gardens. 5" (13 cm).

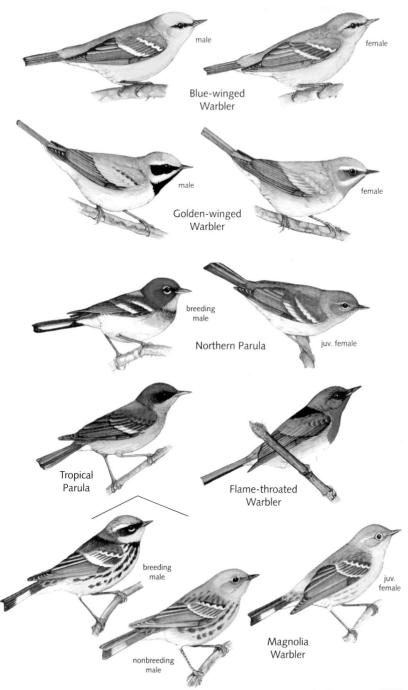

Blue-winged
Warbler

male

female

Golden-winged
Warbler

male

female

Northern Parula

breeding
male

juv. female

Tropical
Parula

Flame-throated
Warbler

breeding
male

nonbreeding
male

juv.
female

Magnolia
Warbler

Yellow Warbler
Dendroica petechia

There are two races in CR; the juvenile female of both races is very similar. <u>Resident race</u>: Often referred to as the Mangrove Warbler, the resident race is a fairly common inhabitant of Pacific coast mangrove swamps; it is uncommon in the Caribbean mangroves north of Moín. Adult male is easily distinguished by its entirely chestnut head; female has chestnut center of crown; juvenile is rather drab. <u>Migrant race</u>: The **rufous streaking on underparts** of bright-yellow adult male is distinctive; note that juvenile male has faint, reduced streaking on breast. The unstreaked female and duller juvenile female have **yellow-edged tail feathers**, which are best seen in flight. Female and juvenile female similar to female Wilson's Warbler (p. 268), but latter has olive tail; also similar to juvenile female Hooded Warbler (p. 268), but latter shows white in tail. Very common NA migrant, from mid-Aug to early May, to 1,500 m. Active and noisy; forages at lower and middle levels of gardens. Emits a near constant, sharp *chip*. 5" (13 cm).

Cape May Warbler
Dendroica tigrina

Breeding male has distinctive **rufous sides of head**; this feature is reduced on nonbreeding male. Female and juvenile show **heavy streaking on underparts** (rather blurred on juvenile female) and a hint of **yellow on sides of neck**. Very rare NA migrant, from late Nov to mid-May, to 2,200 m. Extrapolating from the few records available, could turn up almost anywhere. 5" (13 cm).

Black-throated Blue Warbler
Dendroica caerulescens

Essentially no distinction between breeding and nonbreeding plumages. Adult male and similarly plumaged juvenile male are distinctive. Adult female and juvenile female are quite drab; note narrow white superciliary, **arc below eye**, and **white spot on wing** (absent in some juvenile females). Very rare NA migrant, from Oct to March, mostly at middle elevations, from 500 to 1,400 m. Forages at middle levels of forest and forest edges. 5" (13 cm).

Chestnut-sided Warbler
Dendroica pensylvanica

Breeding male is distinctive; breeding female is very similar, but with reduced chestnut on flanks and reduced facial markings. Nonbreeding adults and juvenile male resemble juvenile female but have some chestnut on flanks. Nonbreeding adults and juveniles often mistaken for a gnatcatcher (p. 236)—due in part to habit of cocking rather long tail up at an angle—but note **eye ring** and **wing bars**; could also be mistaken for nonbreeding adult or juvenile Bay-breasted Warbler (p. 262), but note plain gray face and white eye ring. Very common NA migrant (though scarce in northwestern Pacific), from early Sept to mid-May, to 1,800 m. Forages at all levels of forest edges, second growth, and gardens; often with mixed flocks. Gives a sharp *chip*. 5" (13 cm).

migrant
adult male

juv.
female
(both races)

Yellow Warbler

juv.
female

breeding
male

Cape May
Warbler

breeding
female

male

Black-throated
Blue Warbler

female

breeding
male

Chestnut-sided
Warbler

juv. female

Blackburnian Warbler
Dendroica fusca

Breeding male is distinguished by **intense orange on throat and head**. Breeding female and nonbreeding male and female have yellow-orange on throat and head. Juvenile female and very similar juvenile male have yellow on throat and head; might be confused with juvenile Townsend's and Black-throated Green Warblers, but note **whitish stripes on back**. Common passage migrant, from mid-Aug to late Oct and in April, virtually countrywide, though most numerous at middle elevations. Common winter resident, from mid-Aug to April, from 500 to 1,600 m. Forages mostly at middle and upper levels of forest edges and gardens; often accompanies mixed flocks. 5" (13 cm).

[Compare the following three species with Golden-cheeked Warbler (p. 328).]

Townsend's Warbler
Dendroica townsendi

Breeding male has black chin and throat; all other plumages show less black (to varying degrees); juvenile female has no black on chin and throat. All plumages similar to respective plumages of Black-throated Green Warbler, but note **yellow on lower breast**, **dark ear coverts**, and **streaking on back** (absent in juvenile female). Also compare with Blackburnian Warbler (see above). Very uncommon NA migrant, from Sept to April, at middle elevations and in highlands, between 1,300 and 3,100 m. Forages in middle and upper levels of forest edges, second growth, and gardens. 5" (13 cm).

Black-throated Green Warbler
Dendroica virens

Breeding male has striking black chin, throat, and upper breast; all other plumages show less black (to varying degrees); juvenile has no black on chin, throat, and upper breast. All plumages similar to respective plumages of Townsend's Warbler, but note **mostly whitish underparts**, **olive ear coverts**, and **unstreaked back**. Similar to Blackburnian Warbler, but that species shows whitish stripes on back. Common NA migrant, from Oct to mid-April, at middle elevations and in highlands, between 800 and 3,100 m. Forages in middle and upper levels of forest, forest edges, and gardens. 5" (13 cm).

Hermit Warbler
Dendroica occidentalis

Breeding male has **all-yellow head** with black chin and throat. Other plumages show less black on chin and throat (none on juvenile female) and have vague olive color on crown and ear coverts. Rare NA migrant, from mid-Sept to March, at middle elevations, between 800 and 1,800 m. Forages principally in introduced conifers. 5" (13 cm).

Yellow-throated Warbler
Dendroica dominica

White on side of neck and **plain gray back** are diagnostic. All plumages very similar. Could suggest a Blackburnian Warbler, but note white markings on head. Very uncommon passage migrant; rare winter resident, from mid-Aug to March; mostly at middle elevations, to 1,500 m. Forages methodically at lower and middle levels of second growth and gardens; often found in pine trees. 5" (13 cm).

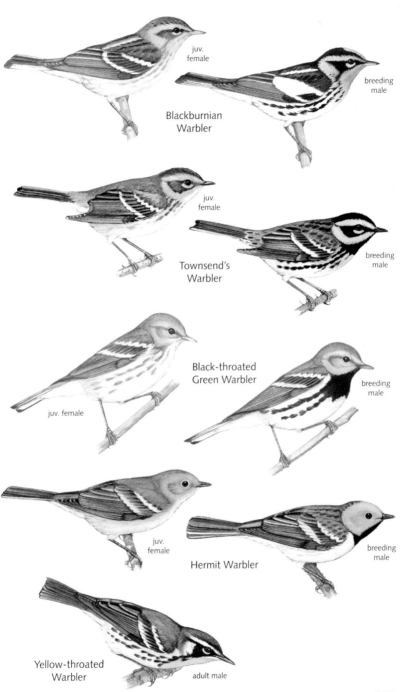

Blackburnian
Warbler

juv.
female

breeding
male

Townsend's
Warbler

juv.
female

breeding
male

Black-throated
Green Warbler

juv. female

breeding
male

Hermit Warbler

juv.
female

breeding
male

Yellow-throated
Warbler

adult male

[The juvenile females of the three species below are extremely similar. It is very difficult to distinguish between them in the field. You are most likely to encounter the Bay-breasted Warbler, however, as the Blackpoll Warbler and the Pine Warbler are both very rare in CR.]

Bay-breasted Warbler
Dendroica castanea

Distinctive breeding male has **black mask** and **reddish-brown crown, throat, and flanks**. Juvenile male and nonbreeding female resemble nonbreeding male, but have just a hint of reddish-brown on flanks. Nonbreeding adults and juveniles are somewhat similar to nonbreeding adult and juvenile Chestnut-sided Warblers (p. 258), but note olive face and lack of eye ring. Common passage migrant, from mid-Sept to mid-Nov and from April to early May, on Caribbean slope, mostly in lowlands but also to 1,800 m. Rare winter resident, from mid-Sept to early May, in lowlands and middle elevations, to 1,400 m. Forages at all levels of forest edges, second growth, and gardens. 5" (13 cm).

Blackpoll Warbler
Dendroica striata

Breeding male could be mistaken for a Black-and-white Warbler (p. 266), but has **all-black crown** and **white ear coverts**. Nonbreeding adults and juveniles are all similar. Very rare NA migrant, from mid-Oct to late March, in lowlands and middle elevations, to 1,400 m. Forages at lower and middle levels of forest edges and second growth. 5" (13 cm).

Pine Warbler
Dendroica pinus

Essentially no distinction between breeding and nonbreeding plumages. Juvenile male very similar to adult female, but has slightly more yellow on belly. Adult male resembles Yellow-throated Vireo (p. 224), but note **faint streaking on sides of breast**. Very rare NA migrant, from late Aug to mid-Nov, along Caribbean coast and in Central Valley. Forages methodically at middle and upper levels of second growth and gardens. 5" (13 cm).

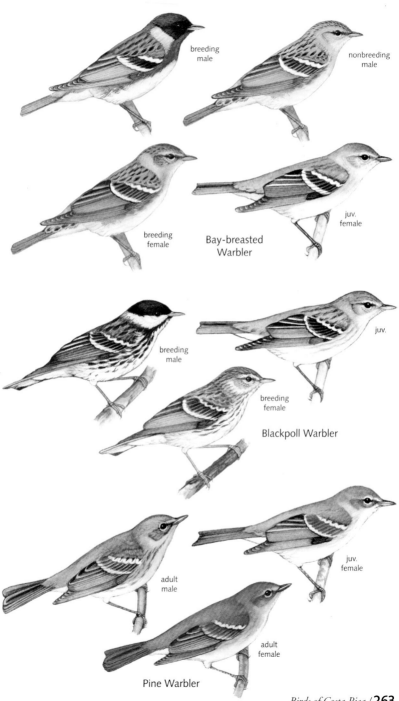

breeding male

nonbreeding male

breeding female

juv. female

Bay-breasted Warbler

breeding male

juv.

breeding female

Blackpoll Warbler

adult male

juv. female

adult female

Pine Warbler

Yellow-rumped Warbler
Dendroica coronata

Identified in any plumage by **yellow on rump and sides of breast** (juvenile female has very faint yellow on sides of breast); also note pale underparts with dark streaking. Breeding male has blue-gray upperparts; all other plumages have brownish upperparts. There are two races of Yellow-rumped Warbler; in CR, the white-throated "Myrtle" is much more likely than the yellow-throated "Audubon's." Widespread; usually an uncommon NA migrant, though in some years irruptive; from mid-Sept to late March; to 1,800 m. Forages on or near ground in fairly open areas; often in small groups. 5" (13 cm).

Prairie Warbler
Dendroica discolor

In breeding male, **black facial markings, black streaking on flanks**, and **rufous streaks on back** are diagnostic. These features are reduced, to varying degrees, in other plumages; in juvenile female, note that the white above and below the eye is bordered by gray. Very rare NA migrant, from late Aug to March. Forages at lower and middle levels of forest edges and second growth; bobs tail continually. 5" (13 cm).

Palm Warbler
Dendroica palmarum

The **chestnut cap** is distinctive in breeding plumage; in all plumages, note **yellow undertail coverts**. Juveniles are virtually identical to nonbreeding adults. Rare NA migrant, from mid-Oct to April, to 800 m. Forages on ground in open areas, usually near water; pumps tail constantly. 5" (13 cm).

Cerulean Warbler
Dendroica cerulea

Breeding male has distinctive **blue upperparts**. All other plumages are very similar to juvenile female, which has **broad, pale superciliary** and distinctive **blue-green upperparts**. Uncommon passage migrant, from late Aug to early Nov and from late March to late April; mostly on Caribbean slope and in Central Valley, to 1,500 m. Forages actively at middle and upper levels of forest, forest edges, and advanced second growth. 5" (13 cm).

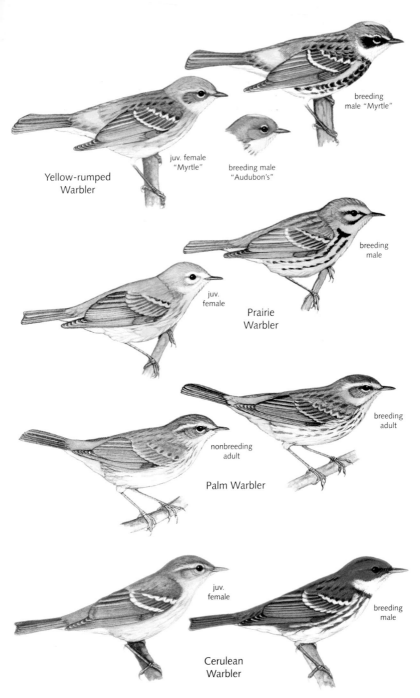

Yellow-rumped
Warbler

juv. female
"Myrtle"

breeding male
"Audubon's"

breeding
male "Myrtle"

juv.
female

Prairie
Warbler

breeding
male

nonbreeding
adult

Palm Warbler

breeding
adult

juv.
female

breeding
male

Cerulean
Warbler

Black-and-white Warbler
Mniotilta varia

Boldly striped black-and-white pattern is diagnostic on both adults; juvenile is slightly drabber. Common NA migrant, from mid-Aug to mid-April, most numerous at middle and upper elevations, to 2,500 m. Forages at middle and lower levels of forest, forest edges, and gardens; often with mixed flocks; creeps on branches and tree trunks. 5" (13 cm).

American Redstart
Setophaga ruticilla

Adult male is striking. Female and juvenile are very similar. Tail pattern is unique in all plumages. Fairly common passage migrant, from early Aug to late Oct and from April to early May; uncommon winter resident, from mid-Aug to early May; to 1,500 m. Forages acrobatically at all levels in forest, second growth, mangroves, and forest edges; often with mixed flocks. Frequently gives tail-fanning display. 5" (13 cm).

Prothonotary Warbler
Protonotaria citrea

The combination of **yellow foreparts**, **gray wings**, and **white posterior underparts** is diagnostic. Female and juvenile are very similar. Fairly common NA migrant, from mid-Aug to late March, mostly in lowlands, to 1,500 m. Forages in lower levels of vegetation, usually near water (especially mangroves). 5" (13 cm).

Ovenbird
Seiurus aurocapilla

Male, female, and juvenile are virtually identical. Most likely mistaken for a migrant thrush (p. 248), but has **striped crown**; also note that it walks on forest floor (instead of hopping). Fairly common NA migrant, from mid-Sept to early May; to 1,500 m. Forages terrestrially in forest and tall second growth, often holds tail cocked up. Gives a hard *chup*. 6" (15 cm).

Worm-eating Warbler
Helmitheros vermivorum

Male, female, and juvenile are virtually identical. Potentially confused with Olive Sparrow (p. 302), but note thin, sharp bill; also somewhat resembles Three-striped Warbler (p. 274), but has **buffy underparts**. Uncommon NA migrant, from late Aug to late April, to 1,500 m. Forages on or near ground in undergrowth and in lower levels of forest; often with mixed flocks. 5" (13 cm).

male

female

Black-and-white
Warbler

male

female

American
Redstart

male

female

Prothonotary
Warbler

Ovenbird

Worm-eating
Warbler

Northern Waterthrush
Seiurus noveboracensis

Male, female, and juvenile are virtually identical. Very similar to Louisiana Waterthrush, but note **flecking on throat** and **thinner superciliary**. Common NA migrant, from mid-Aug to mid-May, mostly in lowlands, to 1,500 m. Terrestrial, prefers edges of ponds and slow-moving streams, also trails; habitually teeters as it walks or stands. Utters a metallic *tsink*. 6" (15 cm).

Louisiana Waterthrush
Seiurus motacilla

Male, female, and juvenile are virtually identical. Very similar to Northern Waterthrush, but note **white throat** and **white superciliary that broadens behind eye**; also has **buffy wash on flanks**. Fairly uncommon winter resident (from late July to mid-April) and passage migrant, mostly at middle elevations, to 2,600 m; rare passage migrant in Caribbean lowlands. Terrestrial, favors fast-flowing streams; habitually teeters as it walks or stands. Call similar to that of Northern Waterthrush. 6" (15 cm).

Wilson's Warbler
Wilsonia pusilla

Male has distincitive **black cap**. Female and similar juveniles have olive cap; both are similar to juvenile female Hooded Warbler and female and juvenile female Yellow Warbler (p. 258), but note **entirely olive tail**. Abundant winter resident (from early Sept to early May) and passage migrant, mostly above 800 m; very uncommon passage migrant in lowlands. Forages actively at all levels in forests, forest edges, second growth, and gardens; often with mixed flocks. 5" (13 cm).

Hooded Warbler
Wilsonia citrina

Adult male has diagnostic **black hood**; paler on juvenile male. Adult female has a much reduced hood; absent on juvenile female. Juvenile female similar to female and juvenile female Wilson's Warbler and female and juvenile female Yellow Warbler (p. 258), but note **white in outer tail feathers**. Very uncommon NA migrant, from late Sept to late April, mostly in wet lowlands, to 1,400 m. Forages low in underbrush, second growth, and forest edges; often flicks tail. 5" (13 cm).

Canada Warbler
Wilsonia canadensis

Adult male has distinctive **dark necklace**; fainter on adult female and juveniles. No other CR warblerlike bird has **plain gray upperparts** and **yellow underparts with white undertail coverts**. Common passage migrant, from early Sept to early Nov; uncommon passage migrant, from early April to early May; to 1,800 m. Forages at all levels in gardens, second growth, and forest edges; also in forests. 5" (13 cm).

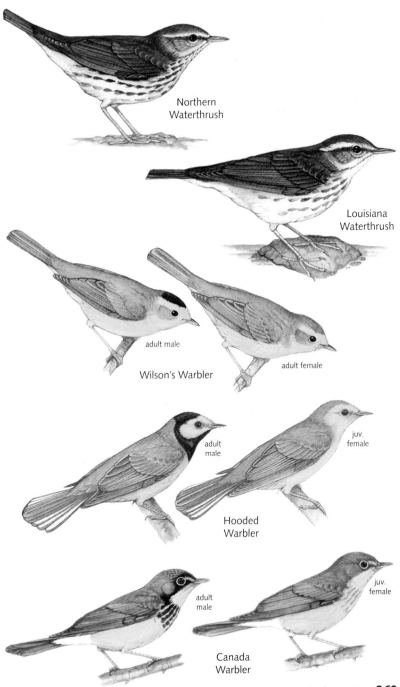

Northern
Waterthrush

Louisiana
Waterthrush

adult male

adult female

Wilson's Warbler

adult
male

juv.
female

Hooded
Warbler

adult
male

juv.
female

Canada
Warbler

[Respective plumages of Mourning Warbler, MacGillivray's Warbler, and Connecticut Warbler are extremely similar. The key diagnostic feature is the eye ring. Of the three species, the Mourning Warbler is by far the most common in CR; the Connecticut Warbler is very rare.]

Mourning Warbler
Oporornis philadelphia

Essentially no distinction between breeding and nonbreeding plumages. Male has no eye ring; some females also lack eye ring, others have a narrow, broken eye ring; juvenile also has a narrow, broken eye ring. Fairly common NA migrant, from early Sept to mid-May, to 1,500 m. Forages inconspicuously, usually within a meter of the ground, in weedy growth, hedgerows, and at forest edges. 5" (13 cm).

MacGillivray's Warbler
Oporornis tolmiei

Essentially no distinction between breeding and nonbreeding plumages. Male has **bold white arcs above and below the eye**. This feature is slightly less distinct on paler headed female and juvenile. Uncommon NA migrant, from mid-Sept to mid-May, to 2,000 m. Forages inconspicuously, usually within a meter of the ground, in weedy growth, hedgerows, and at forest edges. 5" (13 cm).

Connecticut Warbler
Oporornis agilis

Essentially no distinction between breeding and nonbreeding plumages. Female has paler head than male. Male, female, and juvenile have **distinct white eye ring** and **long, extended undertail coverts**. Casual NA migrant, from Oct to March, to 800 m. Forages in lower levels of second growth, forest edges, and gardens, usually near water; walks on ground (Mourning and MacGillivray's Warblers hop). 6" (15 cm).

Kentucky Warbler
Oporornis formosus

Essentially no distinction between breeding and nonbreeding plumages. Female is very similar to male, but has marginally less black on face. The **yellow spectacles** set it apart from all other warblers with yellow underparts and greenish-olive upperparts. Fairly common NA migrant, from mid-Sept to mid-April, mostly at lower elevations, to 1,800 m. Forages on or near ground in mature wet forests (gallery forests in northwest), second growth, and forest edges. Gives a hollow *chup*. 5" (13 cm).

Buff-rumped Warbler
Phaeothlypis fulvicauda

Resembles Sulphur-rumped and Black-tailed Flycatchers (p. 198), but note the **pale superciliary**. A resident warbler. Common in wet lowlands and foothills, to 1,000 m on Caribbean slope and 1,500 m in southern Pacific. Hops and flits along edges of forest streams and on trails and lawns; often attends army-ant swarms; swishes tail from side to side. Sings an accelerating series of loud, piercing notes that can easily be heard above the sound of rushing water. 5" (13 cm).

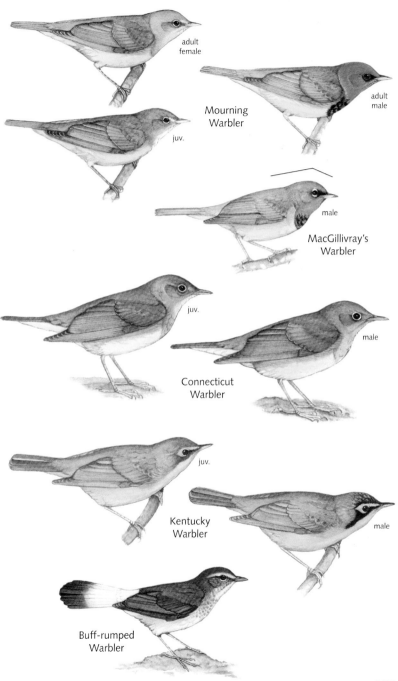

adult
female

adult
male

**Mourning
Warbler**

juv.

male

**MacGillivray's
Warbler**

juv.

male

**Connecticut
Warbler**

juv.

**Kentucky
Warbler**

male

**Buff-rumped
Warbler**

Wood-Warblers

Gray-crowned Yellowthroat $\qquad$ *Geothlypis poliocephala*
Male distinguished by **gray crown** and **miniscule black mask**. Female and similar juvenile told apart from other yellowthroats by a relatively thick (for a warbler) **bicolored bill** and a long tail. A resident warbler. Common and widespread, to 1,500 m. Forages low in brushy fields. From atop shrubbery, male sings sweet, wrenlike phrases, reminiscent of Olive-crowned Yellowthroat, but without the slurred *chrrree* note at the end. 5" (13 cm).

Olive-crowned Yellowthroat $\qquad$ *Geothlypis semiflava*
Male has **extensive black mask with no pale border**. Female has **yellow underparts** with olive-green sides and flanks. A resident warbler. Common in Caribbean lowlands; uncommon at middle elevations of Caribbean slope, to 1,200 m. Prefers low, wet, dense, overgrown sections of otherwise open areas. From exposed perches, male sings sweet, wrenlike phrases—reminiscent of Gray-crowned Yellowthroat, but often ending in a slurred *chrrree*. 5" (13 cm).

Masked Yellowthroat $\qquad$ *Geothlypis aequinoctialis*
Male has **black mask with grayish-blue band above**; also note **yellow belly**. Female shows **gray on sides of head**. A resident warbler. Fairly common in the San Vito area, from 900 to 1,200 m. Found in marshes and wet fields. From exposed perches, male repeats sweet phrases: *twee-lee-lee-lee-leetchwee-lee*. Sometimes the CR/Panama population is considered a distinct species and then called Chiriquí Yellowthroat (*G. chiriquensis*). 5" (13 cm).

Common Yellowthroat $\qquad$ *Geothlypis trichas*
Male has **extensive black mask with whitish band above**; also note **pale buffy belly**. Female and similar juvenile resemble female and juvenile Gray-crowned Yellowthroat, but have thin, dark bill and shorter tail; somewhat similar *Oporornis* warblers (p. 270) have yellow bellies. Uncommon passage migrant, mostly in Caribbean lowlands, from mid-Oct to Nov and from April to early May; uncommon winter resident, to 1,500 m, from mid-Oct to early May. Skulks in marshes and wet thickets. 5" (13 cm).

Collared Redstart $\qquad$ *Myioborus torquatus*
Similar to Slate-throated Redstart, but with **bright-yellow face and throat** and **dark breast band**. Common in highlands, from Tilarán Cordillera south, between 1,500 m and timberline. Forages in middle and lower levels of mature forest, second growth, and forest edges; usually in pairs and often with mixed flocks; frequently makes short sallies and fans its tail. **Endemic to CR and western Panama**. 5" (13 cm).

Slate-throated Redstart $\qquad$ *Myioborus miniatus*
The **dark face and throat** readily differentiate it from the Collared Redstart. A resident warbler. Common at middle elevations, from 700 to 2,100 m. Forages in middle and lower levels of mature forest, second growth, and forest edges; usually in pairs and often with mixed flocks; frequently makes short sallies and fans its tail. Sings a simple song of six or more even notes that increase slightly in pace and volume before stopping abruptly. 5" (13 cm).

Gray-crowned
Yellowthroat

male

female

Olive-crowned
Yellowthroat

male

female

Masked
Yellowthroat

male

female

Common
Yellowthroat

male

female

Collared
Redstart

Slate-throated
Redstart

Rufous-capped Warbler
Basileuterus rufifrons

No other CR warbler combines **rufous on the head** with **plain-yellow underparts**. A resident warbler. Common in northwestern Pacific and in Central Valley, east to Turrialba; to 2,000 m. Also common in intermontane valleys of southern Pacific, from 600 to 1,600 m. Forages in lower levels of woodlands, second growth, forest edges, and shaded coffee plantations; typically holds tail cocked upwards. Sings a spritely jumble of accelerating thin, high notes (similar to song of Black-cheeked Warbler). 5" (13 cm).

Three-striped Warbler
Basileuterus tristriatus

Head pattern somewhat resembles Golden-crowned Warbler and Worm-eating Warbler (p. 266), but note **pale-yellow underparts** and **blackish ear coverts**. A resident warbler. Common at middle elevations, from Tilarán Cordillera south, between 1,000 and 2,200 m. Small groups forage actively in lower levels of mature wet forest and advanced second growth, where, together with Common Bush-Tanagers (p. 278), they are often the core species within mixed flocks. Produces a rapid, high-pitched twittering. 5" (13 cm).

Black-cheeked Warbler
Basileuterus melanogenys

The **rufous crown** and **white superciliary** are diagnostic; also note **grayish breast**. Fairly common in highlands of Central and Talamanca Cordilleras, from 1,600 m to above timberline. Forages actively at lower levels of highland forest and at forest edges; usually two or more birds are present (often with mixed flocks). Song similar to Rufous-capped Warbler, but thinner. **Endemic to CR and western Panama**. 5" (13 cm).

Golden-crowned Warbler
Basileuterus culicivorus

The combination of a **yellow-orange crown stripe** (**bordered by black**) and **yellow underparts** is distinctive. A resident warbler. Fairly common in foothills and middle elevations, from 600 to 1,500 m (to 2,200 m in southern Pacific). Forages actively in lower and middle levels of humid and wet forest and second growth; usually two or more birds are present (often with mixed flocks). Makes dry, rattling wrenlike sounds when foraging; whistles a sweet five-note phrase, the first three notes on the same pitch, the fourth lower, and the fifth sliding up in a somewhat questioning tone. 5" (13 cm).

Wrenthrush
Zeledonia coronata

A somber, rotund, short-tailed bird with a distinctive **golden-russet crown**. Fairly common in highlands, from 1,500 m to above timberline. Stays on or near the ground in dense undergrowth of mature wet forests and paramo. Hard to see; presence best revealed by thin, penetrating call (*tsseee!*) or high-pitched song (*tsee-te-dee*). **Endemic to CR and western Panama**. 5" (13 cm).

Yellow-breasted Chat
Icteria virens

Male, female, and juvenile are virtually identical. No other plain, olive-backed bird combines **white spectacles** and **yellow throat and breast**. Very uncommon NA migrant, from late Sept to late April, to 1,400 m. Prefers concealment of brushy tangles in open areas and along forest edges. Gives a deep, harsh *chewt*. 7" (18 cm).

Rufous-capped
Warbler

Three-striped
Warbler

Black-cheeked
Warbler

Golden-crowned
Warbler

Wrenthrush

Yellow-breasted Chat

Bananaquit

Genus INCERTAE SEDIS. Until recently, the Bananaquit belonged to the monotypic family Coerebidae. Its taxonomic placement is now uncertain. The numerous races of Bananaquit are widespread throughout the neotropics. This small bird is quite active and warblerlike; it is closely related to the wood-warblers (p. 254). Bananaquits, however, build globular nests—quite unlike the warblers—that they use both for raising young and as dormitories.

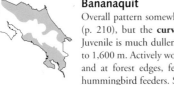

Bananaquit
Coereba flaveola

Overall pattern somewhat resembles the much larger kiskadee-type flycatchers (p. 210), but the **curved bill** and **white wing spot** are diagnostic features. Juvenile is much duller. Very common in wet lowlands and middle elevations, to 1,600 m. Actively works its way through shrubbery and small trees in gardens and at forest edges, feeding on flower nectar, fruits, and insects; comes to hummingbird feeders. Sings a high, scratchy twitter that could be mistaken for a hummingbird. 4" (10 cm).

Tanagers

THRAUPIDAE. The taxonomy of this New World family—which includes the ant-tanagers, bush-tanagers, shrike-tanagers, honeycreepers, and dacnises—is still in some dispute; indeed, there is no single characteristic shared by all members of the family. Many species have fairly stout bills, which indicates a close affinity with the finches; the honeycreepers, however, have long, slightly decurved beaks. Although generally characterized as fruit eaters, most species also eat insects and spiders.

Red-crowned Ant-Tanager
Habia rubica

The male's **red crown patch is bordered by black**; the female has a **golden crown patch**. There is no range overlap with the similar Red-throated Ant-Tanager. Uncommon in Pacific foothills, including the Nicoya Peninsula and the western Central Valley, to 1,200 m; rare in lowlands. Stays fairly low in forests as it forages in small groups, sometimes with mixed flocks; often accompanies army-ant swarms. Active and noisy; groups produce many nonmusical sounds as they move about. The song is a loud, harsh *cheeta cheeta cheeta*. 7" (18 cm).

Red-throated Ant-Tanager
Habia fuscicauda

The Caribbean counterpart of the Red-crowned Ant-Tanager. The male's **red throat** and the female's **yellow throat** are diagnostic; female told apart from Olive Tanager (p. 278) by olive-brown upperparts. Fairly common in Caribbean lowlands and foothills, to 900 m. Favors dense vegetation along streams and forest edges, where foraging groups produce a wrenlike scolding chatter. The sweet, liquid song is also wrenlike. 7" (18 cm).

Black-cheeked Ant-Tanager
Habia atrimaxillaris

On the male, the **dark face** and **pinkish throat** should preclude confusion; female similar but has lighter throat. Relatively common in its limited range around the Golfo Dulce and Osa Peninsula. Small groups, often with mixed flocks, move noisily through the lower levels of wet forest, occasionally coming to forest edges or into second growth. Calls and song wrenlike. **Endemic to Costa Rica**. 7" (18 cm).

Bananaquit

Red-crowned
Ant-Tanager

male

female

Red-throated
Ant-Tanager

male

female

male

Black-cheeked
Ant-Tanager

Tanagers

Common Bush-Tanager
Chlorospingus ophthalmicus

The **triangular white spot behind the eye** is the key field mark on this drab olive-backed bird. One of the most common middle-elevation species, from 600 to 2,200 m. Actively forages at lower and middle levels of forests and adjacent second growth and gardens; almost always in small groups that are regularly accompanied by other species, especially Three-striped Warblers (p. 274). Noisy and nonmusical, it produces high, weak notes that are often slurred together in a rapid twittering. 5" (13 cm).

Ashy-throated Bush-Tanager
Chlorospingus canigularis

On this plain-headed bush-tanager, note the **pale-gray throat bordered by a dark-gray lateral throat stripe** and the yellow-olive breast separating the pale throat and belly. Very uncommon on the Caribbean slope of Central Valley volcanoes and in the Reventazón River watershed; from 400 to 1,200 m. Usually stays high up in the canopy of wet forests, where it typically forages with mixed species flocks. 5" (13 cm).

Sooty-capped Bush-Tanager
Chlorospingus pileatus

The **broad white superciliary** has a jagged, lightning-bolt look to it. Very common in highlands above 2,000 m; fairly common on highest peaks of Tilarán Cordillera. Actively forages at lower and middle levels of forests and forest edges, in groups and in mixed flocks. Sings with a thin, squeaky twittering. **Endemic to CR and western Panama**. 5" (13 cm).

Olive Tanager
Chlorothraupis carmioli

This rather rotund tanager lacks any obvious field marks, but it is greener than the somewhat similar female Red-throated Ant-Tanager (p. 276) and has duller underparts than the female Hepatic Tanager (p. 284). Common in Caribbean foothills, from 300 to 1,000 m; rare in Caribbean lowlands. Groups of up to twenty or more travel through lower levels of mature forests, frequently in the company of other species, especially Tawny-crested Tanagers (p. 280). Flock members produce a variety of shrill or buzzy sounds with an irritated quality. 7" (18 cm).

Rosy Thrush-Tanager
Rhodinocichla rosea

The **rose-colored superciliary and breast** of the male are unique. The female's superciliary and breast are a **warm tawny-orange**. Because it is uncommon and because it skulks, this gorgeous bird is extremely difficult to see in its limited range within the Térraba River watershed; from about 200 to 1,000 m. Forages in leaf litter in dense second growth. Has a rich, liquid voice. 8" (20 cm).

Common
Bush-Tanager

Ashy-throated
Bush-Tanager

Sooty-capped
Bush-Tanager

Olive
Tanager

Rosy
Thrush-Tanager

male

female

Tanagers

Dusky-faced Tanager
Mitrospingus cassinii

The **pale iris** and **olive crown** are diagnostic. Fairly common in wet Caribbean lowlands, rising to about 600 m in Central Cordillera foothills. Noisy flocks of four or more individuals troop through dense vegetation at forest edges and along streams; habitat and bird's wary behavior make it difficult to get a clear view of this species. While it forages, the bird constantly utters a harsh *shpik!*. 7" (18 cm).

White-shouldered Tanager
Tachyphonus luctuosus

The male's **white shoulder patch** is an obvious field mark (male White-lined Tanager's white shoulder patch is barely visible when not in flight). Female distinguished from female Black-and-yellow Tanager (p. 282) by thicker, **bicolored bill** and paler throat. Females of southern Pacific race have gray head; females of Caribbean race have olive green head. Fairly common in wet lowlands and foothills, to 1,000 m. Pairs or small groups typically accompany other species foraging in the lower and middle levels of forests and advanced second growth. Calls with weak sibilant notes. 5" (13 cm).

White-lined Tanager
Tachyphonus rufus

Often travel in pairs; since neither male nor female is particularly distinct, the best key to identification is often their mere co-presence. In flight, the male flashes a bold white wing patch (normally obscured when perched). The characteristic tanager bill distinguishes the rufous female from other similarly colored species. Fairly common in Caribbean lowlands and foothills (to 1,400 m in eastern Central Valley); recently expanding from Panama into southern Pacific. Forages in open areas with brushy habitat. Not very vocal, makes a sweet *chew-wE, chew-wE…*, the last part upwardly inflected. 7" (18 cm).

Tawny-crested Tanager
Tachyphonus delattrii

The male's **bright tawny-orange crest feathers** are conspicuous. Nondescript, brown female best identified by the company she keeps—she often travels in flocks of a dozen or more individuals, including distinctive males. Female distinguished from Thrushlike Schiffornis (p. 214) by larger bill. Common in Caribbean foothills, from 300 to 800 m; uncommon from 800 to 1,200 m; also uncommon in Caribbean lowlands. Moves through understory and lower canopy of mature wet forest in noisy, active flocks that are often joined by other species, especially Olive Tanagers (p. 278). Call notes are sibilant and squeaky. 6" (15 cm).

Dusky-faced
Tanager

male

female
Caribbean race

female southern
Pacific race

White-shouldered
Tanager

male

female

White-lined
Tanager

male

female

Tawny-crested
Tanager

Tanagers

Gray-headed Tanager
Eucometis penicillata

Size, color pattern, upright stance, and hint of a crest could suggest a flycatcher. However, no CR flycatcher, or other tanager, displays such contrast between the **all-gray head** and **bright-yellow underparts**. Fairly common in humid lowlands and foothills of Pacific slope, to 1,200 m; uncommon in northwestern Pacific lowlands and Caño Negro region. Forages in understory of forest and second growth; regularly found accompanying army-ant swarms, also follows troops of White-faced Capuchin Monkeys. Most common vocalizations are a dry sputtering, or high-pitched squeaky notes. 7" (18 cm).

Blue-and-gold Tanager
Bangsia arcaei

Suggests a male euphonia (see species on p. 326), but lacks yellow or tawny on crown and has a **dark-red eye**. Uncommon in Caribbean foothills, from Miravalles Volcano to Turrialba Volcano, between 400 and 1,200 m. Forages mostly in midcanopy of wet forests, often with mixed flocks. **Endemic to CR and Panama**. 6" (15 cm).

Black-and-yellow Tanager
Chrysothlypis chrysomelas

Color pattern of the male is diagnostic, although the **slender bill** and overall slim proportions suggest a warbler rather than a tanager. The female is much more difficult to identify if not in the presence of a male; the somewhat similar female White-shouldered Tanager (p. 280) has a thicker, bicolored bill and a paler throat; distinguished from all similar-looking warblers by **whitish abdomen**. Fairly common in Caribbean foothills and middle elevations, from 400 to 1,200 m. Forages with flocks in forest canopy and forest edges. **Endemic to CR and Panama**. 5" (13 cm).

Sulphur-rumped Tanager
Heterospingus rubrifrons

The **white tufts at sides of breast** are conspicuous; the **yellow rump** is difficult to see if the bird is overhead. Darker gray than either Plain-colored or Palm Tanagers (p. 290). A very uncommon resident of southern Caribbean lowlands and foothills, to 700 m. Forages in midcanopy of forests and forest edges with mixed flocks. Makes high, buzzy notes. **Endemic to CR and Panama**. 6" (15 cm).

White-throated Shrike-Tanager
Lanio leucothorax

The **fierce-looking bill** should distinguish the brightly colored male from all similarly colored orioles (see species on p. 318); it is also the best field mark on the brownish female. Male of Caribbean race has yellow rump and undertail coverts; male of Pacific race has black rump and undertail coverts. Both races uncommon. Caribbean race generally in foothills, to 900 m; southern Pacific race occurs in lowlands. Forages at middle levels of mature wet forest; encountered with mixed flocks. Produces a variety of vocalizations; one of the more common calls is a two-note repetition (*chit-chew, chit-chew…*), with the first note slightly higher than the second. **Endemic from eastern Honduras to Panama**. 8" (20 cm).

Gray-headed
Tanager

Blue-and-gold
Tanager

Black-and-yellow
Tanager

male

female

Sulphur-rumped
Tanager

White-throated
Shrike-Tanager

male
Caribbean race

female

White-winged Tanager
Piranga leucoptera

On the male, combination of **red back**, **bright-white wing bars**, and **small black mask** is diagnostic. The female resembles the female Western Tanager, but has a **bicolored bill** and is brighter yellow underneath. Uncommon at middle elevations, from Tilarán Cordillera south, between 1,000 and 2,200 m. Usually at upper levels of wet forests and forest edges; often with mixed flocks. Makes a thin, weak, rising *tsu-weet*. 5" (13 cm).

Western Tanager
Piranga ludoviciana

Shows **pale bill** and **two wing bars** in all plumages. Female distinguished from female White-winged Tanager by pale bill and greener underparts; also distinguished from female Flame-colored Tanager (p. 286) by unstreaked back. An NA migrant, from Oct to April. Uncommon in northwestern Pacific lowlands, south to Carara; rare in western Central Valley and in southern Pacific, to 2,200 m. Call is a rising *pirdidit*. 7" (18 cm).

Summer Tanager
Piranga rubra

The bright-red male is distinguished from the male Hepatic Tanager by the **pale bill**. Female and juvenile are more **ochre colored** than female and juvenile Hepatic and Scarlet Tanagers (p. 286). During the male's first spring, he still resembles the female, but begins to show red splotches. A very common NA migrant, from mid-Sept to late April. Individuals can be found countrywide, up to 2,500 m, in almost any habitat with some trees. Frequently utters a staccato *chi-ti-duh*. 7" (18 cm).

Hepatic Tanager
Piranga flava

Male distinguished from the male Summer Tanager by **dark bill and lores**. The female resembles an Olive Tanager (p. 278), but is brighter **yellow below** and behaves quite differently; female also similar to female Scarlet Tanager (p. 286), but note heavier, darker bill. Uncommon in wet middle elevations, from 600 to 1,800 m; rare in hills of Osa Peninsula. Pairs or individuals forage fairly high in forests and adjacent gardens. The call is an ascending *chup-chi-dit*. 7" (18 cm).

female

White-winged
Tanager

male

female

Western
Tanager

male

female

Summer
Tanager

male

female

Hepatic
Tanager

male

Tanagers

Flame-colored Tanager
Piranga bidentata

Both sexes have **dusky streaking on the back**, unlike any comparably colored tanager species. Female similar to female Western Tanager (p. 284), but note streaked back and yellow belly. Fairly common in highlands, from about 1,200 m to timberline on Central and Talamanca Cordilleras. Prefers forest edges and garden habitats, where individuals or pairs forage at all levels. Call is a resonant, wooden *kriDECK*. 7" (18 cm).

Scarlet Tanager
Piranga olivacea

Breeding-plumaged male is unmistakable; in nonbreeding plumage, the **black wings** are distinctive. Female is similar to nonbreeding male, but wings are not as dark; female similar to female Summer Tanager (p. 284), but is greener and has darker wings; female also similar to female Hepatic Tanager (p. 284), but bill is paler and less stout. A fairly common and widespread passage migrant; from late Sept to late Nov (when more numerous on the Caribbean side of CR), and again from late March to early May (when more evenly distributed). Stays fairly high in trees at forest edges and in gardens; often several or more individuals are seen together. Generally silent. 6" (15 cm).

[Passerini's Tanager and Cherrie's Tanager were formerly considered conspecific and known as the Scarlet-rumped Tanager (*Ramphocelus passerinii*).]

Passerini's Tanager
Ramphocelus passerinii

Male is virtually identical to male Cherrie's Tanager; females are the key to distinguishing between these species (as is geographic location). The female Passerini's is drabber than the female Cherrie's and lacks orange breast and rump. The **thick, light-blue bill with a dark tip** is a shared trademark of both sexes. A very conspicuous resident of Caribbean lowlands and foothills, to 1,500 m. Numerous birds are generally found together staying low in open areas with ample brush. Calls are varied and frequently given, with a sharp *tsip!* often heard. **Illustration of male same as for Cherrie's Tanager**. 6" (15 cm).

Cherrie's Tanager
Ramphocelus costaricensis

Male is virtually identical to male Passerini's Tanager; female differentiated by **bright orange breast and rump** (no range overlap). Very common in disturbed habitat with thickets and shrubs in southern Pacific lowlands and foothills, north to the Tarcoles River; to 1,800 m. **Endemic to CR and western Panama**. **Illustration of male same as for Passerini's Tanager**. 6" (15 cm).

Crimson-collared Tanager
Ramphocelus sanguinolentus

Not readily confused. Fairly common throughout Caribbean lowlands and foothills, to 1,200 m. Individuals or pairs typically forage a few meters above the ground (slightly higher than Passerini's Tanager) in disturbed habitats. Song is a series of slow-paced, sibilant notes. 7" (18 cm).

male

Flame-colored
Tanager

female

Scarlet
Tanager

breeding
male

nonbreeding
male

female

Passerini's
Tanager

male

Passerini's/Ch
Tanager

fema

Cherrie's
Tanager

Emerald Tanager
Tangara florida

The **black ear patch** distinguishes this brilliant bird from similar bright-green species. Uncommon in Caribbean foothills, from 400 to 1,000 m. Almost exclusively found with mixed flocks in wet forests and at forest edges. 5" (13 cm).

Speckled Tanager
Tangara guttata

Very distinctive; the **spotted underparts** could recall a Sharpbill (p. 224), which shares similar habitat, but note **speckled back** and thicker bill. Fairly common in wet foothills and middle elevations; on Caribbean slope, from Tilarán Cordillera south, and on Pacific slope of Talamanca Cordillera; between 400 and 1,400 m. Forages in forests, forest edges, and gardens; usually with mixed flocks. Produces weak, colorless chipping notes. 5" (13 cm).

Golden-hooded Tanager
Tangara larvata

A very distinctive bird. Juvenile has same pattern as adult, but is much duller. A common species of gardens and forest edges throughout wet lowlands and middle elevations, to 1,600 m. Characteristic call is a buzzy twittering. 5" (13 cm).

Bay-headed Tanager
Tangara gyrola

Reddish-brown head and **deep turquoise-blue underparts** are diagnostic, even on duller plumaged female and juvenile; similar to Rufous-winged Tanager, but note green wings. Common on southern Pacific slope, to 1,500 m; also common at middle elevations and in foothills of Caribbean slope, from 1,500 to 400 m, occasionally to lowlands. Favors middle levels of wet forest habitats, second growth, and gardens. Call is a weak *tsit*. 5" (13 cm).

Spangle-cheeked Tanager
Tangara dowii

The only other highland species with a remotely similar color pattern is the Elegant Euphonia (p. 324), which has an entirely light-blue crown. Fairly common from 1,400 to 3,000 m. Typically with mixed flocks in montane forests and at forest edges. **Endemic to CR and western Panama**. 5" (13 cm).

Rufous-winged Tanager
Tangara lavinia

Similar in all plumages to the Bay-headed Tanager, but note the **rufous wings** and **green underparts**. Uncommon in Caribbean foothills, from 250 to 800 m. Individuals or pairs travel with mixed flocks; forage at middle and upper levels of forests, second growth, and forest edges. Call is a weak *tsit*. 5" (13 cm).

Emerald
Tanager

Speckled
Tanager

Golden-hooded
Tanager

Bay-headed
Tanager

Spangle-cheeked
Tanager

Rufous-winged
Tanager

male

female

Silver-throated Tanager
Tangara icterocephala

Silvery-white throat is not as immediately obvious as the **bright-yellow head**; also note the **black malar stripe** and **black streaking on the back**. Female and juvenile have the same overall pattern as the male, but are duller. Very common in wet foothills and middle elevations, from 400 to 2,000 m; less common in adjacent lowlands. Often in flocks, with or without other species, at middle levels of forest and forest edges. Frequently utters a distinctive buzzy *tseet*. 5" (13 cm).

Plain-colored Tanager
Tangara inornata

Resembles larger Palm Tanager, but without any trace of olive on head; generally keeps violet shoulder patch concealed. Also compare with Sulphur-rumped Tanager (p. 282). Fairly uncommon in Caribbean lowlands, south from the Puerto Viejo de Sarapiquí area. Small groups forage at forest edges and gardens. Rather nondescript vocalizations, as with most members of this genus. **Endemic from CR to northern Colombia**. 5" (13 cm).

Blue-gray Tanager
Thraupis episcopus

In good light, there should be no confusion; in poor light, can look quite gray and could be mistaken for a Palm Tanager (but that species has an obvious two-tone wing). One of the most common birds in gardens throughout the country, to 2,200 m; uncommon in northwestern Pacific. Its simple song is little more than even-pitched squeaks (similar to that of Palm Tanager). 6" (15 cm).

Palm Tanager
Thraupis palmarum

The **black flight feathers** contrast with the otherwise **grayish-olive plumage**. (Compare with Plain-colored Tanager and Sulphur-rumped Tanager [p. 282]). Less numerous than the similar Blue-gray Tanager. Common in gardens below about 1,800 m; uncommon in the Central Valley and very uncommon in northwestern Pacific. Song similar to that of Blue-gray Tanager, but more rapid. 6" (15 cm).

Blue Dacnis
Dacnis cayana

The mostly blue male is distinctive (the male Lovely and Turquoise Cotingas [p. 218] have quite different body forms); the female's **blue head** and **green body** are distinctive. Fairly uncommon in wet lowlands and foothills, to 900 m on Caribbean and to 1,200 m on southern Pacific slope. Favors forest edges and gardens. 4" (10 cm).

Scarlet-thighed Dacnis
Dacnis venusta

The **electric-blue upperparts** and **black underparts** render the male unmistakable. The less colorful female might cause more confusion, perhaps suggesting a warbler, but no other CR species combines light blue-green upperparts with buffy underparts. Fairly common in foothills and middle elevations on Caribbean slope, from Tilarán Cordillera south (on Caribbean slope, descends to the base of mountains during second half of year). Also fairly common on Pacific slope of Talamanca Cordillera (between 400 and 1,500 m) and Tilarán Cordillera (between 1,300 and 1,500 m). Feeds in fruiting trees at forest edges and in gardens. 5" (13 cm).

Silver-throated
Tanager

Plain-colored
Tanager

Blue-gray
Tanager

Palm Tanager

male

female

Blue Dacnis

male

female

Scarlet-thighed
Dacnis

Green Honeycreeper
Chlorophanes spiza

The distinctive turquoise-green male has a black half-hood; the handsome lime-green female has a slightly **decurved yellow bill with a dark culmen**. Fairly common in wet lowlands and middle elevations, to 1,500 m. Found at forest openings, forest edges, second growth, and gardens; often with mixed flocks. 5" (13 cm).

Shining Honeycreeper
Cyanerpes lucidus

Male similar to male Red-legged Honeycreeper, but **bright-yellow legs** are diagnostic. The **blue streaking** on the female's breast is likewise unique. Fairly common in wet lowlands and foothills, to 1,200 m. Feeds at forest edges and gardens. 4" (10 cm).

Red-legged Honeycreeper
Cyanerpes cyaneus

The male's **red legs** and glittering **pale-turquoise crown** distinguish it from the Shining Honeycreeper. The rather nondescript olive-green female might bring to mind a Tennessee Warbler (p. 254), but note the **long, slightly decurved bill**. This is one of the few CR species in which the males molt into a nonbreeding plumage after breeding. In the second half of the year, most males resemble females, but have black wings and tail. In all plumages, flashes **yellow underwing** in flight. Common on Pacific slope and in northern central Caribbean, to 1,200 m. Found in forests, second growth, forest edges, and gardens; typically in small groups. 4" (10 cm).

male

female

Green
Honeycreeper

male

female

Shining
Honeycreeper

nonbreeding
male
(not to scale)

breeding
male

female

underwing

Red-legged
Honeycreeper

EMBERIZIDAE. The rather somber-plumaged birds of this family are found on or near the ground in habitats ranging from open fields and subalpine paramo to rain forest interior. The majority have conical bills that they use to crack open seeds, but they also supplement their diet with fruit and invertebrates. The larger finches and sparrows often forage in leaf litter by scratching with their feet.

Thick-billed Seed-Finch
Oryzoborus funereus

Black male virtually identical to male of Caribbean race of Variable Seedeater, but note seed-finch's **straight culmen**; male very distinct from male of Pacific race of Variable Seedeater. Female Thick-billed Seed-Finch has **rich, warm-brown** coloration; smaller than the similar female Nicaraguan Seed-Finch. Fairly uncommon in weedy areas of wet lowlands and foothills, to 1,200 m. Song is a series of whistles and chirps. 5" (12 cm).

Nicaraguan Seed-Finch
Oryzoborus nuttingi

The male's **huge pink bill** is unmistakable. The female is very similar to female Thick-billed Seed-Finch, though substantially larger; also resembles somewhat larger and slightly darker female Blue-black Grosbeak (p. 310), which favors denser cover. An uncommon resident of wet fields (typically near forest edges) in Caribbean lowlands. Sings a medley of squeaky whistles and chirps. **Endemic from Nicaragua to western Panama.** 6" (15 cm).

Variable Seedeater
Sporophila americana

There are two races in CR, though the females of both races are identical. Female is **drab brown**—less colorful than the rich, warm-brown female Thick-billed Seed-Finch. The **black bill** sets the female apart from the very similar female Yellow-bellied Seedeater and female Slate-colored and Ruddy-breasted Seedeaters (p. 296). Male Caribbean race: Virtually identical to male Thick-billed Seed-Finch, but note seedeater's **curved culmen**. Very common in open areas throughout Caribbean lowlands and foothills, to 1,500 m, extending up Reventazón watershed to Cartago. Sings a fast-paced, disorderly mix of warbles and trills. Male Pacific race: Could be confused with male White-collared Seedeater, but has **black throat** and **lacks wing bars**. Uncommon in northwestern Pacific lowlands, increasingly common in the south, where it can occur up to 1,500 m. Song is richer and more structured than that of Caribbean race. 4" (10 cm).

White-collared Seedeater
Sporophila torqueola

The only CR seedeater with **wing bars**. Fairly common in open areas, including reedy marshes, throughout lowlands and middle elevations, to 1,500 m. Sings a slow series of clear, sweet whistles and chirps (similar to song of Yellow-bellied Seedeater). 4" (10 cm).

Yellow-bellied Seedeater
Sporophila nigricollis

Male is distinctively patterned; note that belly is whitish on some individuals. The **yellowish underparts** set the female apart from the very similar female Variable Seedeater and female Slate-colored and Ruddy-breasted Seedeaters (p. 296). Uncommon and nomadic in open weedy areas of southern Pacific; also known from Cartago and Arenal areas. Song similar to that of White-collared Seedeater, but not as long. 4" (10 cm).

male

male

female

Thick-billed
Seed-Finch

female

male
Caribbean
race

female

Nicaraguan
Seed-Finch

male
Pacific race

Variable
Seedeater

male

Yellow-bellied
Seedeater

female

White-collared
Seedeater

female

Birds of Costa Rica / **295**

Slate-colored Seedeater
Sporophila schistacea

Male's **yellow bill** is distinctive. The **whitish belly and undertail coverts** set the female apart from the very similar female Ruddy-breasted Seedeater and female Variable and Yellow-bellied Seedeaters (p. 294). A rare and irregularly occuring species that travels in small flocks on southern half of both Pacific and Caribbean slopes. Favors tangled growth at forest edges. Song consists of high, metallic, warbling trills. 4" (10 cm).

Ruddy-breasted Seedeater
Sporophila minuta

Male's **rusty underparts** are distinctive. The **buffy underparts and rump** set the female apart from the very similar female Slate-colored Seedeater and female Variable and Yellow-bellied Seedeaters (p. 294). Uncommon in southern Pacific lowlands and Caño Negro region. Flocks wander in open savanna habitat, weedy fields, and marshes. The long, sweet song combines double whistle notes. 4" (10 cm).

Yellow-faced Grassquit
Tiaris olivaceus

The male's **yellow facial markings** are diagnostic; female shows a similar, but indistinct, pattern. Both sexes are more **olive-green** than other seedeaters. Common, mostly at middle elevations, from 600 to 2,200 m; occasionally occurs in lowlands. Favors fields, roadsides, and gardens. Song is a thin, fast twittering. 4" (10 cm).

Blue-black Grassquit
Volatinia jacarina

The male is glossier and has a **thinner and narrower bill** than any similar dark seedeater—there is little range overlap with the rare Blue Seedeater. The female's **streaked breast** is unique among lowland seedeaters; the female migrant Indigo Bunting (p. 312), which is faintly streaked, has a whiter throat and a hint of wing bars. A common bird of open brushy fields, in lowlands and middle elevations, to 1,700 m. Male sings a buzzy *tzeeer* that rises and falls—often given as the bird jumps/flies a foot or so into the air. 4" (10 cm).

Blue Seedeater
Amaurospiza concolor

In poor light, male can look blackish; note the **conical bill**. (Little range overlap with the Blue-black Grassquit.) Female is more **tawny** than similar seedeaters. Male and female perhaps best told apart from similar species by habitat. A rare denizen of middle elevations and highlands, between 1,000 and 2,200 m on both Pacific and Caribbean slopes; also rare on highest hills of Nicoya Peninsula. Favors bamboo clusters along cloud forest edges, where it forages higher off the ground than other seedeaters typically do. Sings with sweet, descending notes. 5" (12 cm).

male

female

Slate-colored
Seedeater

male

female

Ruddy-breasted
Seedeater

male

female

Yellow-faced
Grassquit

female

male

Blue-black
Grassquit

female

male

Blue
Seedeater

Birds of Costa Rica /

Seedeaters, Finches, & Sparrows

Slaty Finch
Haplospiza rustica

The **slender conical bill** is the best way of distinguishing this species from the Peg-billed Finch and the Slaty Flowerpiercer. A rare species known from scattered sightings between 1,500 m and timberline. Forages for seeds, on or near the ground, in grassy areas near highland forests. Call and song are high-pitched and weak. 5" (12 cm).

Peg-billed Finch
Acanthidops bairdii

On both sexes, the **sharp-tipped, slightly upturned bill** is bicolored (the **lower mandible is yellowish**); the female has **buffy wing bars**. (Compare bill with that of Slaty Finch and the Slaty Flowerpiercer.) Fairly uncommon in overgrown bushy areas and forest edges, between 1,500 m and timberline. Feeds mostly on berries, but also eats insects, seeds (especially bamboo seeds), and even flower nectar. Makes a thin, high-pitched *tsip*. Song is a harsh chittering of three or four notes with a softer, querulous ending. **Endemic to CR and western Panama.** 5" (13 cm).

Slaty Flowerpiercer
Diglossa plumbea

The odd bill consists of an **upturned, pinkish lower mandible** and a **dark, hook-tipped upper mandible**; compare bill with that of Slaty Finch and Peg-billed Finch. Common at forest edges and in gardens, from 1,200 m to above timberline. Uses bill to pierce the base of flowers and hence "rob" the nectar. Song is a high, fast twitter. **Endemic to CR and western Panama.** 4" (10 cm).

Grassland Yellow-Finch
Sicalis luteola

The only records consist of several sightings in early May, 1955, on the southwestern flank of Miravalles Volcano, and an unconfirmed sighting near Tarcoles. No other small seedeater-type bird combines bright-yellow underparts and a streaked back. Could appear in open country of Pacific lowlands. 5" (12 cm).

Wedge-tailed Grass-Finch
Emberizoides herbicola

Long tail is distinctive. Rare in intermontane valleys of southern Pacific, mostly between 100 and 500 m. Recent sightings at sea level (Damas, northwest of Quepos) and 800 m (Los Altos de Salitre, above Buenos Aires). Found in fields of tall grass; unfortunately, much of the original habitat has been destroyed to make way for pineapple plantations. Call is a high, sharp *chip*. 7" (18 cm).

Slaty Finch
male
female

Peg-billed Finch
male
female

Slaty
Flowerpiercer
male
female

Grassland Yellow-Finch

Wedge-tailed
Grass-Finch

Large-footed Finch
Pezopetes capitalis

Somber and bulky; the black face and crown stripes show little contrast with the dark-gray hood. Fairly common from Cordillera Central south; from 2,000 m to above timberline. Often scratches in leaf litter with both feet; occurs in undergrowth of highland forests, second growth, and in paramo. Song is a languid medley of sweet whistles and chirps, rather wrenlike in quality. **Endemic to CR and western Panama.** 8" (20 cm).

White-naped Brush-Finch
Atlapetes albinucha

Distinguished by **white crown stripe** and **yellow throat**. Fairly common between 900 and 2,000 m; rare above 2,000 m. Forages at lower levels of second growth, weedy open areas, and forest edges. Voices high, thin notes in both call and song. 7" (18 cm).

Sooty-faced Finch
Lysurus crassirostris

The **flecked malar stripe**, **dark throat**, and **yellow belly** are diagnostic. Fairly common on Caribbean Slope, from Tilarán Cordillera south, between 600 and 1,500 m; rare on Pacific slope of northern Talamanca Cordillera, between 1,200 and 1,600 m. Forages in understory of wet forest. Call consists of two to four piercing notes: *tsee, tsEE*. **Endemic to CR and Panama.** 7" (18 cm).

Yellow-thighed Finch
Pselliophorus tibialis

The **puffy yellow thigh feathers** are diagnostic. Juvenile is entirely dark and could be difficult to identify, though distinctive adults are usually nearby. Common from Cordillera Central south, between 1,400 m and timberline; less common in higher parts of Tilarán Cordillera. Pairs or small groups actively forage in mature forest, second growth, forest edges, and gardens, usually quite low, but sometimes venture high up into trees. Song is high, spritely, and somewhat squeaky. **Endemic to CR and western Panama.** 7" (18 cm).

Stripe-headed Brush-Finch
Buarremon torquatus

Told apart from similar Black-striped Sparrow (p. 302) by **conspicuous white throat** and **black mask** (vs. black eye line). Juvenile Orange-billed Sparrow (p. 302) also has black bill and white throat, but shows white superciliary and black breast band. Uncommon in southern Pacific foothills, from 300 to 1,200 m. Favors dense undergrowth (hence hard to see), but sometimes enters adjacent gardens and forests. Call and song consist of high, penetrating notes. 8" (20 cm).

Chestnut-capped Brush-Finch
Buarremon brunneinucha

The combination of **chestnut crown** and **bright-white throat** is diagnostic. Common at middle elevations, from 900 to 2,500 m. Inhabits understory of wet forest, advanced second growth, and forest edges. Very high, thin notes comprise both call and song. 7" (18 cm).

Large-footed Finch

White-naped
Brush-Finch

Sooty-faced
Finch

Yellow-thighed
Finch

Stripe-headed
Brush-Finch

Chestnut-capped
Brush-Finch

Prevost's Ground-Sparrow
Melozone biarcuata

The **black-and-white facial markings** and **bright reddish-brown crown and nape** are diagnostic. Uncommon in the Central Valley, from 600 to 1,600 m; recent sightings northwest of Monteverde. Forages on or near ground in scrub, grass, hedgerows, shaded coffee plantations, and gardens. Call is a thin *tsip*. Sometimes the CR population is considered a distinct species and then called Cabanis's Ground-Sparrow (*Melozone cabanisi*). 6" (15 cm).

White-eared Ground-Sparrow
Melozone leucotis

Large **white spots in front of and behind eyes** and **bright-yellow on sides of neck** are diagnostic. Fairly common from Tilarán Cordillera to eastern Central Valley, between 1,000 and 2,000 m. Found in undergrowth of humid woodlands, heavily shaded gardens, coffee plantations, and along ravines. Call is a shrill *tsip*. Song begins slowly, then quickly accelerates into a profusion of loud, high notes. 7" (18 cm).

Orange-billed Sparrow
Arremon aurantiirostris

Adult has **bright-orange bill**, **white superciliary**, and **black breast band**. Juvenile (not illustrated) has black bill; distinguished from similar Stripe-headed Brush-Finch (p. 300) by white superciliary and black breast band. Common in lowlands and foothills, to 1,200 m. Pairs or small groups forage in the understory of mature wet forests and tall second growth. Birds on the Pacific side of the country sing a medley of shrill, tinkling notes; vocalization of Caribbean birds lacks the tinkling quality. 6" (15 cm).

Olive Sparrow
Arremonops rufivirgatus

Coloration and pattern reminiscent of a Worm-eating Warbler (p. 266), but note **conical bill**. Similar to Black-striped Sparrow, but note brown-and-beige head (vs. black and gray). Common in northwestern Pacific and western Central Valley, to 900 m. Inhabits understory of forests, forest edges, and adjacent second growth. The song is a series of high notes that accelerate and fall slightly in pitch toward the end; each series lasts four or five seconds. 6" (15 cm).

Black-striped Sparrow
Arremonops conirostris

In addition to the **black-striped gray head**, note the white throat and **gray cheeks**. (Compare with Olive Sparrow.) Told apart from similar Stripe-headed Brush-Finch (p. 300) by black eye line (vs. black mask). Common in wet lowlands and foothills, to 1,500 m. Favors tangled undergrowth at forest edges, overgrown open areas, and shaded gardens. The attention-grabbing song begins slowly with mellow, sweet *chwee* notes that gradually accelerate to a rapid pace toward the end; the performance lasts more than ten seconds. 6" (15 cm).

Stripe-headed Sparrow
Aimophila ruficauda

The **boldly striped head** distinguishes this handsome sparrow. Common in northwestern Pacific lowlands, south to Tarcoles; uncommon in western Central Valley; to 800 m. Recent sightings near Dominical (2004) suggest it may be spreading south along Pacific coast. Small groups forage on ground in brushy areas; often seen along fence rows. Song is a squeaky sputtering. 7" (18 cm).

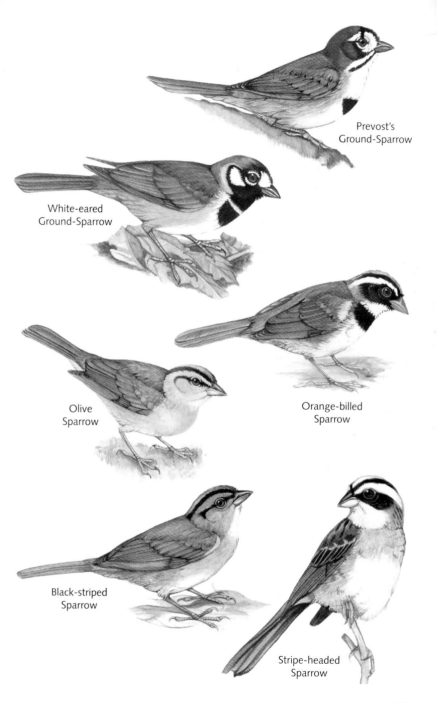

Prevost's
Ground-Sparrow

White-eared
Ground-Sparrow

Olive
Sparrow

Orange-billed
Sparrow

Black-striped
Sparrow

Stripe-headed
Sparrow

Lark Sparrow
Chondestes grammacus

Head pattern and dark breast spot could bring to mind a Prevost's Ground-sparrow (p. 302), but Lark Sparrow has **streaked back**. Accidental NA migrant, known from four recent records: Jacó (Dec 1990); Tortuguero (Oct 1992); Abangaritos (Nov 2000); and Cenizas de Pérez Zeledón, south of San Isidro de El General (March 2005). 6" (15 cm).

Chipping Sparrow
Spizella passerina

At first glance might suggest a juvenile Rufous-collared Sparrow (p. 306), but **unstreaked underparts are grayish;** also note **gray rump**. Accidental NA migrant, known from two records: San Pedro, east of San José (Sept 1977) and a recent sighting in Cahuita (Nov 2001). 5" (12 cm).

Grasshopper Sparrow
Ammodramus savannarum

A small sparrow with a **buffy breast** and **yellow-orange lores**; has dark crown with pale stripe down the middle. Uncommon resident of brushy grasslands on lower Pacific slopes of Guanacaste Cordillera and in upper Tempisque River basin, from 100 to 800 m. Rare winter resident in wet fields of eastern Central Valley. Produces an insectlike buzzy song. 5" (12 cm).

Lincoln's Sparrow
Melospiza lincolnii

Recalls a juvenile Rufous-collared Sparrow (p. 306), but has a **wide, gray superciliary** and a **buffy malar stripe**. A very rare NA migrant, from Nov to May, with scattered reports from Monteverde, Cartago, San Pedro (east of San José), and, more recently, from Tortuguero (Oct 2003). 6" (15 cm).

Botteri's Sparrow
Aimophila botterii

A dull sparrow with **faint lateral throat stripe and postocular stripe**; does not have crown stripe. Rare; found only on open, grassy hillsides and rocky slopes along the Pacific slope of the Guanacaste Cordillera, between 500 and 1,100 m. Song is a short accelerating trill, preceded by several sharp *tsip* notes. 6" (15 cm).

Rusty Sparrow
Aimophila rufescens

Only CR sparrow with **russet crown** (with narrow gray center stripe); has obvious **black lateral throat stripe**. Uncommon and confined to grassy slopes dotted with boulders, dense shrubs, and small trees on the Pacific slope of the Guanacaste Cordillera, between 500 and 1,100 m. In 2005, a small population was discovered south of San Ignacio de Acosta. Sings resolutely with a bright *cheet, chee-chee-chee yew*. 7" (18 cm).

Lark Sparrow

Chipping Sparrow

nonbreeding adult

Grasshopper Sparrow

Lincoln's Sparrow

Botteri's Sparrow

Rusty Sparrow

Seedeaters, Finches, & Sparrows

Rufous-collared Sparrow
Zonotrichia capensis

The **crested black-and-gray head** is distinctive. The juvenile lacks the rufous collar, but still shows a crest on its brown-and-buff head; also note the streaked breast. Both features distinguish it from the juvenile and female House Sparrow. The common sparrow throughout middle and upper elevations, from about 600 m to above timberline. Found in essentially all nonforest habitats, including fields, gardens, and even downtown San José. Its sweet song (*tseeur, tseer, tseer*) is often followed by a higher-pitched trill. 5" (13 cm).

Volcano Junco
Junco vulcani

The glaring **yellow iris** and **pinkish bill** are diagnostic. Fairly common outside of mature forests and in paramo; above 2,700 m. Makes a variety of high, weak utterances. **Endemic to CR and western Panama**. 6" (15 cm).

Old World Sparrows

PASSERIDAE. An Old World family of birds that is represented in Costa Rica by a single species. The House Sparrow was introduced into North America in the 1850s; it thrived and began to radiate throughout the continent, eventually reaching Costa Rica in the mid-1970s. Since then, it has steadily spread across the country. This should be a familiar bird to anyone from Europe, North America, and the many other regions where it has become established.

House Sparrow
Passer domesticus

The smartly attired male should pose no identification problem; the drab female (and very similar juvenile) could be confused with the juvenile Rufous-collared Sparrow, but note rounded head and unstreaked breast. Increasingly common in cities, towns, and villages, to at least 1,400 m. Particularly fond of bus and gas stations, where it nests in exposed open-ended iron girders; typically forages on the ground for spilled seeds and other human-generated scraps. Produces rather simple chirps. 6" (15 cm).

Saltators, Grosbeaks, & Buntings

CARDINALIDAE. Very closely related to the Emberizidae (p. 294) and often considered part of that family. Most species have fairly substantial beaks. Of the species that migrate to Costa Rica, most show strong sexual dimorphism—males are very colorful. The majority of the resident species sing melodiously; few show sexual dimorphism.

Dickcissel
Spiza americana

In all plumages, adults show **yellow superciliary** and **chestnut shoulder patch**. Note distinct black throat patch on breeding male, indistinct throat patch on nonbreeding male, and absence of throat patch on female and juvenile. Juvenile male is browner on the breast than juvenile female. Common passage migrant from early Sept to late Oct and from early April to mid-May, to 1,500 m. Fairly common winter resident, from early Sept to mid-May, principally in grain fields in northwest. Makes an electric buzzing sound. 6" (15 cm).

adult

Rufous-collared
Sparrow

Volcano
Junco

male

House
Sparrow

female

breeding
male

juv.
female

Dickcissel

Streaked Saltator
Saltator striatipectus

The combination of **olive streaking below** and **plain olive above** is distinctive. Fairly common in southern Pacific—though not easy to see in the thickets and scrub it prefers—from sea level (in Coto Colorado Valley) to 1,600 m. Sings two to four sweet, whistled *tsu* notes followed by an upwardly inflected *tsweeee*. 7" (18 cm).

Grayish Saltator
Saltator coerulescens

The only **gray bird** in CR with **white throat and superciliary**. Fairly common in the Central Valley (to 1,800 m) and in sections of Caribbean lowlands; less common on Pacific slope of Tilarán Cordillera; rare around the Gulf of Nicoya. Found in gardens and brushy areas with scattered trees. Song varies with region, but is a pleasant whistled phrase that ends on a rising note. 8" (20 cm).

Buff-throated Saltator
Saltator maximus

Similar to the larger Black-headed Saltator, but **crown is dark grayish-olive** and the **lower throat is peachy-buff** (note broad, black border). Juvenile has sooty throat. Common in wet lowlands and middle elevations, to 1,800 m; uncommon to rare in northwestern Pacific and in western Central Valley. Found in gardens, brushy areas with scattered trees, and at forest edges. Calls with a shrill *tseent*. Sings a melodic series of three double notes, each slightly lower pitched: *cheerilee, cheerilu, tsu-tsu.* 8" (20 cm).

Black-headed Saltator
Saltator atriceps

Distinguished from the similar Buff-throated Saltator by **black crown** and **white throat**. Common in wet Caribbean lowlands and middle elevations, to 1,300 m. Noisy groups forage in thickets, tall second growth, forest edges, and gardens. The distinctive voice is scratchy and harsh in comparison to other saltators. 10" (25 cm).

Slate-colored Grosbeak
Saltator grossus

The male's **thick red bill** and **white throat** are diagnostic. Female has an orange bill; juvenile is uniformly dark gray with a grayish bill. Uncommon in lowlands and foothills of Caribbean slope, to 1,200 m. Forages in mature wet forest, forest edges, and gardens. Makes a sharp *spink* and a harsh *caaah*. The rich song of whistles and warbles is wrenlike or oriole-like in quality. 7" (18 cm).

Streaked
Saltator

Grayish
Saltator

Buff-throated
Saltator

Black-headed
Saltator

Slate-colored
Grosbeak

male

Black-faced Grosbeak
Caryothraustes poliogaster

The thick bill, **black face**, and **yellow head and breast** are diagnostic. Common in Caribbean lowlands and foothills, to 900 m. Noisy groups of up to thirty or more birds travel through all levels of mature wet forest, forest edges, and adjacent gardens; often in mixed flocks. This species has a distinctive, sharp, buzzy call that it emits almost constantly while foraging. 7" (18 cm).

Black-thighed Grosbeak
Pheucticus tibialis

The large bill, **black-and-yellow** coloration, and **white wing spot** are diagnostic. Fairly common at middle and upper elevations, from Miravalles Volcano south, between 1,000 and 2,600 m; occasionally descends to the Caribbean lowlands along mountain bases. Found in gardens and at forest edges. The call note is a sharp metallic *pwik*. The sweet song rambles up and down the scale with phrases that may end in a rapid trill or an emphatically repeated note. **Endemic from CR to western Panama**. 8" (20 cm).

Rose-breasted Grosbeak
Pheucticus ludovicianus

Adult male is unmistakable. The **prominent white wing bars** and **thick, pale bill** differentiate female (adult and juvenile) and juvenile male from other brown, streaked seedeaters and finches. Fairly common NA migrant throughout the country, mostly from Oct to April, to 2,200 m. Found in gardens and at forest edges. Gives a sharp, squeaky *eenk*. 8" (20 cm).

Black-headed Grosbeak
Pheucticus melanocephalus

The **black-and-cinnamon** male is distinctive. Female is very similar to adult female and juvenile male Rose-breasted Grosbeak, but has **noticeably bicolored bill**. Female is further distinguished from juvenile male Rose-breasted Grosbeak by **yellow wing linings** (pink on latter species). Accidental; normal wintering range is only to southern Mexico. Sightings from San Isidro de El General, Santa Rosa National Park, Monteverde, and Cerro de la Muerte. 8" (20 cm).

Blue-black Grosbeak
Cyanocompsa cyanoides

The male's bluish tones and **heavy dark bill** set it apart from any of the similar seedeaters and finches. The female is very similar to the female Nicaraguan Seed-Finch (p. 294), but favors less open habitat. Common in wet lowlands and foothills, and fairly uncommon in northwestern Pacific; to 1,200 m. Dwells in lower levels of mature forest, gallery forest, second growth, and forest edges. The regularly heard song is a descending series of unhurried, sweet whistles that are often followed by a rapid twitter. 7" (18 cm).

Black-faced
Grosbeak

Black-thighed
Grosbeak

male

Rose-breasted
Grosbeak

female

juv.
male

male

Black-headed
Grosbeak

female

male

Blue-black
Grosbeak

female

Blue Grosbeak
Passerina caerulea

The **cinnamon wing bars** distinguish both sexes (breeding male Indigo Bunting lacks wing bars). Uncommon resident in northwestern Pacific (and south to Esterillos) and in western Central Valley. Rare NA migrants add to the population from Oct to April, and also occur in the Caribbean lowlands, chiefly along coast. Prefers open, brushy areas with scattered trees. The call is a sharp, metallic *tchink*. 7" (18 cm).

Indigo Bunting
Passerina cyanea

Breeding male is distinctive (male Blue Grosbeak has wing bars). Female shows **faint streaking on breast** and **narrow wing bars** (compare with female Blueblack Grassquit [p. 296]). Uncommon but widespread NA migrant, from Oct to early May, to 1,500 m. Favors open brushy areas. Call is a sharp, dry *spit*. 5" (13 cm).

Painted Bunting
Passerina ciris

Adult male is unmistakable. The plain greenish female and drab juvenile are "distinguished" by absence of markings (female Yellow-faced Grassquit [p. 296] always shows a trace of facial pattern; female Lesser Goldfinch [p. 324] has dark wings with white patches); the conical bill should distinguish female and juvenile from any warbler. Uncommon NA migrant on Pacific slope and in western Central Valley, from late Oct to early April, to 1,300 m. Found in thickets and lower levels of second growth. Makes a sharp *chip*. 5" (13 cm).

Blackbirds & Orioles

ICTERIDAE. The pointed, conical bill characterizes this diverse New World family. Beyond that, it's difficult to generalize. Some species are melodious singers, while others produce a variety of strange, cacophonous sounds. Males are noticeably larger than the females in some species, while in other species they are more brightly colored. Icterids inhabit almost every CR ecosystem, from open fields to rain forest canopy and from mangrove swamps to city streets.

Bobolink
Dolichonyx oryzivorus

In nonbreeding plumage, this bird is rather sparrowlike, but note **buffy-yellow underparts**, **pointed tail feathers**, and pointed wings. Breeding male has black face and underparts. Very rare passage migrant; most likely in Caribbean lowlands, from mid-Sept to Oct and from April to May. Individuals or small groups visit open fields, especially rice paddies. In flight, whistles a sweet *pink*. 7" (18 cm).

male

Blue
Grosbeak

female

breeding
male

nonbreeding
male

Indigo Bunting

female

male

Painted
Bunting

female

nonbreeding
adult

Bobolink

Blackbirds & Orioles

Red-winged Blackbird
Agelaius phoeniceus

The male's **red-and-yellow shoulders** are distinctive (compare with male Red-breasted Blackbird); female and juvenile are more **heavily streaked** than the female Red-breasted Blackbird. Common in northern central Caribbean lowlands and from Palo Verde region south to Parrita; spreading southeast on both Pacific and Caribbean slopes. Inhabits marshes, wet fields, and edges of mangroves; often in flocks. Several sweet whistled notes are followed by a shrill, raspy *kreeEE!* 9" (23 cm).

Red-breasted Blackbird
Sturnella militaris

Male's **red underparts** are diagnostic; note, however, that male shows red shoulders in flight and could therefore suggest a male Red-winged Blackbird. The female resembles the female Red-winged Blackbird, but has a relatively unstreaked breast with a **pinkish wash**. Fairly common in southern Pacific, from San Isidro de El General south; very uncommon in Caribbean lowlands; to 900 m. Dwells in wet fields and rice paddies. Gives several dry chipping notes followed by a drawn-out, buzzy trill. 7" (18 cm).

Eastern Meadowlark
Sturnella magna

The **broad, black V on the breast**—together with the otherwise **bright-yellow underparts**—readily identifies it. Widespread and fairly common, from sea level to 2,500 m. Mostly terrestrial, in open grassy areas. From an exposed perch, the male whistles a clear, sweet, two-part song: *sweedloo, sweedee.* 8" (20 cm).

Yellow-headed Blackbird
Xanthocephalus xanthocephalus

Male has bright-yellow head and breast, white patch in wing, and otherwise black body. In female and juvenile, black is replaced with brown, and white in wing is reduced or absent. A very casual winter resident, from Dec to March. Possible in freshwater marshes of Palo Verde and Caño Negro regions. Utters a harsh croak. **Not illustrated.** 10" (25 cm).

Melodious Blackbird
Dives dives

Entirely black; even the eye and the bill are black (compare with grackles, cowbirds, and caciques). First recorded in March 1987, now widespread and fairly common, to 1,800 m. Pairs inhabit gardens in all climatic regions. Very vocal; whistles a loud, slurred *wheeur, wheeur, whit-wheeur.* 10" (25 cm).

female

Red-winged
Blackbird

female

Red-breasted
Blackbird

male

Eastern Meadowlark

Melodious
Blackbird

Great-tailed Grackle
Quiscalus mexicanus

The **long tail** (**creased in a distinct V**) and **yellow iris** distinguish male from other black birds. Smaller, paler female probably responsible for most mistaken reports of Nicaraguan Grackle outside of that bird's limited range. Common and widespread, to 2,000 m. Commensal with humans almost anywhere there are even a few dwellings; walks with a swagger; hundreds of noisy individuals roost communally. Produces a wide variety of unmusical sounds. Male 17" (43 cm); female 13" (33 cm).

Nicaraguan Grackle
Quiscalus nicaraguensis

Similar to the larger Great-tailed Grackle; male appears blacker than male Great-tailed Grackle, female has even paler underparts than female Great-tailed Grackle. Uncommon in Caño Negro region, where greatly outnumbered by Great-tailed Grackle. Inhabits riverbanks and borders of marshes. **Endemic to southern Nicaragua and northern CR**. Male 12" (31 cm); female 10" (25 cm).

Bronzed Cowbird
Molothrus aeneus

Male is an **all-black** bird with a **red iris**; female is duller (compare with female Shiny Cowbird [p. 328]); juvenile has a dark iris. This species is much smaller than the very similar Giant Cowbird. Fairly common and widespread, from sea level to 1,900 m. Individuals or flocks of up to one hundred or more forage on the ground (in fields and along roadsides); often perches on utility wires. Females are brood parasites on a variety of passerine species. 8" (20 cm).

Giant Cowbird
Molothrus oryzivorus

Male and smaller female have **red iris** (juvenile has brown iris); male, female, and juvenile show **flat tail** in flight. Note that male has a purplish gloss on its black plumage. Both sexes are larger than Bronzed Cowbird. Generally uncommon throughout Caribbean lowlands and foothills; rare in Central Valley and in southern Pacific; to 1,700 m. Most readily seen at active oropendola (p. 322) nest colonies, where parasitic females attempt to lay their eggs. Male 13" (33 cm); female 11" (28 cm).

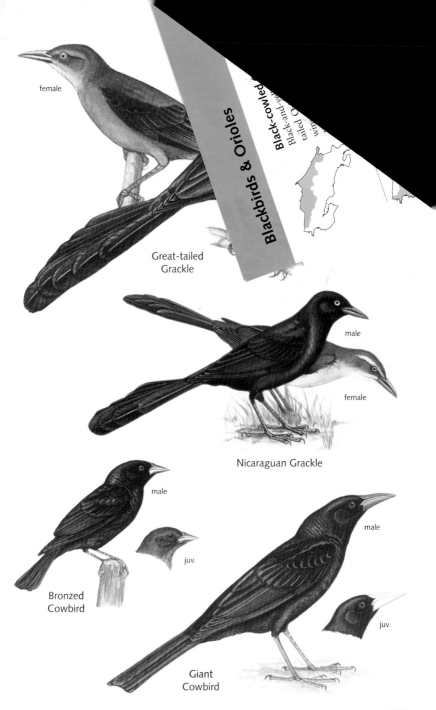

female

Blackbirds & Orioles

Black-cowled

Black-and-y
tailed O

wi

Great-tailed
Grackle

male

female

Nicaraguan Grackle

male

juv.

Bronzed
Cowbird

male

juv.

Giant
Cowbird

...Oriole *Icterus prosthemelas*

... low pattern of adult is very distinctive. Juvenile resembles Yellow-...iole and juvenile Orchard Oriole, but has entirely black tail and no ...g bars. Fairly common in Caribbean lowlands and foothills, to 1,300 m. Recent scattered sightings (since 2003) in southern and central Pacific lowlands may indicate that range is expanding. Favors forest edges, second growth, and gardens. Whistles a series of soft, sweet notes. 8" (20 cm).

Spot-breasted Oriole

Icterus pectoralis

Distinguished from similar, sympatric Streak-backed Oriole by solid-black patch on upper back and distinct **spotting on sides of breast**. Uncommon in lowlands of northwestern Pacific, to 500 m. Found at forest edges and in gardens. Whistles slow, sweet phrases. 9" (23 cm).

Orchard Oriole

Icterus spurius

Male is distinctive. Female and juvenile distinguished from juvenile Black-cowled Oriole by **wing bars**; distinguished from both female and juvenile Baltimore Orioles (p. 320) by **bright-yellow underparts** and **green upperparts**. Common passage migrant from late July to Oct and from March to April; rare winter resident; to 1,500 m. Feeds on flower nectar and fruit at forest edges and in gardens. Often in small groups. 7" (18 cm).

Streak-backed Oriole

Icterus pustulatus

Similar to sympatric Spot-breasted Oriole, but has **streaked back** and no spotting on sides of breast. Fairly common in lowlands of northwestern Pacific, to 500 m. Pairs forage in dry forest canopy, at forest edges, and in gardens. An unaccomplished vocalist; gives a dry wrenlike rattle. 8" (20 cm).

Yellow-tailed Oriole

Icterus mesomelas

Yellow outer tail feathers and undersides of tail are diagnostic (compare with juvenile Black-cowled Oriole). Rare in Caribbean lowlands, to 300 m. Dwells in thickets and dense second growth near water. Sought after as a cage bird for its beautiful voice; it whistles a variety of sweet, mellow, wrenlike phrases. 9" (23 cm).

adult

juv.

Black-cowled
Oriole

Spot-breasted
Oriole

Orchard
Oriole

male

juv. male

female

Streak-backed
Oriole

Bullock's Oriole
Icterus bullockii

The large **white wing panel** and **black eye line** readily identify adult male. Female and juvenile are similar to juvenile Baltimore Oriole, but have **yellow sides of head, throat, and breast**. Casual winter resident in northwestern Pacific, from Oct to March. Call similar to that of Baltimore Oriole. 8" (20 cm).

Baltimore Oriole
Icterus galbula

Black head distinguishes adult male from other orange orioles; **orangish wash on breast** sets female and juvenile apart from somewhat similar female and juvenile Bullock's Oriole and female and juvenile Orchard Oriole (p. 318). Common and widespread NA migrant, from early Sept to early May; to 2,200 m. Feeds on flower nectar and fruit at forest edges and in gardens. Call is a harsh, dry chatter. 8" (20 cm).

Scarlet-rumped Cacique
Cacicus uropygialis

The distinctive **scarlet rump** is usually concealed on perched birds; the **light-blue iris** further distinguishes it from the Yellow-billed Cacique. Common in wet lowlands and foothills on both Caribbean and Pacific slopes, to 1,100 m. Two or more birds typically roam the middle and upper levels of mature wet forest, advanced second growth, and forest edges. Frequently gives loud, ringing whistles. 9" (23 cm).

Yellow-billed Cacique
Amblycercus holosericeus

The **yellow iris** and **pale-yellow bill** are a unique combination among CR black birds (compare with Scarlet-rumped Cacique). Fairly common, virtually countrywide, except in northwestern Pacific lowlands; to timberline. Resides in dense thickets and tangles, where it is usually difficult to see. Behavior and vocalizations (clear, rich whistled song and harsh churring) are quite wrenlike. 9" (23 cm).

Bullock's Oriole — male

female

Baltimore Oriole — male

juv.

female

Scarlet-rumped Cacique

Yellow-billed Cacique

Birds of Costa Rica / **321**

Blackbirds & Orioles

[Displaying males of all three CR oropendola species produce bizarre gurgling and rasping noises. Oropendolas nest in colonies, generally preferring to construct nests in a single tree that is at some distance from nearby trees. The long, pendulous nest is distinctive and conspicuous. The female Giant Cowbird (p. 316) is a brood parasite—look for her near nesting oropendolas.]

Chestnut-headed Oropendola
Psarocolius wagleri

Distinguished from the Montezuma Oropendola by its **pale bill**, **chestnut head**, and black wings. Also compare with the Crested Oropendola. Fairly uncommon in lowlands and middle elevations of Caribbean slope; extremely rare in southern Pacific; to 1,700 m. Favors forests and forest edges, where individuals or flocks forage noisily at upper and middle levels of canopy. Male 14" (36 cm); female 11" (28 cm).

Crested Oropendola
Psarocolius decumanus

Told apart from similar Chestnut-headed Oropendola by **all-black head**. Found only in extreme southern Pacific; first recorded in 1999 and still expanding its range. Uncommon, from 100 to 1,500 m. Small flocks inhabit agricultural areas with scattered trees and forest fragments. Male 17" (43 cm); female 15" (38 cm).

Montezuma Oropendola
Psarocolius montezuma

The only CR oropendola with **colorful facial markings** and **two-toned bill** (compare with Chestnut-headed Oropendola). Very common in Caribbean lowlands; colonies are more thinly distributed at middle elevations of the Caribbean slope, in the Central Valley, and along Pacific slopes of northwestern cordilleras; to 1,500 m. Flocks forage at all levels in forests, forest edges, and adjacent gardens. Male 20" (51 cm); female 16" (41 cm).

Munias

ESTRILDIDAE. An Old World family of birds that resemble finches. Several species are popular in the caged bird trade, and escaped (or introduced) birds have established populations in different parts of the New World.

Tricolored Munia
Lonchura malacca

The adult's large black belly spot distinguishes it from the similarly patterned male Yellow-bellied Seedeater (p. 294). Brownish juvenile is chunkier than seedeaters. In 1999, a small population was discovered near the sugar mill in La Guinea, east of Filadelfia. Numbers of individuals have increased, and they seem to be expanding their range. Prefers tall grass along edges of cane fields and irrigation ditches. Gives a high, thin *dweet, dweet*. 5" (13 cm).

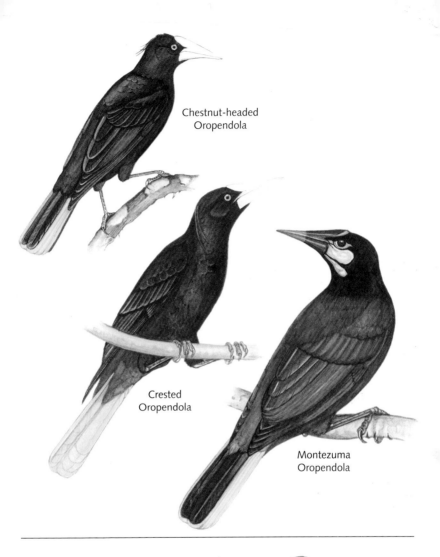

Chestnut-headed
Oropendola

Crested
Oropendola

Montezuma
Oropendola

adult

juv.

Tricolored Munia

FRINGILLIDAE. Most members of this widespread family have conical bills and eat seeds. The euphonias, however, are primarily fruit eaters (many species are particularly fond of mistletoe berries). Long considered members of the tanager family, the euphonias have recently been reassigned to this family. All of the CR members of this family are small; males are brightly colored and females are rather drab. With most male euphonias, observe whether the throat is dark or yellow, and then note the extent of yellow on top of the head. Many female euphonias are trickier to identify, but check the color on the head and belly.

Lesser Goldfinch
Carduelis psaltria

Similar to the Yellow-bellied Siskin, but note **entirely yellow underparts** and **white patches in wings and tail**. Very uncommon in middle and upper elevations, from Tilarán Cordillera south, between 800 and 2,200 m. Pairs or small flocks visit open areas with bushes or a few trees and feed on or near ground on grass seeds. Perched or flying, gives a sweet but melancholy *psee-ee*. 4" (10 cm).

Yellow-bellied Siskin
Carduelis xanthogastra

Similar to the Lesser Goldfinch, but male has **black throat and breast**; both sexes show **yellow patches in wings and tail** (not white). Fairly uncommon in Central and Talamanca Cordilleras, from timberline down to about 1,800 m. Prefers gardens and clearings in forested areas; perches high in trees, but often feeds near ground on seeding plants. Call is high and scratchy; song is a high, thin twittering. 4" (10 cm).

Golden-browed Chlorophonia
Chlorophonia callophrys

The combination of **bright green** and **intense yellow** sets it apart from other highland birds. Common from 1,000 m to timberline. Often in forest canopy, though coming down to eye level at forest edges and in gardens. The soft, mournful, single-note whistle—lasting about one second—alerts one to the presence of these birds. **Endemic to CR and western Panama.** 5" (13 cm).

Olive-backed Euphonia
Euphonia gouldi

Female has **rufous forecrown and vent**. Male distinguished from other male euphonias by **greenish back** and distinguished from female euphonias by **yellow forecrown**. Common in Caribbean lowlands and foothills, to 1,000 m. Mostly in middle and lower levels of wet forest, forest edges, and gardens. The call is a somewhat slurred, shrill *shpreeah-shpree*. 4" (10 cm).

Tawny-capped Euphonia
Euphonia anneae

Male is only CR euphonia with a **tawny crown**; female is only CR euphonia that combines **rufous forecrown** with **gray underparts**. Common in Caribbean foothills, from 400 to 1,700 m. Found in lower and middle levels of mature wet forest and forest edges; often with mixed flocks. Unmusical utterances are harsh and nasal. **Endemic from CR to northwestern Colombia.** 4" (10 cm).

Elegant Euphonia
Euphonia elegantissima

An unmistakable bird with a lovely **powder-blue cap**. Fairly uncommon in middle and upper elevations, from Tilarán Cordillera south, between 1,200 and 2,200 m. Frequents forest edges and gardens. Makes a variety of not very musical sounds. 4" (10 cm).

male

female

Lesser
Goldfinch

male

female

Yellow-bellied
Siskin

male

female

Golden-browed
Chlorophonia

male

female

Olive-backed
Euphonia

male

female

Tawny-capped
Euphonia

male

female

Elegant Euphonia

Thick-billed Euphonia
Euphonia laniirostris

Male set apart from male Yellow-throated Euphonia by **yellow on head that extends beyond the midcrown**. Both sexes set apart from respective sexes of Yellow-throated Euphonia by absence of white on belly. Female virtually identical to female Yellow-crowned Euphonia. (The thick bill is only slightly thicker than the bill of other euphonias—it is not a recommended field mark.) Uncommon in southern Pacific, north to Carara; to 1,100 m. Frequents forest edges and gardens. Call is a loud, sweet *chwee*; also imitates other birds' calls. 4" (10 cm).

Yellow-throated Euphonia
Euphonia hirundinacea

On male, yellow on head limited to forecrown (compare with male Thick-billed Euphonia). Female distinguished from female Thick-billed and Yellow-crowned Euphonias by **white on belly**. Very common in northwestern Pacific foothills and in northern central Caribbean lowlands; uncommon in northwestern Pacific lowlands and western Central Valley; very rare in southern Pacific; to 1,400 m. Inhabits forest edges and gardens. Call is a fairly fast *chee-dee-dee*. 4" (10 cm).

Scrub Euphonia
Euphonia affinis

Male is nearly identical to male Spot-crowned Euphonia, but there is almost no range overlap. Female has **gray hindcrown**. In both sexes, note the absence of white on underparts. Fairly common in northwestern Pacific lowlands, south to Tarcoles; uncommon in foothills, to 1,000 m. Frequents forest and forest edges. Eats mostly berries, especially mistletoe. Gives three high-pitched, even-toned whistles, often followed by two lower-pitched, slower ones. 4" (10 cm).

Yellow-crowned Euphonia
Euphonia luteicapilla

Male combines **dark throat** with **completely yellow crown**. Female is virtually identical to female Thick-billed Euphonia; set apart from female Yellow-throated Euphonia by absence of white on belly. Common in wet lowlands and foothills, to 1,200 m. Favors forest edges and gardens. Calls repeatedly from high in trees with a shrill two- or three-note whistle: *shee-shee-shee*. **Endemic to Nicaragua, CR, and Panama**. 4" (10 cm).

White-vented Euphonia
Euphonia minuta

Both sexes distinguished by **white belly and vent**. Uncommon in wet lowlands and foothills, to 1,200 m. Prefers upper levels of mature forest and forest edges; wags tail constantly. Its vocalizations are a varied assortment of warbled notes and *chip* notes; not as conspicuous as many other euphonias. 4" (10 cm).

Spot-crowned Euphonia
Euphonia imitans

Male is distinguished from the nearly identical male Scrub Euphonia by small crown spots; these are difficult to see in the field, however. Fortunately, there is almost no range overlap. The female is the only euphonia in the southern Pacific with a **rufous forecrown and belly**. Uncommon in southern Pacific lowlands and foothills, to 1,400 m. Forages at middle and upper levels of mature forest and advanced second growth. Produces rolling, buzzy utterances. **Endemic to CR and western Panama**. 4" (10 cm).

Thick-billed
Euphonia

male

female

Yellow-throated
Euphonia

male

female

Scrub
Euphonia

male

female

Yellow-crowned
Euphonia

male

female

White-vented
Euphonia

male

female

Spot-crowned
Euphonia

male

female

Bird distribution is a dynamic phenomenon and many species' ranges expand or diminish over time. A number of species have been added to the CR list in recent years, and others will surely be added in the future. The following three species are newly reported for the country.

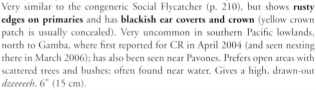

Rusty-margined Flycatcher
Myiozetetes cayanensis

Very similar to the congeneric Social Flycatcher (p. 210), but shows **rusty edges on primaries** and has **blackish ear coverts and crown** (yellow crown patch is usually concealed). Very uncommon in southern Pacific lowlands, north to Gamba, where first reported for CR in April 2004 (and seen nesting there in March 2006); has also been seen near Pavones. Prefers open areas with scattered trees and bushes; often found near water. Gives a high, drawn-out *dzeeeeeh*. 6" (15 cm).

Golden-cheeked Warbler
Dendroica chrysoparia

Told apart from Townsend's, Black-throated Green, and Hermit Warblers (p. 260) by **narrow, dark eye line**; also note **absence of yellow on underparts**. Three recent records of females: Sept 2002 in hills between San Ramón and Palmares de Alajuela, at about 1,500 m; April 2003 near Montaña Azul de Heredia, at about 1,500 m; and Dec 2004 above San Rafael de Oreamuno de Cartago, at 1,700 m. A male was seen in Oct 2005 above Platanillo (southeast of Turrialba), at 1,850 m. Two of the sightings were in agricultural areas with scattered trees, while the other two sightings were in forested areas. This NA migrant was previously known to winter only as far south as Nicaragua. 5" (13 cm).

Shiny Cowbird
Molothrus bonariensis

Male resembles Bronzed Cowbird (p. 316), but has **dark iris** and **purple sheen** to body plumage. Rather nondescript female is pale grayish-brown with **faint streaking on breast**. A female was first seen near Hone Creek (south of Cahuita), in April 2004; since then, there have been continued sightings of both sexes. Forages on ground in open areas and pastures. Females are brood parasites on a variety of passerine species. Whistles high, liquid notes. 8" (20 cm).

female

male

Golden-cheeked
Warbler

Rusty-margined
Flycatcher

female

Shiny
Cowbird

male

Glossary

See Anatomical Features, page XIV, for additional definitions.

accidental. Referring to a species (usually one that is migratory) that is not expected to occur in a given region, but has appeared on one or more occasions. Synonymous with **casual**.

barred. Marked with lines that are horizontal in relation to the upright axis of the bird.

breeding plumage. The distinctive, and usually brightly colored and/or boldly marked, plumage that a bird molts into just prior to the beginning of breeding season. Many North American migrant species appear in Costa Rica in these plumages in March and April. See **nonbreeding plumage**.

breeding resident. A species that breeds in Costa Rica and then migrates out of the country for part of the year (usually to South America during second half of the year).

brood parasite. A species that deposits its egg(s) in the nest(s) of other species, thus freeing itself from all nesting chores.

buffy. Having a creamy, light-brown color.

canopy. The upper level of a forest.

casual migrant. A species that is not expected to migrate to Costa Rica, but occasionally does appear. Synonymous with **accidental**.

commensal. Birds that are commensal with humans benefit by their relationship with human society, either by feeding on human-generated refuse or by nesting on human-made structures.

congeners. Species belonging to the same genus.

congeneric. Belonging to the same genus.

conspecific. Belonging to the same species.

CR. Acronym denoting *Costa Rica*.

cryptic. Describing a combination of plumage pattern and/or bird behavior that makes a bird blend in with its surroundings.

dry forest. Forests of the northwestern Pacific region and western Central Valley that are dry from November to April.

dry lowlands. Lowland habitats of the northwestern Pacific and Caño Negro regions that are dry from November to April.

endemic. Denotes a species with a limited geographic distribution.

fasciated. Marked with fine, wavy barring.

first winter bird. Refers to gulls during the first year of life, from approximately September to April. Gulls take two or more years to reach adult nonbreeding plumage.

foothills. Indicates the elevation ranges from approximately 400 to 800 m (somewhat higher in the southern half of Costa Rica).

gallery forest. Forest that grows along a river or stream.

garden. The term is used in this book as a catch-all for any human-altered environment that still contains some bushes and trees.

highlands. Indicates the upper portions of mountain slopes, from approximately 1,500 to 3,800 m.

humid forest. Forest that remains largely evergreen, but receives less rain than **wet forest**; one indicator of this type of forest is the paucity of epiphytic plants.

irruptive. Term used to denote a population that experiences periodic peaks of abundance.

jizz. In birding parlance, the general impression of a family, genus, or species based on overall size, appearance, and behavior; a subjective but very real tool in the identification process.

lowlands. The elevation range from sea level to approximately 500 m.

mature forest. Forest that has not been disturbed by human activities or cataclysmic natural forces in recent times.

middle elevations. Indicates the elevation ranges from approximately 800 to 1,800 m (somewhat higher in the southern half of Costa Rica).

migrant. A species (or a subset of a species' population) that does not breed in Costa Rica, but passes through and/or spends part of each year in Costa Rica during its annual migratory cycle. The vast majority are species that breed in North America.

morph. One of two or more different color forms in which a species occurs. Since an individual bird remains in a given color morph for all its life, the author prefers this term over the often-used alternative "phase," which could imply that an individual does not spend its entire life in the same color plumage.

NA. Acronym denoting *North America*.

neotropics. The tropics of the Western Hemisphere.

nonbreeding plumage. The drabber, and often less obviously marked, plumage that a bird shows when it is not breeding. Many North American migrant species appear in Costa Rica in these dull plumages. See **breeding plumage**.

paramo. A habitat found above timberline that is comprised of low vegetation.

passage migrant. A North American migrant that rarely, if ever, winters in Costa Rica, but regularly passes through on its way south, then again as it returns north.

passerine. Any of the so-called "perching birds" or "songbirds," or, more technically, any species in the order Passeriformes, which includes all of the species in the second half of this book, beginning with the family Furnariidae (p. 162).

precocial. Referring to species that are relatively mobile when they hatch.

raptor. A bird of prey (i.e., a hawk, eagle, falcon, or owl).

rufous. A reddish-brown color.

SA. Acronym denoting *South America*.

second growth. Vegetation comprised of fast-growing trees, vines, and shrubs that colonize areas affected either by natural causes (fire, flood, volcanic eruptions, landslides, etc.) or cutting by humans.

streaked. Synonymous with **striped**.

striped. Marked with lines that are vertical in relation to the upright axis of the bird.

summer resident. Juvenile North American migrant that does not return north in its first year of life; the following year it returns to North America to breed.

sympatric. Occurring in the same geographic area.

timberline. The upper elevation limit at which trees grow, which occurs in Costa Rica at about 3,100 m.

understory. The lower level of forest habitat, from ground level to about four meters up.

vermiculation. A pattern of wavy lines.

wet forest. Forest that receives enough annual moisture (at least 2.5 meters) for most of the plant species to remain evergreen; wetter than **humid forest**.

winter resident. Refers to North American migrants that spend the North American winter season (September to April) in Costa Rica.

Taxonomic Notes

The following is a list of both English common names and Latin names incorporated in this book that differ from those used in *A Guide to the Birds of Costa Rica* by F. Gary Stiles and Alexander F. Skutch (Cornell University Press, 1989). We provide these as an aid to cross-referencing. Species with the legend "recently added to CR list" will not be found in Stiles and Skutch.

Masked Duck (*Nomonyx dominicus*) – Latin name changed from *Oxyura dominica*.

Black-eared Wood-Quail (*Odontophorus melanotis*) – split from Rufous-fronted Wood-Quail (*O. erythrops*).

Crested Bobwhite (*Colinus cristatus*) – now includes Spot-bellied Bobwhite.

Galapagos Petrel (*Pterodroma phaeopygia*) – English name changed from Dark-rumped Petrel.

Cory's Shearwater (*Calonectris diomedea*) – recently added to CR list.

Manx Shearwater (*Puffinus puffinus*) – recently added to CR list.

Neotropic Cormorant (*Phalacrocorax brasilianus*) – English name changed from Olivaceous Cormorant, Latin name changed from *P. olivaceus*.

Great Egret (*Ardea alba*) – Latin name changed from *Casmerodius albus*.

Green Heron (*Butorides virescens*) – formerly Green-backed Heron (*B. striatus*), which has been split into this species and the following species.

Striated Heron (*Butorides striata*) – see Green Heron.

Agami Heron (*Agamia agami*) – English name changed from Chestnut-bellied Heron.

Roseate Spoonbill (*Platalea ajaja*) – Latin name changed from *Ajaia ajaja*.

White-tailed Kite (*Elanus leucurus*) – split from Black-shouldered Kite (*E. caeruleus*).

Barred Hawk (*Leucopternis princeps*) – English name changed from Black-chested Hawk.

Mangrove Black-Hawk (*Buteogallus subtilis*) – split from Common Black-Hawk (*B. anthracinus*).

Harris's Hawk (*Parabuteo unicinctus*) – English name changed from Bay-winged Hawk.

Red-throated Caracara (*Ibycter americanus*) – Latin name changed from *Daptrius americanus*.

Crested Caracara (*Caracara cheriway*) – Latin name changed from *Polyborus plancus*.

Clapper Rail (*Rallus longirostris*) – recently added to CR list.

Purple Gallinule (*Porphyrio martinica*) – Latin name changed from *Porphyrula martinica*.

Common Moorhen (*Gallinula chloropus*) – English name changed from Common Gallinule.

Southern Lapwing (*Vanellus chilensis*) – recently added to CR list.

Wandering Tattler (*Tringa incana*) – Latin name changed from *Heteroscelus incanus*.

Willet (*Tringa semipalmata*) – Latin name changed from *Catoptrophorus semipalmatus*.

Wilson's Snipe (*Gallinago delicata*) – split from Common Snipe (*G. gallinago*).

Wilson's Phalarope (*Phalaropus tricolor*) – Latin name changed from *Steganopus tricolor*.

Sooty Tern (*Onychoprion fuscatus*) – Latin name changed from *Sterna fuscata*.

Bridled Tern (*Onychoprion anaethetus*) – Latin name changed from *Sterna anaethetus*.

Least Tern (*Sternula antillarum*) – Latin name changed from *Sterna antillarum*.

Large-billed Tern (*Phaetusa simplex*) – recently added to CR list.

Gull-billed Tern (*Gelochelidon nilotica*) – Latin name changed from *Sterna nilotica*.

Caspian Tern (*Hydroprogne caspia*) – Latin name changed from *Sterna caspia*.

Royal Tern (*Thalasseus maximus*) – Latin name changed from *Sterna maxima*.

Sandwich Tern (*Thalasseus sandvicensis*) – Latin name changed from *Sterna sandvicensis*.

Elegant Tern (*Thalasseus elegans*) – Latin name changed from *Sterna elegans*.

Gray-headed Dove (*Leptotila plumbeiceps*) – split from Gray-fronted Dove (*L. rufaxilla*).

Brown-throated Parakeet (*Aratinga pertinax*) – recently added to CR list.

Greater Ani (*Crotophaga major*) – recently added to CR list.

Costa Rican Pygmy-Owl (*Glaucidium costaricanum*) – split from Andean Pygmy-Owl (*G. jardinii*).

Central American Pygmy-Owl (*Glaucidium griseiceps*) – split from Least Pygmy-Owl (*G. minutissimum*).

Striped Owl (*Pseudoscops clamator*) – Latin name changed from *Asio clamator*.

Chestnut-collared Swift (*Streptoprocne rutila*) – Latin name changed from *Cypseloides rutilus*.

Costa Rican Swift (*Chaetura fumosa*) – split from Band-rumped Swift (*C. spinicauda*).

Long-billed Hermit (*Phaethornis longirostris*) – split from Long-tailed Hermit (*P. superciliosus*).

Stripe-throated Hermit (*Phaethornis striigularis*) – split from Little Hermit (*P. longuemareus*).

Canivet's Emerald (*Chlorostilbon canivetii*) – Formerly Fork-tailed Emerald, which has been split into this species and Garden Emerald (*C. assimilis*).

Charming Hummingbird (*Amazilia decora*) – English name changed from Beryl-crowned Hummingbird.

Alfaro's Hummingbird (*Amazilia alfaroana*) – recently split from Indigo-capped Hummingbird (*A. cyanifrons*).

Bronze-tailed Plumeleteer (*Chalybura urochrysia*) – English name changed from Red-footed Plumeleteer.

White-throated Mountain-gem (*Lampornis castaneoventris*) – now includes Gray-tailed Mountain-gem (*L. cinereicauda*).

White-necked Puffbird (*Notharchus macrorhynchos*) – Latin name changed from *Bucco macrorhynchos*.

Pied Puffbird (*Notharchus tectus*) – Latin name changed from *Bucco tectus*.

Striped Woodhaunter (*Hyloctistes subulatus*) – English name changed from Striped Foliage-gleaner.

Scaly-throated Foliage-gleaner (*Anabacerthia variegaticeps*) – English name changed from Spectacled Foliage-gleaner.

Northern Barred-Woodcreeper (*Dendrocolaptes sanctithomae*) – split from Barred Woodcreeper (*D. certhia*).

Cocoa Woodcreeper (*Xiphorhynchus susurrans*) – split from Buff-throated Woodcreeper (*X. guttatus*).

Western Slaty-Antshrike (*Thamnophilus atrinucha*) – split from Slaty Antshrike (*T. punctatus*).

Streak-chested Antpitta (*Hylopezus perspicillatus*) – English name changed from Spectacled Antpitta.

Thicket Antpitta (*Hylopezus dives*) – split from Fulvous-bellied Antpitta (*H. fulviventris*).

Mouse-colored Tyrannulet (*Phaeomyias murina*) – recently added to CR list.

Rough-legged Tyrannulet (*Phyllomyias burmeisteri*) – now includes Zeledon's Tyrannulet (*P. zeledoni*).

Paltry Tyrannulet (*Zimmerius vilissimus*) – English name changed from Mistletoe Tyrannulet.

Northern Scrub-Flycatcher (*Sublegatus arenarum*) – formerly Scrub Flycatcher (*S. modestus*), which has been split into this species and Southern Scrub-Flycatcher.

Slate-headed Tody-Flycatcher (*Poecilotriccus sylvia*) – Latin name changed from *Todirostrum sylvia*.

Olive-sided Flycatcher (*Contopus cooperi*) – Latin name changed from *C. borealis*.

Rusty-margined Flycatcher (*Myiozetetes cayanensis*) – recently added to CR list.

White-ringed Flycatcher (*Conopias albovittatus*) – Latin name changed from *Coryphotriccus albovittatus*.

Thrushlike Schiffornis (*Schiffornis turdina*) – English name changed from Thrushlike Manakin.

Gray-headed Piprites (*Piprites griseiceps*) – English name changed from Gray-headed Manakin.

White-ruffed Manakin (*Corapipo altera*) – split from *C. luecorrhoa*, but maintained former English common name.

Blue-headed Vireo (*Vireo solitarius*) – formerly Solitary Vireo, which has been split into this and two other species, Plumbeous Vireo

(*V. plumbeus*) and Cassin's Vireo (*V. cassinii*), neither yet reliably reported from CR.

Brown-chested Martin (*Progne tapera*) – Latin name changed from *Phaeoprogne tapera*.

Blue-and-white Swallow (*Pygochelidon cyanoleuca*) – Latin name changed from *Notiochelidon cyanoleuca*.

Cliff Swallow (*Petrochelidon pyrrhonota*) – Latin name changed from *Hirundo pyrrhonota*.

Cave Swallow (*Petrochelidon fulva*) – Latin name changed from *Hirundo fulva*.

Scaly-breasted Wren (*Microcerculus marginatus*) – now includes Whistling Wren (*M. luscinia*).

Pale-vented Thrush (*Turdus obsoletus*) – English name changed from Pale-vented Robin.

Golden-cheeked Warbler (*Dendroica chrysoparia*) – recently added to CR list.

Wrenthrush (*Zeledonia coronata*) – English name changed from Zeledonia.

Crimson-collared Tanager (*Ramphocelus sanguinolentus*) – Latin name changed from *Phlogothraupis sanguinolentus*.

Passerini's Tanager (*Ramphocelus passerinii*) – formerly Scarlet-rumped Tanager, which has been split into this and the following species.

Cherrie's Tanager (*Ramphocelus costaricensis*) – see Passerini's Tanager.

Blue-and-gold Tanager (*Bangsia arcaei*) – Latin name changed from *Buthraupis arcaei*.

Variable Seedeater (*Sporophila americana*) – now includes *S. aurita*.

Nicaraguan Seed-Finch (*Oryzoborus nuttingi*) – English name changed from Pink-billed Seed-Finch.

White-naped Brush-Finch (*Atlapetes albinucha*) – now includes Yellow-throated Brush-Finch (*A. gutturalis*).

Chestnut-capped Brush-Finch (*Buarremon brunneinucha*) – Latin name changed from *Atlapetes brunneinucha*.

Stripe-headed Brush-Finch (*Buarremon torquatus*) – now includes Black-headed Brush-Finch (*Atlapetes atricapillus*).

Lark Sparrow (*Chondestes grammacus*) – recently added to CR list.

Streaked Saltator (*Saltator striatipectus*) – split from *S. albicollis*, now known as Lesser Antillean Saltator.

Slate-colored Grosbeak (*Saltator grossus*) – Latin name changed from *Pitylus grossus*.

Blue Grosbeak (*Passerina caerulea*) – Latin name changed from *Guiraca caerulea*.

Shiny Cowbird (*Molothrus bonariensis*) – recently added to CR list.

Giant Cowbird (*Molothrus oryzivorus*) – Latin name changed from *Scaphidura oryzivora*.

Bullock's Oriole (*Icterus bullockii*) – formerly merged with *I. galbula*, which was also called Northern Oriole.

Baltimore Oriole (*Icterus galbula*) – English name changed from Northern Oriole.

Elegant Euphonia (*Euphonia elegantissima*) – English name changed from Blue-hooded Euphonia.

Tricolored Munia (*Lonchura malacca*) – recently added to CR list.

Costa Rica Bird List

Family names are in capital letters.
*Indicates species that are not included in text of field guide.

TINAMIDAE
Great Tinamou	*Tinamus major*
Highland Tinamou	*Nothocercus bonapartei*
Little Tinamou	*Crypturellus soui*
Thicket Tinamou	*Crypturellus cinnamomeus*
Slaty-breasted Tinamou	*Crypturellus boucardi*

ANATIDAE
White-faced Whistling-Duck	*Dendrocygna viduata*
Black-bellied Whistling-Duck	*Dendrocygna autumnalis*
Fulvous Whistling-Duck	*Dendrocygna bicolor*
Muscovy Duck	*Cairina moschata*
American Wigeon	*Anas americana*
Mallard	*Anas platyrhynchos*
Blue-winged Teal	*Anas discors*
Cinnamon Teal	*Anas cyanoptera*
Northern Shoveler	*Anas clypeata*
Northern Pintail	*Anas acuta*
Green-winged Teal	*Anas crecca*
Ring-necked Duck	*Aythya collaris*
Greater Scaup	*Aythya marila*
Lesser Scaup	*Aythya affinis*
Masked Duck	*Nomonyx dominicus*

CRACIDAE
Plain Chachalaca	*Ortalis vetula*
Gray-headed Chachalaca	*Ortalis cinereiceps*
Crested Guan	*Penelope purpurascens*
Black Guan	*Chamaepetes unicolor*
Great Curassow	*Crax rubra*

ODONTOPHORIDAE
Buffy-crowned Wood-Partridge	*Dendrortyx leucophrys*
Crested Bobwhite	*Colinus cristatus*
Marbled Wood-Quail	*Odontophorus gujanensis*
Black-eared Wood-Quail	*Odontophorus melanotis*

Black-breasted Wood-Quail	*Odontophorus leucolaemus*
Spotted Wood-Quail	*Odontophorus guttatus*
Tawny-faced Quail	*Rhynchortyx cinctus*

PODICIPEDIDAE

Least Grebe	*Tachybaptus dominicus*
Pied-billed Grebe	*Podilymbus podiceps*
Eared Grebe	*Podiceps nigricollis*

PROCELLARIIDAE

*Black-capped Petrel	*Pterodroma hasitata*
*Galapagos Petrel	*Pterodroma phaeopygia*
*Parkinson's Petrel	*Procellaria parkinsoni*
*Cory's Shearwater	*Calonectris diomedea*
*Pink-footed Shearwater	*Puffinus creatopus*
*Wedge-tailed Shearwater	*Puffinus pacificus*
*Sooty Shearwater	*Puffinus griseus*
*Short-tailed Shearwater	*Puffinus tenuirostris*
*Manx Shearwater	*Puffinus puffinus*
*Audubon's Shearwater	*Puffinus lherminieri*

HYDROBATIDAE

*Wilson's Storm-Petrel	*Oceanites oceanicus*
*White-faced Storm-Petrel	*Pelagodroma marina*
*Leach's Storm-Petrel	*Oceanodroma leucorhoa*
*Band-rumped Storm-Petrel	*Oceanodroma castro*
*Wedge-rumped Storm-Petrel	*Oceanodroma tethys*
*Black Storm-Petrel	*Oceanodroma melania*
*Markham's Storm-Petrel	*Oceanodroma markhami*
*Least Storm-Petrel	*Oceanodroma microsoma*

PHAETHONTIDAE

| *Red-billed Tropicbird | *Phaethon aethereus* |

SULIDAE

Masked Booby	*Sula dactylatra*
Blue-footed Booby	*Sula nebouxii*
Brown Booby	*Sula leucogaster*
Red-footed Booby	*Sula sula*

PELECANIDAE

| American White Pelican | *Pelecanus erythrorhynchos* |
| Brown Pelican | *Pelecanus occidentalis* |

PHALACROCORACIDAE
Neotropic Cormorant　　　　　　　*Phalacrocorax brasilianus*

ANHINGIDAE
Anhinga　　　　　　　　　　　　*Anhinga anhinga*

FREGATIDAE
Magnificent Frigatebird　　　　　　*Fregata magnificens*
Great Frigatebird　　　　　　　　*Fregata minor*

ARDEIDAE
Pinnated Bittern　　　　　　　　*Botaurus pinnatus*
American Bittern　　　　　　　　*Botaurus lentiginosus*
Least Bittern　　　　　　　　　*Ixobrychus exilis*
Rufescent Tiger-Heron　　　　　　*Tigrisoma lineatum*
Fasciated Tiger-Heron　　　　　　*Tigrisoma fasciatum*
Bare-throated Tiger-Heron　　　　　*Tigrisoma mexicanum*
Great Blue Heron　　　　　　　　*Ardea herodias*
Great Egret　　　　　　　　　　*Ardea alba*
Snowy Egret　　　　　　　　　　*Egretta thula*
Little Blue Heron　　　　　　　　*Egretta caerulea*
Tricolored Heron　　　　　　　　*Egretta tricolor*
Reddish Egret　　　　　　　　　*Egretta rufescens*
Cattle Egret　　　　　　　　　　*Bubulcus ibis*
Green Heron　　　　　　　　　　*Butorides virescens*
Striated Heron　　　　　　　　　*Butorides striata*
Agami Heron　　　　　　　　　　*Agamia agami*
Black-crowned Night-Heron　　　　*Nycticorax nycticorax*
Yellow-crowned Night-Heron　　　　*Nyctanassa violacea*
Boat-billed Heron　　　　　　　　*Cochlearius cochlearius*

THRESKIORNITHIDAE
White Ibis　　　　　　　　　　*Eudocimus albus*
Glossy Ibis　　　　　　　　　　*Plegadis falcinellus*
White-faced Ibis　　　　　　　　*Plegadis chihi*
Green Ibis　　　　　　　　　　*Mesembrinibis cayennensis*
Roseate Spoonbill　　　　　　　　*Platalea ajaja*

CICONIIDAE
Jabiru　　　　　　　　　　　　*Jabiru mycteria*
Wood Stork　　　　　　　　　　*Mycteria americana*

CATHARTIDAE
Black Vulture　　　　　　　　　*Coragyps atratus*

Turkey Vulture	*Cathartes aura*
Lesser Yellow-headed Vulture	*Cathartes burrovianus*
King Vulture	*Sarcoramphus papa*

ACCIPITRIDAE

Osprey	*Pandion haliaetus*
Gray-headed Kite	*Leptodon cayanensis*
Hook-billed Kite	*Chondrohierax uncinatus*
Swallow-tailed Kite	*Elanoides forficatus*
Pearl Kite	*Gampsonyx swainsonii*
White-tailed Kite	*Elanus leucurus*
Snail Kite	*Rostrhamus sociabilis*
Double-toothed Kite	*Harpagus bidentatus*
Mississippi Kite	*Ictinia mississippiensis*
Plumbeous Kite	*Ictinia plumbea*
Black-collared Hawk	*Busarellus nigricollis*
Northern Harrier	*Circus cyaneus*
Tiny Hawk	*Accipiter superciliosus*
Sharp-shinned Hawk	*Accipiter striatus*
Cooper's Hawk	*Accipiter cooperii*
Bicolored Hawk	*Accipiter bicolor*
Crane Hawk	*Geranospiza caerulescens*
Barred Hawk	*Leucopternis princeps*
Semiplumbeous Hawk	*Leucopternis semiplumbeus*
White Hawk	*Leucopternis albicollis*
Common Black-Hawk	*Buteogallus anthracinus*
Mangrove Black-Hawk	*Buteogallus subtilis*
Great Black-Hawk	*Buteogallus urubitinga*
Harris's Hawk	*Parabuteo unicinctus*
Solitary Eagle	*Harpyhaliaetus solitarius*
Roadside Hawk	*Buteo magnirostris*
Broad-winged Hawk	*Buteo platypterus*
Gray Hawk	*Buteo nitidus*
Short-tailed Hawk	*Buteo brachyurus*
Swainson's Hawk	*Buteo swainsoni*
White-tailed Hawk	*Buteo albicaudatus*
Zone-tailed Hawk	*Buteo albonotatus*
Red-tailed Hawk	*Buteo jamaicensis*
Crested Eagle	*Morphnus guianensis*
Harpy Eagle	*Harpia harpyja*
Black-and-white Hawk-Eagle	*Spizastur melanoleucus*
Black Hawk-Eagle	*Spizaetus tyrannus*
Ornate Hawk-Eagle	*Spizaetus ornatus*

FALCONIDAE

Barred Forest-Falcon	*Micrastur ruficollis*
Slaty-backed Forest-Falcon	*Micrastur mirandollei*
Collared Forest-Falcon	*Micrastur semitorquatus*
Red-throated Caracara	*Ibycter americanus*
Crested Caracara	*Caracara cheriway*
Yellow-headed Caracara	*Milvago chimachima*
Laughing Falcon	*Herpetotheres cachinnans*
American Kestrel	*Falco sparverius*
Merlin	*Falco columbarius*
Aplomado Falcon	*Falco femoralis*
Bat Falcon	*Falco rufigularis*
Orange-breasted Falcon	*Falco deiroleucus*
Peregrine Falcon	*Falco peregrinus*

RALLIDAE

Ocellated Crake	*Micropygia schomburgkii*
Ruddy Crake	*Laterallus ruber*
White-throated Crake	*Laterallus albigularis*
Gray-breasted Crake	*Laterallus exilis*
Black Rail	*Laterallus jamaicensis*
Clapper Rail	*Rallus longirostris*
Rufous-necked Wood-Rail	*Aramides axillaris*
Gray-necked Wood-Rail	*Aramides cajanea*
Uniform Crake	*Amaurolimnas concolor*
Sora	*Porzana carolina*
Yellow-breasted Crake	*Porzana flaviventer*
Paint-billed Crake	*Neocrex erythrops*
Spotted Rail	*Pardirallus maculatus*
Purple Gallinule	*Porphyrio martinica*
Common Moorhen	*Gallinula chloropus*
American Coot	*Fulica americana*

HELIORNITHIDAE

Sungrebe	*Heliornis fulica*

EURYPYGIDAE

Sunbittern	*Eurypyga helias*

ARAMIDAE

Limpkin	*Aramus guarauna*

BURHINIDAE

Double-striped Thick-knee	*Burhinus bistriatus*

CHARADRIIDAE
Southern Lapwing	*Vanellus chilensis*
Black-bellied Plover	*Pluvialis squatarola*
American Golden-Plover	*Pluvialis dominica*
Collared Plover	*Charadrius collaris*
Snowy Plover	*Charadrius alexandrinus*
Wilson's Plover	*Charadrius wilsonia*
Semipalmated Plover	*Charadrius semipalmatus*
Killdeer	*Charadrius vociferus*

HAEMATOPODIDAE
American Oystercatcher	*Haematopus palliatus*

RECURVIROSTRIDAE
Black-necked Stilt	*Himantopus mexicanus*
American Avocet	*Recurvirostra americana*

JACANIDAE
Northern Jaçana	*Jacana spinosa*
Wattled Jaçana	*Jacana jacana*

SCOLOPACIDAE
Spotted Sandpiper	*Actitis macularius*
Solitary Sandpiper	*Tringa solitaria*
Wandering Tattler	*Tringa incana*
Greater Yellowlegs	*Tringa melanoleuca*
Willet	*Tringa semipalmata*
Lesser Yellowlegs	*Tringa flavipes*
Upland Sandpiper	*Bartramia longicauda*
Whimbrel	*Numenius phaeopus*
Long-billed Curlew	*Numenius americanus*
Hudsonian Godwit	*Limosa haemastica*
Marbled Godwit	*Limosa fedoa*
Ruddy Turnstone	*Arenaria interpres*
Surfbird	*Aphriza virgata*
Red Knot	*Calidris canutus*
Sanderling	*Calidris alba*
Semipalmated Sandpiper	*Calidris pusilla*
Western Sandpiper	*Calidris mauri*
Least Sandpiper	*Calidris minutilla*
White-rumped Sandpiper	*Calidris fuscicollis*
Baird's Sandpiper	*Calidris bairdii*
Pectoral Sandpiper	*Calidris melanotos*
Dunlin	*Calidris alpina*

Curlew Sandpiper	*Calidris ferruginea*
Stilt Sandpiper	*Calidris himantopus*
Buff-breasted Sandpiper	*Tryngites subruficollis*
Ruff	*Philomachus pugnax*
Short-billed Dowitcher	*Limnodromus griseus*
Long-billed Dowitcher	*Limnodromus scolopaceus*
Wilson's Snipe	*Gallinago delicata*
Wilson's Phalarope	*Phalaropus tricolor*
Red-necked Phalarope	*Phalaropus lobatus*
*Red Phalarope	*Phalaropus fulicarius*

LARIDAE

Laughing Gull	*Larus atricilla*
Franklin's Gull	*Larus pipixcan*
*Bonaparte's Gull	*Larus philadelphia*
*Heermann's Gull	*Larus heermanni*
*Gray Gull	*Larus modestus*
*Ring-billed Gull	*Larus delawarensis*
*Herring Gull	*Larus argentatus*
*Sabine's Gull	*Xema sabini*
*Swallow-tailed Gull	*Creagrus furcatus*
Brown Noddy	*Anous stolidus*
*Black Noddy	*Anous minutus*
*White Tern	*Gygis alba*
*Sooty Tern	*Onychoprion fuscatus*
Bridled Tern	*Onychoprion anaethetus*
Least Tern	*Sternula antillarum*
Large-billed Tern	*Phaetusa simplex*
Gull-billed Tern	*Gelochelidon nilotica*
Caspian Tern	*Hydroprogne caspia*
Black Tern	*Chlidonias niger*
Common Tern	*Sterna hirundo*
*Arctic Tern	*Sterna paradisaea*
Forster's Tern	*Sterna forsteri*
Royal Tern	*Thalasseus maxima*
Sandwich Tern	*Thalasseus sandvicensis*
Elegant Tern	*Thalasseus elegans*
Black Skimmer	*Rynchops niger*

STERCORARIIDAE

*South Polar Skua	*Stercorarius maccormicki*
*Pomarine Jaeger	*Stercorarius pomarinus*
*Parasitic Jaeger	*Stercorarius parasiticus*
*Long-tailed Jaeger	*Stercorarius longicaudus*

COLUMBIDAE

Rock Pigeon	*Columba livia*
Pale-vented Pigeon	*Patagioenas cayennensis*
Scaled Pigeon	*Patagioenas speciosa*
White-crowned Pigeon	*Patagioenas leucocephala*
Red-billed Pigeon	*Patagioenas flavirostris*
Band-tailed Pigeon	*Patagioenas fasciata*
Ruddy Pigeon	*Patagioenas subvinacea*
Short-billed Pigeon	*Patagioenas nigrirostris*
White-winged Dove	*Zenaida asiatica*
Mourning Dove	*Zenaida macroura*
Inca Dove	*Columbina inca*
Common Ground-Dove	*Columbina passerina*
Plain-breasted Ground-Dove	*Columbina minuta*
Ruddy Ground-Dove	*Columbina talpacoti*
Blue Ground-Dove	*Claravis pretiosa*
Maroon-chested Ground-Dove	*Claravis mondetoura*
White-tipped Dove	*Leptotila verreauxi*
Gray-headed Dove	*Leptotila plumbeiceps*
Gray-chested Dove	*Leptotila cassini*
Olive-backed Quail-Dove	*Geotrygon veraguensis*
Chiriqui Quail-Dove	*Geotrygon chiriquensis*
Purplish-backed Quail-Dove	*Geotrygon lawrencii*
Buff-fronted Quail-Dove	*Geotrygon costaricensis*
Violaceous Quail-Dove	*Geotrygon violacea*
Ruddy Quail-Dove	*Geotrygon montana*

PSITTACIDAE

Sulphur-winged Parakeet	*Pyrrhura hoffmanni*
Crimson-fronted Parakeet	*Aratinga finschi*
Olive-throated Parakeet	*Aratinga nana*
Orange-fronted Parakeet	*Aratinga canicularis*
Brown-throated Parakeet	*Aratinga pertinax*
Great Green Macaw	*Ara ambiguus*
Scarlet Macaw	*Ara macao*
Barred Parakeet	*Bolborhynchus lineola*
Orange-chinned Parakeet	*Brotogeris jugularis*
Red-fronted Parrotlet	*Touit costaricensis*
Brown-hooded Parrot	*Pionopsitta haematotis*
Blue-headed Parrot	*Pionus menstruus*
White-crowned Parrot	*Pionus senilis*
White-fronted Parrot	*Amazona albifrons*
Red-Lored Parrot	*Amazona autumnalis*
Mealy Parrot	*Amazona farinosa*
Yellow-naped Parrot	*Amazona auropalliata*

CUCULIDAE

Squirrel Cuckoo	*Piaya cayana*
Yellow-billed Cuckoo	*Coccyzus americanus*
Mangrove Cuckoo	*Coccyzus minor*
*Cocos Cuckoo	*Coccyzus ferrugineus*
Black-billed Cuckoo	*Coccyzus erythropthalmus*
Striped Cuckoo	*Tapera naevia*
Pheasant Cuckoo	*Dromococcyx phasianellus*
Lesser Ground-Cuckoo	*Morococcyx erythropygus*
Rufous-vented Ground-Cuckoo	*Neomorphus geoffroyi*
Greater Ani	*Crotophaga major*
Smooth-billed Ani	*Crotophaga ani*
Groove-billed Ani	*Crotophaga sulcirostris*

TYTONIDAE

Barn Owl	*Tyto alba*

STRIGIDAE

Pacific Screech-Owl	*Megascops cooperi*
Tropical Screech-Owl	*Megascops choliba*
Vermiculated Screech-Owl	*Megascops guatemalae*
Bare-shanked Screech-Owl	*Megascops clarkii*
Crested Owl	*Lophostrix cristata*
Spectacled Owl	*Pulsatrix perspicillata*
Great Horned Owl	*Bubo virginianus*
Costa Rican Pygmy-Owl	*Glaucidium costaricanum*
Central American Pygmy-Owl	*Glaucidium griseiceps*
Ferruginous Pygmy-Owl	*Glaucidium brasilianum*
Burrowing Owl	*Athene cunicularia*
Mottled Owl	*Ciccaba virgata*
Black-and-white Owl	*Ciccaba nigrolineata*
Short-eared Owl	*Asio flammeus*
Striped Owl	*Pseudoscops clamator*
Unspotted Saw-whet Owl	*Aegolius ridgwayi*

CAPRIMULGIDAE

Short-tailed Nighthawk	*Lurocalis semitorquatus*
Lesser Nighthawk	*Chordeiles acutipennis*
Common Nighthawk	*Chordeiles minor*
Common Pauraque	*Nyctidromus albicollis*
Ocellated Poorwill	*Nyctiphrynus ocellatus*
Chuck-will's-widow	*Caprimulgus carolinensis*
Rufous Nightjar	*Caprimulgus rufus*
Whip-poor-will	*Caprimulgus vociferus*

Dusky Nightjar   *Caprimulgus saturatus*
White-tailed Nightjar   *Caprimulgus cayennensis*

NYCTIBIIDAE
Great Potoo   *Nyctibius grandis*
Common Potoo   *Nyctibius griseus*
Northern Potoo   *Nyctibius jamaicensis*

STEATORNITHIDAE
Oilbird   *Steatornis caripensis*

APODIDAE
Black Swift   *Cypseloides niger*
White-chinned Swift   *Cypseloides cryptus*
Spot-fronted Swift   *Cypseloides cherriei*
Chestnut-collared Swift   *Streptoprocne rutila*
White-collared Swift   *Streptoprocne zonaris*
Chimney Swift   *Chaetura pelagica*
Vaux's Swift   *Chaetura vauxi*
Costa Rican Swift   *Chaetura fumosa*
Gray-rumped Swift   *Chaetura cinereiventris*
Lesser Swallow-tailed Swift   *Panyptila cayennensis*
Great Swallow-tailed Swift   *Panyptila sanctihieronymi*

TROCHILIDAE
Bronzy Hermit   *Glaucis aeneus*
Band-tailed Barbthroat   *Threnetes ruckeri*
Green Hermit   *Phaethornis guy*
Long-billed Hermit   *Phaethornis longirostris*
Stripe-throated Hermit   *Phaethornis striigularis*
White-tipped Sicklebill   *Eutoxeres aquila*
Green-fronted Lancebill   *Doryfera ludovicae*
Scaly-breasted Hummingbird   *Phaeochroa cuvierii*
Violet Sabrewing   *Campylopterus hemileucurus*
White-necked Jacobin   *Florisuga mellivora*
Brown Violet-ear   *Colibri delphinae*
Green Violet-ear   *Colibri thalassinus*
Green-breasted Mango   *Anthracothorax prevostii*
Veraguan Mango   *Anthracothorax veraguensis*
Violet-headed Hummingbird   *Klais guimeti*
Rufous-crested Coquette   *Lophornis delattrei*
Black-crested Coquette   *Lophornis helenae*
White-crested Coquette   *Lophornis adorabilis*

Green Thorntail	*Discosura conversii*
Canivet's Emerald	*Chlorostilbon canivetii*
Garden Emerald	*Chlorostilbon assimilis*
Violet-crowned Woodnymph	*Thalurania colombica*
Fiery-throated Hummingbird	*Panterpe insignis*
Blue-throated Goldentail	*Hylocharis eliciae*
White-bellied Emerald	*Amazilia candida*
Blue-chested Hummingbird	*Amazilia amabilis*
Charming Hummingbird	*Amazilia decora*
Mangrove Hummingbird	*Amazilia boucardi*
Alfaro's Hummingbird	*Amazilia alfaroana*
Blue-tailed Hummingbird	*Amazilia cyanura*
Steely-vented Hummingbird	*Amazilia saucerrottei*
Snowy-bellied Hummingbird	*Amazilia edward*
Rufous-tailed Hummingbird	*Amazilia tzacatl*
Cinnamon Hummingbird	*Amazilia rutila*
Striped-tailed Hummingbird	*Eupherusa eximia*
Black-bellied Hummingbird	*Eupherusa nigriventris*
White-tailed Emerald	*Elvira chionura*
Coppery-headed Emerald	*Elvira cupreiceps*
Snowcap	*Microchera albocoronata*
Bronze-tailed Plumeleteer	*Chalybura urochrysia*
White-bellied Mountain-gem	*Lampornis hemileucus*
Purple-throated Mountain-gem	*Lampornis calolaemus*
White-throated Mountain-gem	*Lampornis castaneoventris*
Green-crowned Brilliant	*Heliodoxa jacula*
Magnificent Hummingbird	*Eugenes fulgens*
Purple-crowned Fairy	*Heliothryx barroti*
Long-billed Starthroat	*Heliomaster longirostris*
Plain-capped Starthroat	*Heliomaster constantii*
Magenta-throated Woodstar	*Calliphlox bryantae*
Ruby-throated Hummingbird	*Archilochus colubris*
Volcano Hummingbird	*Selasphorus flammula*
Scintillant Hummingbird	*Selasphorus scintilla*

TROGONIDAE

Black-headed Trogon	*Trogon melanocephalus*
Baird's Trogon	*Trogon bairdii*
Violaceous Trogon	*Trogon violaceus*
Elegant Trogon	*Trogon elegans*
Collared Trogon	*Trogon collaris*
Orange-bellied Trogon	*Trogon aurantiiventris*
Black-throated Trogon	*Trogon rufus*

Slaty-tailed Trogon   *Trogon massena*
Lattice-tailed Trogon   *Trogon clathratus*
Resplendent Quetzal   *Pharomachrus mocinno*

MOMOTIDAE
Tody Motmot   *Hylomanes momotula*
Blue-crowned Motmot   *Momotus momota*
Rufous Motmot   *Baryphthengus martii*
Keel-billed Motmot   *Electron carinatum*
Broad-billed Motmot   *Electron platyrhynchum*
Turquoise-browed Motmot   *Eumomota superciliosa*

ALCEDINIDAE
Ringed Kingfisher   *Ceryle torquatus*
Belted Kingfisher   *Ceryle alcyon*
Amazon Kingfisher   *Chloroceryle amazona*
Green Kingfisher   *Chloroceryle americana*
Green-and-rufous Kingfisher   *Chloroceryle inda*
American Pygmy Kingfisher   *Chloroceryle aenea*

BUCCONIDAE
White-necked Puffbird   *Notharchus macrorhynchos*
Pied Puffbird   *Notharchus tectus*
White-whiskered Puffbird   *Malacoptila panamensis*
Lanceolated Monklet   *Micromonacha lanceolata*
White-fronted Nunbird   *Monasa morphoeus*

GALBULIDAE
Rufous-tailed Jacamar   *Galbula ruficauda*
Great Jacamar   *Jacamerops aureus*

RAMPHASTIDAE
Red-headed Barbet   *Eubucco bourcierii*
Prong-billed Barbet   *Semnornis frantzii*
Emerald Toucanet   *Aulacorhynchus prasinus*
Collared Araçari   *Pteroglossus torquatus*
Fiery-billed Araçari   *Pteroglossus frantzii*
Yellow-eared Toucanet   *Selenidera spectabilis*
Keel-billed Toucan   *Ramphastos sulfuratus*
Chestnut-mandibled Toucan   *Ramphastos swainsonii*

PICIDAE
Olivaceous Piculet   *Picumnus olivaceus*
Acorn Woodpecker   *Melanerpes formicivorus*

Golden-naped Woodpecker	*Melanerpes chrysauchen*
Black-cheeked Woodpecker	*Melanerpes pucherani*
Red-crowned Woodpecker	*Melanerpes rubricapillus*
Hoffmann's Woodpecker	*Melanerpes hoffmannii*
Yellow-bellied Sapsucker	*Sphyrapicus varius*
Hairy Woodpecker	*Picoides villosus*
Smoky-brown Woodpecker	*Veniliornis fumigatus*
Red-rumped Woodpecker	*Veniliornis kirkii*
Rufous-winged Woodpecker	*Piculus simplex*
Golden-olive Woodpecker	*Piculus rubiginosus*
Cinnamon Woodpecker	*Celeus loricatus*
Chestnut-colored Woodpecker	*Celeus castaneus*
Lineated Woodpecker	*Dryocopus lineatus*
Pale-billed Woodpecker	*Campephilus guatemalensis*

FURNARIIDAE

Pale-breasted Spinetail	*Synallaxis albescens*
Slaty Spinetail	*Synallaxis brachyura*
Red-faced Spinetail	*Cranioleuca erythrops*
Spotted Barbtail	*Premnoplex brunnescens*
Ruddy Treerunner	*Margarornis rubiginosus*
Buffy Tuftedcheek	*Pseudocolaptes lawrencii*
Striped Woodhaunter	*Hyloctistes subulatus*
Lineated Foliage-gleaner	*Syndactyla subalaris*
Scaly-throated Foliage-gleaner	*Anabacerthia variegaticeps*
Buff-fronted Foliage-gleaner	*Philydor rufum*
Buff-throated Foliage-gleaner	*Automolus ochrolaemus*
Ruddy Foliage-gleaner	*Automolus rubiginosus*
Streak-breasted Treehunter	*Thripadectes rufobrunneus*
Plain Xenops	*Xenops minutus*
Streaked Xenops	*Xenops rutilans*
Tawny-throated Leaftosser	*Sclerurus mexicanus*
Gray-throated Leaftosser	*Sclerurus albigularis*
Scaly-throated Leaftosser	*Sclerurus guatemalensis*
Plain-brown Woodcreeper	*Dendrocincla fuliginosa*
Tawny-winged Woodcreeper	*Dendrocincla anabatina*
Ruddy Woodcreeper	*Dendrocincla homochroa*
Olivaceous Woodcreeper	*Sittasomus griseicapillus*
Long-tailed Woodcreeper	*Deconychura longicauda*
Wedge-billed Woodcreeper	*Glyphorhynchus spirurus*
Strong-billed Woodcreeper	*Xiphocolaptes promeropirhynchus*
Northern Barred-Woodcreeper	*Dendrocolaptes sanctithomae*

Black-banded Woodcreeper	*Dendrocolaptes picumnus*
Cocoa Woodcreeper	*Xiphorhynchus susurrans*
Ivory-billed Woodcreeper	*Xiphorhynchus flavigaster*
Black-striped Woodcreeper	*Xiphorhynchus lachrymosus*
Spotted Woodcreeper	*Xiphorhynchus erythropygius*
Streak-headed Woodcreeper	*Lepidocolaptes souleyetii*
Spot-crowned Woodcreeper	*Lepidocolaptes affinis*
Brown-billed Scythebill	*Campylorhamphus pusillus*

THAMNOPHILIDAE

Fasciated Antshrike	*Cymbilaimus lineatus*
Great Antshrike	*Taraba major*
Barred Antshrike	*Thamnophilus doliatus*
Black-hooded Antshrike	*Thamnophilus bridgesi*
Western Slaty-Antshrike	*Thamnophilus atrinucha*
Russet Antshrike	*Thamnistes anabatinus*
Plain Antvireo	*Dysithamnus mentalis*
Streak-crowned Antvireo	*Dysithamnus striaticeps*
Spot-crowned Antvireo	*Dysithamnus puncticeps*
Checker-throated Antwren	*Myrmotherula fulviventris*
White-flanked Antwren	*Myrmotherula axillaris*
Slaty Antwren	*Myrmotherula schisticolor*
Dot-winged Antwren	*Microrhopias quixensis*
Rufous-rumped Antwren	*Terenura callinota*
Dusky Antbird	*Cercomacra tyrannina*
Bare-crowned Antbird	*Gymnocichla nudiceps*
Chestnut-backed Antbird	*Myrmeciza exsul*
Dull-mantled Antbird	*Myrmeciza laemosticta*
Immaculate Antbird	*Myrmeciza immaculata*
Spotted Antbird	*Hylophylax naevioides*
Bicolored Antbird	*Gymnopithys leucaspis*
Ocellated Antbird	*Phaenostictus mcleannani*

FORMICARIIDAE

Black-faced Antthrush	*Formicarius analis*
Black-headed Antthrush	*Formicarius nigricapillus*
Rufous-breasted Antthrush	*Formicarius rufipectus*
Black-crowned Antpitta	*Pittasoma michleri*
Scaled Antpitta	*Grallaria guatimalensis*
Streak-chested Antpitta	*Hylopezus perspicillatus*
Thicket Antpitta	*Hylopezus dives*
Ochre-breasted Antpitta	*Grallaricula flavirostris*

RHINOCRYPTIDAE

Silvery-fronted Tapaculo *Scytalopus argentifrons*

TYRANNIDAE

Yellow-bellied Tyrannulet	*Ornithion semiflavum*
Brown-capped Tyrannulet	*Ornithion brunneicapillus*
Northern Beardless-Tyrannulet	*Camptostoma imberbe*
Southern Beardless-Tyrannulet	*Camptostoma obsoletum*
Mouse-colored Tyrannulet	*Phaeomyias murina*
*Cocos Flycatcher	*Nesotriccus ridgwayi*
Yellow Tyrannulet	*Capsiempis flaveola*
Yellow-crowned Tyrannulet	*Tyrannulus elatus*
Greenish Elaenia	*Myiopagis viridicata*
Yellow-bellied Elaenia	*Elaenia flavogaster*
Lesser Elaenia	*Elaenia chiriquensis*
Mountain Elaenia	*Elaenia frantzii*
Torrent Tyrannulet	*Serpophaga cinerea*
Olive-striped Flycatcher	*Mionectes olivaceus*
Ochre-bellied Flycatcher	*Mionectes oleagineus*
Sepia-capped Flycatcher	*Leptopogon amaurocephalus*
Slaty-capped Flycatcher	*Leptopogon superciliaris*
Rufous-browed Tyrannulet	*Phylloscartes superciliaris*
Rough-legged Tyrannulet	*Phyllomyias burmeisteri*
Paltry Tyrannulet	*Zimmerius vilissimus*
Northern Scrub-Flycatcher	*Sublegatus arenarum*
Black-capped Pygmy-Tyrant	*Myiornis atricapillus*
Scale-crested Pygmy-Tyrant	*Lophotriccus pileatus*
Northern Bentbill	*Oncostoma cinereigulare*
Slate-headed Tody-Flycatcher	*Poecilotriccus sylvia*
Common Tody-Flycatcher	*Todirostrum cinereum*
Black-headed Tody-Flycatcher	*Todirostrum nigriceps*
Eye-ringed Flatbill	*Rhynchocyclus brevirostris*
Yellow-olive Flycatcher	*Tolmomyias sulphurescens*
Yellow-margined Flycatcher	*Tolmomyias assimilis*
Stub-tailed Spadebill	*Platyrinchus cancrominus*
White-throated Spadebill	*Platyrinchus mystaceus*
Golden-crowned Spadebill	*Platyrinchus coronatus*
Royal Flycatcher	*Onychorhynchus coronatus*
Ruddy-tailed Flycatcher	*Terenotriccus erythrurus*
Sulphur-rumped Flycatcher	*Myiobius sulphureipygius*
Black-tailed Flycatcher	*Myiobius atricaudus*
Bran-colored Flycatcher	*Myiophobus fasciatus*

Tawny-chested Flycatcher	*Aphanotriccus capitalis*
Tufted Flycatcher	*Mitrephanes phaeocercus*
Olive-sided Flycatcher	*Contopus cooperi*
Dark Pewee	*Contopus lugubris*
Ochraceous Pewee	*Contopus ochraceus*
Western Wood-Pewee	*Contopus sordidulus*
Eastern Wood-Pewee	*Contopus virens*
Tropical Pewee	*Contopus cinereus*
Yellow-bellied Flycatcher	*Empidonax flaviventris*
Acadian Flycatcher	*Empidonax virescens*
Alder Flycatcher	*Empidonax alnorum*
Willow Flycatcher	*Empidonax traillii*
White-throated Flycatcher	*Empidonax albigularis*
Least Flycatcher	*Empidonax minimus*
Yellowish Flycatcher	*Empidonax flavescens*
Black-capped Flycatcher	*Empidonax atriceps*
Black Phoebe	*Sayornis nigricans*
Long-tailed Tyrant	*Colonia colonus*
Bright-rumped Attila	*Attila spadiceus*
Rufous Mourner	*Rhytipterna holerythra*
Dusky-capped Flycatcher	*Myiarchus tuberculifer*
Panama Flycatcher	*Myiarchus panamensis*
Ash-throated Flycatcher	*Myiarchus cinerascens*
Nutting's Flycatcher	*Myiarchus nuttingi*
Great Crested Flycatcher	*Myiarchus crinitus*
Brown-crested Flycatcher	*Myiarchus tyrannulus*
Great Kiskadee	*Pitangus sulphuratus*
Boat-billed Flycatcher	*Megarhynchus pitangua*
Rusty-margined Flycatcher	*Myiozetetes cayanensis*
Social Flycatcher	*Myiozetetes similis*
Gray-capped Flycatcher	*Myiozetetes granadensis*
White-ringed Flycatcher	*Conopias albovittatus*
Golden-bellied Flycatcher	*Myiodynastes hemichrysus*
Streaked Flycatcher	*Myiodynastes maculatus*
Sulphur-bellied Flycatcher	*Myiodynastes luteiventris*
Piratic Flycatcher	*Legatus leucophaius*
Tropical Kingbird	*Tyrannus melancholicus*
Western Kingbird	*Tyrannus verticalis*
Eastern Kingbird	*Tyrannus tyrannus*
Gray Kingbird	*Tyrannus dominicensis*
Scissor-tailed Flycatcher	*Tyrannus forficatus*
Fork-tailed Flycatcher	*Tyrannus savana*

Genera INCERTAE SEDIS

Thrush-like Schiffornis — *Schiffornis turdina*
Gray-headed Piprites — *Piprites griseiceps*
Rufous Piha — *Lipaugus unirufus*
Speckled Mourner — *Laniocera rufescens*
Barred Becard — *Pachyramphus versicolor*
Cinnamon Becard — *Pachyramphus cinnamomeus*
White-winged Becard — *Pachyramphus polychopterus*
Black-and-white Becard — *Pachyramphus albogriseus*
Rose-throated Becard — *Pachyramphus aglaiae*
Masked Tityra — *Tityra semifasciata*
Black-crowned Tityra — *Tityra inquisitor*

COTINGIDAE

Lovely Cotinga — *Cotinga amabilis*
Turquoise Cotinga — *Cotinga ridgwayi*
Yellow-billed Cotinga — *Carpodectes antoniae*
Snowy Cotinga — *Carpodectes nitidus*
Purple-throated Fruitcrow — *Querula purpurata*
Bare-necked Umbrellabird — *Cephalopterus glabricollis*
Three-wattled Bellbird — *Procnias tricarunculatus*

PIPRIDAE

White-collared Manakin — *Manacus candei*
Orange-collared Manakin — *Manacus aurantiacus*
White-ruffed Manakin — *Corapipo altera*
Lance-tailed Manakin — *Chiroxiphia lanceolata*
Long-tailed Manakin — *Chiroxiphia linearis*
White-crowned Manakin — *Pipra pipra*
Blue-crowned Manakin — *Pipra coronata*
Red-capped Manakin — *Pipra mentalis*

OXYRUNCIDAE

Sharpbill — *Oxyruncus cristatus*

VIREONIDAE

White-eyed Vireo — *Vireo griseus*
Mangrove Vireo — *Vireo pallens*
Yellow-throated Vireo — *Vireo flavifrons*
Blue-headed Vireo — *Vireo solitarius*
Yellow-winged Vireo — *Vireo carmioli*
Warbling Vireo — *Vireo gilvus*

Brown-capped Vireo	*Vireo leucophrys*
Philadelphia Vireo	*Vireo philadelphicus*
Red-eyed Vireo	*Vireo olivaceus*
Yellow-green Vireo	*Vireo flavoviridis*
Black-whiskered Vireo	*Vireo altiloquus*
Scrub Greenlet	*Hylophilus flavipes*
Tawny-crowned Greenlet	*Hylophilus ochraceiceps*
Lesser Greenlet	*Hylophilus decurtatus*
Green Shrike-Vireo	*Vireolanius pulchellus*
Rufous-browed Peppershrike	*Cyclarhis gujanensis*

CORVIDAE

White-throated Magpie-Jay	*Calocitta formosa*
Black-chested Jay	*Cyanocorax affinis*
Brown Jay	*Cyanocorax morio*
Azure-hooded Jay	*Cyanolyca cucullata*
Silvery-throated Jay	*Cyanolyca argentigula*

HIRUNDINIDAE

Purple Martin	*Progne subis*
Gray-breasted Martin	*Progne chalybea*
Brown-chested Martin	*Progne tapera*
Tree Swallow	*Tachycineta bicolor*
Mangrove Swallow	*Tachycineta albilinea*
Violet-green Swallow	*Tachycineta thalassina*
Blue-and-white Swallow	*Pygochelidon cyanoleuca*
Northern Rough-winged Swallow	*Stelgidopteryx serripennis*
Southern Rough-winged Swallow	*Stelgidopteryx ruficollis*
Bank Swallow	*Riparia riparia*
Cliff Swallow	*Petrochelidon pyrrhonota*
Cave Swallow	*Petrochelidon fulva*
Barn Swallow	*Hirundo rustica*

TROGLODYTIDAE

Band-backed Wren	*Campylorhynchus zonatus*
Rufous-naped Wren	*Campylorhynchus rufinucha*
Rock Wren	*Salpinctes obsoletus*
Black-throated Wren	*Thryothorus atrogularis*
Black-bellied Wren	*Thryothorus fasciatoventris*
Bay Wren	*Thryothorus nigricapillus*
Riverside Wren	*Thryothorus semibadius*
Stripe-breasted Wren	*Thryothorus thoracicus*
Rufous-breasted Wren	*Thryothorus rutilus*

Spot-breasted Wren	*Thryothorus maculipectus*
Rufous-and-white Wren	*Thryothorus rufalbus*
Banded Wren	*Thryothorus pleurostictus*
Plain Wren	*Thryothorus modestus*
House Wren	*Troglodytes aedon*
Ochraceous Wren	*Troglodytes ochraceus*
Sedge Wren	*Cistothorus platensis*
Timberline Wren	*Thryorchilus browni*
White-breasted Wood-Wren	*Henicorhina leucosticta*
Gray-breasted Wood-Wren	*Henicorhina leucophrys*
Nightingale Wren	*Microcerculus philomela*
Scaly-breasted Wren	*Microcerculus marginatus*
Song Wren	*Cyphorhinus phaeocephalus*

CINCLIDAE

| American Dipper | *Cinclus mexicanus* |

SYLVIIDAE

Tawny-faced Gnatwren	*Microbates cinereiventris*
Long-billed Gnatwren	*Ramphocaenus melanurus*
White-lored Gnatcatcher	*Polioptila albiloris*
Tropical Gnatcatcher	*Polioptila plumbea*

TURDIDAE

Black-faced Solitaire	*Myadestes melanops*
Black-billed Nightingale-Thrush	*Catharus gracilirostris*
Orange-billed Nightingale-Thrush	*Catharus aurantiirostris*
Slaty-backed Nightingale-Thrush	*Catharus fuscater*
Ruddy-capped Nightingale-Thrush	*Catharus frantzii*
Black-headed Nightingale-Thrush	*Catharus mexicanus*
Veery	*Catharus fuscescens*
Gray-cheeked Thrush	*Catharus minimus*
Swainson's Thrush	*Catharus ustulatus*
Wood Thrush	*Hylocichla mustelina*
Sooty Robin	*Turdus nigrescens*
Mountain Robin	*Turdus plebejus*
Pale-vented Thrush	*Turdus obsoletus*
Clay-colored Robin	*Turdus grayi*
White-throated Robin	*Turdus assimilis*

MIMIDAE

| Gray Catbird | *Dumetella carolinensis* |
| Tropical Mockingbird | *Mimus gilvus* |

BOMBYCILLIDAE
Cedar Waxwing   *Bombycilla cedrorum*

PTILOGONATIDAE
Black-and-yellow Silky-Flycatcher   *Phainoptila melanoxantha*
Long-tailed Silky-Flycatcher   *Ptilogonys caudatus*

PARULIDAE
Blue-winged Warbler   *Vermivora pinus*
Golden-winged Warbler   *Vermivora chrysoptera*
Tennessee Warbler   *Vermivora peregrina*
Orange-crowned Warbler   *Vermivora celata*
Nashville Warbler   *Vermivora ruficapilla*
Flame-throated Warbler   *Parula gutturalis*
Northern Parula   *Parula americana*
Tropical Parula   *Parula pitiayumi*
Yellow Warbler   *Dendroica petechia*
Chestnut-sided Warbler   *Dendroica pensylvanica*
Magnolia Warbler   *Dendroica magnolia*
Cape May Warbler   *Dendroica tigrina*
Black-throated Blue Warbler   *Dendroica caerulescens*
Yellow-rumped Warbler   *Dendroica coronata*
Golden-cheeked Warbler   *Dendroica chrysoparia*
Black-throated Green Warbler   *Dendroica virens*
Townsend's Warbler   *Dendroica townsendi*
Hermit Warbler   *Dendroica occidentalis*
Blackburnian Warbler   *Dendroica fusca*
Yellow-throated Warbler   *Dendroica dominica*
Pine Warbler   *Dendroica pinus*
Prairie Warbler   *Dendroica discolor*
Palm Warbler   *Dendroica palmarum*
Bay-breasted Warbler   *Dendroica castanea*
Blackpoll Warbler   *Dendroica striata*
Cerulean Warbler   *Dendroica cerulea*
Black-and-white Warbler   *Mniotilta varia*
American Redstart   *Setophaga ruticilla*
Prothonotary Warbler   *Protonotaria citrea*
Worm-eating Warbler   *Helmitheros vermivorum*
Ovenbird   *Seiurus aurocapilla*
Northern Waterthrush   *Seiurus noveboracensis*
Louisiana Waterthrush   *Seiurus motacilla*
Kentucky Warbler   *Oporornis formosus*
Connecticut Warbler   *Oporornis agilis*

Mourning Warbler	*Oporornis philadelphia*
MacGillivray's Warbler	*Oporornis tolmiei*
Common Yellowthroat	*Geothlypis trichas*
Olive-crowned Yellowthroat	*Geothlypis semiflava*
Masked Yellowthroat	*Geothlypis aequinoctialis*
Gray-crowned Yellowthroat	*Geothlypis poliocephala*
Hooded Warbler	*Wilsonia citrina*
Wilson's Warbler	*Wilsonia pusilla*
Canada Warbler	*Wilsonia canadensis*
Slate-throated Redstart	*Myioborus miniatus*
Collared Redstart	*Myioborus torquatus*
Golden-crowned Warbler	*Basileuterus culicivorus*
Rufous-capped Warbler	*Basileuterus rufifrons*
Black-cheeked Warbler	*Basileuterus melanogenys*
Three-striped Warbler	*Basileuterus tristriatus*
Buff-rumped Warbler	*Phaeothlypis fulvicauda*
Wrenthrush	*Zeledonia coronata*
Yellow-breasted Chat	*Icteria virens*

Genus INCERTAE SEDIS

Bananaquit	*Coereba flaveola*

THRAUPIDAE

Common Bush-Tanager	*Chlorospingus ophthalmicus*
Sooty-capped Bush-Tanager	*Chlorospingus pileatus*
Ashy-throated Bush-Tanager	*Chlorospingus canigularis*
Black-and-yellow Tanager	*Chrysothlypis chrysomelas*
Rosy Thrush-Tanager	*Rhodinocichla rosea*
Dusky-faced Tanager	*Mitrospingus cassinii*
Olive Tanager	*Chlorothraupis carmioli*
Gray-headed Tanager	*Eucometis penicillata*
White-throated Shrike-Tanager	*Lanio leucothorax*
Sulphur-rumped Tanager	*Heterospingus rubrifrons*
White-shouldered Tanager	*Tachyphonus luctuosus*
Tawny-crested Tanager	*Tachyphonus delattrii*
White-lined Tanager	*Tachyphonus rufus*
Red-crowned Ant-Tanager	*Habia rubica*
Red-throated Ant-Tanager	*Habia fuscicauda*
Black-cheeked Ant-Tanager	*Habia atrimaxillaris*
Hepatic Tanager	*Piranga flava*
Summer Tanager	*Piranga rubra*
Scarlet Tanager	*Piranga olivacea*
Western Tanager	*Piranga ludoviciana*

Flame-colored Tanager	*Piranga bidentata*
White-winged Tanager	*Piranga leucoptera*
Crimson-collared Tanager	*Ramphocelus sanguinolentus*
Passerini's Tanager	*Ramphocelus passerinii*
Cherrie's Tanager	*Ramphocelus costaricensis*
Blue-gray Tanager	*Thraupis episcopus*
Palm Tanager	*Thraupis palmarum*
Blue-and-gold Tanager	*Bangsia arcaei*
Plain-colored Tanager	*Tangara inornata*
Emerald Tanager	*Tangara florida*
Silver-throated Tanager	*Tangara icterocephala*
Speckled Tanager	*Tangara guttata*
Bay-headed Tanager	*Tangara gyrola*
Rufous-winged Tanager	*Tangara lavinia*
Golden-hooded Tanager	*Tangara larvata*
Spangle-cheeked Tanager	*Tangara dowii*
Scarlet-thighed Dacnis	*Dacnis venusta*
Blue Dacnis	*Dacnis cayana*
Green Honeycreeper	*Chlorophanes spiza*
Shining Honeycreeper	*Cyanerpes lucidus*
Red-legged Honeycreeper	*Cyanerpes cyaneus*

EMBERIZIDAE

Blue-black Grassquit	*Volatinia jacarina*
Slate-colored Seedeater	*Sporophila schistacea*
Variable Seedeater	*Sporophila americana*
White-collared Seedeater	*Sporophila torqueola*
Yellow-bellied Seedeater	*Sporophila nigricollis*
Ruddy-breasted Seedeater	*Sporophila minuta*
Nicaraguan Seed-Finch	*Oryzoborus nuttingi*
Thick-billed Seed-Finch	*Oryzoborus funereus*
Blue Seedeater	*Amaurospiza concolor*
Yellow-faced Grassquit	*Tiaris olivaceus*
*Cocos Finch	*Pinaroloxias inornata*
Slaty Finch	*Haplospiza rustica*
Peg-billed Finch	*Acanthidops bairdii*
Slaty Flowerpiercer	*Diglossa plumbea*
Grassland Yellow-Finch	*Sicalis luteola*
Wedge-tailed Grass-Finch	*Emberizoides herbicola*
Sooty-faced Finch	*Lysurus crassirostris*
Yellow-thighed Finch	*Pselliophorus tibialis*
Large-footed Finch	*Pezopetes capitalis*
White-naped Brush-Finch	*Atlapetes albinucha*

Chestnut-capped Brush-Finch	*Buarremon brunneinucha*
Stripe-headed Brush-Finch	*Buarremon torquatus*
Orange-billed Sparrow	*Arremon aurantiirostris*
Olive Sparrow	*Arremonops rufivirgatus*
Black-striped Sparrow	*Arremonops conirostris*
Prevost's Ground-Sparrow	*Melozone biarcuata*
White-eared Ground-Sparrow	*Melozone leucotis*
Stripe-headed Sparrow	*Aimophila ruficauda*
Botteri's Sparrow	*Aimophila botterii*
Rusty Sparrow	*Aimophila rufescens*
Chipping Sparrow	*Spizella passerina*
Lark Sparrow	*Chondestes grammacus*
*Savannah Sparrow	*Passerculus sandwichensis*
Grasshopper Sparrow	*Ammodramus savannarum*
Lincoln's Sparrow	*Melospiza lincolnii*
Rufous-collared Sparrow	*Zonotrichia capensis*
Volcano Junco	*Junco vulcani*

CARDINALIDAE

Streaked Saltator	*Saltator striatipectus*
Grayish Saltator	*Saltator coerulescens*
Buff-throated Saltator	*Saltator maximus*
Black-headed Saltator	*Saltator atriceps*
Slate-colored Grosbeak	*Saltator grossus*
Black-faced Grosbeak	*Caryothraustes poliogaster*
Black-thighed Grosbeak	*Pheucticus tibialis*
Rose-breasted Grosbeak	*Pheucticus ludovicianus*
Black-headed Grosbeak	*Pheucticus melanocephalus*
Blue-black Grosbeak	*Cyanocompsa cyanoides*
Blue Grosbeak	*Passerina caerulea*
Indigo Bunting	*Passerina cyanea*
Painted Bunting	*Passerina ciris*
Dickcissel	*Spiza americana*

ICTERIDAE

Bobolink	*Dolichonyx oryzivorus*
Red-winged Blackbird	*Agelaius phoeniceus*
Red-breasted Blackbird	*Sturnella militaris*
Eastern Meadowlark	*Sturnella magna*
Yellow-headed Blackbird	*Xanthocephalus xanthocephalus*
Melodious Blackbird	*Dives dives*
Great-tailed Grackle	*Quiscalus mexicanus*
Nicaraguan Grackle	*Quiscalus nicaraguensis*
Shiny Cowbird	*Molothrus bonariensis*
Bronzed Cowbird	*Molothrus aeneus*

Giant Cowbird	*Molothrus oryzivorus*
Black-cowled Oriole	*Icterus prosthemelas*
Orchard Oriole	*Icterus spurius*
Yellow-tailed Oriole	*Icterus mesomelas*
Streak-backed Oriole	*Icterus pustulatus*
Bullock's Oriole	*Icterus bullockii*
Spot-breasted Oriole	*Icterus pectoralis*
Baltimore Oriole	*Icterus galbula*
Yellow-billed Cacique	*Amblycercus holosericeus*
Scarlet-rumped Cacique	*Cacicus uropygialis*
Crested Oropendola	*Psarocolius decumanus*
Chestnut-headed Oropendola	*Psarocolius wagleri*
Montezuma Oropendola	*Psarocolius montezuma*

FRINGILLIDAE

Scrub Euphonia	*Euphonia affinis*
Yellow-crowned Euphonia	*Euphonia luteicapilla*
Thick-billed Euphonia	*Euphonia laniirostris*
Yellow-throated Euphonia	*Euphonia hirundinacea*
Elegant Euphonia	*Euphonia elegantissima*
Spot-crowned Euphonia	*Euphonia imitans*
Olive-backed Euphonia	*Euphonia gouldi*
White-vented Euphonia	*Euphonia minuta*
Tawny-capped Euphonia	*Euphonia anneae*
Golden-browed Chlorophonia	*Chlorophonia callophrys*
Yellow-bellied Siskin	*Carduelis xanthogastra*
Lesser Goldfinch	*Carduelis psaltria*

PASSERIDAE

House Sparrow	*Passer domesticus*

ESTRILDIDAE

Tricolored Munia	*Lonchura malacca*

Index of Scientific Names

This index lists all the birds described in the species accounts.
For a complete list of birds in Costa Rica see page 341.
For the most recent taxonomic changes see page 335.

Basileuterus culicivorus	274	Camptostoma obsoletum	190
Basileuterus melanogenys	274	Campylopterus hemileucurus	122
Basileuterus rufifrons	274	Campylorhamphus pusillus	174
Basileuterus tristriatus	274	Campylorhynchus rufinucha	238
Bolborhynchus lineola	96	Campylorhynchus zonatus	238
Bombycilla cedrorum	254	Caprimulgus carolinensis	110
Botaurus lentiginosus	20	Caprimulgus cayennensis	112
Botaurus pinnatus	20	Caprimulgus rufus	110
Brotogeris jugularis	96	Caprimulgus saturatus	110
Buarremon brunneinucha	300	Caprimulgus vociferus	110
Buarremon torquatus	300	Capsiempis flaveola	188
Bubo virginianus	108	Caracara cheriway	52
Bubulcus ibis	22	Carduelis psaltria	324
Burhinus bistriatus	62	Carduelis xanthogastra	324
Busarellus nigricollis	32	Carpodectes antoniae	218
Buteo albicaudatus	42	Carpodectes nitidus	218
Buteo albonotatus	44	Caryothraustes poliogaster	310
Buteo brachyurus	42	Cathartes aura	30
Buteo jamaicensis	46	Cathartes burrovianus	30
Buteo magnirostris	42	Catharus aurantiirostris	246
Buteo nitidus	42	Catharus frantzii	246
Buteo platypterus	42	Catharus fuscater	246
Buteo swainsoni	46	Catharus fuscescens	248
Buteogallus anthracinus	44	Catharus gracilirostris	246
Buteogallus subtilis	44	Catharus mexicanus	246
Buteogallus urubitinga	44	Catharus minimus	248
Butorides striata	24	Catharus ustulatus	248
Butorides virescens	24	Celeus castaneus	160
Cacicus uropygialis	320	Celeus loricatus	160
Cairina moschata	4	Cephalopterus glabricollis	220
Calidris alba	74	Cercomacra tyrannina	176
Calidris alpina	76	Ceryle alcyon	148
Calidris bairdii	76	Ceryle torquatus	148
Calidris canutus	76	Chaetura cinereiventris	118
Calidris ferruginea	76	Chaetura fumosa	118
Calidris fuscicollis	76	Chaetura pelagica	118
Calidris himantopus	76	Chaetura vauxi	118
Calidris mauri	74	Chalybura urochrysia	128
Calidris melanotos	74	Chamaepetes unicolor	10
Calidris minutilla	74	Charadrius alexandrinus	64
Calidris pusilla	74	Charadrius collaris	64
Calliphlox bryantae	138	Charadrius semipalmatus	64
Calocitta formosa	230	Charadrius vociferus	64
Campephilus guatemalensis	160	Charadrius wilsonia	64
Camptostoma imberbe	190	Chiroxiphia lanceolata	222

Chiroxiphia linearis	222	Contopus sordidulus	202
Chlidonias niger	84	Contopus virens	202
Chloroceryle aenea	148	Coragyps atratus	30
Chloroceryle amazona	148	Corapipo altera	222
Chloroceryle americana	148	Cotinga amabilis	218
Chloroceryle inda	148	Cotinga ridgwayi	218
Chlorophanes spiza	292	Cranioleuca erythrops	162
Chlorophonia callophrys	324	Crax rubra	10
Chlorospingus canigularis	278	Crotophaga ani	102
Chlorospingus ophthalmicus	278	Crotophaga major	102
Chlorospingus pileatus	278	Crotophaga sulcirostris	102
Chlorostilbon assimilis	126	Crypturellus boucardi	2
Chlorostilbon canivetii	126	Crypturellus cinnamomeus	2
Chlorothraupis carmioli	278	Crypturellus soui	2
Chondestes grammacus	304	Cyanerpes cyaneus	292
Chondrohierax uncinatus	34	Cyanerpes lucidus	292
Chordeiles acutipennis	112	Cyanocompsa cyanoides	310
Chordeiles minor	112	Cyanocorax affinis	230
Chrysothlypis chrysomelas	282	Cyanocorax morio	230
Ciccaba nigrolineata	106	Cyanolyca argentigula	230
Ciccaba virgata	106	Cyanolyca cucullata	230
Cinclus mexicanus	250	Cyclarhis gujanensis	228
Circus cyaneus	40	Cymbilaimus lineatus	174
Cistothorus platensis	242	Cyphorhinus phaeocephalus	244
Claravis mondetoura	90	Cypseloides cherriei	116
Claravis pretiosa	90	Cypseloides cryptus	116
Coccyzus americanus	100	Cypseloides niger	116
Coccyzus erythropthalmus	100	Dacnis cayana	290
Coccyzus minor	100	Dacnis venusta	290
Cochlearius cochlearius	26	Deconychura longicauda	170
Coereba flaveola	276	Dendrocincla anabatina	170
Colibri delphinae	130	Dendrocincla fuliginosa	170
Colibri thalassinus	130	Dendrocincla homochroa	170
Colinus cristatus	14	Dendrocolaptes picumnus	168
Colonia colonus	200	Dendrocolaptes sanctithomae	168
Columba livia	84	Dendrocygna viduata	4
Columbina inca	88	Dendrocygna autumnalis	4
Columbina minuta	88	Dendrocygna bicolor	4
Columbina passerina	88	Dendroica caerulescens	258
Columbina talpacoti	88	Dendroica castanea	262
Conopias albovittatus	210	Dendroica cerulea	264
Contopus cinereus	202	Dendroica chrysoparia	328
Contopus cooperi	202	Dendroica coronata	264
Contopus lugubris	202	Dendroica discolor	264
Contopus ochraceus	202	Dendroica dominica	260

Geotrygon veraguensis	92	Icterus bullockii	320
Geotrygon violacea	92	Icterus galbula	320
Geranospiza caerulescens	40	Icterus mesomelas	318
Glaucidium brasilianum	108	Icterus pectoralis	318
Glaucidium costaricanum	108	Icterus prosthemelas	318
Glaucidium griseiceps	108	Icterus pustulatus	318
Glaucis aeneus	120	Icterus spurius	318
Glyphorhynchus spirurus	170	Ictinia mississippiensis	36
Grallaria guatimalensis	184	Ictinia plumbea	36
Grallaricula flavirostris	184	Ixobrychus exilis	24
Gymnocichla nudiceps	178	Jabiru mycteria	18
Gymnopithys leucaspis	178	Jacamerops aureus	152
Habia atrimaxillaris	276	Jacana jacana	60
Habia fuscicauda	276	Jacana spinosa	60
Habia rubica	276	Junco vulcani	306
Haematopus palliatus	66	Klais guimeti	136
Haplospiza rustica	298	Lampornis calolaemus	134
Harpagus bidentatus	34	Lampornis castaneoventris	134
Harpia harpyja	46	Lampornis hemileucus	134
Harpyhaliaetus solitarius	44	Lanio leucothorax	282
Heliodoxa jacula	122	Laniocera rufescens	214
Heliomaster constantii	134	Larus atricilla	80
Heliomaster longirostris	134	Larus pipixcan	80
Heliornis fulica	62	Laterallus albigularis	56
Heliothryx barroti	124	Laterallus exilis	56
Helmitheros vermivorum	266	Laterallus jamaicensis	56
Henicorhina leucophrys	244	Laterallus ruber	56
Henicorhina leucosticta	244	Legatus leucophaius	192
Herpetotheres cachinnans	52	Lepidocolaptes affinis	172
Heterospingus rubrifrons	282	Lepidocolaptes souleyetii	172
Himantopus mexicanus	68	Leptodon cayanensis	32
Hirundo rustica	236	Leptopogon amaurocephalus	194
Hydroprogne caspia	80	Leptopogon superciliaris	194
Hylocharis eliciae	128	Leptotila cassini	90
Hylocichla mustelina	248	Leptotila plumbeiceps	90
Hyloctistes subulatus	164	Leptotila verreauxi	90
Hylomanes momotula	146	Leucopternis albicollis	40
Hylopezus dives	184	Leucopternis princeps	40
Hylopezus perspicillatus	184	Leucopternis semiplumbeus	40
Hylophilus decurtatus	228	Limnodromus griseus	78
Hylophilus flavipes	228	Limnodromus scolopaceus	78
Hylophilus ochraceiceps	228	Limosa fedoa	68
Hylophylax naevioides	180	Limosa haemastica	68
Ibycter americanus	48	Lipaugus unirufus	214
Icteria virens	274	Lonchura malacca	322

Nyctidromus albicollis	110	Pelecanus erythrorhynchos	16
Nyctiphrynus ocellatus	112	Pelecanus occidentalis	16
Odontophorus gujanensis	12	Penelope purpurascens	10
Odontophorus guttatus	12	Petrochelidon fulva	232
Odontophorus leucolaemus	12	Petrochelidon pyrrhonota	232
Odontophorus melanotis	12	Pezopetes capitalis	300
Oncostoma cinereigulare	196	Phaenostictus mcleannani	178
Onychoprion anaethetus	82	Phaeochroa cuvierii	124
Onychorhynchus coronatus	200	Phaeomyias murina	190
Oporornis agilis	270	Phaeothlypis fulvicauda	270
Oporornis formosus	270	Phaethornis guy	120
Oporornis philadelphia	270	Phaethornis longirostris	120
Oporornis tolmiei	270	Phaethornis striigularis	120
Ornithion brunneicapillus	188	Phaetusa simplex	82
Ornithion semiflavum	188	Phainoptila melanoxantha	252
Ortalis cinereiceps	10	Phalacrocorax brasilianus	16
Ortalis vetula	10	Phalaropus lobatus	78
Oryzoborus funereus	294	Phalaropus tricolor	78
Oryzoborus nuttingi	294	Pharomachrus mocinno	144
Oxyruncus cristatus	224	Pheucticus ludovicianus	310
Pachyramphus aglaiae	216	Pheucticus melanocephalus	310
Pachyramphus albogriseus	216	Pheucticus tibialis	310
Pachyramphus cinnamomeus	214	Philomachus pugnax	78
Pachyramphus polychopterus	216	Philydor rufum	164
Pachyramphus versicolor	216	Phyllomyias burmeisteri	190
Pandion haliaetus	32	Phylloscartes superciliaris	192
Panterpe insignis	122	Piaya cayana	102
Panyptila cayennensis	118	Picoides villosus	158
Panyptila sanctihieronymi	118	Piculus rubiginosus	158
Parabuteo unicinctus	32	Piculus simplex	158
Pardirallus maculatus	58	Picumnus olivaceus	158
Parula americana	256	Pionopsitta haematotis	96
Parula gutturalis	256	Pionus menstruus	96
Parula pitiayumi	256	Pionus senilis	96
Passer domesticus	306	Pipra coronata	222
Passerina caerulea	312	Pipra mentalis	222
Passerina ciris	312	Pipra pipra	222
Passerina cyanea	312	Piprites griseiceps	214
Patagioenas cayennensis	86	Piranga bidentata	286
Patagioenas fasciata	86	Piranga flava	284
Patagioenas flavirostris	86	Piranga leucoptera	284
Patagioenas leucocephala	86	Piranga ludoviciana	284
Patagioenas nigrirostris	86	Piranga olivacea	286
Patagioenas speciosa	86	Piranga rubra	284
Patagioenas subvinacea	86	Pitangus sulphuratus	210

Stelgidopteryx serripennis	234	Threnetes ruckeri	120
Sterna forsteri	82	Thripadectes rufobrunneus	166
Sterna hirundo	82	Thryorchilus browni	242
Sternula antillarum	82	Thryothorus atrogularis	242
Streptoprocne rutila	116	Thryothorus fasciatoventris	242
Streptoprocne zonaris	116	Thryothorus maculipectus	238
Sturnella magna	314	Thryothorus modestus	240
Sturnella militaris	314	Thryothorus nigricapillus	240
Sublegatus arenarum	192	Thryothorus pleurostictus	240
Sula dactylatra	14	Thryothorus rufalbus	240
Sula leucogaster	14	Thryothorus rutilus	238
Sula nebouxii	14	Thryothorus semibadius	240
Sula sula	14	Thryothorus thoracicus	240
Synallaxis albescens	162	Thryothorus zeledoni	240
Synallaxis brachyura	162	Tiaris olivaceus	296
Syndactyla subalaris	164	Tigrisoma fasciatum	20
Tachybaptus dominicus	8	Tigrisoma lineatum	20
Tachycineta albilinea	232	Tigrisoma mexicanum	20
Tachycineta bicolor	232	Tinamus major	2
Tachycineta thalassina	232	Tityra inquisitor	216
Tachyphonus delattrii	280	Tityra semifasciata	216
Tachyphonus luctuosus	280	Todirostrum cinereum	196
Tachyphonus rufus	280	Todirostrum nigriceps	196
Tangara dowii	288	Tolmomyias assimilis	194
Tangara florida	288	Tolmomyias sulphurescens	194
Tangara guttata	288	Touit costaricensis	96
Tangara gyrola	288	Tringa flavipes	70
Tangara icterocephala	290	Tringa incana	72
Tangara inornata	290	Tringa semipalmata	70
Tangara larvata	288	Tringa melanoleuca	70
Tangara lavinia	288	Tringa solitaria	70
Tapera naevia	100	Troglodytes aedon	242
Taraba major	176	Troglodytes ochraceus	242
Terenotriccus erythrurus	198	Trogon aurantiiventris	142
Terenura callinota	182	Trogon bairdii	142
Thalasseus elegans	80	Trogon clathratus	144
Thalasseus maximus	80	Trogon collaris	142
Thalasseus sandvicensis	82	Trogon elegans	142
Thalurania colombica	126	Trogon massena	144
Thamnistes anabatinus	176	Trogon melanocephalus	140
Thamnophilus atrinucha	176	Trogon rufus	140
Thamnophilus bridgesi	176	Trogon violaceus	140
Thamnophilus doliatus	174	Tryngites subruficollis	72
Thraupis episcopus	290	Turdus assimilis	250
Thraupis palmarum	290	Turdus grayi	250

Index of English Common Names

This index lists all the birds described in the species accounts.
For a complete list of birds in Costa Rica see page 341.
For the most recent taxonomic changes see page 335.

Falcon, Orange-breasted	50	Flycatcher, Yellowish	206
Falcon, Peregrine	50	Flycatcher, Yellow-margined	194
Falcon, Aplomado	50	Flycatcher, Yellow-olive	194
Finch, Large-footed	300	Flycatcher, Least	204
Finch, Peg-billed	298	Foliage-gleaner, Buff-fronted	164
Finch, Slaty	298	Foliage-gleaner, Buff-throated	164
Finch, Sooty-faced	300	Foliage-gleaner, Lineated	164
Finch, Yellow-thighed	300	Foliage-gleaner, Ruddy	166
Flatbill, Eye-ringed	200	Foliage-gleaner, Scaly-throated	164
Flowerpiercer, Slaty	298	Forest-Falcon, Barred	52
Flycatcher, Acadian	204	Forest-Falcon, Collared	54
Flycatcher, Alder	204	Forest-Falcon, Slaty-backed	54
Flycatcher, Ash-throated	208	Frigatebird, Great	18
Flycatcher, Black-capped	206	Frigatebird, Magnificent	18
Flycatcher, Black-tailed	198	Fruitcrow, Purple-throated	218
Flycatcher, Boat-billed	210	Gallinule, Purple	58
Flycatcher, Bran-colored	198	Gnatcatcher, Tropical	236
Flycatcher, Brown-crested	208	Gnatcatcher, White-lored	236
Flycatcher, Dusky-capped	208	Gnatwren, Long-billed	236
Flycatcher, Fork-tailed	206	Gnatwren, Tawny-faced	236
Flycatcher, Golden-bellied	210	Godwit, Hudsonian	68
Flycatcher, Gray-capped	210	Godwit, Marbled	68
Flycatcher, Great Crested	208	Golden-Plover, American	66
Flycatcher, Nutting's	208	Goldentail, Blue-throated	128
Flycatcher, Ochre-bellied	198	Goldfinch, Lesser	324
Flycatcher, Olive-sided	202	Grackle, Great-tailed	316
Flycatcher, Olive-striped	194	Grackle, Nicaraguan	316
Flycatcher, Panama	208	Grass-Finch, Wedge-tailed	298
Flycatcher, Piratic	192	Grassquit, Blue-black	296
Flycatcher, Royal	200	Grassquit, Yellow-faced	296
Flycatcher, Ruddy-tailed	198	Grebe, Eared	8
Flycatcher, Rusty-margined	328	Grebe, Least	8
Flycatcher, Scissor-tailed	206	Grebe, Pied-billed	8
Flycatcher, Sepia-capped	194	Greenlet, Lesser	228
Flycatcher, Slaty-capped	194	Greenlet, Scrub	228
Flycatcher, Social	210	Greenlet, Tawny-crowned	228
Flycatcher, Streaked	212	Grosbeak, Black-faced	310
Flycatcher, Sulphur-bellied	212	Grosbeak, Black-headed	310
Flycatcher, Sulphur-rumped	198	Grosbeak, Black-thighed	310
Flycatcher, Tawny-chested	198	Grosbeak, Blue	312
Flycatcher, Tufted	206	Grosbeak, Blue-black	310
Flycatcher, White-ringed	210	Grosbeak, Rose-breasted	310
Flycatcher, White-throated	204	Grosbeak, Slate-colored	308
Flycatcher, Willow	204	Ground-Cuckoo, Lesser	102
Flycatcher, Yellow-bellied	204	Ground-Cuckoo, Rufous-vented	102